# Let's Stick a Little Bit More!

The first Airfix Ready-to-Run diesel locomotive was the Brush Type 2 Class 31; but what would it look like as a plastic construction kit? Here we see it visualised exclusively for this publication by John Rimmer.

## A Further Appreciation of Vintage Plastic Kits

by

Steve Knight

Irwell Press Ltd.

Copyright IRWELL PRESS LIMITED
ISBN 978-1-906919-49-8

### The Author

Stephen Knight was born in Kingston, Surrey in 1961. From a young age, he was fascinated by railways and witnessed the closing years of Southern steam from the family home in Basingstoke. In 1987, he discovered a built-up Kitmaster 'Pug' in a box of second-hand model railway items he had purchased. It was love at first sight. From then on, he determined to find out as much as possible about these fascinating models, culminating in the publication of this book. In 1990 Steve founded the Kitmaster Collectors Club, which now has more than 200 members. He is married, with two sons, a cat and a rabbit, and lives in Essex.

### The Model Maker

Marcus Archer was born in Chester in 1959, the year Kitmaster appeared in the shops. He attended a school in Chester with a railway line at the bottom of the playground. His father was a commercial artist and Marcus inherited his love of painting and his endless patience. He started building kits as a boy and even then paid special attention to correct painting and lining. Today, he enjoys building the occasional Kitmaster and Airfix model and as Exhibition Officer of the Kitmaster Collectors Club he has regular opportunities to put them on public display. He is especially noted for some of his extraordinarily detailed conversion work on these kits.

### Acknowledgements

The Author would like to acknowledge the help and assistance of the following people without whom this book would have been less than it is now: Keith and Patricia Anthony, Marcus Archer, Mrs Rose Barker, Lawrence Blake, David Brown, Claire Cannon, the Late Michael Catalani, Linda Cuthbertson, Peter Corley, Roy Cross, Mrs W.Crozier, Howard Corn & David Gould (The Eagle Society), James Day, Roger Dent, John Emmerson (BRM), Merl Evans, Mr Fergusson, Cyril Ferry, Tom Freeman, Nick Gillman, Peter Gurd, Pat Hammond, Chris Hawkins (Irwell Press), Peter Hilton, Corinne Lawrence (RPC Containers), Major W.S.Lee, Richard Lines (Hornby Hobbies), Joe Lock, Luciano Luppi, David Luesby, Wendy Meadway, Rod Moore, Robert and Janet Parker, John Rimmer, Kenneth Rush, Kathleen Shaw, Graham Short, Tony Palm, Harold Skinner, George Smith and Kevin Grindlay (Dapol Railways), Hazel Smith and T.Eric Smith CBE (Rosebud), David Stocks, Mrs. W.Sweeting, John Wells, Mario Wens, Andy Wright, Tony Wright, Reed Packaging Group, Ordnance Survey Publications, Hunting Aerofilms Ltd., Warners Group Publications plc/British Railway Modelling, PECO/The Railway Modeller, Northants Herald & Post, Chronicle & Echo, Evening Telegraph, Citizen Newspapers, the staff of the Northamptonshire Museums and Information Service and the members of the Airfix and Kitmaster Collectors Clubs and the Braintree & Halstead Model Railway Club.

Grateful thanks for permission to reprint material is extended as follows: PECO Publications & Publicity Ltd. ('Railway Modeller'); 'Model Railways'/Argus Publications Ltd. ('Model Railway News'); Ian Allan Ltd. ('Model Railway Constructor'); Warners Group Publications plc ('British Railway Modelling' and 'Collectors Gazette'); Magpie Publications & Publicity Ltd. ('Model Railway Collector'); Link House Publications Ltd. ('Model Railway Enthusiast'); Mattel Ltd. ('Rosebud News').

Copyright 2012 Stephen Knight. Kitmaster and the Kitmaster Logo are trademarks of Dapol Ltd. Chirk, Clywd 1985. Airfix, Products in Plastic and the Airfix logo are trademarks of Hornby Hobbies plc 2006. Neneware, Rosebud, Rosebud Dolls and the Rosebud Logo are trademarks of Mattel Inc. Leicester 1969.

First published in the United Kingdom as *Let's Stick Together* in 1998 by Irwell Press Ltd, 59A High Street, Clophill, Bedfordshire, MK45 4BE
This updated and expanded edition published 2012.
Printed by Konway Press

# Contents

**4**     **Preface and Acknowledgements**

**6**     **Chapter One - An Introduction to Rosebud Kitmaster**
Who Were Rosebud?
The Rosebud Kitmaster Story
The Raunds Site
The Kitmaster Concept

**26**     **Chapter Two The Rosebud Kitmaster Story**

**54**     **Chapter Three - The Models in Detail**
1. BR Mk1 Coaches
2. Midland Pullman Cars
3. Presentation Sets
4. Prototype *Deltic*
5. Rebuilt Royal Scot
6. Battle of Britain
7. Ariel Arrow Super Sports Model
8. Motorised Bogies KM1 & KM2
9. BR 350HP Class 08 Diesel Shunter
10. BR Standard Class 4MT Mogul
11. Continental Prototypes, Early American General, Italian Tank, Swiss Crocodile, Baureihe 23 (German), 241P Mountain (French), DB B4yge Coach, SNCF A9 myfi Coach, New York Central Hudson
12. BR Standard Class 9F *Evening Star*
13. Canadian National U-4-A
14. LNER A3 Pacific *Flying Scotsman*
15. GWR 34XX *City of Truro*
16. Nescafe/Telegadget *Lord of the Isles*
17. GNR Stirling 8ft Single No.1
18. Stephenson's *Rocket*
19. SR Schools Class V *Harrow*
20. LMS Class 8P Pacific *Duchess of Gloucester*
21. LMS Beyer Garratt
22. LNER Class J94 Saddle Tank.
23. GWR 61XX Prairie Tank.

**124**     **Chapter Four - Rumours and Postulations**

**128**     **Chapter Five - Collaborations**
Nabisco and the Hermes Supply Company.
The Humbrol Connection Peco Interiors.

**138**     **Chapter Six - Chassis and Motorisation Kits**
[A] Arby Perfecta Kits, [B] N & KC Keyser, [C] SMRSChassis Kits.

**144**     **Chapter Seven - Rise and Fall - the Airfix Reintroductions**
Airfix Rolling Stock
Photographic Archive.
Airfix Catalogue Artwork.

**194**     **Chapter Eight - The Airfix Models in Detail**
24 Park Royal Railbus. A guest article by John Wells
25 BR Class 04 Drewry 204HP Shunter.

**198**     **Chapter Nine - Middlesex Toy Industries - Scalecraft**

**202**     **Chapter Ten - The Kitmaster and Airfix Compendium**
Introduction and Notes.
Table One Production Details.
Table Two Release Dates and Prices.
Table Three Press Coverage.
Table Four Names and Numbers.
Table Five Airfix Reintroductions
Table Six Rosebud Kitmaster Media Campaign
Kitmaster Publications.
Retail & Dealer Catalogues, Colour Charts, Colour Card.
Collecting Kitmaster Models.
Appendix 1 Index to model railway journal entries.

*Note: A number of pictures in the Introductory sections are repeated later in the text for continuity and completeness.*

# Rosebud

**BRITAIN'S FINEST DOLL**

An example from the superb Rosebud collection of lightweight plastic dolls, fully jointed, with **Mama** voice, sleeping eyes and eyelashes. Packed **in** attractive four colour box.

*Sole Concessionaires:*
**L. REES & CO. LTD.**
31-35 WILSON STREET, LONDON, E.C.2
TELEPHONE: MONARCH 2651 (7 lines) • CABLES: ELREESONIA, AVE., LONDON

BIF 1951
APRIL 30—MAY 11
EARLS COURT & OLYMPIA
SEE OUR EXHIBIT

# Preface to the First Edition

In 1962 the precariously balanced finances of the Rosebud organisation finally tipped against Kitmaster and the company was sold outright to Airfix. I was too young at that time to remember anything of the brightly coloured Kitmaster boxes which had rapidly established themselves as favourites in model shops throughout the land. I first came across Kitmaster models in a box of old locomotives purchased from a jumble sale many years later. Where does the fascination with these models lie?

Could it be a yearning for the brash kitsch of a bygone age, or the wonderfully eccentric planning behind the Kitmaster concept; or perhaps enthusiasm born from a realisation that these were, and still are, some of the finest scale railway kits ever produced? They are certainly varied and interesting, to the point of becoming idiosyncratic. In an attempt to provide something for everyone, we are faced with a range of kits that lines up a diminutive L&Y Pug next to a towering Hudson locomotive; models that are geographically and historically in two different worlds.

Here lies the magic: the unanswered questions, the enigmas lost in the mists of time, submerged under a mountain of dusty paperwork. My research over the last eight years has taken me far and wide in search of the answers. I hope you will enjoy the fruits of my labour, for this is truly the story of a remarkable company with a remarkable product. At the time advanced and innovative, Kitmaster and Airfix models are today cherished collectors' pieces in their own right. Wherever they are, Kitmaster models always manage to create a sense of excitement in people. The older ones fondly remember them from their heyday, saving their pocket money to buy the latest model. Younger observers are fascinated by the wealth of detail in these vintage 'toys', which once used to keep their fathers and uncles very creatively occupied on a Saturday evening! For me, they will always hold a certain magic, as through the pages of this book I hope to bring Rosebud Kitmaster to life for a whole new generation of model makers. Whilst space constrains the amount of detail it is possible to provide in a work of this nature, you will find a series of essays on particular models in the range. I apologise whole-heartedly and in advance for the choice of models. If your particular favourite is not covered, it is only because I chose them in no particular order and wrote them over a period of years. I do hope that you will not be too disappointed!

**Stephen Knight, Halstead 1998.**

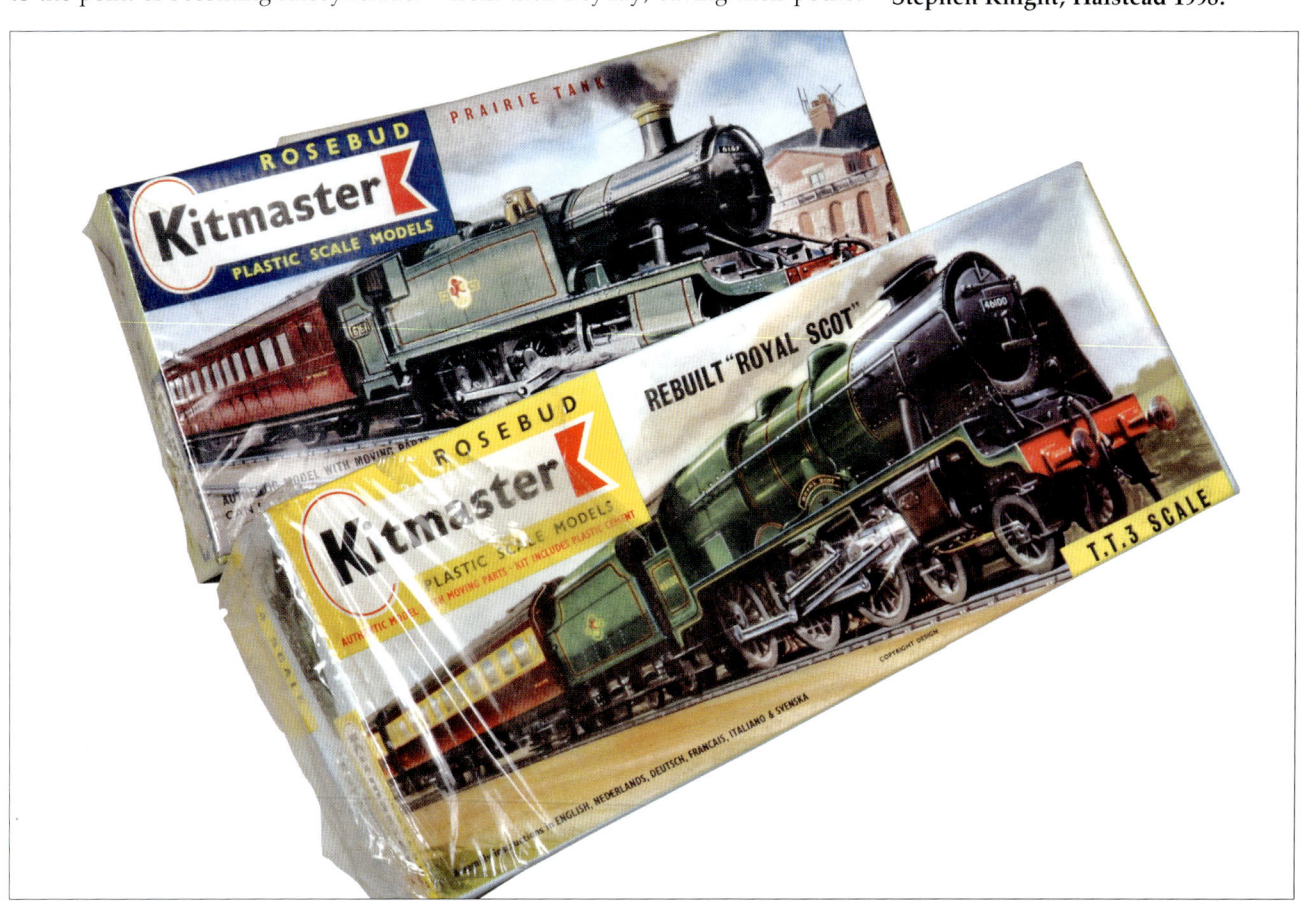

# Preface to the Second Edition

Since the first publication of *Let's Stick Together* 12 years ago, a lot has happened. No sooner was the book issued than the 'phone began to ring with ex-Rosebud employees saying *'Why didn't you talk to me?'* In fact I had made strenuous efforts to contact as many key players as possible before writing the first edition, but of course the added publicity of a book launch, local radio and press coverage and word-of-mouth led inexorably to more former employees coming out of the woodwork. Add to this the discovery of the artwork for the last three kits, some interesting test shots and more information on certain aspects of the kits and the pressure for a second edition became overwhelming. The past ten years also saw the publication of further essays in the Models in Detail series in The Kitmaster Collectors Club journal *'Signal'*, which have now been collated into the main text. Recent re-discovery of some important Airfix artwork and transparencies combined with major advances in colour reproduction have also allowed us to bring you many more full-colour plates throughout the text. I sincerely hope that you enjoy reading this new edition of the book as much as I have enjoyed editing it.

**Stephen Knight, Halstead 2012.**

## Mr. Eric Smith introduces his SALES TEAM

**THE NEWS BEHIND THE NEWS**

ROSEBUD DOLLS, now selling and distributing direct to the wholesale trade, have appointed 6 new representatives to cover the complete country. No matter where you are, there's a representative to give you the maximum service and advice on Rosebud dolls, and to take care of your problems personally. Each is specially trained and knows the best method of boosting your sales of Rosebud dolls. You can depend on your Rosebud representative —make a note of his name.

**ROSEBUD**
Rosebud Dolls Limited, Raunds, Northamptonshire. Tel: Raunds 191 (5 lines)

Mr. R. G. NOBLE — Sales Director

1. Mr. L. E. Ambler — ALSO NORTHERN IRELAND
2. Mr. D. H. Birch
3. Mr. A. L. Brown
4. Mr. F. L. Wood
5. Mr. D. Parr
6. Mr. A. Bowden-Stuart

**SALES AREAS:**
1. Scotland, Northern England and Northern Ireland
2. Lancashire and Yorkshire
3. North Wales and the Midlands
4. East Anglia and South Coast
5. Greater London
6. South Wales and the West Country

# Chapter 1: An Introduction to Rosebud Kitmaster - A Rose by any other name...

The story of Rosebud is really the story of one remarkable businessman. The Managing Director of the Rosebud group of companies was Thomas Eric Smith, always known as T. Eric Smith. He was born on 22nd April 1916 in the East End of London; his father and mother had their own business making and selling toys. Eric spent his formative years learning the toy trade and left school at just 13 years old. He was immediately set to work for the family business, but his father proved a hard taskmaster. He put Eric to work in his first week cleaning out the toilets, much to the annoyance of his mother. So one might say that he learned the business from the bottom! When Eric was fifteen his father died and from 1931 he had to support his mother, himself and the business. The family had two factories in east London making beech horses, dolls houses and forts.

By the outbreak of war in 1939, the family business, Masks Ltd, was mostly producing heads for soft fabric dolls. The old factories were heavily bombed over a three-day period in 1940. The first factory was hit on a Sunday night, followed by the second factory on the following Monday lunchtime and, just to make things worse, the Smith family house was struck that very same Monday night. With nowhere to live, nowhere to work and no possessions to speak of, Eric and his mother were forced to leave London.

Sheltering away from the bombing in Northamptonshire, Eric and his mother took stock of their situation. The war was at its height. London was taking a regular pounding from the Luftwaffe. There was little point in trying to set up their business in the capital again. But life in the Salvation Army hostel in Rothwell was grim and soul destroying. Eventually, they decided to move back to London and to start again.

Having set off on the long journey down the A6 back to London, Eric began to have second thoughts. He stopped the car in Kettering, went into a newsagent to buy some tobacco and casually asked the proprietor if he knew of any vacant factories thereabouts. He was told of one near Rushden, further down the A6. When he reached Rushden he asked again in a similar shop. This time it was a customer who answered 'Go to Raunds and ask for Alderman Corby OBE' he was told. Eric had never heard of Raunds in his life, but soon located it. 'I drove into town and stopped the first man I saw in the street' he recalls. 'I told him I was looking for Alderman Corby OBE. He drew himself up to a full six feet and said "I am Alderman Corby OBE". I said that I'd been told he could help me find a vacant factory site. He looked over his shoulder and said "See that building there? That's it. Do you want to look around it?" We'd stopped right outside Frost's Ironmongers in Grove Street. Well, we looked it over and I agreed a three-year let at an annual rent of £100 per year.' So they never did make it back to London but settled instead in Raunds; even bringing some of their East End girls up to Raunds to help them. The girls didn't stay long; they hated the countryside, the quiet and slow pace of life in Raunds, and soon pined for London.

No sooner had Masks Ltd been relocated into the former boot factory in Grove Street than Eric Smith was called up for active service. He joined the RAF and was posted abroad, not returning until 1946. Mrs A.R.Smith had set up business in the shop and former mechanics workshop of the Advance Garage, also a part of the former boot factory in Grove Street, Raunds. During his service career, Eric had conceived some new and exciting ideas for toys which he now wanted to put into practice. His best ideas involved the low cost construction of dolls using glues and sawdust, known as composites. Some of his early experiments were conducted in the kitchen ovens of the family and their friends in the Raunds area. Before the Second World War, most dolls were made in Germany with heads of porcelain. These expensive German dolls were effectively made extinct by the war thereby creating a market opportunity. T. Eric Smith founded his own toy making company, called Nene Plastics Ltd, on a new site in the former William Nicholls boot factory in Grove Street, Raunds, Northamptonshire. Nene Plastics' first range of dolls was branded Starlight Dolls, although this name does not appear to have been registered. Initially, the area behind his mother's business was used for production and offices, but soon he took over other parts of the former boot and shoe factory, together with the frontages on Grove Street that had been Frost's Ironmongery and several other businesses including a hairdresser. These buildings were eventually designated Plant Two (Doll final assembly) and Plant Three (Doll head/wig production).

There were plenty of local women who were very pleased to work for the new enterprise, Nene Plastics Ltd, making its premier doll range, Starlight Dolls. At about that time, in 1946, British Overseas Airways Corporation began a new air service to South America and called it 'The Starlight Service'. Eric had liked the

**Rosebud used BRS parcels as well as British Railways parcel services for their deliveries. Here a pair of Bristol Longwell Green FCG6 cabbed lorries prepare to set off from Wellingborough for Milwall Docks with another consignment of Rosebud Dolls for export.** (*Northampton Evening Echo*)

7

February, 1959     GAMES & TOYS     67

# *Now available*
## ROSEBUD
# Kitmaster
## PLASTIC SCALE MODEL
## RAILWAY KITS

These models are the first of a whole range of engine kits planned by Rosebud Kitmaster Limited to appeal to modellers everywhere. Packed in attractive boxes, complete with step by step instructions, these models are precision moulded and authentic in every detail.

**NATIONAL ADVERTISING** will ensure a steady demand. Stock Rosebud Kitmaster for 1959 and use attractive free Display Material available on request.

See them on
Stand No. 8 CORN EXCHANGE
BRIGHTON

- STEPHENSON'S ROCKET
- DIESEL ELECTRIC
- EARLY AMERICAN GENERAL
- CORONATION CLASS Duchess of Gloucester
- SCHOOL CLASS—Harrow
- SADDLE TANK

Authentic models with moving parts.
Can be used on OO and HO gauge tracks.

ROSEBUD
Kitmaster
REGD. TRADE MARK
PLASTIC SCALE MODELS

Rosebud Kitmaster Limited
Raunds, Northamptonshire

KM2

*Left.* This rare colour advertisement appeared in the Toy industry newspaper "Games & Toys" in February 1959 and announced the new Kitmaster range ahead of the 1959 Brighton Toy Fair. The first kits were actually issued two months later and reached the shops in time for a may 1959 launch.

Raunds factory. On 20th March 1947 Eric registered the trademark 'Rosebud' for dolls, No.657461. With the retirement of his mother in 1953 T Eric Smith acquired her business, Masks Ltd., together with the parts of the Grove Street site which had been used by that company. By the beginning of 1953 a new PVC plant, making beach balls(!) had come on stream. In September 1953 a 10,000 sq.ft. site, to the west of the existing plant, was cleared for construction of a new injection moulding plant which would boast 25 moulding machines turning out 25,000 dolls per day at peak supply. The new plant, formally designated Plant One and often referred to as the 'New' factory, went into production on 1st February 1955. Boasting a full suite of offices, toilets, rest areas and a loading bay, it was the epitome of modern manufacturing and a big improvement on the improvised facilities of the 100-year-old former boot factory. Plant One was commissioned to set about making the injection moulded parts for Nene Plastics' two main product lines: 'Rosebud' dolls and 'Neneware' kitchenware. However, by the summer of 1955, doll production was far outstripping everything else. At the end of that year, with sales soaring 63% to top 5,000,000 dolls, Eric decided to drop 'Neneware' and 'Masks' and to concentrate on Miss Rosebud - the foremost Nene Plastics Ltd doll by far. To reflect this change of emphasis, during 1955 the name of the company was changed to Rosebud Dolls Ltd. He also took his first steps away from the Raunds site. Premises in Rock Street, Wellingborough were acquired. This was formerly C.E. & H.B. Groome's leather workshop. Although it was initially used for doll production, to alleviate space pressure in Raunds, Rock St was eventually converted into a warehouse.

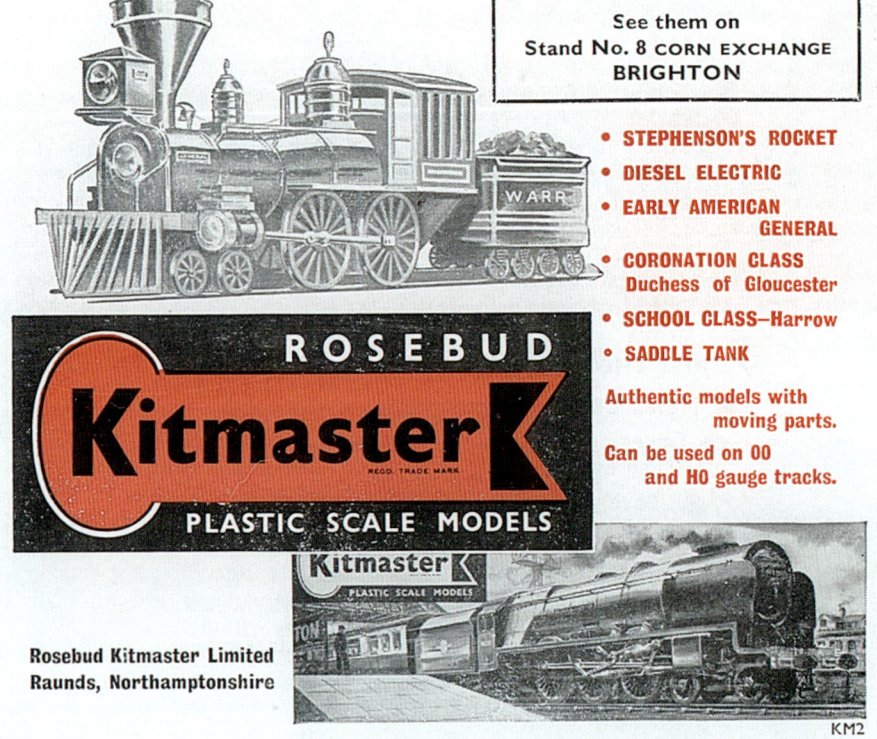

name and coined it for his new doll making venture. By May 1947 Eric had secured orders form the USA for $100,000 worth of dolls and adopted the slogan 'Dollars for Dolls' to spearhead his export drive. The new seven inch high composite dolls were shown at the British Industries Fair at Olympia, an event which became a regular fixture in the Rosebud year, together with the Harrogate and Brighton Toy Fairs. These dolls were immensely popular with British audiences and remained in production, albeit in PVC, for many years.

Eric soon settled into his newly adopted home town. He became a town councillor and after marrying his wife Hazel, on 12th June 1946, moved into an imposing house called Ashfields Hall. This Victorian property had been constructed for a former partner in the Nicholls Boot factory, also called Smith, who had left and started his own successful footware company. The street in Raunds which is today called Smith Court is named after the bootmaker, not the dollmaker.

At the beginning of 1946, Nene Plastics employed 39 people in the

8

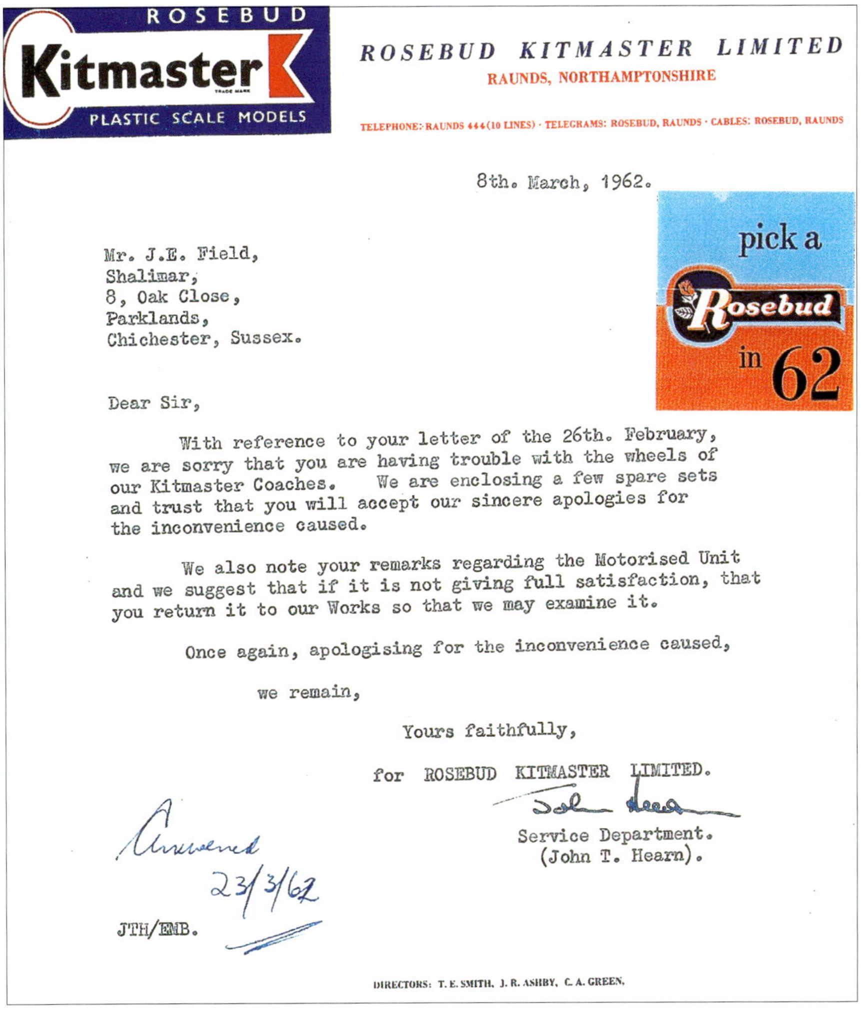

**ROSEBUD Kitmaster**
PLASTIC SCALE MODELS

**ROSEBUD KITMASTER LIMITED**
RAUNDS, NORTHAMPTONSHIRE

TELEPHONE: RAUNDS 444 (10 LINES) · TELEGRAMS: ROSEBUD, RAUNDS · CABLES: ROSEBUD, RAUNDS

8th. March, 1962.

Mr. J.E. Field,
Shalimar,
8, Oak Close,
Parklands,
Chichester, Sussex.

pick a *Rosebud* in 62

Dear Sir,

With reference to your letter of the 26th. February, we are sorry that you are having trouble with the wheels of our Kitmaster Coaches. We are enclosing a few spare sets and trust that you will accept our sincere apologies for the inconvenience caused.

We also note your remarks regarding the Motorised Unit and we suggest that if it is not giving full satisfaction, that you return it to our Works so that we may examine it.

Once again, apologising for the inconvenience caused,

we remain,

Yours faithfully,

for ROSEBUD KITMASTER LIMITED.

Service Department.
(John T. Hearn).

Answered
23/3/62

JTH/EMB.

DIRECTORS: T. E. SMITH, J. R. ASHBY, C. A. GREEN.

It was managed by Bill Crozier and despatched Rosebud Dolls as finished products direct to Millwall docks for shipment abroad, as well as to the UK market. In 1955 the shareholding of Nene Plastics was as follows: T. Eric Smith 81.5% (Managing Director) Hazel Smith 15% (Eric's wife and chief dress designer) R.F. Ruff 2.5% (Company Secretary) W.S. Lee 1% (Major Lee, Works Manager) The company had an impressive portfolio of products in plastic *(continued page 14)*

**These ads from H A Blunt and Gamages show how retailers began to promote the new range. The interesting Rosebud letter carries their "Pick a Rosebud in 62" pictorial slogan and confirms that the motorised bogie was, indeed a genuine Rosebud production, even though T Eric Smith could not recall it when interviewed in 1995!**

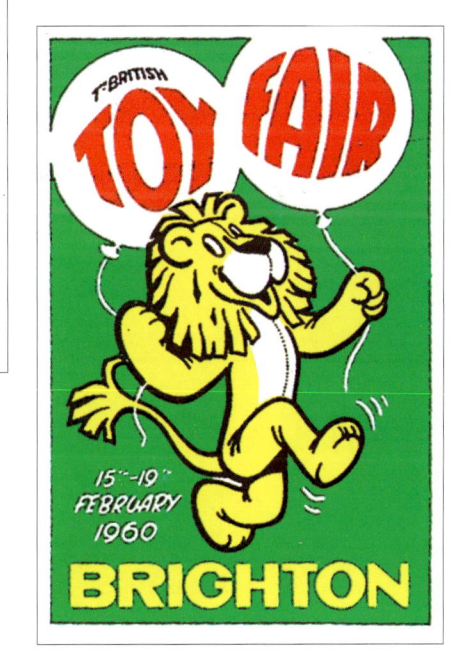

1st BRITISH TOY FAIR
15th–19th FEBRUARY 1960
BRIGHTON

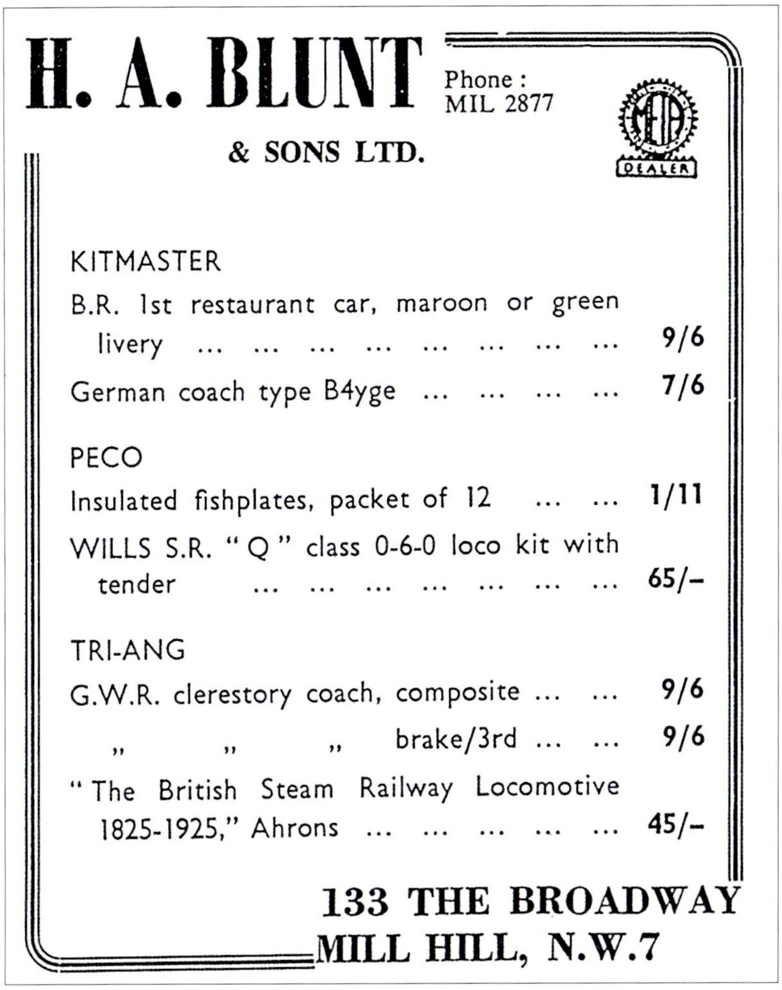

## H. A. BLUNT & SONS LTD.
Phone: MIL 2877

**KITMASTER**
B.R. 1st restaurant car, maroon or green livery ... ... ... ... ... ... ... 9/6
German coach type B4yge ... ... ... ... 7/6

**PECO**
Insulated fishplates, packet of 12 ... ... 1/11

WILLS S.R. "Q" class 0-6-0 loco kit with tender ... ... ... ... ... ... ... 65/-

**TRI-ANG**
G.W.R. clerestory coach, composite ... ... 9/6
 ,,   ,,   ,,   brake/3rd ... ... 9/6

"The British Steam Railway Locomotive 1825-1925," Ahrons ... ... ... ... 45/-

**133 THE BROADWAY MILL HILL, N.W.7**

## GAMAGES
THE BEST
**PLASTIC KIT CENTRE**
Always something new and unusual from home and abroad.

**NEW!** FOR YOUR LAYOUT — ROSEBUD **Kitmaster** PLASTIC SCALE MODELS

Presenting for the first time something QUITE different—models of new and old locomotives (to "OO" and "HO" standards), with movable parts and the full details of the real thing.

No. 2 **DIESEL ELECTRIC SHUNTER 4/6**

No. 3 **EARLY AMERICAN GENERAL 6/6**

Also available now—Kit No. 1. Stephenson's Rocket, 4/6. Kit No. 5. School's Class Harrow, 7/6.

Other interesting locomotives which will be available in 1959 are—
Coronation Class    Battle of Britain Class
Stirling    Giant Swiss Crocodile
and many others.

Post and Packing 9d. if outside our van area.

**GAMAGES · HOLBORN · LONDON · E.C.I. HOL 8484**

9

*Top.* The former Co-Operative Wholesale corset factory in Wellingborough provided much-need extra space as Rosebud outgrew even the expanded premises at Grove Street, Raunds. Outside the gate is the company pantechnicon featured in our rear cover painting.

*Lower Left.* Rosebud introduced a high-quality in-house magazine called, imaginatively, "Rosebud News" in 1952. It carried news of new product success, developments on the site and the fortunes of the Rosebud cricket team!

*Lower right.* Masks Ltd was Eric Smith's Mother's company, set up to make dolls heads (always known as masks) from "composition" – a mixture of glue and sawdust. It was eventually bought by Eric and amalgamated into Rosebud.

Rosebud Dolls Ltd was an important exhibitor at the bi-annual British Industries Fair, held every year in London & Manchester. Their detailed display for the BIF was kept in a special cabinet at Raunds and is seen in the upper picture. The lower shots show Rosebud's internal sales display cabinet, situated inside the Canteen area, and used to show off new products to visiting Buyers.

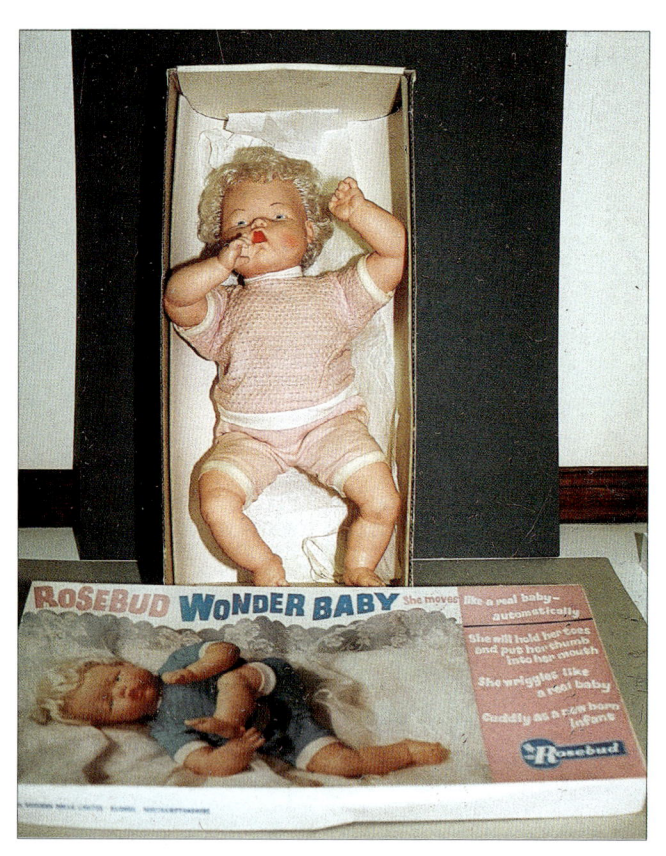

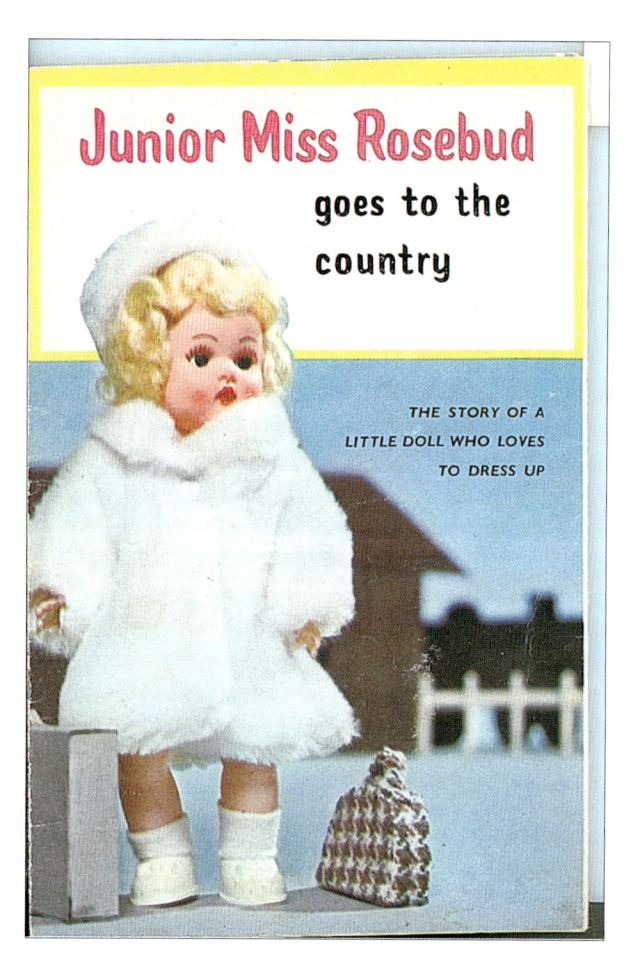

*Top Left.* A 1959 mini-catalogue for Junior Miss Rosebud, a seven inch doll aimed at pre-teen girls.
*Top Right.* Rosebud launched the Rosebud Wonder Baby in 1964 and it bankrupted them. Scaling almost lifesize, the baby could eat, drink and "urinate", as well as having hair that could grow. But she was extremely ugly and very expensive. This disastrous piece of marketing, with thousands of unsold units in stock and dealers returning the unloved, hideous dolls forced Eric Smith to call in the Receiver.

*Bottom Left & Right.* "She'd Love a Rosebud" was a long-running slogan for dolls. Here we see a trade advertisement promoting Rosebud's heavy-weight campaign in women's weekly titles in the run up to Christmas 1954. It was also displayed on London Underground carriage boards. To the right is a page from the Northampton Evening Chronicle's 1953 Coronation special edition.

12

*Top Left.* "Harrogate, Brighton, Nuremburg – tomorrow we conquer the world!" *"Pick a Rosebud in '62"* prepares to take on Europe! Playpets were the forerunner of Aquatoys – hours of bath time fun; and the kids loved them too!
*Lower.* Large-scale advertising campaigns in the Press and on the new fangled-ITV (From 1953) meant Rosebud was a household name in the UK.

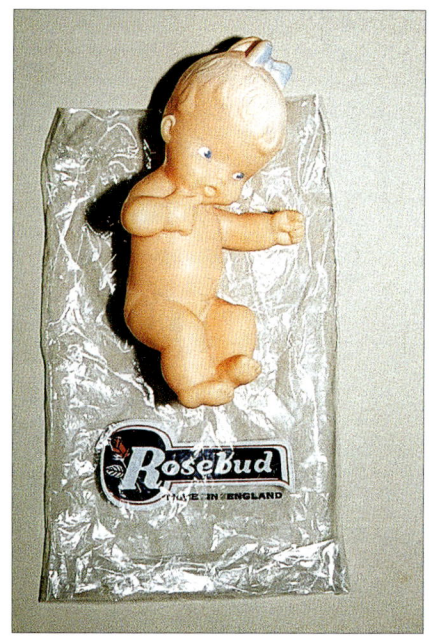

*Top and left.* Rosebud Aquatoys were designed for bath-time fun, sold in simple poly bags from a counter-top trade pack. Baby Rosebud (at top right) was also available in "washable PVC".

*Lower Left.* Rosebud Easi-Build was a polystyrene injection moulded constructional toy available in two sets and four different colours.

*Below*. Dennis Franklin, Technical Manager chats with Bob Parker, Site Chemist during 1998.

at this time. In polyethylene were: children's buckets, 'Neneware', pails, washing-up bowls, sink-tidies, measuring jugs, beakers, soap dishes, egg trays and 'aquatoys', which included swimming fish for the bathtub. In polyvinylchloride there were children's inflatable balls, Rosebud Doll parts and rotary cast toys such as the 'puppy'. In cellulose acetate were 'Teddy Bear' and 'Miss Rosebud' dolls. The plastic bucket was, according to Eric, the first product to be advertised on a full half-page and in colour in the *Daily Express* newspaper. Eric and his management team travelled down to Fleet Street to see the paper being 'put to bed' and printed with their ground-breaking advertisement in it.

14

Rosebud's site chemist, Mr Robert Parker, had trained at ICI in Welwyn Garden City and by 1955 was living with his wife Janet, Rosebud's Personnel Officer, in a caravan on the Rosebud site, for there was still an acute housing shortage following the war. His skill enabled Rosebud to capitalise on all the latest polymer developments and he was instrumental in the later switch to Polystyrene needed for Easi-Build and Kitmaster products. T.Eric Smith says that Easi-Build and Kitmaster were not the first polystyrene products they made. Bob and Dennis Franklin seem to remember a pull-along dog toy that had a polystyrene base which may well have been the first use of the material by Rosebud. Certainly, Rosebud was one of the first British companies to make full use of injection moulding machines.

The name Rosebud was originally coined when a young girl, who was visiting the factory, was presented with a choice of dolls from the factory display cabinet by T.Eric Smith. The girl chose a new design which Hazel Smith had only just dressed and placed on display. The girl thanked 'Uncle Eric' and then her mother asked her why she had chosen that doll and what she liked best about it. 'She has lovely rosebud lips' said the girl. Eric adopted it as the name for that design of doll. 'Miss Rosebud', as the doll was known, was very successful. Soon all of the other dolls were being given Rosebud names in line with the new trademark.

Although there is another possible aspect to the use of Rosebud as a trademark for toys, it is discounted by Eric Smith. Orson Wells' seminal 1941 film *Citizen Kane* opens with the dying words of the protagonist, closely modelled on millionaire publishing tycoon William Randolph Hearst. Those words are 'rose bud'. The journalist narrating the film in flashback tries to discover what 'rose bud' means, but only at the very end of the film is it revealed that Rose Bud was the name of the toy manufacturer who made Hearst's (sic) boyhood toboggan, seen being thrown into the furnace in the closing shot. Is there a link? Certainly the *cognoscenti* seem to think there is, but Eric is steadfast in his version, which is repeated in *Pollock's Directory of British Dolls*, quoting the 'rosebud lips' scenario as the origin of the name. Rosebud was an established name for both girls and boys in the late 1950s.

*Top.* **The Baby Rosebud series, six inch dolls in hard plastic, became very popular.**

*Left.* **The Walking Teddy Bear was interesting, but made in rigid plastic, he was not very cuddly!**

Hazel Smith was Rosebud's chief dress designer for the dolls costumes and went to great lengths to research the very latest styles around the world, always keeping abreast of the latest trends and fashions. Eric attributes much of Rosebud's success to Hazel's skill as a designer, rating her second only to her contemporary designer at Ideal Toys in New York at the time. Even the 'Evening Telegraph' attributed most of Rosebud Dolls success to *the great demand for the Rosebud series because of their originality of dress*, whilst 'Toys and Games', reviewing the Rosebud Dolls display at Harrogate said: *the 'Miss Rosebud' dolls in particular, with their real nylon stockings and high-heeled shoes, were outstanding and their outfits the last word in fashion.*

From an early point in the business, the sole sales concessionaire for Rosebud Dolls was L.Rees & Co Ltd, an association which lasted from 1947 to 1958. In the very first edition of the house newsletter 'Rosebud News' in 1953, Mr Sydney Myers, a Director of L.Rees & Co Ltd, wrote an excellent article detailing how the dolls were marketed and sold around the world. The change from L.Rees to direct supply of wholesalers was highlighted in Rosebud's 1959 trade advertising and again at the Harrogate and Brighton shows, proudly boasting *Selling Direct to the Wholesale Trade*. L.Rees & Co had regularly advertised Rosebud Dolls to the trade throughout the early 1950s, including special Accession and Coronation advertising. Following the 1958 switch to direct distribution, Rosebud began to advertise in the trade magazine 'Toys and Games' themselves. A further major change occurred towards the end of 1963 when the sales policy was switched from distribution

*Right top.* Rosebud Dolls used their own Dodge Q pantechnicon for deliveries to their London concessionaires, L.Rees and Co.

*Right centre.* In 1967, W&H Models were able to re-import many of the kits *en masse* from unsold exported stock.

*Right bottom.* Most Kitmaster kits could be ordered from Gamages, Selfridges and Hamleys if you could not find them in your local shop.

*Left and above.* Nene Ware encompassed a number of household utensils, including (left) Mugs and right, an egg tray and soap dish. Also shown is a hard plastic toy iron and hollow moulded telephone in PVC.

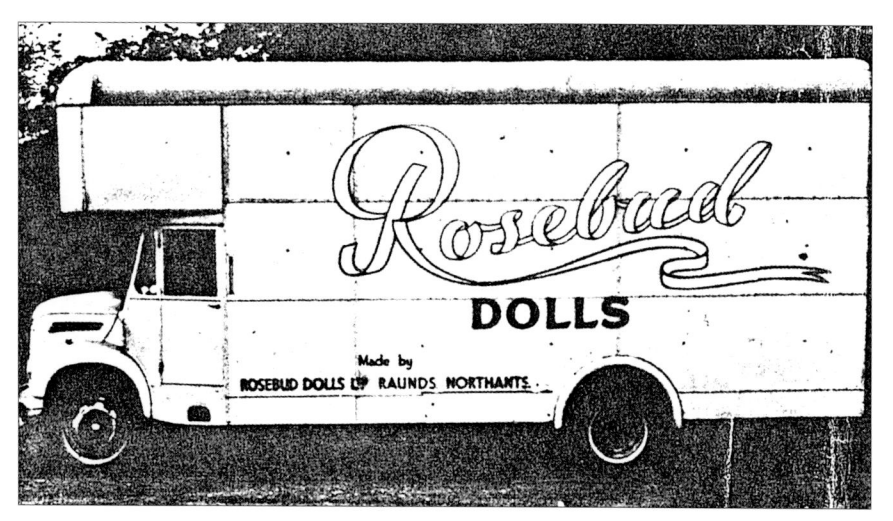

# KITMASTER!

WE ARE PLEASED TO ANNOUNCE THAT WE HAVE BEEN ABLE TO RECOVER FROM ABROAD, A CONSIGNMENT OF THESE FAMOUS PLASTIC LOCOMOTIVE KITS. UNFORTUNATELY, DUE TO VERY HIGH HANDLING, SHIPPING AND CLEARANCE CHARGES, WE CANNOT OFFER THE KITS AT THE ORIGINAL PRICES, BUT EVEN AT THE NEW FIGURE, THESE REPRESENT GOOD VALUE FOR MONEY. STOCK IS LIMITED, AND IN SOME CASES ONLY 2-3 DOZEN KITS ARE AVAILABLE—SO IT'S FIRST COME FIRST SERVED.

| | | |
|---|---|---|
| KIT No. 4 | LMS/BR CORONATION CLASS LOCO AND TENDER KIT | PRICE 16/6 + 1/6 P. & P. |
| KIT No. 5 | SR/BR SCHOOLS CLASS LOCO AND TENDER KIT | PRICE 11/6 + 1/6 P. & P. |
| KIT No. 8 | ITALIAN 0.6.0. TANK KIT | PRICE 5/- + 1/- P. & P. |
| KIT No. 9 | G.N. STIRLING 8' SINGLE AND TENDER KIT | PRICE 11/6 + 1/6 P. & P. |
| KIT No. 10 | BR DELTIC DIESEL | PRICE 16/6 + 1/6 P. & P. |
| KIT No. 11 | SR/BR BATTLE OF BRITAIN CLASS LOCO AND TENDER KIT | PRICE 16/6 + 1/6 P. & P. |
| KIT No. 12 | SWISS CROCODILE ELECTRIC ARTICULATED LOCO | PRICE 16/6 + 1/6 P. & P. |
| KITMASTER 12V DC 2-RAIL MOTOR BOGIE | | PRICE 28/10 + 1/- P. & P. |

IT IS REGRETTED THAT NO OTHER KITS ARE AVAILABLE EXCEPT THOSE AS SHOWN ABOVE

## W & H (MODELS) LTD

Telephone: 01-935-8835

14 New Cavendish Street, London, W.1.

---

Postage will be paid by Hamley Brothers Ltd.

No Postage stamp necessary if posted in Great Britain or Northern Ireland

BUSINESS REPLY CARD
LICENCE No. W.D. 217

**HAMLEY BROTHERS LTD.,**
200-202 Regent Street,
London, W.1.

via wholesalers to direct supply of retailers, something that has become more popular in recent years.

In October 1958 the Rosebud Kitmaster Ltd company was incorporated to make plastic construction kits by the injection method, using excess capacity in the Rosebud Dolls Ltd. injection room. The announcement in 'Toys and Games' that December quoted the Company Registration number as No.612977: *Private Company. Registered 15th October 1958. Capital £10000 in £1 shares. Objects: To carry on business of general engineers and engineering contractors, manufacturers and designers of and dealers in spare parts, kits, models, games and articles of all kinds made from plastics and plastic materials, etc. The permanent directors are: Thomas E. Smith (chairman), Broadfield House, Raunds, Nothants and John R. Ashby 22 Beaufort Drive, Barton Seagrave, near Kettering. Secretary: P.F.Minney. Registered office: Grove Street, Raunds, Northants.* Also in December 1958, the trade-mark Rosebud Kitmaster was registered, No. 778268 for: *Kits of parts (sold complete) for assembling into toy models; and toy models made therefrom. Registered by: T.E.Smith, Grove St, Raunds, Northants.*

Injection technology was well understood by Rosebud, T. Eric Smith having two patents, dating from 1950, on the subject numbers 667091 and 667906. T.Eric Smith says that they decided to move into kit manufacturing 'because at the time it was a growing industry. We went into the train side because it was different.' T.E Smith was Managing Director whilst J.R. Ashby acted as the Finance Director. John Ashby, who had replaced R.H.Ruff as Company Secretary on his retirement in 1954, was formerly with

**Gaily coloured Trade Displays were issued to retailers in 1959 (above) and cheaper two-colour versions again in 1960, below.**

W.J.Thompson & Co Ltd, the chartered accountants who audited Nene Plastics Ltd. books and was consequently familiar with their operations. He later became a Director. By 1962 there were two more named directors of Rosebud Kitmaster Ltd, D.H.Birch (who was originally Rosebud's Sales Representative for Lancashire & Yorkshire) and Charles A.Green as Works Director. Mr Green later became Works Director at Rosebud-Mattel and eventually at Smith's Containers.

To spearhead their 1959 sales campaign and help launch the Kitmaster project, Eric recruited a crack team of seasoned toy industry sales reps. They were headed by ex-Cascelloid marketing manager R.G.Noble, who had overseen the launch of the very first Palitoy trainsets, now the Sales Director. Working with him were two former Trix

*Above.* A range of Rosebud toys from the period: (L to R) Chatty Kathy, Baby Miss Rosebud, Squuezy squeaky Cat, Aquatoy baby doll and 15" Miss Rosebud. *Below left.* The cheapest Baby Rosebud (left in picture) had jointed arms only, whilst the more expensive version had both jointed arms and legs (right). *Below.* A counter-top trade pack of washable PVC baby dolls know as "Vinyl Babies".

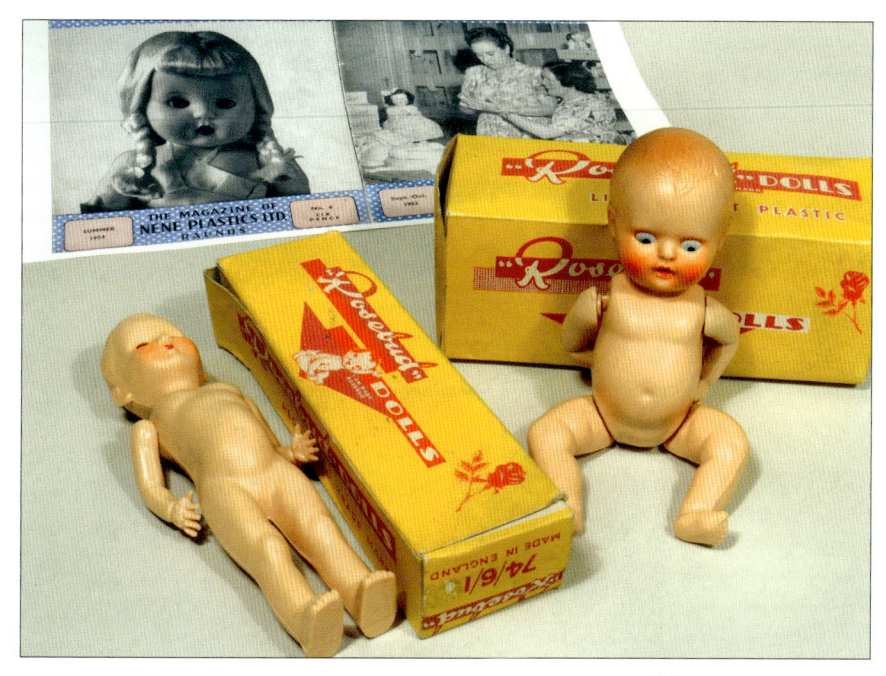

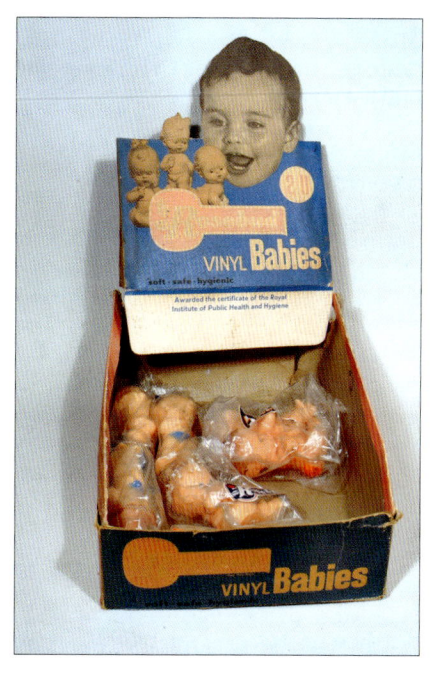

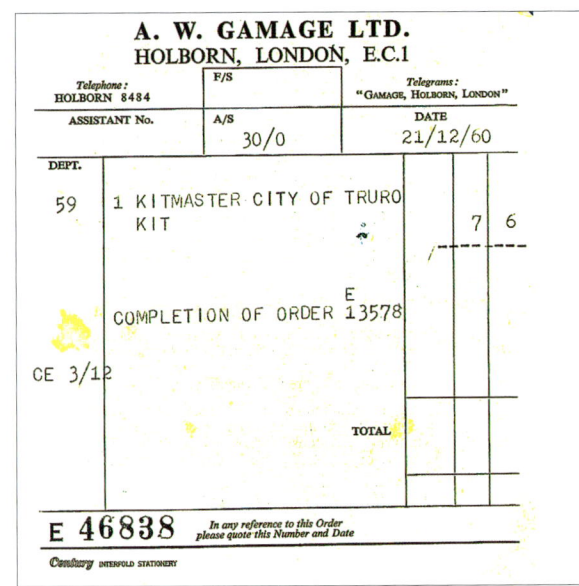

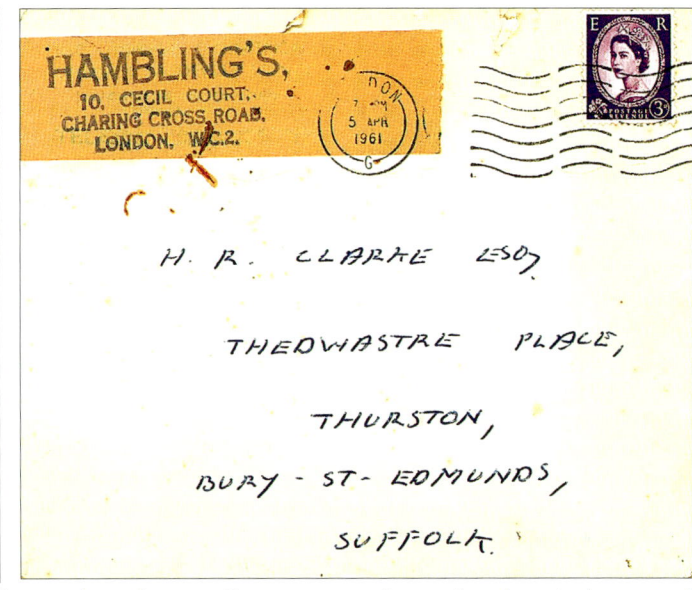

With their traditional large Christmas railway display and annual catalogues, Gamages was always the place to be sure of obtaining the latest Rosebud Kitmaster kit. Hambling's, on the other hand, would sell you metal wheels and axles to make your model more authentic.

*Above.* A London Transport trolley bus makes its way up a virtually deserted High Holborn, past the impressive frontage of Gamages store. The 621 ran from North Finchley to High Holborn and was withdrawn in November 1961. B.K.B. Green, Initial Photographics.

*Below.* A French edition of the 1959 catalogue.

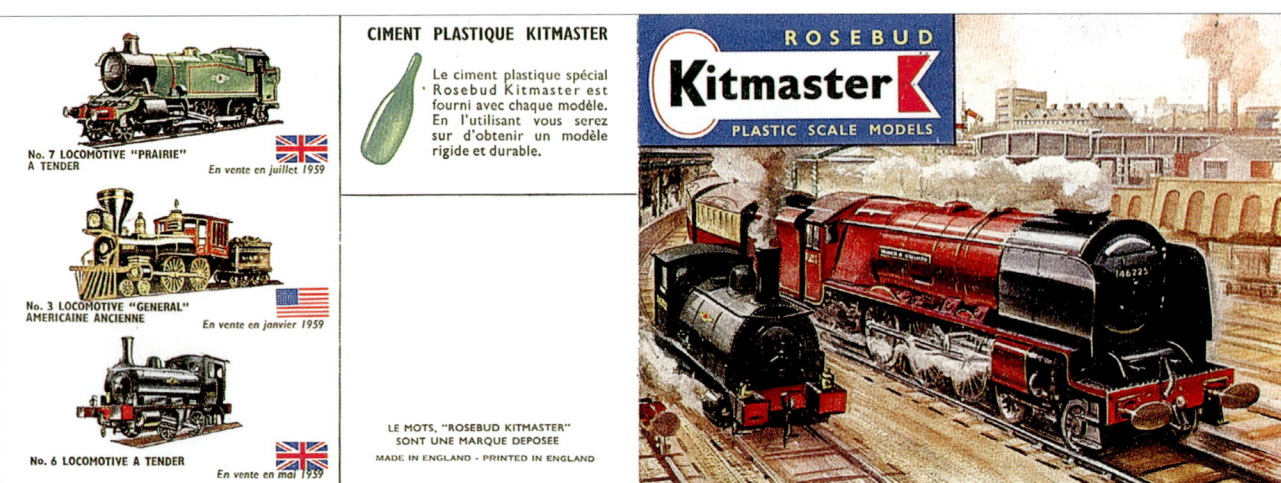

20

employees, L.E.Ambler (covering Scotland, N.Ireland and Northern England) whilst Mr A L Brown covered the Midlands. Two former Chad Valley reps covered London (Mr D Parr) and the Eastern Counties (Mr Frank L Wood). As noted above, D.H. Birch covered the North West whilst Mr A Bowden-Stuart covered the South West. These last two were the only existing Rosebud reps in the new team.

The Company Secretary of Rosebud Dolls was Mr J.R.Ashby, but Rosebud Kitmaster Ltd. had its own Company Secretary to comply with the Companies Act. This was Mr.P.G.Minney, who held the post from 1958 until 1960. Philip Minney was the General Office Manager for Rosebud Dolls Ltd. from 1951 until 1960 and oversaw a team of four workers in that capacity. His role was rather low-key in the Kitmaster organisation; Ashby was a much more powerful figure, and it seems as though he was appointed very much 'on paper' only. His job expanded rapidly when Rosebud wound up their long partnership with L.Rees & Co. Rees had been responsible for representing Rosebud products to the trade. However, in 1958 that long association ended and Rosebud had to recruit its own salesforce. This required a trebling, to twelve people, in the General Office staff and immediately wiped out any cost savings over the previous arrangement. Rosebud Kitmaster also used the Rosebud Dolls sales team. Philip Minney left Rosebud in 1960 and went to Bassett-Lowke, where he remained until 1969. He is now retired and lives in Worcestershire.

Rosebud Kitmaster Ltd. had no premises of its own, but a part of the 'New' factory, known as Plant One or just 'P1', at Raunds was converted for use by Kitmaster (see site plan). In April 1959, T.Eric Smith disclosed to the trade press that main doll production would be re-located to Wellingborough. New 25,000 sq.ft. premises were found in Westfield Road, which had been a former Co-Operative Wholesale Society corset factory. According to the press release, the new site was to be used for 'the dressing and assembling of dolls, and when full production is reached, in the course of the next few weeks, approximately 200 personnel will be employed.' It proved spacious and ideally suited to Rosebud's needs. Production transferred there in late 1959, leaving Raunds to concentrate on Kitmaster and a wide range of vinyl toys. The Wellingborough Rock Street site became the main warehouse at this time.

Rosebud Dolls Ltd continued to trade successfully throughout 1963, but had to lay off staff that summer due to a lack of orders. By early 1964, things were looking dire. Mr J.R. Ashby decided to leave at this point as did a number of junior staff. Problems with export credits and introduction of direct-to-retailer sales, with no wholesaler to act as a buffer, caused bigger and bigger problems for Eric. Eventually, on 15th June 1964, he was forced to call in the Receiver. Rosebud Dolls Ltd was put into administrative receivership and the Receiver issued a short statement to the press: 'In order to safeguard the position generally, the debenture holders of Rosebud Dolls ltd. have appointed Mr E.C.Baillie, chartered accountant, as Receiver from June 15th 1964.' Within a few days of coming into the company, the Receiver issued a written statement to all of the 240 strong workforce. It read: *I have now had an opportunity of looking into certain aspects of the business and have arranged increased schedules for the factory. Following my appointment as Receiver, I now confirm that I have taken over responsibility for your employment on the same terms you had with Rosebud Dolls Limited, with immediate effect. Yours faithfully, E.C.Baillie, Receiver.*

Having survived a period in Receivership, Rosebud Dolls Ltd started to rebuild itself and became Europe's leading manufacturer of dolls. Eric bought himself a Rolls Royce and was always to be seen travelling abroad to find new buyers for British-made dolls.

**Rosebud supplied factory-built models, packed in strong cardboard boxes, together with fold out trade displays which would also hold a selection of 1960 catalogues.**

**E.Rankine Gray (ERG) were one of the first commercial manufacturers of plastic assembly kits of railway subjects. Moulded in clear cellulose acetate, these mid-1950s kits also included white metal and turned brass parts. Only Rosebud marketed 100% plastic moulded kits of trains at this point.**

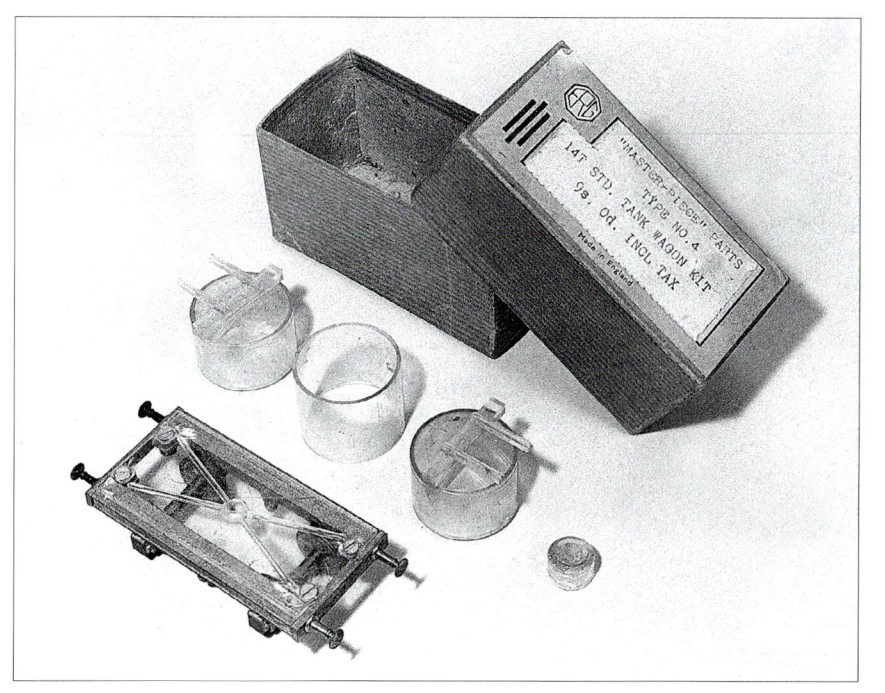

Amongst their most popular brands were the Rosebud Talking Doll, Chatty Kathy, and a licensed Bugs Bunny. Dolls were being produced in every size from 4 inches up to 34 inches and in many different styles and colours. They even developed a smooth injection moulded articulated teddy bear that swivelled its head as it walked. Advanced stuff for the time! T. Eric Smith made something of a faux-pas when he turned down the opportunity to produce under licence the then-new Action Man toys. Eric reasoned that boys would never play with dolls; which proves that you can't win them all! Although Rosebud had been rumoured to be a take-over target for the UK chemicals and fibres giant Cortaulds, it was eventually to fall prey to forces from the other side of the Atlantic. During 1967, Eric was persuaded to sell his successful business to Mattel Inc of America, thereby forming Rosebud-Mattel Ltd, the world's largest doll manufacturer. Mattel was, at that time, run by Elliott and Ruth Handler and was built around the success of the Barbie doll. Ruth Handler, the 85-year-old inventor of the Barbie doll, died in Los Angeles on 29th April 2002.

*Right.* **The end is nigh – 29 January 1963 and all Rosebud Kitmaster stock has been sold to Airfix Products Ltd.**

*Below.* **Visiting a trade fair, Mattel meets Rosebud. Left to Right: Elliot Handler, Hazel Smith, Ruth Handler, Eric Smith.**

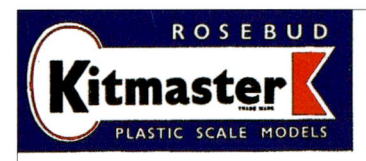

---

ROSEBUD KITMASTER LIMITED
RAUNDS, NORTHAMPTONSHIRE

TELEPHONE: RAUNDS, 444 (10 LINES) · TELEGRAMS: ROSEBUD, RAUNDS
CABLES: ROSEBUD, RAUNDS

J. A. Barclay.,
4, 'Linkstone' Warren Road,
Liverpool 23,
Lancs.               29/1/63.

Dear Sir,

We thank you for your letter of the _____

We wish to notify you that Messrs. Airfix Ltd., Haldane Place, Garratt Lane, LONDON.S.W.18, have purchased all the stock and manufacturing rights of the Rosebud Kitmaster.

We are therefore no longer carrying spare parts etc., for the Kitmaster range.

May we take this opportunity of thanking you for the support that you have given us in the past.

Yours faithfully,

FOR ROSEBUD DOLLS LIMITED.

Sales Department.
(JOHN T. HEARN).

JTH/SAC.

DIRECTORS: T. E. SMITH, J. R. ASHBY  C. A. GREEN, D. H. BIRCH

## AIRFIX—KITMASTER

*RAILWAY MODELLER DECEMBER 1962*

READERS have wondered over the past few months what was happening to the popular Kitmaster range, and we are pleased to announce that the plastic moulds and stock of kits have been purchased by Airfix, who will continue to market them as at present. We understand they have plans for development and incorporation into their own series of kits later on.

Ruth Handler was instrumental in the takeover of Rosebud Dolls in 1967 by her Mattel Inc company. Barbie, named after Mrs Handler's daughter Barbara, was launched in 1959 and revolutionised the existing pattern for dolls, which until then were almost invariably babies. With her model looks and improbable physique – if human, the original Barbie would measure 39-18-33 – she became loved by girls worldwide, attacked by feminists and the subject of endless cultural and political debate. More than one billion of the dolls have been sold in 150 countries and 95 per cent of American girls own one. When Mrs Handler noticed the enthusiasm with which her daughter played with paper dolls of teenagers and adults, she became convinced that there was a gap in the market for a doll that would allow girls to dream about the future: 'My whole philosophy of Barbie was that through the doll, the little girl could be anything she wanted to be,' Mrs Handler wrote in 1994. 'Barbie represented the fact that a woman has choices. I believed it was important to a little girl's self-esteem to play with a doll that has breasts.'

Mrs Handler, born Ruth Mosko and the youngest of 10 children, married her high-school sweetheart, Elliot Handler, who co-founded the company Mattel. Male executives on the board of Mattel initially rejected her design out of hand but Mrs Handler persevered. When 'Barbie Teenage Fashion Model' made her first appearance at the 1959 Toy Fair in New York, she was an instant hit. Barbie went on to make a fortune for Mattel which, by the early 1960s, had annual sales of $100 million. The Handlers were ousted from the board of Mattel in 1975. Her most enduring creation, however, went from strength to strength. Barbie has inspired artists from Andy Warhol to the pop group Aqua. There is a Barbie in the Smithsonian Institute, and a Barbie was selected in 1976 to be buried in the official time capsule celebrating the bicentennial of the United States. Barbie – who now has nearly a billion outfits

*Top.* Another interesting Rosebud toy from circa 1963/4 was the Red Devils Parachutist, shown here with a yellow EasiBuild set.
*Above.* The deal to form Rosebud-Mattel Ltd is signed In the Boardroom at Mattel Inc. Seated are Hazel Smith (left) and Ruth Handler; standing are Eric Smith (with pipe) and Elliot Handler. On the wall behind them is a photograph of Barbara Handler, Ruth's daughter and the original model for Barbie.

**A rare colour advert introducing Aquatoys, from "Toys & Games".**

in her wardrobe – was joined by Ken in 1961 and the first black Barbie appeared in 1981.

During the mid-1960s, Rosebud issued a number of interesting doll-related toys including a Red Devils parachutist kit, hand-launched, with figure and 'chute. These were a source of amusement to the workers on the production line who frequently 'fired' them into the air instead of packing them away properly! The company logo had been stylised by this time to remove the rose and used a more modern condensed bold typeface with white lettering on a red background. It was, it has to be said, rather dull compared to the two original logos, both of which were designed by Hazel Smith. The Rosebud name disappeared for ever in 1971 when Rosebud-Mattel Ltd became just Mattel (UK) Ltd.

Having sold the company, Eric and Hazel went on a world cruise and tried to adapt to a new life of quiet retirement. However, it was not to be. Frustrated by the lack of telephone calls from the bank, traders and business contacts, Eric decided that he wanted another business to run. He was, in his words, 'tired of being a nobody'. Eric was also bored with life away from England. He says he returned to England for two main reasons: the country is the only place where the grass is always green, and the only country in which you can speak to a policeman! Whilst highly subjective, there is no doubt that the globetrotting life of a tax exile did not suit Eric or Hazel.

Eric started to look around for another suitable market opportunity. Working on a hunch, he chose the emergent field of plastic containers. In a remarkable turn of events, Eric returned to Raunds and approached Rosebud-Mattel to negotiate re-purchase of the Raunds site! In 1969, he

was successful and Rosebud-Mattel moved out and consolidated on their second site in Wellingborough. This was a former Co-Op corset factory purchased by Eric for £10,000 when the Grove Street site became too crowded. Both Eric and Hazel moved back into their purpose-built architect designed bungalow, Broadfield House, on the hill overlooking the factory. This large property with all the latest modern conveniences had been constructed to Eric's design during 1956 and included a plate glass window so large that it took six men to carry the single pane during construction. Measuring some 9ft high by 18ft long and half an inch thick, this beautiful window gave panoramic views across the rolling Northamptonshire countryside behind Raunds. Later on, Eric also purchased the adjoining field from the farmer, Mr Groom, and had a small practice golf course constructed on it. When they first arrived in Raunds, Eric and Hazel lived at Ashfields Hall in Raunds, another palatial residence which was used to host the Nene Plastics Christmas Party until the workforce outgrew even this grand venue. It was opportune that they should move out in August 1956, as the Hall caught fire on 4th June 1961 and was destroyed. Eric's bungalow survived up to the last reorganisation of the Reed Packaging site in 1989 when it was demolished after access was removed by further site development, the wonderful window removed by the simple, if crude, expedient of driving a bulldozer shovel through it. According to witnesses to the demolition, it exploded with a crack which could be heard all across the town.

Having re-acquired the old site from Mattel, Eric set about razing the oldest parts of the dolls factory, referred to as the 'Old' factory, an ancient hotchpotch of buildings including Plant Two and Three. He kept the part, then known as the 'New' factory or Plant One. He built an entirely new factory on the site and imported a single second-hand German blow-moulding machine to work with a material known as HDPE, High Density Polyethylene, a versatile polymer made by BP. The first 13 employees were mostly former Rosebud/Mattel staff, including Mrs Rose

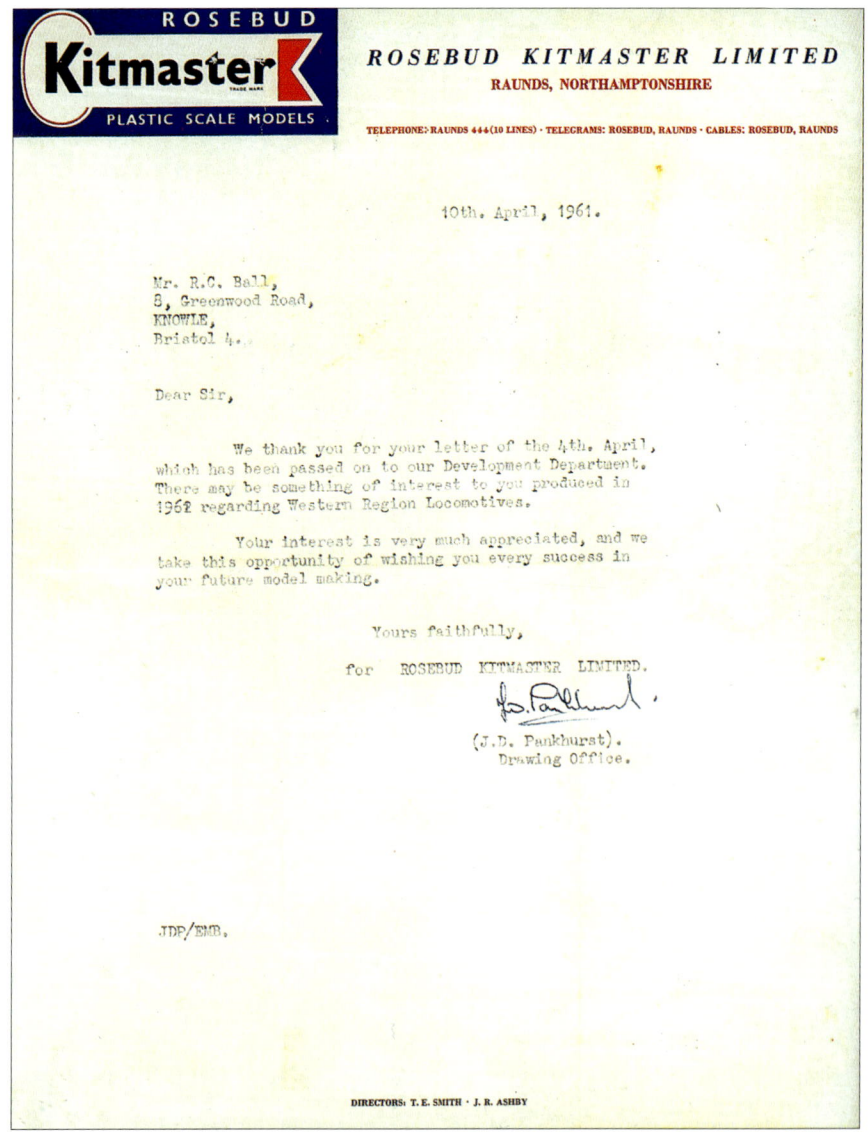

**This April 1961 letter promises something of interest to modellers of the Great Western during 1962…**

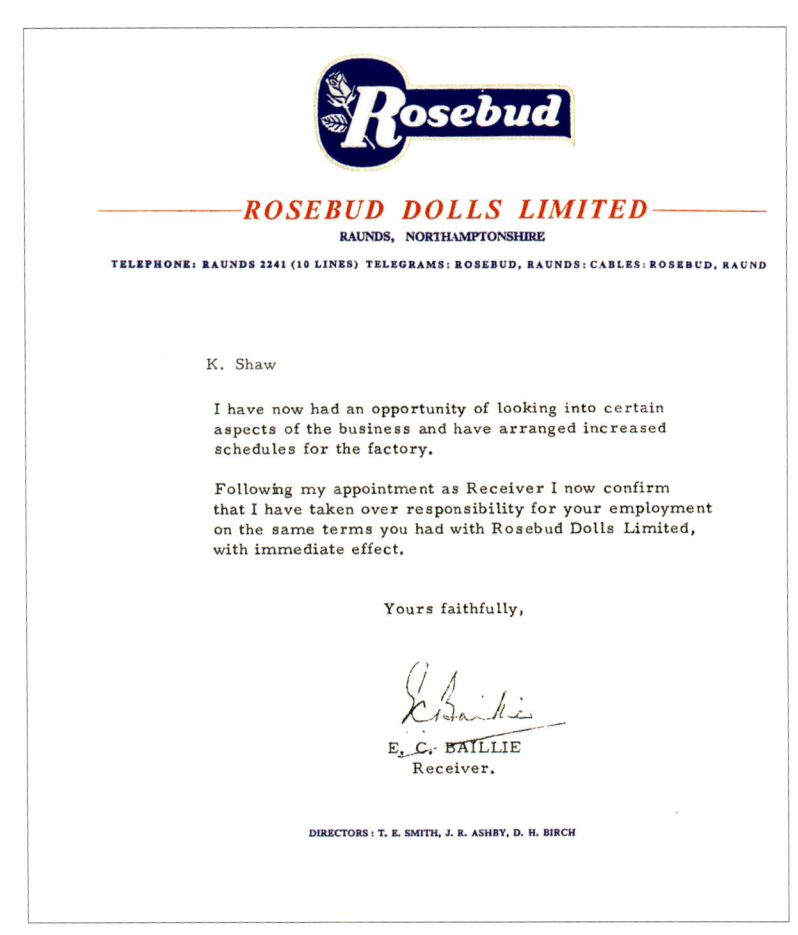

Following the financial difficulties at Rosebud, a Receiver was appointed and this letter sent to all members of staff.

The Northampton Evening Telegraph Tuesday June 18th, 1964 two crashes share the front page – one at Rosebud and the other on the Midland main line.

Barker, a stalwart of Masks Ltd, Nene Plastics Ltd and Rosebud Dolls Ltd who became Wages Clerk together with Eric's loyal handyman and chauffeur, Cyril Ferry who was persuaded to rejoin Eric in the new company, 'Smiths Containers Ltd'. Cyril Ferry, who always referred to T.Eric Smith as 'The Boss', remained a close friend, having acted as gardener, chauffeur, handyman, waiter, decorator and machine-hand in his time with Eric's companies. When Cyril's daughter announced her engagement in 1970, Eric insisted on driving her in his Rolls Royce on the big day, even purchasing a chauffeur's cap for the occasion. Cyril himself was a little wary of driving it; 'Eric came down one day and said "Come on, we're taking the Roller out". We went down to Stanwick and then on the back road to Thrapston, which is a lovely straight road. Suddenly, Eric pulled over and got out. He turned to me and said "Right Cyril, it's your turn, you drive now". I told him I couldn't, not the Rolls. "Don't be so bloody stupid! How's the car going to get to the airport the next time I come back? Is it going to drive itself there? Now get in!" So I got in and drove it. It was superb. So quiet you couldn't hear the wind or the engine, just a gentle purr. I drove him everywhere in it, including up to Gleneagles and Turnberry to play golf. I loved driving it, but eventually, he changed it for a limited edition Mercedes. The Merc was nice, but it wasn't the same. I loved that Rolls Royce.'

On 7th January 1970, with Cyril Ferry at the controls and Eric Smith watching, the first blow-moulded half-gallon plastic bottle in Britain came off the new production line at Smith's Containers, Grove Street, Raunds. It was an instant success; new machines were installed within weeks and the product range increased at a huge rate. Now the company, which is known as RPC Containers Ltd, has seven UK sites including Halstead in Essex, where by coincidence the Collectors Club is based, and turnover exceeds some £22m per year. T.Eric Smith finally retired to the Channel Islands in 1988 and eventually passed away on 13th June 2006, the day after his 60th Wedding Anniversary, aged 90. Hazel Smith followed some three months later on 29th September 2006, both passing away in the General Hospital at St Helier, Jersey.

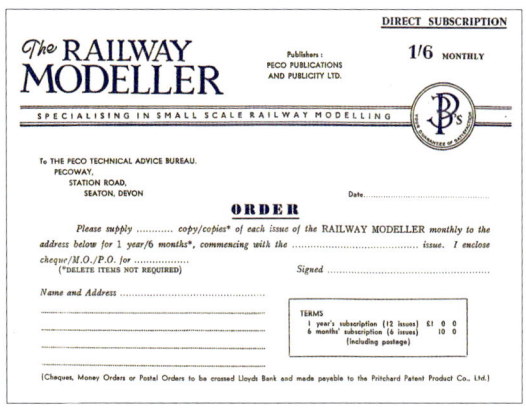

When you could pop down to your local model shop and buy both Airfix AND Kitmaster kits, it was pretty close to heaven! Four classics from the archives: Airfix BR Standard class 4 Mogul in the Type 4 box used from 1974 onwards. The superb Kitmaster model of Andre Chapelon's 241P "Montagne" (Mountain) design for the Paris-Marseille route. The largest kit issued by Airfix up to that point was the famous Avro Lancaster B Mk 1, seen here in the striking Type 1 box art around 1957. Still fondly remembered and the subject of frequent requests to "re-manufacture" the tools is Patrick Stirling's GNR No.1 8ft Single.

# Chapter 2: The Rosebud Kitmaster Story

Although Airfix products Ltd in the UK had introduced a polystyrene kit of the Ferguson Tractor in 1948, they were only initially available through Ferguson sales reps and were always supplied fully constructed. It was not until 1955 that the tractor became available as a kit, through Woolworths. The advent of the mass-produced plastic assembly kit had therefore come in 1952, when American toy manufacturer Gowland & Gowland started a mass production line for plastic construction kits. They initially offered waterline models of famous sailing ships, such as the *Santa Maria* and a range of 1/32nd scale model cars, known

*Above.* Not the first Airfix kit, but perhaps the most fondly remembered is the Spitfire Mk1 coded BT-K from 1955. Their 1978 Mark 1a kit was re-issued in 2005 onwards to mark Airfix' 50th Anniversary carrying the BT-K markings, which are entirely fictional and thought to have been copied from a larger Aurora kit. In 2009 James May, assisted by a team of Telford schoolchildren, built a life-size replica of the blue Airfix kit and adorned it with decals for – you've guessed it – BT-K!

*Below.* Original Airfix oil painting for Evening Star, thought to be by Charles Oakes, but unsigned.

*Marcus Archer built and painted the Kitmaster class 08 Shunter seen here. It was the first Kitmaster model to hit the shops in May 1959.*

as *Highway Pioneers*. The Gowland & Gowland company, based in Santa Barbara, California immediately licensed the new range of kits to Revell Inc of Venice, California, for distribution in Europe from its plant at Bunde in Germany. In the UK, the *Highway Pioneers* range was not made available until 1955 and was distributed not by Revell but by Baileys Agencies (1953) Ltd. By today's standards, they are crude models with not enough detail, but they represent a landmark in the development of the plastic kit which leads directly to the introduction of the Kitmaster range just three years later. By an ironic twist of fate, the *Highway Pioneers* tooling now resides in Chirk together with the remaining Kitmaster tools, as both are now owned by Dapol Ltd.

The Kitmaster range of plastic assembly scale kits was introduced in the period 1959 to 1962 by Rosebud Kitmaster Ltd. The revolutionary growth in UK plastic injection moulding capabilities during this time led directly to the introduction of a range of 4mm, 3.5mm and 3mm scale assembly kits moulded in the still-new plastic polystyrene. Polystyrene is much more rugged and durable than cellulose acetate, which had previously been used for trains. It can be easily welded with a liquid cement and forms a rigid structure, unlike polyvinyl chloride which was the softer, more elastic compound used to make Rosebud Dolls. Two competing ranges of plastic kits were introduced in the late 1950s, the Rosebud Kitmaster series of famous locomotives and the Airfix Railway and Trackside series. Both ranges brought unheard-of detail to contemporary modelling, at an affordable price. However, Rosebud kits were always more expensive than comparable Airfix types. In fact, whenever Airfix re-introduced an extant Kitmaster kit it was

**One of the obvious attractions of collecting these models is the superb artwork – like this de luxe Presentation Set No.2 featuring artwork by Ken Rush.**

28

A bizarre change of direction in mid 1963 saw the Flying Scotsman project, by then well advanced, dropped in favour of a 1:16th Scale motorcycle – the Ariel Arrow Super Sports. But at a hefty 5s 6d each, they were not going to rescue Rosebud from the financial quagmire.

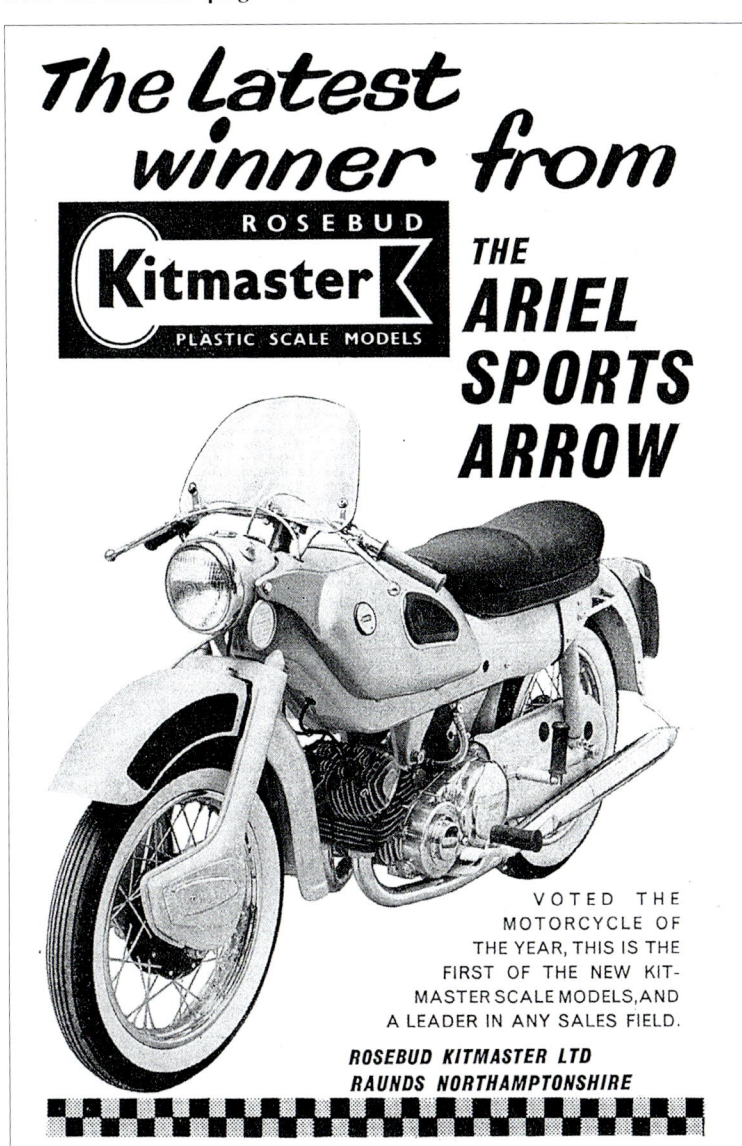

invariably accompanied by a hefty price reduction in relation to the original Kitmaster price. For example, in 1959 a Kitmaster Pug cost a not insubstantial 4s 6d, but by 1965 Airfix had reissued the Pug at just two shillings! Whilst there had been attempts at using injection moulded polystyrene for Railway kits before Kitmaster, these were limited to a few highly specialised manufacturers. An early example was E.Rankine Grey, or E.R.G., who, in 1956, introduced two wagon kits, one a box van and the other a 14t standard tank wagon. However, these kits used a combination of whitemetal, brass and plastic parts and were extremely rudimentary. Rosebud really were the first company to make 100% injected plastic rolling stock kits and proudly proclaimed this 'World First' in their 1959 Trade catalogue.

Rosebud Dolls Ltd employed a number of toolmakers over the years. At one point there were twelve people working in the toolroom. Some were experienced toolmakers who came from other local companies whilst others started their careers with Rosebud. One such was Mr Sydney Smith, who finished his National Service in 1954 and immediately joined Rosebud as an apprentice, firstly in the Maintenance Department and then in the tool room. He recalls that whilst the earlier patterns were made from brass, the later ones were nickel-plated copper which could be used to die-sink the tools directly by electro-etching. Mr Smith remembers the toolmakers taking the first 'shots' from a number of products as a perk of the job. Whilst his wife was ill at home with a cold, he brought her the very first shot of the Swiss Crocodile to while away her time!

Initially, Rosebud's Assistant Technical Manager Dennis Franklin undertook all of the work on the Kitmaster project himself, but it soon got to be too much for one man. Dennis needed help and so, with Eric's agreement, recruited staff for the tool room. Some of the railway patterns which were made in-house were by a couple of young

It was not long before motorisation kits appeared to enable Kitmaster Models to move under their own power (above). Beginning with the L&Y Pug, the Arby Perfecta kit range also covered the Italian tank, the Prairie and the Battle of Britain.

toolmakers, Gordon Wilby and John Marshall, who had joined Rosebud from Mettoy in Northampton. However, it was Dennis Franklin, above all, who was responsible for the birth of Kitmaster and the selection and design of the first two series of kits. He travelled extensively to research locomotives and carriages and to secure drawings from manufacturers and railway companies alike. It was Dennis who decided that they should make all of the locomotives to one constant scale; 4mm to the foot, irrespective of their country of origin. In the end this proved a fatal flaw in the product range, cutting off the vast Continental European and American markets which were so firmly embedded in 3.5mm scale modelling. This was pointed out in no uncertain terms by Mr Sidney Pritchard of PECO to Dennis Franklin. However, Dennis remained a staunch supporter of the 'constant scale' concept.

During the period of Kitmaster production, the toolroom was attempting to turn out a new tool each month, but this was said to be impossible. Finally, T.Eric Smith came into the toolroom one Friday evening and told them all that, in future, the work would be contracted out. Three of them, including Sid Smith, left immediately and within hours were on the payroll at John Orme & Co in Higham Ferrers. Orme had previously done work for Rosebud, including making special tools, to Rosebud's own designs, for doll assembly. Such tools included the first ever machine for stitching dolls' hair to their heads, designed at Raunds by Jack Branson, a Rosebud development engineer, after he saw a worker stow a needle by sticking it into a reject dolls head. Another Orme production for Rosebud was the first rotary casting machine for dolls and toys; the prototype was constructed from Mecanno by Dennis Franklin, Robert Parker and Sid Wilding.

Eventually, a number of toolmakers left, causing a re-think in the strategy. When Mr Fergusson, a Scottish marine model-maker, joined the toolroom in 1962, all work on railway subjects had been postponed, mainly due to the resignation of the pattern and toolmakers. He worked on the new motorcycle range, preparing the Ariel Arrow tool and working up drawings and patterns for a Matchless racing bike which never saw the light of day. He left Rosebud in 1964. John Marshall, a tall, avuncular gentleman complete with handlebar moustache, was one half of the famous Rosebud pattern making team for the Kitmaster project.

John has had a long and varied career. He started work on rebuilding De Havilland Vampire airframes at Little Staughton airfield near St Neots in the early 1950s. This is where he first met Gordon Wilby, the other half of the Kitmaster pattern-making team with whom he would develop a close friendship. Both were also members of the Rushden & Wellingborough Model Aero Club. Both men were excellent hobby modellers in their spare time. Immediately post-war, Gordon Wilby showed some of his work at a model competition at Rushden School, which was judged by W.J.Bassett Lowke. As a result, Gordon was offered a job with Bassett Lowke at their Northampton factory. In 1959 Gordon answered an ad in the local press for model makers from Rosebud Dolls and left. 'Not long after, I got a call from Gordon asking me to join him at Rosebud' says John. 'I recall that the first diesel shunter was in production, the Schools was coming out and so our first project together as a team was the Deltic, during summer 1959. John and Gordon were earning the above-average wage of £10 per week. Later still both men moved to John Orme & Co Ltd where they worked on sub-contract to Rosebud.

Their job was to develop silver-soldered brass masters from which the tools could be made. The work was divided between them with Gordon doing most of the locomotives whilst John did their tenders and the coaches. Consequently, whilst John did extensive work on the patterns for the Mk1 coaches and Blue Pullman he only did the tenders for the Mountain, DB23 and Truro and simply modified Gordon's work as required on the Beyer-Garratt. The Swiss Crocodile was, however, all his own work. John recalled that around the time they left Rosebud, the Pullman was being tried out from the moulds in black plastic! He pointed out, interestingly, that all Rosebud's instruction sheets were printed in-house on a RotaPrint machine which was housed next to their design workshop in the 'top secret' area of Beech House used for such work. John enjoyed his time with Rosebud, especially the chance to work closely with some of the great model designers such as Frank Roche and Michael Catalani. John has especially fond memories of Rosebud's in-house artist of the time, Tom Chapman, who had joined Rosebud from Mettoy around 1960. Interestingly, John has an example of the Schools locomotive without any lining. This was a very early shot from the tool before the decision to add raised 'lining' was taken. It has to be said that, of course, it looks much better without it! Another interesting item from that time is a test shot of the Diesel Shunter (Class 08) in the same yellow plastic used for the Rocket.

John was working on the eight-wheel LNER tender for the A3 Flying Scotsman at Whitsun 1961 when he was offered, and accepted, a job at Mettoy in Northampton. The owner of the famous Corgi model cars brand was happy to pay him £13 per week plus travelling expenses! At that time, fellow pattern maker Ron Green was completing patterns for the Ariel Arrow motorcycle. According to John, another project running at the time, but later abandoned, was a working model of a Singer Slantomatic Sewing Machine, which would have been ideal for Rosebud's regular target audience of young teenage girls.

Dennis Franklin and his team undertook the specialist pattern-making required for the railway subjects until he left Rosebud in 1960, just as his masterpiece, the Beyer-Garratt, was about to be released. From that point onwards, the railway pattern-making was subcontracted out to John Orme and Co and to freelance model makers, such as Jack Gain from Birmingham.

Rosebud never supplied free finished kits, but made their workers buy them at trade price! Jack Gain designed his own chassis for many of the locos in order to motorise them for his own layout. His motorised version of the Rocket is said to have became the pattern for the Tri-ang model. Halfway through the model making for City of Truro, Jack asked Rosebud for more money to finish the complicated pattern. Rosebud refused and tried to find another modeller to finish the pattern, even advertising in the Classified section of *Railway Modeller* in June 1960! No modeller, when faced with the complexity of the pattern, would touch it for the money Rosebud were offering and so they had to go back to Jack with a better offer. His work has been described by fellow pattern-maker, Mr Fergusson as 'beautiful, exemplary models'. He used carbon arc resistance soldering to build the brass patterns and used techniques which were peculiar to his trade as a silversmith, very different to Mr Fergusson's work on the Ariel Arrow which involved soldering and gas blowtorch, techniques picked up in his marine model-making career.

The principal Design Engineer of British Trix Ltd, Michael Catalani, on the demise of the Trix factory in Northampton, briefly came to work for Rosebud in May 1960. He had been about halfway through the development work for the British Trix Mk1 coaches at the time Dufay Ltd (the owner of the Trix brand) decided to centralise operations in Birmingham. Michael, who was then living at Wootton in Northampton, rang round some local companies looking for work and was invited to an interview with Rosebud Kitmaster on 22nd April 1960. This turned out to be an auspicious day, being both T.Eric Smith's and Michael Catalani's birthday. How could he fail to get the job with Eric in such an ebullient mood? Michael began work almost immediately. Although he had been mid-way through the development of the British Trix BR Mk1 coaches, his input into the Kitmaster Mk1 tooling was limited as the tools were at a very late stage by then. However, he did work on the drawings for the Pullman Cars, which were in the process of being redrawn from the Metro-Cammel master drawings. However, within three weeks of leaving Trix, Dufay Ltd had enticed him back with the promise of his own 'branch' office in Northampton and he left Rosebud's employ. T.Eric Smith was in Scotland at the time of Michael's departure, which, according to Michael, was probably just as well!

### KITMASTER "BATTLE OF BRITAIN"

THE Kitmaster "Battle of Britain" appears to have preceded the "Deltic" in production. However, we doubt if any of the many Kitmaster fans will quibble about the order!

As can be seen from our illustration, the Bulleid Pacific fully maintains the high standards set by its predecessors, though the air-smoothed casing leaves little opportunity for the intricate detail of some of the other models. As can be seen, the full character of the prototype has been captured, the B.F.B. wheel, the massive motion and the relatively high-pitched cylinders.

As readers will know, there is little basic difference, other than the name and number, between the "Battle of Britain" and West Country classes; in point of fact there are more variations between individual locomotives than between the nominal classes. Therefore we have two classes to select from, while one could stretch a point and give this model a Merchant Navy name and number. Here, of course, there are slight differences of size, but we doubt if they are sufficient to be noticeable on a layout.

Once again this is an excellent model of a popular prototype, and should be as well received by enthusiasts as previous items in this range. It retails at 10/6.

Rosebud launched their range in early 1959 as an 'exciting series of famous locomotives' whilst Airfix concentrated on the lucrative trackside accessories and freight rolling stock. Growth for both ranges was strong throughout 1960. It was not until 1961 that Airfix brought out their first locomotive, the Drewry Class 04 0-6-0 diesel shunter and followed it with a Park Royal Railbus. Rosebud warned buyers to 'watch for a new model every month' and to be sure to 'collect them all'. Inevitably this was followed up with 'have you got them all yet?' which is almost a motto for the Collectors Club. Remarkably, this rapid rate of introduction, one new kit each month, was initially maintained.

Tool making was, and remains, formidably expensive. Each of the larger tools, such as the Duchess and Battle of Britain, cost £10,000, an astonishing sum at the time, equal to two or three decent suburban houses. They were created from original patterns supplied by Rosebud at the London & Scandinavian Metallurgical Company in Wimbledon, south-west London. The tool making process was long and complex, but is summed up here by Dennis Franklin. 'First I did a breakdown of the loco into individual piece part drawings which I then handed over to Gordon and John, our two model makers. They made the master patterns. What happened to those, I do not know. I wish to God we'd got our hands on them. They

**Although Hornby Dublo had produced the Rebuilt West Country Class and Tri-Ang would soon produce their own, rather crude, version of the original air-smoothed Bulleid Light Pacific, it was the new Kitmaster model that garnered favourable reviews throughout 1960. The kit was further improved by Airfix for their 1968 re-issue by the addition of 'scissors' brake gear.**

might have gone to Airfix, or they might have remained at London & Scan. Then London & Scan. would mount them onto perspex and take a silicon rubber cast. From the cast they took a positive in epoxy resin. At that time we carried out inspection and then detailing such as rivets. The cavity epoxy male was then sprayed with a microns-thick active metal silver layer to excite the surface. It could then be electroplated with nickel, then backed up with copper to the thickness we wanted, normally 25 thousands of an inch. The cores could be cut directly out of steel or plated depending on their complexity.

'The sideframes, wheels and motion would all be machined from solid. It's a damn sight easier than trying to make wheels that fine with all the spokes at that size. We also machined all the gates and runners into the finished tool. The amount of plating done determined the cost of the tools. Some of them would be in the vats for weeks. Smaller locos were running at about £6-7000, but something like a Duchess cost us £10,000. That was a huge amount of money in 1959. After laying out and balancing, the steel tool was then spark-eroded from the plated masters. Finally they were case-hardened for durability. We wanted the tools to last and to have a useful life of more than one million shots. We were shifting up to 100,000 units per year of the more popular kits, I should think. You only damaged the tools if they were put up on the press wrongly.

'I personally found the laying-out and balancing of the tools the most interesting part and I learnt a lot during my time on the Kitmaster project. We had to balance up dead sizes and run sizes. We had to lay out, in conjunction with Lon Scan, the position of the relevant parts and where the runners would be machined in. We had to work out the projected area of each part and then balance it up so that the top half of the tool had the same projected area as the bottom half and the left hand side had the same projected area as the right half. Next we had to put the runners and gates in so that it all filled at the same time. Technically that is what you wanted to do, to get the same pressure on each tie-bar. You can do it by altering the size of the gates or the size of the runner to get it to fill pretty evenly. You will always get one part that fills last. To ease the operator's task, they were instructed always to look at that last part. If that part was full, he could put it in the box, if it

**When Kitmaster launched the impressive Midland Pullman sets in 1961 they were the epitome of Modern Image modelling, as evidenced by this contemporary Peco instructional.**

**Another stalwart of both the Airfix and Kitmaster ranges was the Southern Railway "Schools" Class V, the most powerful 4-4-0 in Europe.**

33

wasn't full, the whole thing was rejected.

'For obvious reasons I was on tenterhooks when a new tool came in. The number of times I would go through the parts list and then when the first shots were off... I'd heave a big sigh of relief.'

Airfix reduced the diameter of the sprues, which in original Kitmaster kits are rather thick. Dennis commented: 'Hydraulic pressure on the end of the ram and therefore on the leading material could be as much as 20,000 psi, but because of the tremendous pressure drop across the ram, cylinder, gates and runners, by the time you get to the other end of the tool you might only have 5 or 10 psi! We had worked with polystyrene before, for bases of push-along toys. They had wheels in polythene for toughness. We also experimented with high density polystyrene for dolls, before we settled on blow-moulded H.D. polyethylene for arms and legs. With Kitmaster we were working exclusively with polystyrene. The sprue diameter is judged in various ways. If the material was too hot in the tool it would blister, if it were too cold it would freeze solid in a narrow runner. You have to get the right combination of sprue size and temperature profile across the tool. When we started we were using a Windsor 1044 twin interlocked screw machine. You couldn't get a lot of pressure on it. Then we got a Windsor SH1 and an SH4. They were very modern and ran at higher pressures, but Airfix may have been using an Ankhewerk or something else. If you're producing 200,000 per year and you can save 5g of material by reducing the sprue sizes, it counts. We decided to use larger runners and to hell with the expense!'

However, by the end of 1960, delays were setting in, and promised introduction dates began to slip, by up to six months in some cases. The ever-expanding Kitmaster stable had reached some thirty models when things started to go wrong. The problem was mostly cash flow; tooling up for a different kit each month had financially drained Rosebud by the end of 1961. It had taken too long for Rosebud to get their distribution and marketing strategy sorted out and the projected growth in plastics modelling had not fully materialised. Consequently, revenues were not enough to fund the ambitious launch programme and market conditions were also far from ideal. Compounding the difficulty, the production area for Rosebud Dolls was being compromised by the expanding tools and stock of Rosebud Kitmaster. Eric Smith took the decision to look at a buyer for the Kitmaster business. At the end of 1962 he successfully negotiated the sale of all tools and remaining stock to Airfix Ltd. In October 1962, Christopher Brown of West Bromwich purchased a Kitmaster Battle of Britain kit. On inspection he found that one side of the front bogie was missing and the left-hand coupling rod was badly moulded and unusable. He wrote to Rosebud for a replacement part, but on hearing nothing by mid-November, wrote again. This time his letter was answered, by John Hearn (Sales Manager of Rosebud Dolls Ltd.) to inform him '...that Messrs Airfix Ltd., Haldane Place Garratt Lane, London S.W.18 have purchased all the stock and manufacturing rights of the (sic) Rosebud Kitmaster.'

At this point, it is worth considering the British outline model scene at that time. The growth of OO scale model railways between 1950 and 1960 had been astonishing. Nearly all of the models which are today thought of as the 'classic' core of railway modelling were introduced during this period. These include the Jinty Tank, Electra, 3MT and Britannia from Tri-ang, the Standard Class 4MT tank, MetroVick Co-Bo and Bulleid Pacific from Hornby Dublo and the Trix Britannia and Standard Class 5MT. Vast sums of money were being invested in new tooling and new models by a large number of manufacturers. Firms such as Meccano (Hornby-Dublo) and Lines Bros (Tri-ang) were releasing upwards of a dozen new models each year during the decade. Add to that ready-to-run releases from Graham Farish, Playcraft and British Trix and you begin to appreciate the scale of this expansion.

Unfortunately for Rosebud, the year 1961 saw a sharp decline in revenues for all these manufacturers as the OO gauge market became saturated. Too many new releases meant that fragmentation was occurring. No single company was receiving enough income to fund their ambitious product development programmes. An editorial in *The Model Railway Constructor* of January 1962 noted that many companies including, specifically, Kitmaster and Hornby-Dublo, had been forced to cancel or curtail new product introductions planned for 1962. In fact the March 1962 issue, in an Editorial report from the Toy Fair, mentions specifically the suspension of issue of the SR Tank, LNER A3 and Canadian National 4-8-4. The same article also noted that 'Kitmaster have, however, introduced the first in a series of large scale motorcycle kits.' This was, of course, the Ariel Arrow Super Sports in 1:16th scale.

Sometime after 1961 Rosebud introduced a set of Lego-like construction sets known as Rosebud Easi-Build. These were simple injection moulded construction kits. There were two Easi-Build sets, known as A and B. Each set is a single sprue of parts which interlock to make simple toys rather like a stripped down plastic Meccano. They are not toy bricks like Airfix Betta Builda or Lego, but were designed as constructional toys. Although one kit

**When Airfix received the Kitmaster tools, the first to be reintroduced was the virtually new Ariel Arrow Super Sports motorcycle, as it needed the least changes. This is the November 1963 Type II header.**

will make several simple models which are illustrated on the card, the best results are obtained by combining sets A and B, or preferably numerous sets of each type!

Easi-Build appears to have been moulded in several colours including yellow, green, red and blue plastic and came in a clear plastic bag with an instructional header (253 x 213 mm) showing exploded diagrams on one side and made up toys on the other. Priced at a premium 2s 6d, they feature the same Rosebud logo as the famous dolls. These kits can sometimes be found unopened even today but do not appear to have sold well. 1962 was not only a bad year for Kitmaster. Hornby Dublo cut its programme in half and struggled on for a further two years, the end finally coming in 1964 with a Lines Brothers agreed takeover to form Triang-Hornby. As has been noted above, the agreed takeover by Airfix went ahead at the end of the 1963 season. An interesting twist in the story then occurred. The Hermes Supply Company of Ravensbury Terrace, Wandsworth, London SW18, a fully-owned subsidiary of Airfix Products Ltd., secured a contract to supply certain kits from the excess stock of Kitmaster on behalf of Nabisco Foods Ltd. Nabisco at that time manufactured Shredded Wheat breakfast cereal and ran a promotion which enabled collectors to get free or reduced price Kitmaster models. This promotion ran throughout 1962 and 1963, after the sale of Kitmaster to Airfix Ltd. Airfix and Hermes together continued to supply Nabisco promotional kits until January 1964. More information can be found in the separate section on Nabisco. As for the other players, British Trix, which had been sold in 1957, was again sold in 1962 and survived long enough to be taken over by the Swiss Liliput company in 1970. Graham Farish, who had ceased all production for a while during 1957, stopped all OO production in 1976 in favour of concentrating efforts on the growing N gauge market.

When Kitmaster was sold, the moulds and all remaining stock in the UK were acquired by Airfix. Importers in each country disposed of residual overseas stocks. This led to some kits being available for a prolonged period after liquidation. Indeed, some distributors had tremendous problems clearing their warehouses. The Italian importer rediscovered a warehouse full of Kitmasters in 1969 and, despite prolonged advertising, could not shift them. Eventually they were given to local Children's Homes. A similar fate is said to have befallen a large number of kits imported into Sweden. After years of storage they were circulated to the Occupational Therapy departments of several big Swedish hospitals, where long-stay patients were encouraged to make them up! During 1967, W&H were able to offer most of the original series of twelve models which had been re-imported.

Airfix originally planned to incorporate at least some of the models into the successful Airfix Rolling Stock range. However, during a period around the transition from Kitmaster to Airfix, the tools were put into storage in a warehouse with a leaking roof. Water coming through the holes was channelled onto tarpaulins covering part of tools, but found its way into some of them, causing the case-hardened steel to oxidise and thereby produced tiny pits in the surface of the tool. When Joe Chubbock, toolmaker, and John Grey, MD of Airfix went to inspect their new acquisitions they were horrified at the damage which the ingress of water had caused. The rust damage to the worst-affected tools was thought to be irreversible and a decision was taken to scrap those tools straight away. Although the coach tooling was rusty, a report from the 1964 Toy Fair, in Peco's trade newsletter, *News Special*, mentioned that the '...the former

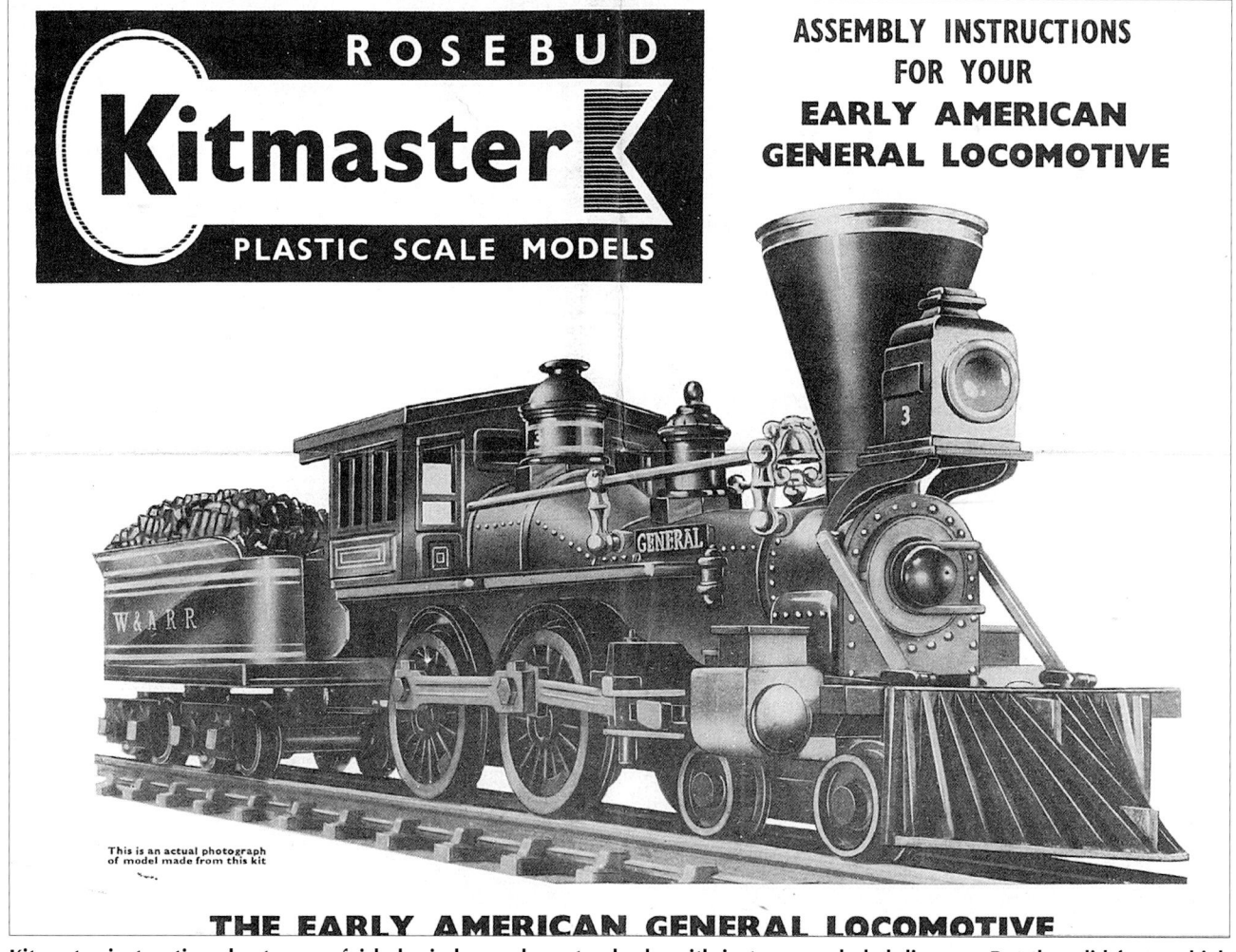

**Kitmaster instruction sheets were fairly basic by modern standards, with just one exploded diagram. But they did feature high quality illustrations of the completed models.**

Kitmaster coach dies are being rebuilt and their introduction is still in the future.' The same report noted the reintroduction of the Kitmaster L&Y Pug locomotive and asserted that 'Airfix have long established the principle of saying nothing of new productions until they are actually available.' During the 1965 Interplas exhibition in London, the Airfix reps were questioned about future Kitmaster reissues. A carefully worded letter was sent by Airfix to prospective stockists explaining that the ongoing programme of reintroductions '...over the last eighteen months...' would continue wherever the models could be '...sensibly incorporated into our own Railway range.' In the end, only nine of them were reissued; the Ariel Arrow, Pug, J94, Prairie, City of Truro, Schools, Battle of Britain, Mogul, and Evening Star. The omissions from the British Outline range were particularly surprising, especially when some of the tools were so new. The Beyer-Garratt, Diesel Shunter, Duchess, Deltic and Mk1 coaches were all omitted.

However, the greatest shock was the news that none of the Continental prototypes would be re-issued. Airfix had two separate distribution companies in America – Airfix Craftmaster and USAirfix, both of whom regularly imported and re-packaged Airfix kits for the huge US market. Why Airfix Products Ltd. would not let Airfix Craftmaster take the mould for the NYC Hudson loco or The General 4-4-0, we shall probably never know. The situation is made even more bizarre when one realises that Airfix had issued their own HO scale rolling stock kit - the Interfrigo refrigerator van. This last kit is all that remains of the HO production of Airfix and Kitmaster. All of the other tools were scrapped, variously by Airfix and Palitoy in the period from 1964 to 1982, when Dapol acquired the remaining tools.

More disaster followed. The unused tools were stored at Haldane Place on the lowest shelf of the racking in the Airfix storeroom. The River Wandle, which flowed past the outer wall of the factory, unexpectedly flooded one night and submerged the tool room in 3ft of water. This inevitably caused all the tools on the lower shelf to go rusty and they were condemned as insurance write-offs and scrapped. This is why so few tools survived into the Palitoy era.

After the collapse and subsequent acquisition of Airfix in 1980, the Haldane Place factory in Wandsworth was systematically cleared. Most of the documentation, records and artworks were transferred to the Palitoy Design office, located in a converted snooker hall in Coalville. The machines were sent to France, whilst the tools were despatched to another Palitoy site at Glenfield, near Leicester. To avoid paying rates on the vacant building, the roof was removed. It was sold and eventually the buildings were demolished and replaced by a Texas DIY store.

Airfix had become part of the Palitoy group, owned by the US conglomerate General Mills. The entire stock and most moulds of Airfix were located in the warehouse at Glenfield, near Leicester before production of Airfix kits was transferred to the Palitoy factory in France. During a visit to Glenfield in 1984 by David Boyle, proprietor of Dapol Model Railways, whilst negotiating the purchase of Mainline Railways from Palitoy, he witnessed the wholesale destruction of many priceless moulds in response to an order to 'clear the warehouse'. In order to stop the carnage, during which the Beyer-Garratt and Stirling Single moulds were opened and '...a sledgehammer put across the face of the tools...' David contacted the management of Palitoy and offered to buy the Airfix trackside range, along with Mainline, from them on the spot. Dapol initially acquired eight moulds in spring 1985.

The collapse of Palitoy's European businesses, Mainline, Airfix and Action Man, was the direct result of a re-organisation of the business by the American managers in Cincinnati. They decided to abandon all European product development. Instead, subsidiary companies would be offered a 'shopping list' of US designed products which they could re-package for sale in Europe. This was a disaster for Airfix. Palitoy UK had carefully stored the entire Airfix archive in a specially-constructed room at Coalville, but with the redundancy of the entire design team and closing of the Mainline sites in Coalville, this was put at nought. Artwork, drawings, archive photographs, mock-ups and roughs were unceremoniously thrown into a skip. Even framed artwork was thrown out. Employees were offered the chance to buy any item from the site for just £5! Some material was rescued by employees, some was donated to the Bethnal Green Museum of Childhood. Much important historical material was destroyed but luckily some of the railway artwork from the ex-Kitmaster kits has survived in private hands. Fortunately, the team from Replica Railways, visiting the factory to buy

*Above and right.* These two images from noted lensman Tony Wright show the stunning detail incorporated in the front end of the Kitmaster NYC Hudson and the life-like appearance possible with their 9F kit, seen here exiting Stoke Tunnel on the Wolverhampton MRC club layout "Stoke Bank".

clearance stock, was able to rescue a lot of Airfix catalogue artwork and transparencies, together with original BR General Arrangement drawings from Derby Works which had all been thrown into a skip. Much of that rescued artwork is reproduced here.

Although eight of the ex-Kitmaster tools had arrived with the Mainline business, there were some unaccounted for. The missing tools were eventually located in the French factory, at Calais, after David Boyle obtained permission to search it from Palitoy management. The tools had been marked with the name of the model when they were acquired by Airfix. How they got to Calais is quite interesting. The story begins with Airfix Products Ltd whilst they were still independent and based at Haldane Place. When Airfix introduced ready-to-run railways in 1976 they lost no time in exploiting their position as a major plastic kit manufacturer. Right from the start Airfix Railways trainsets were available with a couple of Trackside Series kits included for good measure. These kits were late mouldings in grey plastic, in polybags and lacking separate packaging. Various subjects were included in these sets, mostly buildings such as the Water Tower or fittings such as the Signal Gantry with very occasionally a set of figures included. Scarcest of these is a polybagged set of Civilians, which, at the time of release, was long since deleted! This activity clearly forged a link between the RTR system and the Railway and Trackside kit series. With the acquisition of the entire Airfix business by Palitoy in late 1980 all of the Airfix RTR models and the Railway series tools came under new ownership. Integration of Airfix items into Palitoy's Mainline Railways range was relatively quick, with many items packed in Mainline boxes carrying Airfix branding on their underframes. However, no mention was made of the former Airfix railway kits.

### Table A : Design Groups of Kitmaster railway vehicles

| British Steam Designs | | | Continental | Diesels | Coaches |
|---|---|---|---|---|---|
| *Standard Designs* | *Pre-Grouping* | *Big Four* | | | |
| 9F | Pug | Duchess | Hudson | Shunter | BSK |
| 4MT | Rocket | Schools | General | Deltic | SK |
| | Truro | Bulleid | Baureihe | Pullman | CK |
| | Stirling | Prairie | Mountain | | FO |
| | | SR USA | Crocodile | | A9myfi |
| | | A3 | Italian | | B4yge |
| | | J94 | CN U4a | | Kitchen |
| | | Rb Scot | | | Parlour |
| | | Garratt | | | |

These were stored in the infamous warehouse at Glenfield near Leicester, along with many other Airfix tools. At some point during 1983 it was decided to re-introduce these kits into the Mainline Railways range, as accessories. A selection was made and in order to prove the feasibility of the project, these moulds were shipped to Palitoy's Calais factory, where test shots could be made. This would allow Palitoy management to assess the state of each tool and the attractiveness and suitability of each kit.

These tests are known to have taken place as the Kitmaster archive contains the unopened bag with test shots for the J94 tank engine in it. Merl Evans, Technical Manager at Bachmann and a former Palitoy employee at their Coalville plant, kindly supplied these. However, the numbering on the bag, which is an in-series Mainline catalogue number, is described by Charles Manship in his seminal tract on collecting Airfix and Mainline Railways as the Diesel Shunting Locomotive. It is true that the bag does have 'Shunting

**Top.** The Midland Pullman required a motor bogie of sorts and Rosebud's solution was to use the KM1 Motor Bogie. It was ingeniously designed to fit inside a BR Mark One coach body, but could equally well be adapted for Pullman use.

**Below.** Everything you needed in 1961 to build a Midland Pullman set.

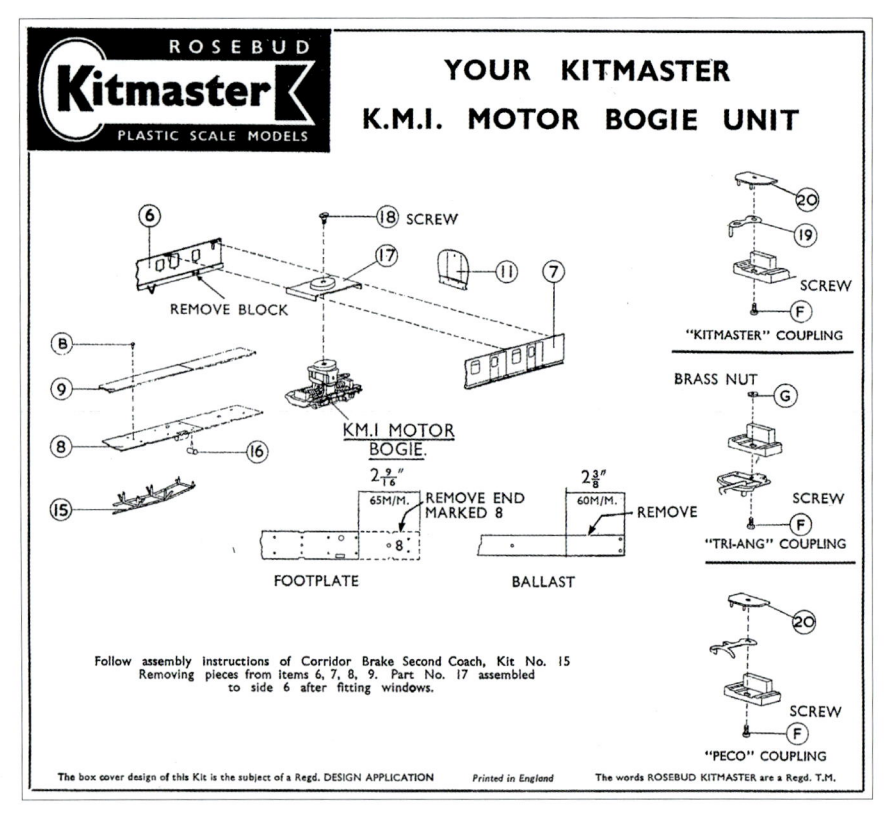

Locomotive' written on it, but it is clearly the J94 which is inside. The table shows which models were considered for Mainline releases, with their projected catalogue numbers.
    37-467 Platform Figures
    37-468 Railway Workmen
    37-469 Scammel Scarab
    37-470 Drewry Shunter
This last number was eventually allocated to the J94 test shot instead.

There are some similarities between this list and the manifest list of tools recovered from Calais by Dapol Model Railways when they acquired that

business from Palitoy. The selection here explains why some tools remained at Leicester whilst others went to France, a fateful move which ensured the ultimate destruction of many of those remaining at Leicester. This included many rare Kitmaster tools that had been previously stored by Airfix in their secondary warehouse at Charlton in Kent.

Ultimately, Palitoy abandoned the idea of re-issuing these kits as a result of a changed policy from General Mills (the Palitoy US parent company) which would end European product development and lead to exclusively US-sourced products for the European market. It was this decision from Palitoy that led them to firstly agree a sale to Dapol of the Railway and Trackside construction kit tooling. In 1986 the non-railway Airfix range was sold to Humbrol, with production of the famous aircraft kits remaining in France, at the Heller plant in Trun. Dapol set about releasing all of the Airfix trackside models, in a second deal with Palitoy. Oddly, they were unable to agree on the Airfield Control Tower kit. Palitoy maintained that it was not a 'trackside' kit, although the 1962 advertisements and the Airfix complaint slip clearly show it in the 'Trackside' range! When released in 1959 Pattern No 4017, it was

**Crowded shelves in the Model shop! Eleven rare and classic kits of the 1950s and 1960s, beginning, at top, with the Airfix James Bond Aston Martin DB9 in 1:24th scale, with working ejector seat. It squares up to a classic 1:32nd scale 1950s motor car kit by J & R Randall Ltd in their Merit range. Central is the extremely rare Airfix *Southern Cross* ship kit in 1:600th scale – only sold on board the Shaw Savill liner. In the foreground is a 1:1200th waterline model of *K.M. Bismarck* made by Eagle Wall Ltd. Next, middle, is Kitmaster's Beyer-Garratt, a classic kit by any measure, still much in demand today. Aurora issued the rather wonderful Regulus II cruise missile in 1959 following the success of an earlier Revell model, but theirs was in the senior ¼ in scale (1:48th). Airfix launched their range of 1:12th scale Famous Figures with the Lifeguard Trumpeter. It is still in production today with Hornby. Tri-ang (bottom) launched their plastic kit range under the FROG (acronym for 'Flies Right Off the Ground') brand first used for their pre-war flying tinplate models. They specialised in Cold War jets and airliners of the 1950s in 1:96th scale. The Faller kit of the Convair 440, made in West Germany, was in a similar scale of 1:100 and also part of series, which included the Vickers Viscount. Lindbergh of the USA made fairly simple kits in 1:48th but always with striking box art, while the Douglas Skyrocket in this selection is another rare Cold War experiment from the stable of Revell Inc, many of whose boxes featured superb paintings by Jack Lanemaker.**

*Tom Wright's Deltic on Stoke Bank.*

clearly a trackside kit, but upon reintroduction in the 12th Airfix catalogue it had become 03305-1 numbered in the AFV/Diorama range. Subsequently it became 03380-2 in the 13th Catalogue, but was listed with Series 3 Aircraft Kits! It was reissued again in 1991 in the Airfield series.

When Dapol shot the mould marked 'Drewry Shunter' they found it to be the original Kitmaster Deltic. This tool had been earmarked for scrapping by Airfix and indeed the tool for the clear parts was destroyed. The search of the Calais factory also unearthed the Rocket, Prairie, City of Truro, Pug and J94. All of these were eventually incorporated into the Dapol range, but it was some time before the Drewry became available again. Over 2,000 Deltics were produced in the initial run. The tool has been repaired several times at Dapol. The initial issue of the J94 by Dapol, catalogue number C34, only ran to 2,400 kits and the tool was only engraved with the Dapol logo for the very last batch. The J94 tool became unusable before the disastrous fire at Dapol's old factory in Winsford, but during the inferno, a girder fell on it and destroyed it forever. It was scrapped and the kit deleted from the Dapol range.

Dapol have also produced new decal sheets for some of the locomotives in the last ten years; names such as *Kings Wimbledon* began to appear on the Schools, *92* and *257 Squadron* names were marketed for the Battle of Britain and even the Prairie got a new number – 4141. Now, after more than forty years of continuous production, these fine kits are still giving hours of enjoyment to the young modeller and providing a priceless source of parts for 'Kitbashers' everywhere. As this book went to press it would appear that Dapol are considering re-tooling the Kitmaster Stirling single for re-issue.

**A lot of the Kitmaster artwork was produced by freelance artist Kenneth Rush. Ken's distinctive style of the period uses a lot of highlights and speed whiskers to convey power & speed and his perspectives are very condensed by comparison with, say, later Roy Cross images. The Deltic and DB Class 23 show this well, whilst the adoption of a "standardised" layout for boxes after kit No. 27 did somewhat restrict this, as evidenced on the German B4yge coach.**

---

### Are you a Kitmaster collector, too?

Are you making and collecting these authentic scale models of some of the world's most famous locomotives? Take the Deltic Diesel, for instance. It's just out—the latest to be issued—and like all Kitmasters it has moving parts and works on OO and HO gauge tracks. To ensure complete authenticity it was made from British Railways blueprints and officially checked by B.R. designers. That's how correct to the last detail *all* Kitmaster models are!

**AT MODEL AND TOY SHOPS EVERYWHERE!**

**ROSEBUD Kitmaster PLASTIC SCALE MODELS**

ROSEBUD KITMASTER LIMITED

C10

**10 AUTHENTIC MODELS TO MAKE!**

| | | | |
|---|---|---|---|
| No. 1 | Stephenson's Rocket 4/6d. | No. 6 | Saddle Tank 4/6d. |
| No. 2 | Diesel Electric Shunter 4/6d. | No. 7 | Prairie Tank 6/6d. |
| No. 3 | Early American General 6/6d. | No. 8 | Italian Tank 6/6d. |
| No. 4 | Coronation Class 10/6d. | No. 9 | Stirling 8' Single 7/6d. |
| No. 5 | Schools Class Harrow 7/6d. | No. 10 | Deltic Diesel 10/6d. |

moulding with the commensurate detail it could give. An advance mention in the 'Model Railway News' of March 1959 said: 'Rosebud Kitmaster, a new name to the hobby ...will introduce a model of British Railways Class DEJ3 Shunter as a complete plastic assembly kit at the reasonable price of 4s 6d.' This was the first mention to the public of a Kitmaster product. Rosebud had informed the trade at the Harrogate Toy Fair in January 1959 and splashed out on lavish two-colour full page adverts in the trade magazine 'Toys and Games' to promote the first four releases. Reviewing the Toy Fair, 'Toys and Games' said: *Introduced for the first time to the trade were the Rosebud Kitmaster plastic scale models of famous trains, past and present. The detail of these models was amazing, as each is built to scale with actual moving parts and can be used on OO and HO gauges; twelve models are planned to make their debut during 1959 with prices ranging from 4s 6d for the Diesel Electric No.2 to the Battle of Britain Class No.11 at 10s 6d. All are packed in attractive boxes, complete with instructions and special plastic cement. National advertising in hobby and modelling publications and boys' weeklies is planned to commence in April and carry on until the end of the year, so that interest is steadily increased. Striking counter displays of an actual model appearing from a tunnel are also available to all stockists, who will be supplied through their usual Rosebud wholesalers.*

The same report also noted that November and December 1959 would see a concerted £30,000 campaign of TV advertising by Rosebud to support the launch of several news dolls including Miss Rosebud (14½in and 20in), 'Delightful teenagers, impeccably dressed', Rosebud Sisters (11- 13- 15- and 17-inches) and 'a charming new Baby Rosebud' range in four sizes from 10 to 18 inches.

'DEJ3' was the original Eastern Region designation of the 350HP 0-6-0 diesel electric shunter designed by the LMS and built at Derby Works. However, as the article points out, what actually emerged from Grove Street was a model of the DEJ4 350HP Class 08 locomotive, being the ubiquitous British Railways standard design constructed at Doncaster Works. For more information please see the section in *The Models in Detail* dealing with this kit. This was the first Kitmaster model to be available in the shops, despite carrying the series number 2! You have to Read The Runes in this game...

Eric Smith got the idea for plastic assembly kits from America. He brought back a sample of an early US kit for the wood-burning 4-4-0 locomotive 'The General'. Branded Trail-Blazers and manufactured by Advance Molding Corporation of 54 West 21st St New York, it was partnered by a Mail Coach (Catalogue No. 34/98) and a Day Car. He discussed the possibilities of doing something similar with Dennis Franklin,

### The Kitmaster Concept

The idea of easily built, inexpensive scale railway kits was a good one. At the time of introduction, ready to run rolling stock left much to be desired. Tri-ang offered crude under-scale length coaches, many 'freelance' designs and a noticeable lack of detail in their mouldings. Indeed in the 1966 publication, the *Tri-ang Hornby Book of Trains*, Rovex describe how each new model may differ considerably from the prototype: 'Some dimensional divergences are deliberately made ...to make use of standard components ...to hold down costs.' The alternative, Hornby Dublo, system was also lacking in detail and attention to scale. At the time Hornby Dublo were just starting to introduce the so called 'Super Detail' coaching stock. Whilst it represented an improvement on the earlier all-tin-plate construction, the printed tin-plate sides still looked primitive by comparison to Kitmaster's highly detailed coach moulding. Tin-plate was the order of the day at British Trix, whilst Graham Farish offered a composite of tin and plastics. Only Rosebud Kitmaster seized the full possibilities of plastic injection

41

Assistant Technical Manager. This project would be something of a 'labour of love' for Dennis as both his father and grandfather were enginemen with the erstwhile London, Midland and Scottish railway at Wellingborough. Dennis' first task was to redesign, at Eric's insistence, 'The General' for re-issue in the UK. The original US issue was 3.5mm/ft. Dennis would have preferred to ignore this locomotive in favour of something not already covered as a kit subject.

The choice of locomotives was, from the outset, rather esoteric. This was due to the direct involvement of T.Eric Smith and Dennis Franklin in the selection of prototypes to be modelled. Eric Smith himself states that his favourite model of them all is the first one, The Rocket. The first batch of four was released in April 1959, four years into the British Transport Commission's 'Modernisation Plan' which would inexorably lead to the death of British steam power. Kitmaster failed to grasp the marketing opportunity provided by the plan. The first series of ten kits to be advertised contained only one production series diesel, no electric locomotives and no BR Standard Steam designs. The eventual inclusion of the BR Class 9F and Class 4MT designs came far too late to affect sales figures. There were no concessions made to the wave of optimistic enthusiasm gripping the country at the beginning of the new decade. A sense that only steam engines would sell certainly pervaded the Rosebud camp.

There were, however, some very interesting foreign designs, including the famous Italian State Railways Class 835 'Caffetierra' tank engine and the massive Be6/8 Krokodil of the Swiss Federal

*Top.* Rosebud introduced colourful packaging for their composite Presentation Sets from late 1959. These three were all painted by Ken Rush from pictures and models supplied by Rosebud. From top to bottom they are: Set P3 with TT Royal Scot and four BR Mk1 coaches, Set P2 with Battle of Britain and three BR Mk1 coaches and Set P1; 100 YEARS OF BRITISH STEAM LOCOMOTIVE HISTORY with Rocket, the Stirling Single and the Duchess.

*Left.* Powering your Kitmaster models was easiest if you used Kitmaster Motor Bogies. The KM1 Motor Bogie fitted into a suitably modified BR BSK Coach, whilst freight locomotives could be pushed only by the natty little powered Box Van, KM2.

Fitting the KM1 Bogie involved bending or cutting the steel ballast weight in the coach – no easy job for a young boy! But the plastic yoke made the ultimate fitting of the bogie easy and allowed easy removal for maintenance.

Railways. Unfortunately, Kitmaster had not properly researched the export market for these kits. Together with the later kits of the SNCF 241P Mountain and the DB Class 23 2-6-2, these were produced to the British scale of 4mm to 1ft, in order to maintain a 'constant scale' across the series. Suffice to say, these models found only limited acceptance in their intended markets.

The first four kits were, however, a promising start. The BR Class 08 Diesel shunter was a good choice, preceding the Tri-ang and Hornby Dublo models by several years. The Duchess was a popular prototype, although here Hornby had stolen a march on Kitmaster, whilst Southern enthusiasts everywhere welcomed the Schools Class 4-4-0. The Rocket was such a delightful and diminutive model that most people looked favourably on it although it was difficult to incorporate into any contemporary model scene.

From thereon it was rather an uneven choice. Models came in every size, shape, form and livery. What was needed was a coherent plan backed up by some solid market research. But, alas, it was not to be. There were high points of course; the Bulleid Pacific, the Pug and Prairie were all rapturously welcomed. But the Italian tank and the Crocodile were less than enthusiastically received.

*Right.* A 1970s view of the site after Reed Packaging had redeveloped most of it.

## The Raunds Site

The small town of Raunds in Northamptonshire, which lies between the A6 and the A1 Trunk roads, near Wellingborough, was for many years the home of Rosebud Dolls and Rosebud Kitmaster. Rosebud's original Grove Street premises are no longer in existence, having been redeveloped in 1970 by T.Eric Smith for the Smiths Containers site. The Rosebud factory was situated at the junction of Brook Street and Grove Street in buildings which started life as Nicholl's Boot Factory. After the recession of the 1930s, the boot factory was broken up into separate units, part of it becoming Frost's Ironmongery. Other parts became the Tivoli Cinema, the Advance Garage and another small boot workshop. When, in 1940, T.Eric Smith's mother moved their toy-making company from London to Raunds and formed Masks Ltd., she took over the redundant Advance Garage premises. In 1946, T.Eric Smith himself acquired Frost's Ironmongery to provide offices for his new company, Nene Plastics Ltd and it was duly converted. Other buildings in the former boot factory were converted for use as, variously, a showroom, canteen, production area, solvent store, carpentry and maintenance workshop and further offices.

The new office boasted five telephone lines with the number Raunds 191, but by 1960 this had been doubled to ten lines with a new number, Raunds 222. The manufacturing plant was arranged through numerous outbuildings and parts of the old boot factory at the rear of the former shops. Components for the dolls passed down a chute under the Central Road to reach the final assembly area. In 1954 Rosebud began construction of the so-called 'New' factory at Raunds. This was to house new doll-making injection moulding machines, but would eventually house the Rosebud Kitmaster production area. The New factory, which became Plant 1, was adjacent to the rather ramshackle Old factory, which was designated Plant 2 and 3, and contained a suite of offices along the south wall. When Rosebud-Mattel moved out to Wellingborough and sold the site back to T.Eric Smith in 1969, he demolished the Old factory and Grove Street offices, replacing them with a brand new factory for the Smiths Containers business. The 1969 Ordnance Survey aerial photograph shows the cleared site of the old factory with just the new Plant 1 left, but by 1970 a completely new plant had arisen, Phoenix-like, from the ashes. This adjoined the former Kitmaster New factory, which is still in existence as part of the RPC Containers site. Further building work has taken place at RPC from 1984 onwards and no trace of the original Grove Street premises exists,

*Middle.* **This rear view of Plant 1 (The New Factory) was taken in 1969, prior to the demolition of the older buildings on the site. It clearly shows the boiler house and loading bay at the rear of the injection shop. Eric Smith appears to be lurking inside…**
*Above.* **The New Factory building encompassed a suite of offices (on left in picture) and abutted straight on to the old cottages in Beech Hill, the nearest of which was used as a solvent store for many years.**

This RAF aerial photograph clearly shows the old boot factory as it was after the construction of the new mould shop, but prior to demolition of the older buildings in 1969.

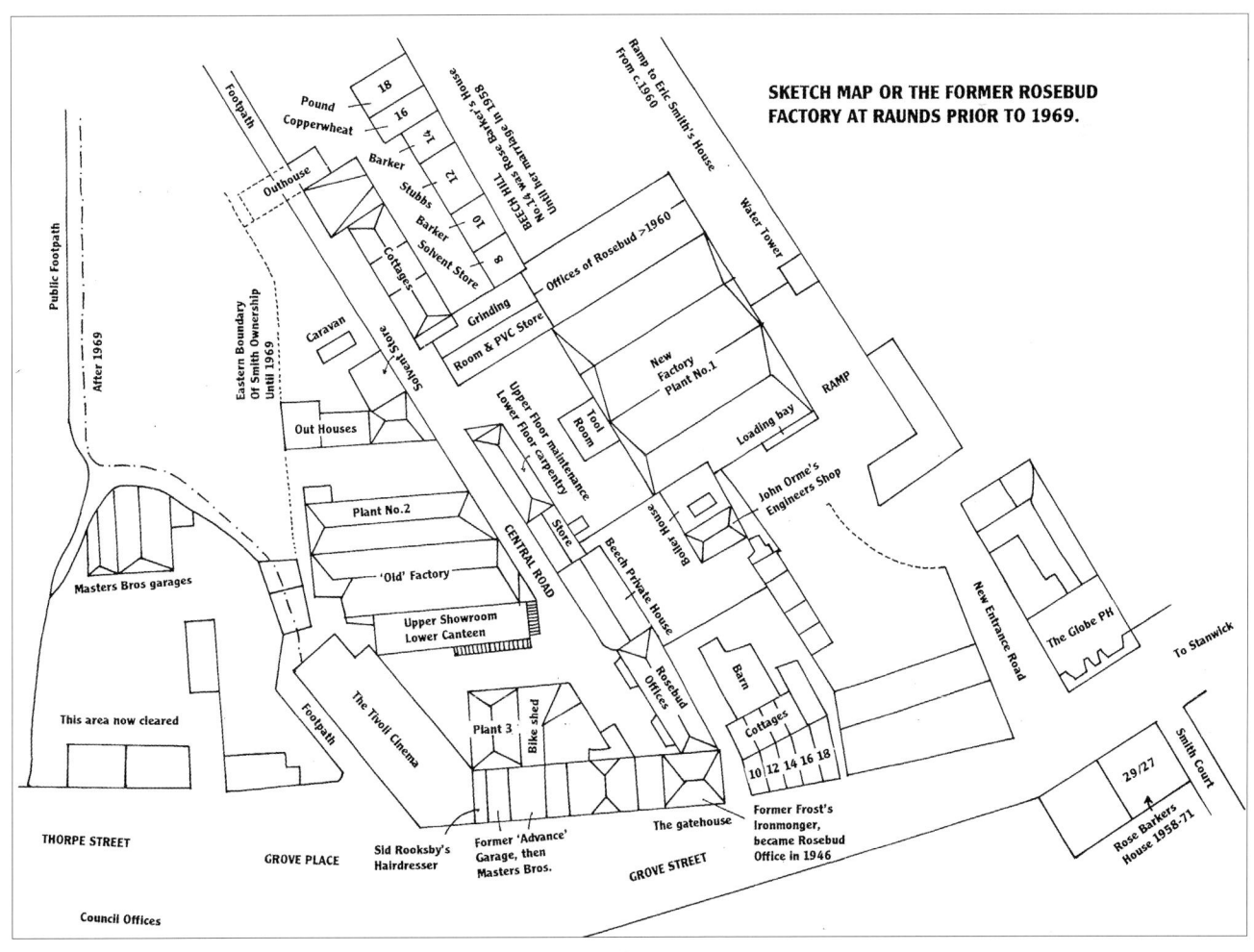

**SKETCH MAP OR THE FORMER ROSEBUD FACTORY AT RAUNDS PRIOR TO 1969.**

45

*Top.* Workers are busy with the injection moulding machines in the new Plant 1.

*Below.* The same scene after Rosebud moved out – soon to be filled with blow-moulding machines for Smith's Containers Ltd.

*Top.* **A view looking up Beech Hill. The Canteen, the building with the white door on the left, also contained the Showroom.**

*Middle.* **The site included a lot of waste ground. This is the rear of Beech Hill for instance; the building with the lamp bracket was the Development Department!**

*Bottom.* **The Canteen with the Showroom further up the slope.**

except the New Factory building. In 2012 RPC Containers vacated the entire site and as this book goes to press it is being offered redevelopment. Should this take place the last remaining Rosebud building will disappear forever.

A separate office was set up in New York by a Manufacturer's Agent called Mark Price, a personal contact of Eric Smith. He traded as the Rosebud Corporation of America Inc but, according to T.Eric Smith, the project was not a success. The venture came to nothing. The address did appear on the rear of the 1960 trade catalogue and on certain 1959 catalogues showing the office address in Fifth Avenue, New York but Rosebud had effectively abandoned the US market. There were no other subsidiary offices.

Distribution to the UK model trade was initially via A.A.Hales Ltd who were at that period, 1959, based at 60 Station Road, New Southgate, London N11. By 1960 A.A.Hales had re-located to 26 Station Court, Potters Bar, Hertfordshire and had been joined in distributing the kits by Messrs. E. Kiel & Co of Russel Gardens, Wick Lane, Wickford, Essex. By 1960, Cyril Tilley was delivering a van load of Kitmaster kits to Kielkraft every week.

Rosebud used two vans and drivers, the vans being an old Morris Commercial and a larger Dodge truck, whilst the second driver was Harold Skinner. These delivered the bulk kits direct to the wholesale warehouses each week. The drivers also picked up raw materials from suppliers around the country, for example the castings for the KM1 and KM2 motor bogies came from Stalybridge. In addition, there was the daily staff pick-up shuttle from Corby and the villages.

Both Kielkraft and A.A.Hales Ltd. used self-employed Sales Representatives to travel around the model and toy shops promoting their full catalogues of products. Eric Smith had his carpenter, Jack Woods, fabricate some special travelling display cases for these salesmen. The wooden cases open to reveal shelves containing made up examples of the locomotives. Eric still retains his own personal show-case together with his own collection of Kitmaster locomotives constructed from some of the first test shots from each new mould tool.

*Top.* The ground where chemist Bob Parker would park his caravan, at the rear of the Showroom/Canteen.

*Right.* A lovely view down Beech Hill to the Gatehouse, which housed Eric's office and to the left, the Print Shop where the instruction sheets were produced.

*Above.* The view along Grove Street today is very different. The trees mark the eastern boundry of the Rosebud site, the Grove Street frontage has been swept away to be replaced by the modern offices of RPC Containers, which are set further back from the road.

*Left.* It's 1970 and Eric Smith has just produced his first blow-moulded 1 gallon plastic container. Smiths Containers is about to take off in Raunds again!

*Below.* This rare view from the archives of Northants Libraries & Museum Service shows Grove Street around 1930 with the former boot factory and ironmongers on the left. The Gatehouse, leading to Beech Hill can clearly be seen behind the parked car.

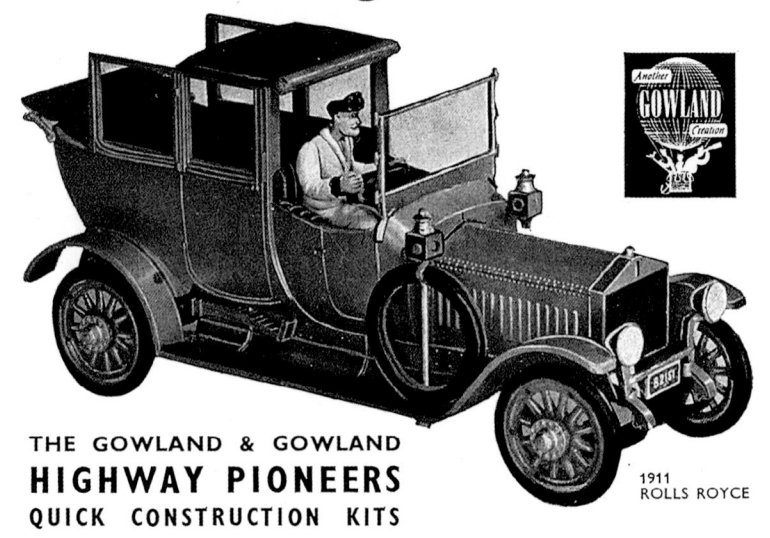

**A Rush Job**

The box artwork varied dramatically according to which artist was given the commission. The best of this box artwork which makes these kits so attractive to collectors has been described as a 'design icon of the sixties'. It is primarily the work of Ken Rush, although other illustrators were used. Ken is a freelance illustrator who was much in demand during the early 1960s for box artwork. He left the RAF in 1950 and immediately began work illustrating books, magazines and children's comics, including *The Eagle*. He also accepted commissions for Revell, Airfix and Frog, where he was house artist from 1972-74 responsible for a large number of aircraft paintings including the D.H. Sea Venom, Gloster Gladiator, Lockheed Neptune and Maryland. In 1968 he was asked to illustrate a set of Brooke Bond PG Tips Tea trade cards entitled *History of the Motor Car*.

Rush was a freelance, as were most of the artists illustrating kit boxes at the time, and had no particular affinity for the models he was asked to illustrate. He returned to railway subjects in the mid-1970s with some work for Airfix-GMR, illustrating the first Airfix Railways catalogue. His signature may be seen on the GWR Prairie tank train set in the Trade version of this catalogue and on the Wild West 4-4-0 locomotive set in the Retail catalogue. Throughout the early years of the 1960s, his studio in Soho was crammed with commissions for Revell (ships, including Sinking of the Tirpitz and Ben Ledi), Frog (aircraft), Airfix (cars and trains) and of course, Rosebud Kitmaster. Ken confirms that he painted the artwork for the majority of the early kits including the Motorised Box Van, BR Mk1 coaches and most of the first series of twelve kits. He also did several other aircraft illustrations including the Red Arrows display team for the front cover of the 1966 Farnborough Air Show programme.

When Ken and his wife paid a visit to the erstwhile Cumberland Toy and Model Museum, in Cockermouth, curator Rod Moore took the opportunity to interview them. It soon became obvious that identifying which kits Ken was responsible for would not be easy, as Rosebud had omitted the artist's name on all their boxes...

'The sky is normally pretty distinctive; Ken's work is pretty detailed' said his wife. Ken agreed 'Yes, but there was lots of overhang on these boxes. I normally signed in the track, somewhere they can't cut it off, using a different colour, blue or pale brown, something like that.' Rod then asked if he still had any artwork for them 'I just handed over the artwork and that was that. In those days they would buy the copyright, now

*Top.* Gowland & Gowland were one of the first companies to mass produce a series of plastic assembly kits – Highway Pioneers hit British streets in 1955.

| Table B (1) Kits Illustrated by Ken Rush | | |
|---|---|---|
| **Definitely** | **Possibly** | **Certainly Not!** |
| Evening Star | City of Truro | BR Mogul |
| Prairie | Hudson | DB Coach |
| Crocodile | P1 Set | SNCF Coach |
| P2 Set | Motor Bogie KM 1 | Pullmans |
| Italian Tank | | Beyer-Garrett |
| BR Coaches CK, SK, BSK, RFO | | |
| DB Class 23 | | |
| Box Van KM 2 | | |
| Duchess | | |
| Royal Scot | | |
| 1959 & 60 Trade & retail catalogues | | |
| Biggin Hill | | |
| P3 Set | | |
| Flying Scot | | |
| USA Tank | | |
| CN U-4-A | | |

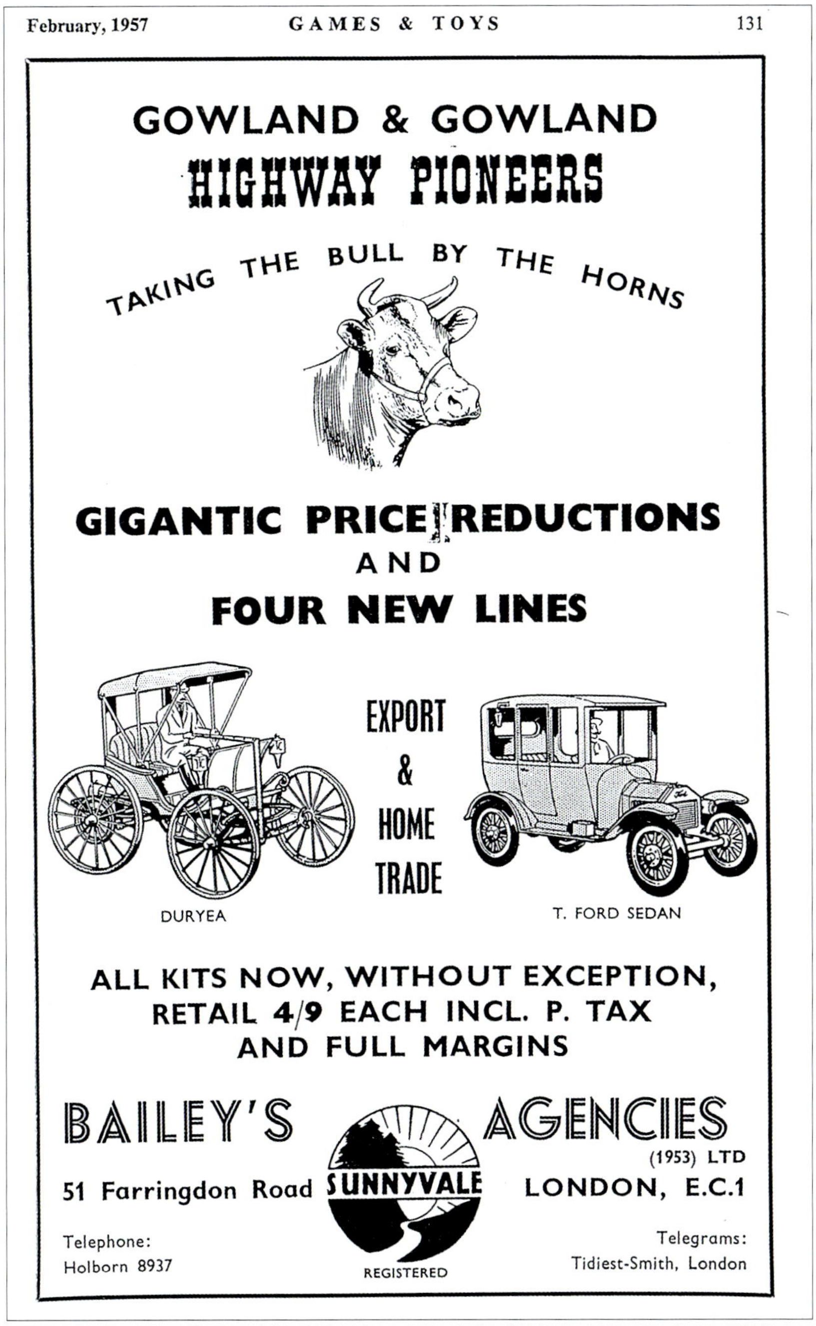

*Left.* 1957 saw big cuts in the prices charged for Highway Pioneers, but 4s 9d was still high compared to Airfix. It was however, the starting point for Rosebud Kitmaster pricing – the first kits retailed at 4s 6d.

*Above.* A Japanese retailer advert for Rosebud Kitmaster.

Hot on the Heels of Gowland was International Molding Corporation's "Trailblazers" series of Old Timer Railroad models (to use the vernacular). A super little range of HO freight and passenger cars in garishly coloured (mostly yellow) plastic. It featured a rather good model of The General locomotive, a veteran of the Civil War and featured in a 1950s film. It was spotted by Eric Smith at a US Trade Show and brought back to Raunds. With just one simple change (metal bogie screws were swapped for plastic pins) Rosebud produced "The World's First ALL Plastic Railway Construction Kit". Shown here fully painted, it was a shameless rip off from the Trailblazers original, shown here in black.

the law is different. Normally, I had to buy the kit to get an example of it; this was not an era where you got the artwork back!' Rod was interested in Ken's path into kit illustration. 'I started off doing press advertisements for Airfix. I would get a photograph of the new model and add a line drawing over it. Then my wife would take it to the lab and have a bleach-out print made. All of the photograph disappeared leaving you with a perfect line drawing. They used them in their Stop Press ads, I remember. I did them for years. I had so much work in those days, the average wage was about fifteen hundred a year and we were making five hundred a week! Still, I paid for it with a nervous breakdown; that's when I met my wife, she was nursemaid to me, until gradually I could start working again. I got a lot of kits to do. I sort of got known for them. Frog paid the worst. Revell was OK. I did the Sinking of the Tirpitz for them.'

His wife chips in 'Oh yes, your ships were beautiful weren't they? I really liked those more than the cars.' Ken agrees 'I liked doing the ships. The trains were good too. Rosebud Dolls it was, near Northampton.' Rod prompts him by mentioning Raunds. 'Yes that's right. There was never any credit for the artist on the box. If there's a way of masking it off, they will. It's mean, but they do it. There's no signature on any of them. It makes me seem like an impostor, but it's absolutely true. I'd just like to find it on one of them'.

Ken rummages through another pile of Kitmaster kits in the museum. 'The Duchess of Gloucester was one of mine. I know the technique I used you see; I'm fairly certain the French Mountain was one of mine too. This sort of treatment here (he points at the box) and the highlights. They used to say to me "Get out your pot of highlights". I did a very long box of an aerial view of a big station with lots of track, like Victoria*. I've got the actual box tops for that one and a long train passing a castle* cut out at my home; they're too big to take anywhere.'

*Actually Waterloo, on the P2 Set and a Royal Scot at Conway Castle on the P3 set.

'Sometimes I got about a hundred pounds for an image, but that was for something really complicated. I did the pictures about twice the size of the box. I've got one for Airfix, they're more or less the same working size. If you went up too much, in reduction it could suffer. Or on the other hand, it could sharpen it to a certain point and then you'd lose detail. So it had to be a balance, ease of work against size. I don't have many left at home. I might have prints or proofs, but apart from a half-finished American Old Timer I was doing for Airfix (Jupiter or 119), I haven't got any of the originals. It's sad in a way. I did so many of them, if I'd kept the copyright I'd have been a rich man by now!' Ken still works for a living, editing and interviewing for a ballet magazine, but the days of his illustrations appearing in your local toy shop are long gone. According to Ken the following list sums up his work for Rosebud Kitmaster:

**The Export Drive**
Rebuilding the British economy following the Second World War was a long and painful process. As an editorial in *Rosebud News*, written by George Lindgren, MP for Wellingborough noted, 'Sales of your dolls abroad are providing export credits to buy food and clothing for your families and friends'. It went on to ask the workforce of war-torn Britain to strive even harder to meet export targets. T.Eric Smith was very keen on exporting his products, especially to the USA, and made many trips there, including one memorable six week visit sailing on R.M.S. Queen Mary, during which he took orders for more than a million dolls. Naturally then, Rosebud Kitmaster felt it their duty to try to 'do their bit' for British exports. As a consequence, most Kitmaster publications and kits were written in several languages. The little 1959 catalogue for example, is known in at least six different languages. Whilst the French and German translations were presumably straight-forward to accomplish, the Swedish and Dutch versions seem to have caused problems!

Technical translator and Kitmaster collector, Tony Palm, comments on the languages used: 'It is interesting to note

*Below.* **The Hobby Line Berkshire locomotive was a direct contemporary of Kitmaster and competition for their NYC Hudson both at home and in the US market. Hobbyline also developed models of a typical small steam switcher in C&O livery and FA-type diesel units.**

that the linguistic capabilities of Rosebud Kitmaster were not the best. In fact, the quality of the language used on the box cover of the SNCF Mountain was so poor that the text had to be blocked out with a thick black stripe, presumably following reactions from French distributors. With some difficulty, one can make out the legend 'Societe National Chemin de fer Francaise' - a grotesque rendering of 'Société Nationale des Chemins de fer Français'. The correct version was then overprinted above the name '241P Mountain'. Likewise, the quality of the Swedish text on the assembly instructions in several kits was appalling. It seems as though someone from the factory had just bought an English-Swedish dictionary and scribbled down the first words he came across to make a 'translation'. Naturally, the results were diabolical.' Tony ends by saying that he has not had the opportunity to check the other languages used in the kits, but assumes that they are probably just as bad!

Unfortunately, Rosebud's French customers had to suffer a further blow to their national pride when the instruction sheet for the SNCF A9myfi coach described it as '...forming part of the Mistral express, famous for its high speed runs between Paris and Lille..' It should, of course, have read 'Paris and Lyon', a mistake which *European Railways* called 'An obvious blunder inviting ridicule' in their review of the kit.

Happily, Genova-based collector Luciano Luppi says the Italian was of reasonable standard. The reprinted Format 2 instructions for the first twelve kits were quite good, with just one mistake; the words 'plastic cement' were translated as 'plastic concrete', whilst the 1959 Italian catalogue translates 'Stirling Single' as 'Stirling Peculiar' and 'Saddle Tank' as 'The tender can be fitted with a saddle'!

To aid their overseas distributors still further, Rosebud made available factory-assembled and finished kits. These could be displayed on flat-packed cardboard Trade Displays which were designed to be counter top mounted or put in a shop window. Each built kit is properly assembled and painted according to the Rosebud painting notes in the kit. The completed models were then packed in special foam filled boxes. The foam liners are cut-to-shape and appear to have been made professionally. The boxes are plain cardboard constructions which do not exactly match the retail boxes for each kit. They carry a simple label 'Built Up Kit' and the Series number for that loco. The kits were built as 'out-work' by Rosebud workers, who could earn extra money for this task. Cyril Ferry and Keith Anthony both remember making and painting the kits for these trade sample boxes. Cyril was able to complete so many that the proceeds paid for his annual summer holiday in Switzerland! Neither man enjoyed building the DB Class 23, preferring instead the Pullman cars, a much easier task which would earn them more money! Packed in their foam lined boxes, these kits were despatched world-wide to interested dealers. The Club has an interesting example of a completed Mk.1 coach which was presented to a former worker at Metropolitan Cammell in Birmingham in recognition of help rendered in furnishing the drawings of the Midland Pullman and Met-Cam Mk.1 coaches. It is also packed in a foam-lined shipment box.

The 1960 design for a simplified Trade Display is much smaller than the earlier full-colour 1959 version and certainly would not take a full-length box. Packed flat, it folds up into a box shape with pre-punched slots where the 'sleepers' should be and a slot at left to take a fistful of 1960 catalogues set on end. The printing on the 1960 version is in two colours only to further reduce costs. Rosebud Kitmaster models were widely distributed abroad with residual stocks still surfacing as far apart as Brisbane, Bombay and Buenos Aires.

*Above.* **The Swiss Crocodile box art portrayed the reciprocating cranks rather well.**

*Below.* **A 1959 Kitmaster catalogue for the US market with dollar prices and Rosebud corporation of America address. (See also pages 20 and 114 for alternative versions of this catalogue.**

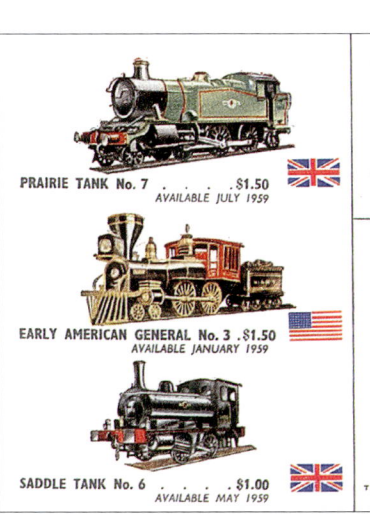

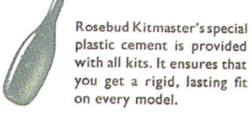

*Above*. A pre-assembled Kitmaster Mk 1 BSK, factory built and presented to a staff member at Metro-Cammell in thanks for help with the forthcoming Blue Pullman project.

*Below*. A refurbished Kitmaster 4-CEP unit originally built by Alan Williams, who used to run it around his office at Ian Allan in Shepperton according to colleague Chris Leigh.

*Bottom*. Devoid of lining, the MK1 coaches looked very smart in Southern Region Stock Green livery.

# Chapter 3: The Models In Detail
## Models in Detail - 1
### The British Railways Standard Mk1 Coaches
### Nos. 13, 14, 15, 17, 18, 20, 21 and 28

Perhaps the second most famous model(s) from the Kitmaster stud, after the Beyer-Garratt, these superb OO coach kits are still much sought after today. Embodying unheard-of detail when first released in 1959, such as flush-glazed windows and correctly aligned brake gear, they soon became the first choice for discerning modellers. They had significant advantages over the other available proprietary brands of Mk1, Tri-ang Railways and Hornby Dublo.

Firstly, the Kitmaster models were to scale length from the BR drawings, unlike Tri-ang's nine inch coaches and the Hornby Dublo 'Super -Detail' coaches, which were only a scale 57ft long. Although correct for the Full Brake (BG), this is too short, by some 8ft, from the actual 65ft length of the Brake Second (BSK), Full Second (SK) and the Corridor Composite (CK). All of these, together with the First Class Open Restaurant, were correctly modelled by Kitmaster at a scale 65ft. In fact, Richard Lines has gone on record as saying that the Tri-ang ten inch coaches owed more

| TABLE B (2) - British Railways Standard Mk1 Coach Codes ||
|---|---|
| General Codes: | |
| F First Class | O Open Stock |
| S Second Class | K Corridor or Kitchen |
| T Third Class | B Brake Compartment or Buffet |
| C Composite 1st/3rd or 1st/2nd | R Restaurant |
| U Unclassified | |
| Common Coach types: | |
| MLV Motor Luggage Van | RSO Restaurant Second Open |
| BG  Gangwayed Brake | BSK Corridor Brake Second |
| SO  Open Second | BCK Corridor Brake Composite |
| TSO Tourist Open Second | BFK Corridor Brake First |
| SK  Corridor Second | CK  Corridor Composite |
| FO  Open First | FK  Corridor First |
| RB/RMB  Miniature Buffet | RFO Restaurant First Open |
| RBR Rebuilt Buffet Restaurant | RK  Kitchen |

*Attention to detail on the underframes, bogies and roofs leant an air of authenticity to Kitmaster coaches which was sadly lacking in their contemporary offerings from Hornby-Dublo, Trix and Tri-ang.*

MAY 1960

# NEWS SPECIAL

**CANDID, UNBIASED, UP - TO - THE - MINUTE NEWS
THE STOP PRESS OF THE MODEL RAILWAY WORLD**

*From our Staff Reporters and Special Correspondents*

| No. 33 | FREE | MAY 1960 |

## PERFECTA'S LATEST

THE latest Perfecta kit, designed to convert the Italian tank kit to power drive, is now released, and we illustrate above the various components contained therein.

The main difference with this kit is that it incorporates combined ballast weight stiffeners which are located between the frames, adding useful weight and stiffness to the chassis. There are some small detail differences, principally the provision of a grub-screw for the worm-wheel. The kit is designed to use the Tri-ang XT60 motor, which has the worm already fixed to the shaft.

It is possible to add extra ballast weight to the body, and it is suggested that a mixture of lead shot and plasticine is used to fill the boiler. This, however, is a matter for the individual modeller to decide for himself. Obviously a supply of suitable lead sheet could influence matters.

Once again a very detailed instructional sheet, complete with full-size templates for cutting the footplate and mainframes, is supplied, and if these instructions are faithfully followed even the beginner can make a success of motorizing the kit—provided he has not assembled it first, for, as with the previous Perfecta, it is difficult, if not altogether impossible, to motorize an already assembled Kitmaster loco.

The price of the Perfecta kit No. 2 is 8/9 and the Tri-ang TTX60 motor retails at 12/10, making a total of 21/7 per loco, with 1/6 extra if Peco couplings are to be added.

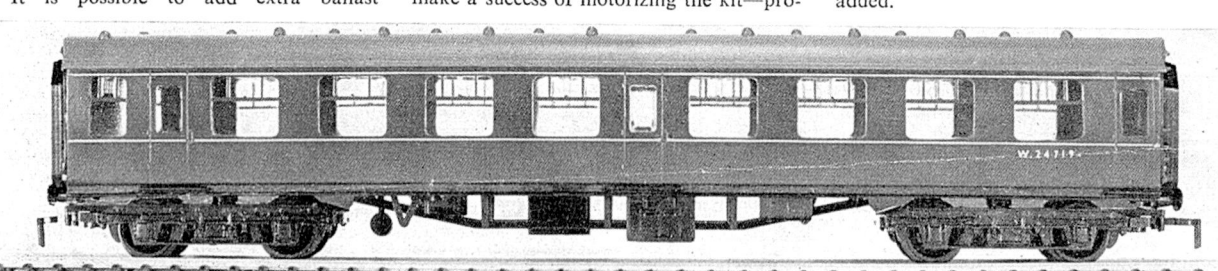

## KITMASTER COACHES

WE illustrate above and below the latest Kitmaster coaches for OO gauge, but feel that they hardly need any further recommendation. Indeed, we know that 4mm. scale modellers have taken these superb models to their hearts, and the only vestige of complaint comes from those with strict period layouts who cannot reconcile a modern flush-sided coach with the rest of their stock.

We would, however, make two observations that may assist readers. First and foremost it is vital to secure the windows firmly in place with cement. There is a natural tendency to use very little for fear of getting some on to the glazing, so we would suggest that some additional fillets placed after the glazing has set will simplify matters. It is also easier to carry out painting, lining and lettering before the sides are fixed. If you want a removable roof it is possible to cement a piece of hardwood into the roof and hold it down with a long screw. This is particularly useful if you intend adding the Peco interior fittings and maybe lighting at a later date.

Finally, we learn that some enthusiasts are buying the kits for the sake of the bogies alone, which at 6/6 is still excellent value for money!

---

to Kitmaster than any of their other competitors, whilst Pat Hammond in his definitive history of Rovex, claims that the 'Completely Knocked Down', or CKD, coach kits were introduced by Tri-ang to compete directly with Kitmaster coaches. As noted elsewhere, British Trix was developing its own series of BR Mk1 coaches at this time as well and must have been influenced by the Rosebud design. Michael Catalani certainly investigated a flush glaze system for the Trix coaches, but it was rejected on the grounds of cost. It is strangely ironic therefore, that thirty years later, Hornby Hobbies have re-introduced the former Tri-ang Mk1 coaches with flush-glazing that owes much to the pioneering work done by Kitmaster.

Secondly, because they came in kit form, they were easier to convert into other prototypes among the then rapidly emerging Mk1 fleet. A 57 ft BG could be made from two BSKs, for example, far more easily than with an early Tri-ang model, which was a one piece moulding for sides, ends and floor. Many such conversions were described in the model press at the time and subsequently, and an index is provided in the appendices. Two interesting examples appeared in *MRC* July and August 1962 describing a catering vehicle

56

## MORE KITMASTER TT-3

SAMPLES of the brake/2nd and compo from the Kitmaster initial range of TT-3 coaches are now to hand and we illustrate them below. The quality and specifications are exactly the same as in the previous pair reviewed last month. Both retail at 5/11 per kit and are supplied complete with all necessary transfers and cement, in the basic maroon and green colours of the range. It will be noted that Kitmaster are behind with their scheduled release dates, but they are doing everything in their power to make up the leeway.

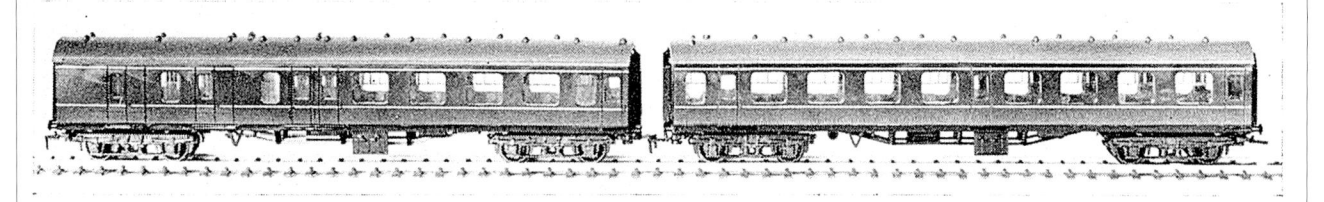

---

MODEL RAILWAY NEWS      MARCH, 1960

# GAMAGES
## ALWAYS Something NEW!
### EXCITING NEWS for MODEL RAILWAY ENTHUSIASTS

**ROSEBUD 'KITMASTER'**

No. 13 & 14

The terrific success of the "Kitmaster" Plastic Locomotive Kits is being followed up this year with true to scale "OO" Coaches. In July a motorised Box-wagon and an electric-motor Bogie will become available, so that you will be able to build your models and run them on your layout too!

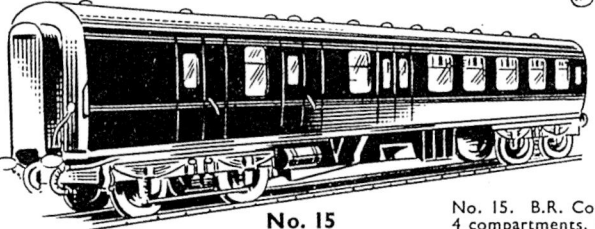

No. 13 B.R. Corridor Composite Coach, with 7 compartments—three 2nd and four 1st class.

No. 14. B.R. Corridor 2nd Class Coach with 8 compartments.

**ONLY 6/6 EACH**

Post and Packing 8d.

No. 15. B.R. Corridor/Brake 2nd Class Coach with 4 compartments, plus Guards and Luggage.

No. 15

**1960 MODEL BOOK**

Not many left of this issue! The most popular of all. Have you got YOURS? A veritable mine of information; including interesting Photos, Facts and Figures about Railways, Aircraft, Ships and Cars. Once again we include a special PLASTICS section, and also details and prices of most models and accessories stocked at Gamages. 132-pages. Covers in FULL COLOUR.

**STILL ONLY 1/-**

Post 6d.

**DUE IN APRIL**
A NEW SERIES FOR 'TT' ENTHUSIASTS
Rebuilt ROYAL SCOT LOCOMOTIVE & TENDER
No. 16. TT3   **6/11**
This is the first of a series. Coaches and a motorised Bogie will follow at regular intervals.

**GAMAGES · HOLBORN · LONDON · E.C.1**   HOL 8484   Open Thursdays until 7 p.m

---

and an open brake second conversion. The catering vehicle was actually needed to run with the Kitmaster restaurant coach, which had no kitchen facilities of its own. These coaches ran as a three-set with a diagram 700 or 701 RK and a full Restaurant Second Open RSO. It was perhaps a strange choice of vehicle from that point of view. Finally, the extra weight provided by full length ballast and the overall appearance of the flush glazing produced coaches which ran smoothly and looked accurate.

The only drawback to the Kitmaster Mk1s, up to the release of the RFO, was the lack of any interior detail. The Tri-ang and Dublo models at least had optional rudimentary interiors, whilst the Kitmaster coaches offered nothing. For the 4mm scale coaches, this was solved by the enterprising Pritchard Patent Product Co (PECO) who rapidly introduced a range of cardboard interior kits to fit the OO Kitmaster coaches. These fine kits include all interior partitions, tables, mirror, doors, pictures and even a selection of passengers! Peco realised that the Standard Corridor 2nd could be built in two variants, as an Open Second (SO) or as a Corridor Compartment Second (SK). Accordingly, both interior kits were produced, along with those for the Corridor Brake Second (BSK) and the Corridor Composite (CK). No kit was needed for the Restaurant car, since a detailed plastic interior was provided when the kit was finally introduced in summer 1961. See also 'PECO Interiors' section of this guide. There is also, unusually for Kitmaster, a continuous flaw in the Composite coaches. In both TT and OO scales the spacing of the First class windows is uneven, giving a smaller end compartment than in the prototype. Whether this was due to a drawing inaccuracy on the part of BR or Rosebud, we shall probably never know.

**Notes on the Diagrams and Decals**

The maroon versions of all these coaches are described as E.R., W.R. and L.M. Regions on the box, whilst the green version is shown as Southern Region.

BSK Corridor Brake Second OO [15] TT [17]
Maroon version has transfers for:
Diagram 181 M34090/105/671 E34422/590/35157
Diagram 182 W34152/297/763
Green version has transfers for:

57

Diagram 182 S34256/621/158/945/279/35020
Diagram 181 Three-a-side seating with folding armrests
Diagram 182 Four-a-side seats without armrests

CK Corridor Composite OO [13] TT [18]
Maroon version has transfers for:
Diagram 126 M15627/019/243 E15307/144/16017
Diagram 128 W15111/598/430
Green version has transfers for:
Diagram 128 S15042/573/888/903/580/873
Diagram 126 Three-a-side seating with folding armrests
Diagram 128 Four-a-side seats without armrests

SK Corridor Compartment Second OO [14] TT [20]
Maroon version has transfers for:
Diagram 146 M24133/405/861 E24222/531/25027
Diagram 147 W24165/341/719
Green version has transfers for:
Diagram 147 S24320/305/169/326/318/311
Diagram 146 Three-a-side seating with folding armrests
Diagram 147 Four-a-side seats without armrests

TSO Corridor Open Second
Peco manufactured an interior kit for a diagram 89/93 TSO with 2+2 seating which shares a common body shell with the SK kits listed above. The body shell is also common to the following diagrams:
Dia 94 SO Open Second with 2+1 seating
Dia 60 RS Second Class Restaurant with 2+1 loose seats Nos. Sc1014-17
Dia 61 RU Unclassified Restaurants with 2+1 loose seats Nos. E1018-57
Dia 149 SK Gloucester RC&W prototype M25456
Dia 150 (Later AA204) SK Metro-Schlieren bogies M25283-5

RFO Open Restaurant First Class OO [28] TT [21]
Maroon and Green versions both have transfers for:
Diagram 36 M4/5/6/S9/W7/8/E1/2/3/10/11
The body shell is also common to the following diagrams:
Dia 71 FO Open First with 2+1 fixed seating Nos. M3000-2

Although these coach tools were eventually scrapped by Airfix, an interesting report from the 1964 Toy Fair, carried in the Peco trade journal *News Special* No.3 of March 1964, indicated that 'the former Kitmaster coach dies are being rebuilt and their introduction is still in the future.' How much work was done is not known, but these tools were amongst those said to be heavily pitted after storage in a warehouse with a leaking roof. The decision to scrap them entirely was made easier by the arrival of Tri-ang's 'CKD' kits for Mk1 coaches of similar pattern at competitive prices.

| Technical Data | |
|---|---|
| Kit Numbers | OO Scale 13 14 15 28 |
| | TT Scale 17 18 20 21 |
| Box Type | 4 [13/14/15] 3 [28] |
| | 6 [17/18/20/21] |
| Instruction format: | 2 [13-15/17/18/20/21] 3 [28] |
| Length of Completed Model: | 262 mm (13-15 28) |
| | 197 mm (17-21) |
| Release Dates: | 4/60 and 7/61 (OO Kits) |
| | 6/60-8/60 (TT Kits) |
| Conversion/detailing kit: | PECO Interiors for [13-15] |
| Reviews: | MRN, MRC, RM: 3/60 |
| 1st Advert: | KC13/4/60 |
| Issue Prices: | 6s 6d (13/14/15); 9s 6d (28) |
| | 5s11d (17/18/20); 6s 6d (21) |

Current Market Price
| | Made | Unmade |
|---|---|---|
| Green | £4-8 | £10-20 |
| Maroon | £3-6 | £9-15 |

**Chocolate and cream suited the Mk1s, as shown by this beautifully constructed CK by Marcus Archer.**

*Above.* Kitmaster coaches were very useful for conversion to other Mk1 diagrams, the modular and flexible nature of the Mk 1 concept lending itself to "cut & shut" projects. Here we see a Western Region Diagram 19 RKB and a Southern Region Diagram 23 RKB.

*Below.* The only "catering" vehicle in the Kitmaster Mk1 portfolio was the Restaurant First Open – in reality a standard open first class trailer designed to run with a dedicated kitchen car. It was the only Kitmaster Mk1 to be supplied complete with detailed interior mouldings.

*Bottom.* Two Kitmaster BSKs could joined together to make a 57ft full brake (BG).

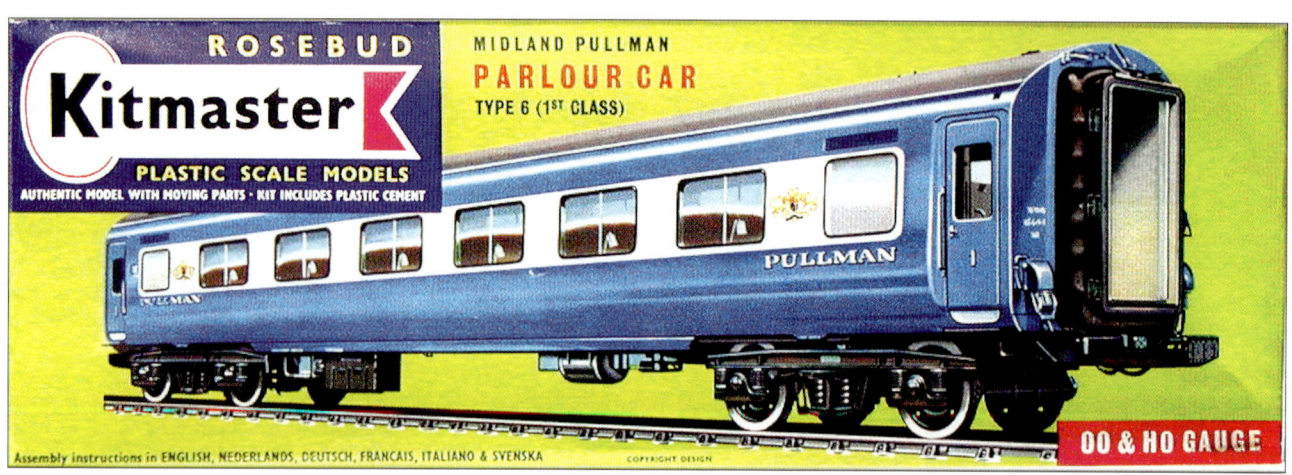

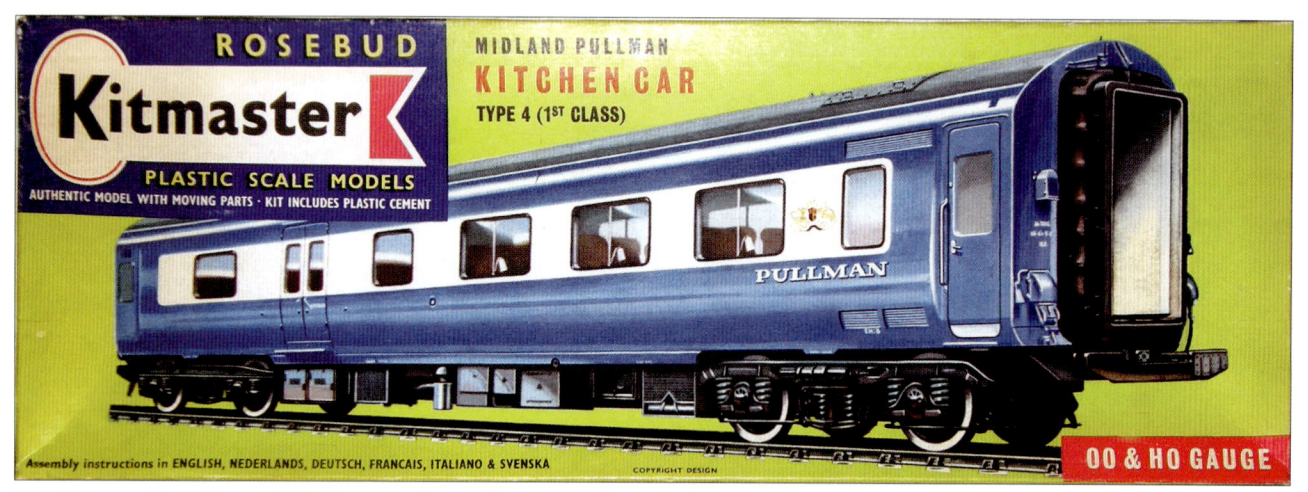

The Metropolitan-Cammell Pullman train coaches were the very latest in modernisation-era motive power when Kitmaster issued these kits during 1961.

The Pullman Power car contains many complex compound curves which give it a very distinctive front end look. Tri-ang sadly failed to capture it, but as can be seen here in the display model built by Marcus Archer, Kitmaster nailed it.

# The Models In Detail - 2
## Nos. 31, 32 and 33: The Metropolitan-Cammell Pullman Cars

Diesel Multiple units are not, perhaps, the most glamorous of subjects for modelling, but the famous Blue Pullman trains introduced in 1959 were certainly stylish and striking as they snaked through the craggy gorges of the Derbyshire Peak District and threaded the rolling Wiltshire countryside. From their inception, the model railway manufacturers were relatively quick to add Blue Pullmans to their range, both Tri-ang Railways and Rosebud Kitmaster making forays into this area. However, the task for modellers trying to put together complete sets for either the Midland Pullman or the South Wales Pullman was made quite difficult because not all of the vehicles were made available in proprietary form and a certain amount of confusion still persists.

Introduced into service on 4th July 1960, the prototype Metropolitan-Cammell diesel-electric multiple units rapidly established an image and identity for the British Transport Commission's Modernisation Plan. They were the blue-streak flag bearers of a new age of ultra-modern, ultra-comfortable and ultra-stylish rail travel. 'Britain's Most Modern Train' proclaimed the 1961 Kitmaster Catalogue, and so they were. A heavy promotional campaign by British Railways, Metro-Cammell and the Pullman Car Company had ensured that the 'Blue Pullman' was a household name by the end of 1961 and consequently the three kits of the Midland Pullman were very well received.

An article in the December 1965 issue of *Rail News* shows a Midland Pullman six-car set leaving Hadley Wood Tunnel at the southern end of the East Coast Main Line. According to the paper, the unit covered the 186 miles between London and Leeds in 166 minutes. This run was to assess their suitability for use on the Great Northern routes from Kings Cross after transfer of Manchester Pullman services to the newly electrified West Coast route at the beginning of 1966. As is now well recorded, these trials were for naught and the two units were transferred to the Western Region to supplement their existing three eight-car units with a new twelve-car formation.

Coming, as they did, towards the end of the Kitmaster programme, the Midland Pullmans embodied many refinements, including a common sprue for bogie parts in all three kits. However, they also suffered from deteriorating quality control in the mouldings and a lack of attention to accuracy in the tooling stage, some parts being misnumbered, or even omitted completely! Even given these shortcomings, they are still fondly remembered and have accrued considerable value in recent years.

The Kitmaster Pullman Cars were modelled strictly on the Midland Pullman sets as running between St Pancras and Manchester Central, although the 1961 catalogue artwork clearly shows a Western Region power car, lettered 'Midland Pullman'. The WR units had tell-tale route indicator blinds on the power car sides, in order that they might operate over several different routes. The Kitmaster models are easily distinguished from the later Tri-ang 'Blue Pullman' cars by the extra fine detail on the body mouldings, the air conditioning motors and Kitmaster logo on the underside of the floor and the fact that they have the correct pattern Metro-Schlieren bogies. The Tri-ang units have incorrect BR coach bogies. In fact, two patterns of Metro-Schlieren bogie were employed, the larger heavy duty one is the power bogie supporting the traction motors, whilst the smaller one is the 'standard' version. Metropolitan Cammell had obtained UK rights for the bogie from its German manufacturer in the mid-1950s and persuaded the BTC to experiment with the design for possible widespread use on the burgeoning fleet of Mk1 coaches. Three Mk1 corridor second coaches (M24281-3), then under construction by Metro-Cammell, were thus duly fitted with Schlieren bogies for the trial. After 150,000 miles of running on the London Midland Region, the wear characteristics of the Schlieren pattern were pronounced good enough to equip the new diesel Pullmans then in the design stage at Metro-Cammell. The eventual ride quality when in service with the Blue Pullman was not as good, however, and as a consequence, the more advanced Commonwealth bogie design was adopted for all future coaching stock requirements.

When examining motorised models of the Blue Pullmans, it should be noted that the Tri-ang Power Bogie fitted to their power car is virtually identical to the Kitmaster KM1 Power Bogie, often found fitted to Kitmaster power cars, since both were modelled on the BR1

**EXPRESS SUCCESS!**

**MIDLAND PULLMAN**

BRITAIN'S MOST EXCITING TRAIN

**MANCHESTER & LONDON**
**LONDON & LEICESTER,**
**LOUGHBOROUGH & NOTTINGHAM**

2nd October, 1961 until further notice
(except at Bank Holiday periods)

### Table C BTC Type Designation of Metropolitan Cammell Pullman Cars

| TYPE | CODE | Set | Modelled by & number | | Description |
|---|---|---|---|---|---|
| 1 | DMBS | WR | Triang | R.555 | Driving Motor Brake Second |
| 2 | DMBF | MR | Kitmaster | Km 31 | Driving Motor Brake First |
| 3 | TKF | WR | Not Modelled | | Trailer Kitchen First |
| 4 | MKF | MR | Kitmaster | Km 32 | Motor Kitchen First |
| 5 | MPS | WR | Not Modelled | | Motor Parlour Second |
| 6 | TPF | MR | Kitmaster | Km 33 | Trailer Parlour First |
| 6 | TPF | WR | Tri-ang | R.426 | Trailer Parlour First |

### Table D : Arrangement of Vehicles and Allocations

**Midland Pullman (St. Pancras to Manchester and Leicester)***

| Car | A | B | C | D | E | F |
|---|---|---|---|---|---|---|
| Config | DMBF | MKF | TPF | TPF | MKF | DMBF |
| Type | 1 | 4 | 6 | 6 | 4 | 1 |
| Set No | M60090 | M60730 | M60740 | M60741 | M60731 | M60091 |
| | M60092 | M60732 | M60742 | M60743 | M60733 | M60093 |
| Model | Km31 | Km32 | Km33 | Km33 | Km32 | Km31 |
| 1st | 12 | 18 | 36 | 36 | 18 | 12 |
| First Class | | | | | | Total 132 |

**South Wales Pullman (Paddington to Cardiff, Bristol, Birmingham)**

| Car | A | B | C | D | E | F | G | H |
|---|---|---|---|---|---|---|---|---|
| Config | DMBS | MPS | TKF | TPF | TPF | TKF | MPS | DMBS |
| Type | 2 | 3 | 5 | 6 | 6 | 5 | 3 | 2 |
| Set No | W60094 | W60644 | W60734 | W60744 | W60745 | W60735 | W60645 | W60095 |
| | W60096 | W60646 | W60736 | W60746 | W60747 | W60737 | W60647 | W60097 |
| | W60098 | W60648 | W60738 | W60748 | W60749 | W60739 | W60649 | W60099 |
| Model | R.555 | -- | -- | R.426 | R.426 | -- | -- | R.555 |
| 1st | - | - | 18 | 36 | 36 | 18 | - | - |
| 2st | 18 | 42 | - | - | - | - | 42 | 18 |
| First Class | | | | | | Total 108 | | |
| Second Class | | | | | | Total 120 | | |

Bogie. K's also produced a motor bogie for the Pullman, in 1962. Priced at £2.2s.9d, there were optional correct pattern sideframes at 1s.6d per pair. These gave a much more authentic look to the models. The complete arrangement of power and trailer cars for these sets when introduced were as shown in the following tables.

For their 1963 catalogue, Tri-ang chose to model the South Wales Pullman 8-car sets which were a mixture of First and Second Class. The Tri-ang power car units are therefore Second Class (DMPS), and their Parlour cars are the Western Region First Class Parlours (TPF). The Kitmaster power cars were correctly modelled from all-First Class Midland sets together with Midland First Class Kitchen and Parlour cars, so it is impossible to create an authentic Western Region composite set with first and second class, since Western Region Second Class Motor Parlour cars (MPS) do not exist. Only Kitmaster produced a catering vehicle of any sort and it was, as noted above, a Motor Kitchen First (MKF). These are the only catering vehicles ever produced for Blue Pullmans, so any stalwart wishing to put together a complete South Wales set will also need a pair of Midland Kitchen cars to convert to Trailer Kitchen Firsts. As can be seen from Table C, there are six different types of coach for these trains, of which only four have been modelled. The major differences between Midland and Western sets is in the positioning of the power bogies on the parlour and kitchen cars, and the addition of narrower second class seating bays to the two extra coaches of Western sets, together with destination route indicator blinds on the sides of the power cars. When running, the motor bogie ends of the power cars were adjacent to each other. For example, on a Midland set the motor kitchens and driving motor brake firsts were coupled with their power bogies together and likewise on Western sets, the DMBS and MPS power bogies were adjacent. The Kitmaster models each contain sufficient parts to make up three bogies, either motor or trailing; very useful if you need sideframes to convert Tri-ang units! So, to produce a complete South Wales 8-Car set, some conversions will be necessary. These can be summarised as follows.

**Trailer Kitchen First.** In a simple conversion from the Kitmaster Motor Kitchen First, the powered bogie is exchanged for a second trailing bogie.

**Motor Parlour Second.** This is more complex. The best way to approach it is by converting a Parlour First using either the Kitmaster or Tri-ang version. The major problem is the re-arrangement of the seating to give seven bays instead of six. I have seen this done with a Kitmaster Mk1 RFO interior, which gives good results and has the appropriate 1+2 spacing across the aisle and also the correct spacing for the new window bays. The drawback is that all glazing must be cut

```
Technical Data
Kit Numbers: OO Scale 31 32 33
Box Type:3
Instruction format: 3
Length of Completed Model        280 mm (31)
                                 285 mm (32/33)
Release Dates: 12/61 (31); 1/62 (32/33)
Conversion/detailing kit:        Chris Leigh bogie castings
                                 K's Pullman motor bogie & sideframes
                                 Fox Decals
                                 Railmatch Paint
Reviews: MRN 12/61 MRC 1/62 RM 12/61
1st Advert BOP 2.62 (With Humbrol)Issue Prices  10s 6d (All kits)
Current Market Price    Made     Unmade
Power                   £20      £50
Kitchen                 £45      £50
Parlour                 £18      £25
```

*Right.* **Kitmaster Trade Packs normally contained one dozen kits of the same subject in a strong cardboard shipping carton, seen here packed with a selection of shrink-wrapped larger kits.**

*Bottom.* **There was plenty of publicity for the new Pullman services – leaflets like this one were widely distributed and many different posters proclaimed the smart new era of diesel Pullman travel.**

and re-spaced. It is also possible to approach this conversion by cutting up the seating bays of a Tri-ang second class driving car and splicing them together, but you will need to destroy five dummy Tri-ang trailers for each pair of Parlour Seconds, and that could be expensive! The finished coach body will then require the addition of the power bogie and exhaust pipe removed from the Kitchen car above. A trailing bogie can then be fitted at the other end. Southern Pride Models do now supply a brass etched inlay that neatly replaces the 1st class glazing of Tri-ang Parlour Cars with new 7-bay second class windows.

**Multiple Unit Working**
The original Midland sets were eventually reallocated, as noted above, to the Western Region. In order that they might work together as a twelve car set, the power cars were modified for Multiple Unit control. This involved cutting away the front skirt, thereby revealing the conventional buffer beam and coupling used for shunting 'dead' units. Also added were multiple unit control jumper cables on either side of the cab front. This conversion would be quite straightforward should you be contemplating a twelve car formation! Perhaps the best book on the subject is Ian Allan Profile Series No.10 The Blue Pullmans, issued in 1985. It is, sadly, long out of print, but can often be found on Preservation Society bookstalls. For a modern account of the Blue Pullmans, with many detailed photographs, see the 'British Railways Illustrated' *Summer Special No.10* (2002): *DIESEL DAWN 'Without Superior in Europe' Or: What To Do With The BLUE PULLMANS?*

In addition to the Southern Pride etched window inlays for all six vehicle types, complete numbering and logos for both sets are available from Fox Transfers. Cast whitemetal sideframes from original Kitmaster items can be obtained from Chris Leigh via good model shops, whilst Railmatch make the correct Nanking Blue paint for these units.

There were three Kitmaster Presentation Sets issued in 1960 and 1961. Top is the "100 Years of British Steam Locomotives" set, today the easiest to find. In the lower picture is set P3, the TT Royal Scot and coaches, which is perhaps the scarcest of the three.

# The Models In Detail - 3
## P1, P2 and P3. The Presentation Boxed Sets

Perhaps some of the most attractively packaged and some of the rarest items in the Kitmaster portfolio are the Presentation Sets. These large, brightly coloured boxes brought together numerous kits at a bargain price and often included special tools and paint. Boxed Presentation Sets were introduced very early in the Kitmaster range. There are three boxed sets in existence, two in OO and one for TT. The 1960 retail catalogue did not mention them, but the 1960 Trade catalogue actually had colour pictures of the boxes, previewing them for release throughout 1960. In fact the planned introduction dates were shown as: P1 Current, P2 4/60, P3 8/60. In reality, the P2 set did not appear until 10/60, when W&H and H.A.Blunt began advertising it. All three were noted in the 1961 catalogue with prices of 27s 6d (P1) and 37s 6d (P2/P3).

The first to be issued was the 'One Hundred Years of British Steam Locomotive History' Set, in 1960. It had three kits, which were illustrated on the specially produced box cover. Set P1, *One Hundred Years of British Steam Locomotive History* had the following contents:
No.1 Rocket
No.4 Coronation Class
No.9 Stirling 8ft Single
Booklet *The Steam Locomotive*
Capsule of polystyrene cement
Eight capsules of paint
Paintbrush
Emery file
Pair of tweezers (marked 'Sheffield')
Three lengths of Wrenn straight track, 3½, 9 and 12 inch, each fitted with a card label printed in red on blue 'supplied by G & R Wrenn Ltd'
Kitmaster 1959 or 1960 Catalogue

Although these sets had specially commissioned artwork for the box lids, inside they had only the lower halves of each individual kit box, together with a small box for the paint, tweezers etc. They did not include the original kit box tops. In this early P1 set the three kits were not individually wrapped. This set, with its striking painting of the three famous locomotives lined up together, was very well received and many were sold. Consequently, they are the most common among collectors today, though in only a very few is *The Steam Locomotive* booklet still present. These particular sets have now become very valuable as a consequence.

The second set brought together the Bulleid Light Pacific with three BR Mk1 coaches in a most attractive boxed set, again with a special cover, which proclaims it to be a 'Complete Train Kit'. The truly superb Ken Rush painting on the lid captures the excitement of the unrebuilt Pacific 34057 Biggin Hill pulling out of Waterloo station with a rake of green coaches on a West of England express. Unfortunately, the painting appears to have been made from a standard issue BR photograph of the scene, as the locomotive is clearly a 'Merchant Navy', with a curved tender rave, and the coaches are Bulleid steam stock, complete with roof tanks and double rain strip, rather than the Mk1 Standard coaches included in the kit! The Set P2 'Battle of Britain Complete Train Kit' was made up as follows:
No.11 Battle of Britain Class locomotive
No.13 Green BR Mk1 CK
No.14 Green BR Mk1 SK
No.15 Green BR Mk1 BSK
*The Steam Locomotive* booklet
Tube of Humbrol brand polystyrene cement
Eight capsules of Humbrol brand paint
Paintbrush
Emery file
Pair of tweezers (marked 'Sheffield')
Four pieces of Wrenn straight track each with card label red on blue G & R Wrenn
Kitmaster 1960 Catalogue

The loco kit is moulded in black plastic; any green ones you may see are Airfix productions. From this set onwards, the kits were supplied in plastic bags, so that parts were not lost. At the same time acetate wrappers were added to protect the outside of the sets. All instructions were multilingual from Set P2 onwards.

The final release in the series was for TT modellers. Scheduled for August 1960, it actually saw the light of day just in time for Christmas that year. It represents excellent value for money, bringing five kits together in one box. Once again, specially commissioned artwork, by Ken Rush, adorns the lid, this time featuring the Royal Scot locomotive and rake of maroon coaches passing Conway Castle on the North Wales Coast line of the LMR. Contents of the Set P3 'Royal Scot Complete Train Kit' were much like the other two.
No.16 Rebuilt Royal Scot Locomotive
No.17 BR Standard Corridor Brake 2nd Maroon
No.18 BR Standard Corridor Composite Maroon
No.20 BR Standard Corridor Second Maroon
No.21 BR Standard Restaurant 1st Maroon
*The Steam Locomotive* booklet
Half ounce capsule of Humbrol/ Kitmaster polystyrene cement
Eight capsules of paint
Paintbrush
Emery file
Pair of tweezers (marked 'Sheffield')
Lengths of Wrenn straight track
Kitmaster 1960 Catalogue

All of these kits were supplied in protective plastic bags in open box trays, with no lids. As has been mentioned above, the distinctive feature of these sets was the artwork and that elusive little booklet, *The Steam Locomotive*. It was written by the contemporary railway journalist J.N.Maskelyne, Assoc.I.Loco.E, who had a regular column in *Model Railway News* at the time. 'JNM' was paid the princely sum of £50 for his scribblings about the early history of the steam locomotive in Britain. The booklet measures 6x4½in. approximately and is printed in black on white. The cover shows the Britannia Pacific 70012 JOHN OF GAUNT emerging from Audley End tunnel on the Cambridge-Liverpool Street line. The book was specially commissioned by Kitmaster for the P1 Presentation Set '100 Years of British Steam Locomotive History', issued in 1960. It includes two adverts, one for Kitmaster locomotives which features the official BR shot of the Schools Class locomotive, the other for Rosebud Dolls with the original Rosebud logo – the one that includes a rose!

Although written for and about the first presentation set, it was later included with the other two sets and is referred to on the box covers. The author unfortunately died during 1960 and many adverts refer to 'the late author'. The book deals with the development of the steam locomotive between 1829 and 1937 and appears to have been written during 1959, the last year of the author's life. He was a distinguished technical journalist and engineer and had several of his books about locomotive practice and operation published by Percival Marshall & Co, the parent group of *Model Railway News*.

**Airfix Presentation Set No.1**
Airfix also produced four Presentation Sets during the late 1950s. These were Galleons, Sports Cars, Aircraft and, starting in 1957, the No.1 Trackside Presentation Set. This was originally an attractive red and yellow Type 1 box with special artwork, but later a more general Presentation Box was used, distinguished from the other three by a simple adhesive label. The set originally contained all Type 1 kits:

1 No.4005 Signal Box
2 No.4007 Platform Section
1 No.4009 Booking Hall
1 No.4012 Platform Fittings
1 No.4013 Station Accessories
Set of Airfix enamel Paints
Paint brush
Tube of Airfix polystyrene cement

However, when it was re-issued, the Signal Box was replaced by a No.4014 Footbridge. Early re-issues retain Type 1 kit packaging, but later all kits were in Type 2 packaging, whilst the paints were now a standard set of intermixable Airfix enamels which could also be bought separately. All of the Airfix Presentation Sets from this period are extremely rare indeed.

## Technical Data

**Kit numbers**
P1   100 Years of British Steam Set
P2   Battle of Britain Set
P3   The Royal Scot Set

**Box dimensions mm/ins**
P1   442 x 216 x 39   16½ x 8½ x 1½
P2   660 x 225 x 39   25½ x 8¾ x 1½
P3   750 x 216 x 39   30 x 8½ x 1½

**Presentation Set Numbers and Contents**
P1   1/ 4/ 9            100 Years of Steam
P2   11/13/14/15        Battle of Britain
P3   16/17/18/20/21     Royal Scot

**Release Dates**
10/59   (P1)
7/60    (P2)
12/60   (P3)
There were no Reviews for these sets
1st Advert MRN 1/62 (P2)

**Issue Prices**
P1   27s 6d
P2   37s 6d
P3   37s 6d

**Current Market Price Unmade**
P1      £70-120
P2      £150-200
P3      £150-200
Airfix  £70-100

**The original issue of the Trackside Presentation set.**

*Left.* Airfix Presentation Set No.1 featured a selection of Trackside kits to build a small country station. It was issued in a brightly coloured dedicated Type 1 style box. This was soon replaced with a generic box style that could be used for a variety of subjects by simple addition of a sticky label – seen here.

*Below.* Kitmaster set P2 brought together the Battle of Britain and three Mk1 green coaches. Notice the peculiar "hybrid" Bulleid/BR Mk1 coaches on the artwork.

Controversy rages to this day about the correct shade of blue for the Deltic. With poor quality undercoat, inferior colour film and the vagaries of the carriage washing plant, it is inevitable that differences would persist between ex-works and in-traffic pictures of Deltic. Here seen in as-preserved condition at Locomotion and in traffic below at Acton Bridge.

# The Models In Detail - 4
## No.10: The Prototype Deltic Diesel

This much sought after kit has a chequered history. The English Electric Deltic prototype was running trials throughout Britain in 1958/59 and was an obvious choice for a kit. The striking blue livery with those distinctive speed whiskers (the first *go faster* stripes?) on the nose combine with the sheer size of the original to produce a most pleasing model. Combined with Ken Rush's highly individual style of artwork and a box art where he surpassed himself for excitement, with bold sweeps of line and colour and you can see why this is a favourite kit for many people.

The Deltic was unique, at the time, in being the only locomotive model without any motion or connecting rods. The Kitmaster principle of unpowered locos driven from behind by a motorised coach or van did not work well. This is because the loco valve gear was often too stiff to turn freely when pushed from behind. The Deltic did not have this problem and acted just like a twelve wheel coach in practice. It could easily be driven by the KM1 motor bogie running in a coach behind it though it is necessary to weight the loco correctly to make it adhere to the track in this configuration. The officially recommended weight was 4oz evenly distributed. However, an entry in *Railway Modeller* quotes this as being insufficient and recommends 7oz evenly distributed above the bogies as being more useful. The problem was entirely solved by K's, who produced a six-wheel power bogie specially to fit the Deltic. Priced £2.3s.6d, it could be fitted with cast sideframes to match at an additional cost of 3s.6d. This bogie is based on that company's successful design for tender drive units, but is fitted with disc rather than spoked wheels. The sideframes fit onto stretchers which, whilst whitemetal, are equivalent to the plastic stretchers in size and position. Thus, the kit sideframes can be used with equal ease. Interestingly, there are significant detail differences in the Kitmaster and K's sideframes.

When Kitmaster's tooling was acquired by Airfix in 1962, it included the Deltic. However, by this time, production series Deltic deliveries had commenced to British Railways. The Class 55 Deltics were sufficiently different from the prototype to make a conversion difficult. The cab detail and window patterns were wrong, a new bogie sideframe was needed and the length was reduced. Additionally, Kitmaster had moulded the speed whiskers on the sides. Perhaps this explains why Airfix never released the model. Nevertheless, an item appeared in 'Mixed Freight' in the *Railway Modeller* of August 1961, showing a Kitmaster Deltic painted in the new two-tone green livery, as delivered to Eastern Region!

Airfix did continue to provide Deltics, via the Hermes Supply Co, to fulfil the Shredded Wheat promotion throughout 1963 and into late January 1964. The tooling passed to Dapol at the time they acquired all the other Airfix railway kit tools. It is said that David Boyle did not intend to release the kit at first. However, when Dapol shot the mould marked 'Drewry' they found it to be the original Kitmaster Deltic. This tool had been earmarked for scrapping by Airfix due to the poor state of the central cores, and indeed the tool for the clear parts was destroyed. On the original manifest of tools acquired by Dapol, this item was shown as 'Drewry'. Only later was its true identity discovered. One thousand kits were run off as an experiment. Because it was not intended to release it as such, the kit retained the Rosebud Kitmaster logo, whereas all the other kits were re-engraved with the Dapol logo. Early Dapol kits do not

**Deltic at Acton Bridge with the Merseyside Express.**

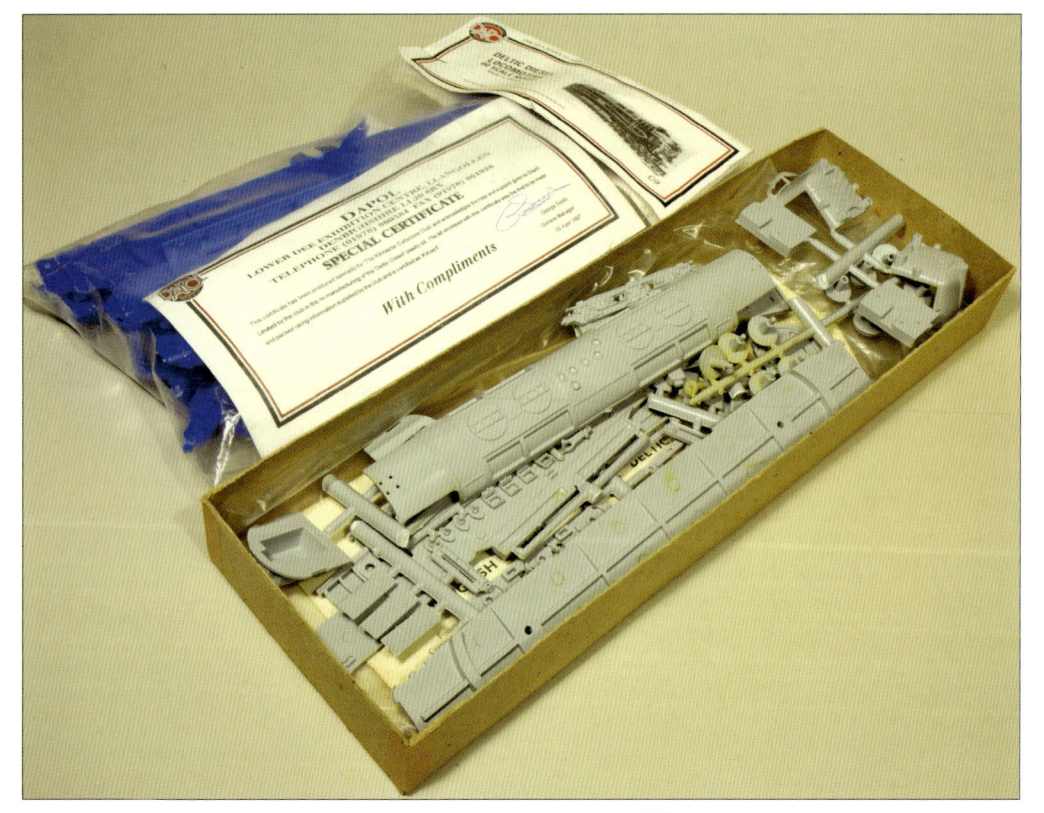

*Top.* Kitmaster Deltic descends Stoke Bank on the former Wolverhamton MRC layout.

*Middle.* Stylised Kitmaster Deltic artwork on the box top

*Bottom.* Two Deltic re-issues by Dapol. The grey moulding was issued in 1984 when the tool was rediscovered and sold without instructions, decals or glazing in a poly bag through W&H. The later bagged blue version had a copy of the Nabisco instruction sheet and a new decal; still no glazing though! The *With Compliments* slip states that this was the first shot to be run in blue at Dapol from the refurbished tools.

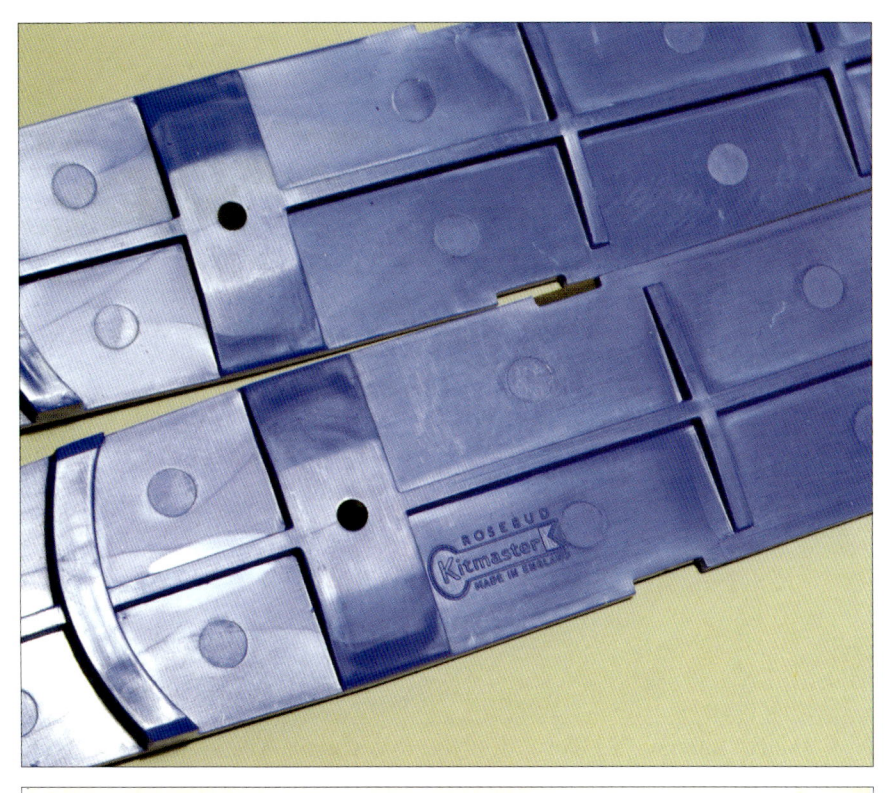

include the transparent window components or any instructions or the decal, whilst later issues lack only the glazing parts.

The Dapol-produced Kitmaster Deltic retains the Rosebud Kitmaster logo on the underside of the floor. This version of the kit can only be distinguished from the original by the colour of the plastic; Kitmaster originally shot the mould in ultramarine blue plastic, whilst early Dapol issues used light grey plastic. Later Dapol issues used ultramarine plastic, but of a lighter colour density than the original. Interestingly, early examples of the Deltic did not have the logo on the underside, but it was added during the early lifetime of the Rosebud kit. The tool, although once stated by Dapol to be 'beyond economic repair' has now been refurbished and with assistance from the Kitmaster Collectors Club, has re-appeared with a proper instructional header card and waterslide decal. In addition, South Eastern Finecast have a Flushglaze kit, No. 99, for this loco. During 2007, incidentally, Bachmann Industries (Europe) Ltd working with the National Railway Museum, produced a superb ready-to-run model of the Deltic – the 'Ice Cream Cart' in North London lineside *argot*.

*Top*. The original tool without the Kitmaster logo (top) as supplied in boxed kits and the engraved tool used for Nabisco bagged issues.

**Middle.** The 1960 Kitmaster Trade Price list also featured Deltic.

*Lower*. Most Kitmaster instruction sheets are black, but during 1962, a batch were printed in blue at Grove Street. This one was further overprinted by Hermes Supply Co to add the wording "With Compliments of Nabisco Foods" above the title.

*Top.* The kit-bashed Kitmaster OO Royal Scot. *Middle.* Kitmaster TT Royal Scot box top. *Bottom.* The kit-bashed OO and issued TT Royal Scots compared.

72

# The Models In Detail - 5
## No.16: The TT3 Rebuilt 'Royal Scot' Class Locomotive

This rather pleasing model was the only locomotive in the ill-fated TT ('Table Top') range. TT3 scale was introduced by Tri-ang in 1956 to take advantage of new smaller motors and to exploit the smaller space required by the 3mm scale. In spite of heavy promotion and an even heavier catalogue from Tri-ang, TT never really caught on in the UK and was finally withdrawn in 1966. The Kitmaster models were, as usual, accurate scale models. They did not, however, enjoy the same competitive advantages over Tri-ang as their OO big sisters. This was because Tri-ang pioneered their new standards for track, locomotives and coaches right from the beginning of TT. The coaches were scale length, unlike the OO types, and they were significantly cheaper than Kitmaster.

The Royal Scot was therefore a risky step for Rosebud. A large amount of effort went into the tooling, for a comparatively small market. It is ironic to reflect that, had they tooled it up for 4mm scale, it would have been an instant best seller; the first commercial model for 4mm scale was by Mainline, released in the 1980s. The decision in 1961, not to produce the KM3 Motor Bogie, was another major blow for the scale. Without it, the Royal Scot became virtually redundant, there being no locomotive motorising kit available for it at the time. This understandable decision, however, reflected the generally poor sales of TT items in the early years of production. The only power bogie made for TT was by K's, and was not really suitable for the BSK. Subsequently an etched nickel-silver chassis by Chris Thane has been derived from Comet patterns and this does fit the kit. However, the 3SMR chassis No.620 is not the correct wheelbase for this loco, although it claims to be so. Immediately after the initial release, Mike Bryant motorised one for *Model Railway Constructor* using a spare Tri-ang A1A-A1A motor bogie. It was apparently successful, but Tri-ang Class 31s in TT are a bit too thin on the ground today to contemplate such butchery! Because the connecting rods are so fine in 3mm scale, Kitmaster took the unusual step of including two sets of valve gear. The instructions note that for static display purposes, the scale size plastic valve gear and rods give the best appearance, whilst for running on a TT layout, slightly larger metal coupling rods and pistons are supplied, for added strength. The 'Royal Scot' locomotive was featured on the cover of the P3 Presentation Set, together with the four TT coaches also included in the set. The model has transfers and nameplates for three 'Royal Scots', 46100 Royal Scot, 46110 Grenadier Guardsman and 46149 The Boy Scout.

---

**DUE IN APRIL**
A NEW SERIES FOR 'TT' ENTHUSIASTS
Rebuilt ROYAL SCOT LOCOMOTIVE
& TENDER
No. 16. TT3    **6/11**
This is the first of a series. Coaches and a motorised Bogie will follow at regular intervals.

C.1    HOL 8484    Open Thursdays until 7 p.m

---

# Kitmaster
# NEW TT3 SERIES

Here's big news for TT enthusiasts! The full range of Kitmaster's exciting new TT3 series is in the shops now. Four *perfect scale* models of B.R. Coaches to build yourself . . . plus the famous Re-built 'Royal Scot'. If you're a TT collector you must own all the models in the TT3 series. Hurry! See them at your favourite model shop today.

TT3 No. 16 Re-built 'Royal Scot' 6/11d.
TT3 No. 17 Corridor Brake Second Coach 5/11d.
TT3 No. 18 Corridor Composite Coach 5/11d.
TT3 No. 20 Corridor Second Coach 5/11d.
TT3 No. 21 Restaurant First Coach  6/6d.

*Sixteen OO gauge models now available.*
*Ask at your usual MODEL or TOY SHOP.*

ROSEBUD KITMASTER LIMITED

**ROSEBUD Kitmaster**
PLASTIC SCALE MODELS

# NOW...

*A cut-away model showing the motor installed.*

## 'BATTLE of BRITAIN'

Now you can have the popular Battle of Britain Pacific Locomotive to add to your stud of power-driven Kitmaster models. All the parts you need. Nickel-silver tyres, current collectors, gears, axle sleeves, bearings, wires and weights, plastic parts, etc., conveniently packaged together. Complete with well-detailed, illustrated Instructional. Price only **11/8**, including Purchase Tax.

Apart from the Battle of Britain, there are three other Perfecta Kits to power-drive Kitmaster locomotives. No. 1 for the 0-4-0 Saddle Tank, price 8/9, No. 2 for the 0-6-0 Italian Tank, price 8/9, and No. 3 for the ever-popular 2-6-2 Great Western Prairie Tank, price 11/8. Motors extra. If you have not already obtained these do so without delay as supplies are now limited.

For Kitmaster Coaches—Peco Interiors add the final touch of realism. Four types now available— Nos. 13, 14K, 14SO, 15. All at one price, 2/9 each.

| COMPLETE COST ! | | |
|---|---|---|
| KITMASTER LOCOMOTIVE KIT | 10 | 6 |
| PERFECTA KIT ... | 11 | 8 |
| XT60 MOTOR ... ... | 12 | 10 |
| PECO COUPLING HOOKS | 1 | 6 |
| | 36 | 6 |

## PERFECTA KIT 4

COMPLETE REVISED PECO CATALOGUE 1/6, by post 2/-

SOLE SALES CONCESSIONAIRES :—

TRADE ENQUIRIES TO THE MANUF.

**THE PRITCHARD PATENT PRODUCT Cº Lᵀᴰ**
**PECOWAY—STATION ROAD—SEATON—DEVON**
TEL & GRAMS —SEATON 542

PLEASE TELL YOUR FRIENDS ABOUT THE **RAILWAY MODELLER**

Peco regularly advertised Perfecta kits on full pages within Railway Modeller, as they were both distributor of the kits and publisher of the magazine.

# The Models In Detail - 6
## No.11 : Bulleid 'Battle of Britain' Class Pacific

The Bulleid Pacific kit, No.11, was amongst the first batch of kits to be introduced. Making its appearance in early 1960, it rapidly established a position of fame amongst kit constructors. It predated the Tri-ang version by several years and as a consequence, became extremely popular with Southern Region (Railway) modellers. Many photographs of club and exhibition layouts of the time show motorised Kitmaster Battle of Britains. Airfix also had some considerable success with this loco and it continues as a mainstay of the Dapol kit fleet. It is impossible to estimate how many kits have been produced over the years, but it must be pushing 300,000 kits. There are certainly still large numbers of unmade Airfix kits in circulation.

The model is 34057 Biggin Hill, as running in 1958 in original condition. This locomotive was never rebuilt and the air-smoothed casing remained to the end of Southern steam, in July 1967. The high-sided 5,500 gallon tender of the kit was often 'cut down' on other locomotives of the class in order to reduce axle loading on the lightly laid West of England routes, where Bulleid's light Pacifics were regular performers. The kit has the original unorthodox BR(SR) style lining moulded on the boiler, cab and tank sides. This livery did not follow the 'standard' BR lining pattern with a boxed-in running number. Instead, the lines were continued straight across the cab sides and onto the tender. The resultant 'sleek' appearance of the unrebuilt locos contrasted sharply with the 'stocky' look of the rebuilt version, which more closely resembled a Britannia Pacific in appearance. The lining can be easily removed from the kit parts with a sharp knife and replaced by a suitable modern alternative: Kemco Waterslide BR/SR lining might be best, but standard BR (GWR) lining from PC Pressfix can be used if preferred.

The original Kitmaster tool had no brake gear and front steps for the loco, and these were added by Airfix in a major re-tooling which replaced the symbolic vacuum pipe with a scale example and added an NMRA buckeye coupling to the tender drawbar. For some unexplained reason, the front bogie retained the original Kitmaster coupling.

The Battle of Britain was a popular choice for motorisation, as has been noted, but this was made considerably easier by the issue of Arby Perfecta Kit No.4 in November 1960. This utilised the Tri-ang XT.60 motor (originally developed for use in TT locos and the Lord of the Isles) to provide traction. Pick-up was by nickel silver strips brushing the surface of steel rim tyres fitted over the plastic Boxpok wheels. The plastic axles were covered by metal sleeves running in brass frame bushes to improve the free-running performance of the chassis. To provide adhesion, a large custom casting was placed between the frames with the motor bolting straight to it. By all accounts it was quite a successful conversion, and many can still be found today.

Only one article on motorising this loco ever appeared in the model railway press despite the popularity of the kit. Since the proposed conversion involved butchering a Hornby Dublo A4, it was not very practical. However, in 1969 Ray Simmons wrote three excellent articles for Airfix Magazine covering detailing and motorising the kit.

Although basically a good model, and generally engineered to scale, there are many areas where Kitmaster compromised or deviated from the prototype to simplify production. The appearance of the finished model can therefore be considerably enhanced by the addition of detail parts, obtainable mostly from the workshop of the late, famed Bulleid 'guru' Albert Goodall. With Hornby Hobbies' release of the air-smoothed light Pacifics in 2006, an accurate and very detailed model of this popular prototype is now available.

## KITMASTER "BATTLE OF BRITAIN"

THE Kitmaster "Battle of Britain" appears to have preceded the "Deltic" in production. However, we doubt if any of the many Kitmaster fans will quibble about the order!

As can be seen from our illustration, the Bulleid Pacific fully maintains the high standards set by its predecessors, though the air-smoothed casing leaves little opportunity for the intricate detail of some of the other models. As can be seen, the full character of the prototype has been captured, the B.F.B. wheel, the massive motion and the relatively high-pitched cylinders.

As readers will know, there is little basic difference, other than the name and number, between the "Battle of Britain" and West Country classes; in point of fact there are more variations between individual locomotives than between the nominal classes. Therefore we have two classes to select from, while one could stretch a point and give this model a Merchant Navy name and number. Here, of course, there are slight differences of size, but we doubt if they are sufficient to be noticeable on a layout.

Once again this is an excellent model of a popular prototype, and should be as well received by enthusiasts as previous items in this range. It retails at 10/6.

*Above.* Original Airfix catalogue artwork by Wendy Meadway, circa 1976, showing added brake gear. *Below.* Kitmaster box artwork. *Bottom.* The superb Airfix Type 3 box featuring a Roy cross painting of "Biggin Hill"

# IMPROVE YOUR LAYOUT...

## BUILD AUTHENTIC
# Kitmaster
## LOCOS & COACHES

You can improve your layout without heavy additional cost by assembling these plastic scale model railway kits. Serious model railway enthusiasts all over Britain—and the rest of the world too — collect Kitmaster's international range of locomotives and coaches for OO and TT tracks. New! Coach electric motor bogies to *motorize* all Kitmaster locos. Ask about them at model shops everywhere.

OO KITS: 1 Rocket 4/6. 2 Diesel Electric Shunter 4/6. 3 Early American 'General' 6/6. 4 Coronation Class 10/6. 5 Schools Class 'Harrow' 7/6. 6 Saddle Tank 4/6. 7 Prairie Tank 6/6. 8 Italian Tank 4/6. 9 Stirling 8 foot Single 7/6. 10 Deltic Diesel 10/6. 11 Battle of Britain 10/6. 12 Swiss 'Crocodile' 10/6. 13, 14, 15 B.R. Coaches 6/6 each. TT3 SERIES: 16 Rebuilt "Royal Scot" 6/11. 17 Corridor Brake Second Coach 5/11. 18 Corridor Composite Coach 5/11.

**ROSEBUD Kitmaster** PLASTIC SCALE MODELS

No. 10 Deltic Diesel
No. 11 Battle of Britain Class
No. 12 Giant Swiss "Crocodile"
No. 13 Corridor Composite Coach

MOTORS
KM1 Coach Electric Motor Bogie for OO gauge 27/6d.
KM3 Coach Electric Motor Bogie for TT3 gauge 27/6d.
KM2 Electric Motorized Box Wagon for OO gauge 35/-

*Above*. The original Kitmaster box for the Ariel Arrow showing the odd scale; 1:16 and out of sequence kit number: 60.

*Below*. Airfix made good use of the Ariel Arrow tool, issuing it first as a bagged Series 2 kit, then promoting it to Series 3 with nice Roy Cross artwork and also using as the basis for a wacky "Weird-oh" of their own – the bizarre *"Ton Up Tony"* now a rare Airfix collectable.

# The Models In Detail - 7
## No.60: The Ariel Arrow Super Sports Model

The Ariel Arrow is perhaps the most elusive of the Kitmaster models. In production for just five months from March 1962, it was a big risk for Rosebud. When the locomotive range was suddenly curtailed, before the last three advertised models had been released, to announce a large scale motorcycle kit was indeed brave. Rosebud had no experience of this market as no British motorcycle kits then existed. The decision to produce it can possibly be attributed to the 'suggestion' scheme run by Rosebud. Since two of their employees were stalwarts of the Wellingborough Motorcycle Touring Club and one of those had owned an ex-WD Ariel cycle, it may have been at their instigation that the 1960 Motorcycle of the Year was chosen as the next subject for a Kitmaster kit. In fact, there was to have been a whole series of them. The second, No.61, was in the pattern-making stage when the company was sold to Airfix. It would have been a Matchless circuit racing machine. Drawings and some patterns were made, but the project was never completed by Kitmaster or, indeed, resurrected by Airfix.

The Ariel Arrow Super Sports Model, to give it its proper name, was produced in a standard, but dimensionally unique, Kitmaster card box. It was numbered out of sequence, as No.60. This was meant to be the first number in a new series of kits, allowing the railway range to continue using the 1-59 block of numbers. The introduction was noted in an editorial from the 1962 Toy Fair by *Model Railway Constructor* at the same time as they announced that kits 35, 36 and 37 had been suspended.

The large scale, 1:16, meant changes to the normal assembly method, with both the main superstructure and chassis being assembled as separate parts. In order to produce this kit, Kitmaster worked from a real Ariel Arrow which was taken into the Design Office and meticulously studied and drawn. These were in addition to the manufacturer's drawings which were also made available to the pattern maker, Mr Fergusson of Kettering. Perhaps the most interesting feature was the wheels. To enable the spokes to appear as fine as possible, Rosebud elected to mould the wheels in clear plastic. One simply painted carefully over the spokes to obtain the desired effect. When the tooling was acquired by Airfix, they retooled these parts in the same opaque yellow plastic used for the rest of the bike; consequently the two kits are easily distinguished.

Oddly, the Rosebud Kitmaster logo does not appear on the model at all, but is instead on the stand. This was duly re-engraved by Airfix. Airfix do not seem to have changed the thick Kitmaster mould sprues on this model. The lack of a coupling to retool led directly to the incorporation of this kit into the Airfix range as early as July 1963. In fact the early reintroduction date would indicate that very few changes were made. However, they did think it worth changing the registration number in the artwork from ONV 989, which is a Northamptonshire number, to 697 AOH, which is a Birmingham number. The Rosebud factory was, of course, in Northamptonshire; Airfix chose not to use a Wandsworth number, but the area registration which covered the Ariel Motorcycles factory in Birmingham. The original Kitmaster kit has ONV 989 on the box whilst the decals are for 697 AOH. Additionally, the price was reduced dramatically at the same time, coming down from 5s 11d as a Kitmaster model to the meagre 2s of an Airfix Series 1 kit. Later the kit was re-issued as Series 2 and finally ceased production in 1980. An interesting kit issued in 1964, pattern No.311, was 'Ton-up-Tony'. This was described by Airfix as a 'Wheird-ohs' kit and formed part of a series of three, the others being Flame-Out Freddie (Monstrous T33C pilot) and Toilway Daddy (Barely Humanoid Dragster driver!). This latter other was licensed directly from Hawk plastic models of America. The Airfix contribution to the extensive Hawk Weird-ohs range involved the addition of a grotesque caricature of a demented biker astride the aforementioned Ariel Arrow! It is actually quite a sought-after kit for Airfix collectors, mainly, one suspects, because not many people bought it!

*Above*. Airfix Type 2 header by Charles Oakes.

*Below*. Airfix Type 3 header by Roy Cross.

The Kitmaster motorised bogies drew heavily on the Tri-ang design.

80

# The Models In Detail - 8
## KM1 and KM2 - The Motorised Bogies

The motorisation of Kitmaster models was made infinitely easier by the introduction, in 1960, of two ready-to-run motor bogie units. These are the KM1 Motorised BR1 Bogie for passenger stock and the KM2 Motorised Box Van for freight stock. The power bogies were designed to fit inside a Standard BR Mk1 BSK coach. The appropriate Kitmaster coach number is shown on the box panel of each motor bogie; KM1 fits Coach No.15 (OO BSK) and KM3 would have fitted Coach No.17 (TT BSK). The KM3 power bogie was shown in the 1960 and 1961 catalogues, but was never actually commercially produced. This was documented in an official press statement in *Railway Modeller* of July 1961. Interestingly, the *Airfix Magazine* of November 1960 described a test run of a TT motor bogie sample they had received. This was presumably a limited factory built coach fitted with a prototype bogie to promote the Royal Scot and TT Coach range. Interestingly, a June 1960 advertisement in *Model Railway News* from Southgate Hobby Shop offered a 'motorised Utility Van to drive your Kitmaster Locomotives'. The unit was said to be available in 'red or green', presumably maroon and SR green, and cost 45s each. They were heralded as a 'Southgate Speciality'. Any further details would be appreciated.

Occasionally, KM1 power bogies are found fitted to Kit No.31 (Pullman Power Car) which has the fitting to take it and the instruction showing how to fit it. A lot of work is involved in replacing the cast metal sideframes of BR1 pattern with the driving bogie Metro-Schleiren pattern sideframes. Fitting it to the BSK involves considerable modification to the coach, including bending up the existing steel ballast weight, and fitting a plastic yoke supplied in the kit.

The Motorised Box Van was designed to run behind a Kitmaster locomotive, thereby pushing it along. The principle was first demonstrated at the 1961 Brighton Toy Fair, using a standard KM1 motor bogie inside an RB3 Refrigerator Van. It was critically acclaimed at the time, especially by *Model Railway Constructor* who thought it 'an economical way to motorise your Kitmaster fleet.' The construction is very similar to the KM1 motor bogie, except that the ballast weight is different and the sideframes are not die cast. Instead, black plastic sideframes are fitted to the bogie whilst the body is a separate one piece moulding in brown bauxite coloured plastic. The body moulding is almost identical to the Hornby Dublo ventilated van, even down to the tool marks on the inside but, conspicuously, it carries the Rosebud Kitmaster logo on the underside. The unit comes with a choice of couplings; in a separate enclosure are parts to enable the fitting of either Peco Simplex or Tri-ang Tension Lock couplings as an alternative to the standard Kitmaster hook and eye coupling.

Despite their superficial similarity to the Tri-ang designed motor bogie used in their Diesel Multiple Unit, it is certain that Tri-ang did not produce them, as Richard Lines emphatically stated in a letter to the Club. (See 'Rumours & Postulations'). Cyril Ferry, a former Rosebud employee, used to drive up to Stalybridge to collect the raw castings for these and also remembered an armature winding machine being installed in the Design & Development Dept. at Grove Street. Although former employees and out-workers can remember making assemblies, such as the choke, or assembling and packing them, most metallic parts seem to have been subcontracted to outside manufacturers and the designer remains a mystery.

A complete parts list for the KM1 and KM2 motor bogies was unearthed in the 1959 diary of Kathleen Shaw, who was one of the women who assembled these units at Raunds. Kath says that they had a test track leading back from the end of the production line to the packing stage. Each completed bogie was simply popped onto this track and allowed to run under power direct to the packing station. In this way every bogie could be quickly tested and any faults rectified before being packed into their respective boxes. Kath's entry is for August 1959, but the bogie did not actually reach the shops until July 1960. These are the parts list for KM1 and 2 in Kathleen Shaw's diary, August 1959:

845 1 Insulator
846 2 Worm
847 3 Armature Segment
848 1 Commutator
851 2 Magnet extrusion
853 1 Magnet
854 2 Axle
855 4 Wheel
895 1 Magnet screw
896 1 Brush plate
897 1 Brush spring
898 1 Retaining plate
900 2 Felt pad
901 2 Bearing retainer
902 1 Spring
903 1 Pick-up spring
904 2 Bearing
905 4 Retaining plate screw
912 1 Bogie frame KM1
913 1 Bogie frame KM2
972 2 Bearing small
981 2 Brush contact
1116 1 Shaft
1117 1 Commutator insulator
1121 2 Carbon brush
Wire 0.0048in diameter
1 Suppressor
1 Choke
*2 Sideframe moulding (KM2 only)*
*2 Coupling plates*
*2 10BA screws 1 Maintenance Sheet*
*1 Instruction sheet (KM1 only)*
*2 Couplings*
These last parts in italics are not in Kath's list, but are included here for completeness.

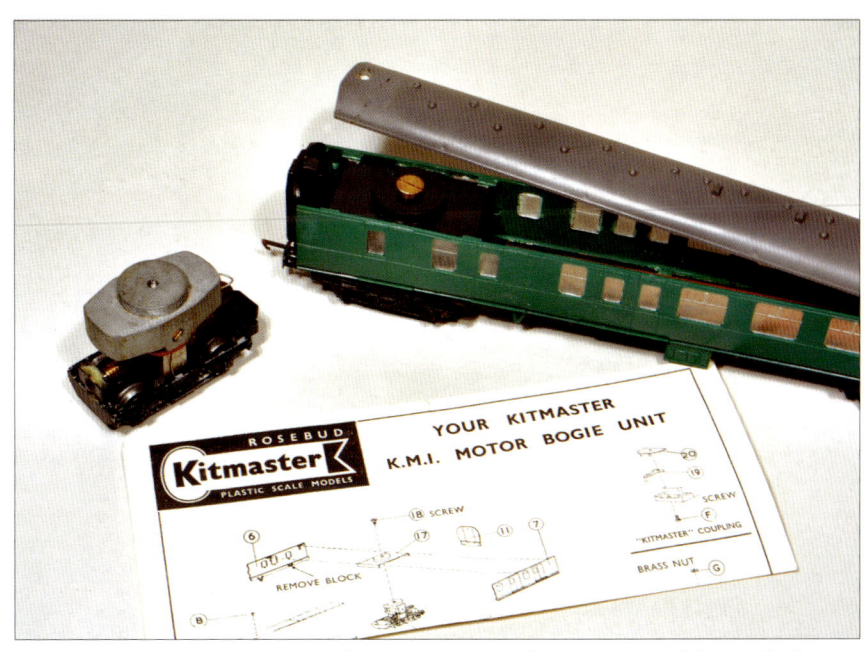

**A plastic yoke was supplied with KM1 which could be cemented into a built BSK below the roof line to support the motor bogie.**

*Top.* A Kitmaster Class 08 marshals a train of Scalecraft Road Railers in the scene modelled by Marcus Archer.
*Middle and bottom.* These two interesting models were built by David Smith of Keighley using Kitmaster Class 08 kits for the Bachmann catalogue, prior to the introduction of their ready-to-run model. A third model in BR blue Is on page 83.

82

# The Models In Detail - 9
## No.2: The 350HP Diesel Shunter

Whether nestling behind the shed, lurking in the bay platform or simply pottering about in the yard, the humble diesel shunter became a ubiquitous sight throughout Britain's railway network. In this appreciation of the famous Kitmaster model, we turn the spotlight on the diesel electric shunter. The diesel electric shunter was one of the first of the new series designs for the emergent British Railways and it is therefore not surprising that several re-classifications have been made during their lifetime. Consequently we must start by considering the various designations which have been given to these locos under British Railways ownership. Altogether, they have been reclassified four times since construction. Originally, they were designated into classes and sub-classes by the Eastern Region. This was followed by two sets of general BR designations in the late 1950's and early 1960s culminating in the advent of the computerised TOPS numbering system in October 1968.

'DEJ3' was the original Eastern Region designation of the 350HP 0-6-0 diesel electric shunter designed by the LMS and built at Derby Works. In October 1968, under the TOPS numbering system, this would become Class 11, of which over one hundred were constructed between 1948 and 1952. The designation DEJ3 was arrived at as follows: DE for diesel electric, J indicating the wheel arrangement 0-6-0, design number 3 of this type. The J, incidentally, had long been used for dozens of 0-6-0 steam locomotive classes.

**Catalogue shots from Bachmann featuring the Kitmaster 08 kits used as prototypes for their own model.**

'DEJ4' is the 350HP 0-6-0 Class 08 locomotive, the ubiquitous British Railways standard diesel-electric design constructed at Doncaster Works. Originally, the DEJ4 designation applied to both machines fitted with English Electric power and traction equipment and those fitted with Blackstone engines. This was soon changed, however, to allow two sub-classes depending on variant of prime mover, the Blackstone powered machines becoming D3/3 (later 3/1B), whilst EE examples became D3/2 (Later 3/1A).

Two more variants, which were powered by Crossley engines, had initially been given the design numbers DEJ5 and DEJ6, although externally they were identical to DEJ4 locos. The DEJ5 machines were powered by Blackstone, but had GEC traction motors, whilst DEJ6 had Blackstone engines driving BTH motors. DEJ5 was then re-classified as D3/4 (later 3/1C) whilst DEJ6 was allocated D3/5 followed by 3/1D. These two groups were eventually amalgamated to form a separate TOPS class; Class 10. Confused? You soon will be!

All surviving EE and Blackstone machines at the 1968 re-organisation of the capital fleet were grouped together within Class 08, whilst the Crossley engined examples were designated Class 10. No Class 10 machines survived long enough to carry the 10.xxx number. All of the Class 08 locomotives which survived long enough to carry their full TOPS number eventually received the English Electric 6KT 6-cylinder engine, developing 261 KW of power, giving a top speed of 20 mph. Many of the non-standard locomotives were disposed of to industrial concerns while numerous examples of both TOPS classes were exported. Although built as vacuum brake only, many of the survivors have now received air braking or, in some cases, dual braking systems.

The final development of the basic English Electric 0-6-0 diesel electric shunter design is the Class 09. Utilising the same EE 6KT power plant as Class 08, but uprated to 298KW (400HP) these engines are all air-braked and are re-geared to have a top speed of 27 mph, to match the specific requirements of the Southern Region. Only thirty were built and all initially were allocated to the SR. In recent years, however, they have become more widely dispersed, one at least being allocated to Sheffield Tinsley. Tinsley itself was home to Britain's most unlikely shunter design, the three-strong Class 13 hump shunters. These were formed from specially weighted and modified Class 08s adapted to work in pairs as master and slave units. The

| Table E - Summary of Classes: | | | | | | |
|---|---|---|---|---|---|---|
| **BR Class Designations** | | | | Locomotive Running Numbers | | Engine/Electrical Equipment |
| 1st BR | 2nd BR | 3rd BR | TOPS | 1957 Nos. | 1964 Nos. | |
| DEJ3 | D3/8 | 3/8A | 11 | 12045-12138 | 12045-12138 | EE |
| DEJ4 | D3/2 | 3/1A | 08 | 13000-13116 | | EE |
| | | | 08 | 13127-13136 | | EE |
| | | | 08 | 13152-13365 | D3000-4192 1 | EE |
| DEJ4 | D3/3 | 3/1B | 08 | 13117-13126 | D3117-3126 | Crossley |
| DEJ5 | D3/4 | 3/1C | 10 | 13137-13151 | D3137-3151 | Blackstone/GEC |
| | | | 10 | | D3439-3453, D3473-3502, D3612-3651 | Blackstone/GEC |
| DEJ6 | D3/5 | 3/1D | 10 | 13152-13166 | D3152-3166 | Blackstone/BTH |
| | D3/13 | 3/9 | 12 | 15211-15236 | 15211-15236 | EE/ SR Boxpok |
| *Later Classes:* | | | | | | |
| | | | 09 | | D3665-3671, D4099-4114 | EE |
| | | | 09 | | D3719-3721 | EE |
| | | | 13 | | D4500 Ex D4188 + 3698 | EE |
| | | | 13 | | D4501 Ex D4190 + 4189 | EE |
| | | | 13 | | D4502 Ex D4187 + 3697 | EE |
| Note 1 : With exceptions for listed sub-classes. | | | | | | |

'slaves' had the entire upper section of their cabs removed and were then permanently connected to the suitably modified 'master' units. All were withdrawn with the end of hump shunting in 1985.

**The Rosebud Kitmaster Class 08**
This excellent scale model is extremely important in the history of British outline modelling because it was the first ever plastic assembly kit of a locomotive to be issued in the UK. An advance mention in the *Model Railway News* of March 1959 said 'Rosebud Kitmaster, a new name to the hobby, will introduce a model of British Railways Class DEJ3 shunter as a complete plastic assembly kit at the reasonable price of 4s 6d.' This was the first mention anywhere of a Kitmaster product. However, as the *Railway Modeller* news article pointed out, what actually emerged from the Kitmaster factory in Grove Street was a model of the DEJ4 350HP Class 08 locomotive. The detail differences, if apparent externally, are not too great however and the model is a good representation of a type which could eventually be seen all over the network. This was the first Kitmaster model to be available in the shops, despite carrying the series number 2! It featured in numerous publicity and promotional pieces which produced favourable reviews in all three model railway journals of the time in March and April 1959.

The Kitmaster model was notable for its superb attention to detail. Not only was it fitted with correct outside-frame cranks and scale width coupling rods, but it was also possessed of a pair of correct pattern vacuum tanks under the front buffer beam and a wealth of bodyside detail. From the modeller's point of view, it is important because it is still, after thirty years, relatively common and does not command a high price second-hand. It is ideally suited, therefore, to a motorisation and detailing project. This model is still a favourite amongst discerning modellers of today and many have been supplied by the Kitmaster Collectors Club for enthusiasts to motorise.

The only drawback to this model is the amount of moulded-on detail, all of which has to be removed if a full restoration to prototype is undertaken. This would necessarily include removal of both front ladders on the bonnet sides, all handrails and the lamp brackets. This criticism actually applies to all of the models except the Hornby Dublo/Wrenn loco which has individually fitted front ladders. It is interesting to note that most of the proprietary models depict the cab front with four electric marker lights, whereas locomotives in the initial batches built in 1952/3 were delivered with only two, set immediately above each buffer. Indeed, the very first Rosebud production kits, as shown in the instructional photograph, were modelled with only two marker lights, but the later production batches definitely have all four. The tool was modified very early on in its life, probably during 1959.

**The Bachmann prototype model**
The first indications that Bachmann would be producing a model of the Class 08 shunter came in 1995. During late 1995, Graham Hubbard, CEO of Bachmann Industries (Europe) Ltd. contacted the Kitmaster Collectors Club for the supply of three 350HP Diesel Shunter kits together with a complete rake of BR Mk1 coaches. These were duly forwarded by the Club and formed the basis for the Bachmann proving and photographic models which appear in that company's 1996 catalogue and are reproduced here. The models were built

A very early example of the 08 with only two marker lights. (A. Wakeford).

84

professionally, by David Smith of Keighley MRC, and use Branchlines chassis. The development models were first shown to the public at the 1996 Warley M.R.C. exhibition, with the production models released in 1999.

The British model manufacturers have rightly devoted much effort to the BR Shunter classes and it is quite possible to model virtually the entire fleet of 1955-1965 prototypes. Whilst many have been available in Ready-to-Run form, the others are available as whitemetal or resin (Class 01,02,05,07,14) kits. Special mention should be made here of the super little Drewry diesel-mechanical (Class 04) modelled so effectively by Airfix. This plastic bodyline kit, the only 'true' Airfix locomotive, is still in production with Dapol. Until the release of Bachmann's own ready-to-run Class 04, the Airfix kit on the Bachmann Class 03 chassis provided an excellent model of a widely used type.

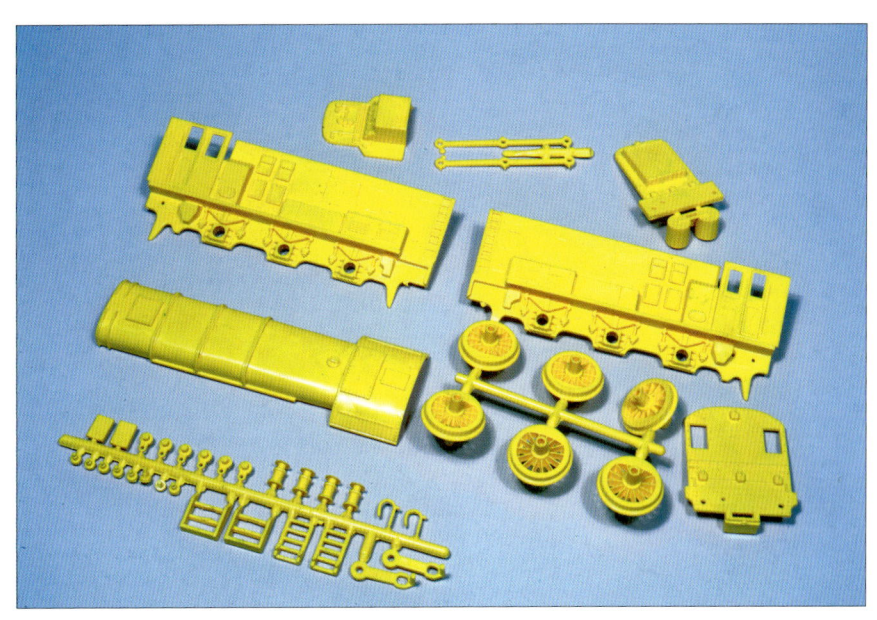

Test shot in Rocket yellow with four marker lights.

| Table F - The Models | | | | | |
|---|---|---|---|---|---|
| Manufacturer | Cat. No. | Type | Class | Date | Status |
| Hamblings | | DEJ3 | 11 | 1954 | Deleted |
| Kirdon Electric | | DEJ3 | 11 | 1955 | Not Produced |
| Triang-Hornby | R152 | DEJ3 | 11 | 1956 | Deleted, mould used for Devious Diesel |
| Rosebud Kitmaster | 2 | DEJ4 | 08 | 1959 | Deleted, mould scrapped by Airfix. |
| Hornby Dublo/Wrenn | 2231 | DEJ4 | 08 | 1961 | Deleted |
| Hornby Railways | R050 | DEJ4 | 08 | 1976 | Current in Railroad range |
| Hornby Railways | R050 | DEJ4 | 09/08 | 2004 | Current |
| Lima | L205107 | | 09 | 1978 | Deleted |
| Bachmann | 32-115 | DEJ4 | 08 | 1999 | Current |

The full majesty of Roy Cross' painting of the BR standard Mogul is revealed with the removal of the additional elements needed for a box top.

# The Models In Detail - 10
## No.30 The British Railways Standard Class 4MT Mogul

The advent of the British Railways Class 4MT Mogul was a major milestone in British outline modelling. Only in latter years has another proprietary model of this locomotive been produced and the Mogul in its time has spawned a whole plethora of adapting, conversion and motorisation kits. Favourably received at the time of initial launch, it was rapturously welcomed back to model shop shelves everywhere when Airfix announced the 1967 reintroduction of an improved and retooled model. Resplendent in a Series 4 box with full colour Roy Cross artwork, this kit became a mainstay of the Airfix Railways offerings for many years. The picture depicts 76067 on a standard 50-55 foot turntable, but on close inspection it is noticeable that this loco has a 2-2-4-0 wheel arrangement! The forward half of the coupling rod is quite obviously 'missing' and only the rear driving wheels are actually coupled. Why Roy allowed such an obvious omission to escape his normally powerful scrutiny is hard to say. Certainly all of the other details are faithfully rendered. In the transparency shown here, without the additional Airfix graphics, you can really see the turntable and the foreground in detail. Mysteriously, the Mogul was dropped from the range at the time of issue in the Type 7 boxes so it never received a new piece of artwork, unlike the Schools, Truro and Pug. The locomotive is portrayed in amazing detail considering the age and cost of the original Kitmaster issue. It utilises a very good representation of the standard BR2A tender which was widely deployed by modellers until the arrival of the Bachmann-produced Mainline Standard Class 4 in 1980. Because of the inter-changeability of parts between Standard locos, the Mogul kit has proved a valuable source of parts for 'kit-bashers' over the decade. Indeed, it was only in 2008 that a ready-to-run model finally became available with the introduction of the superb Bachmann offering.

*Above.* Original Kitmaster box art work.

*Left.* Airfix Type 4 box artwork.

*Below.* Built Kitmaster Standard class 4MT Mogul

87

Kitmaster box art for The General (HO), Swiss Crocodile (OO), German Baureihe 23 (OO) and NYC Hudson (HO).

# The Models In Detail - 11
## The Kitmaster Continental Prototypes

Only one company in the history of railway modelling has produced rolling stock in all three popular scales of the 1960s- Rosebud Kitmaster. Remarkable as it may seem, Kitmaster appears to have been the only producer to dabble in 4mm, 3.5mm and 3mm at the same time. Such notions were not to be entertained by Airfix, though after the agreed sale of Kitmaster to Airfix in 1963, there were high hopes for the new combined range. Airfix originally planned to incorporate at least some of the models into the successful Airfix Rolling Stock range. However, the greatest shock was the news that none of the Continental prototypes would be re-issued. Airfix had issued their own HO scale rolling stock kit - the Interfrigo refrigerator van. This last kit is all that remains of the HO production of Airfix and Kitmaster.

### The Continental Prototypes
The choice of locomotives was, from the outset, rather esoteric. This was probably due to the direct involvement of T.Eric Smith in the selection of prototypes to be modelled. There were some very interesting foreign designs, including the famous Italian State Railways Class 835 'Caffettiera' tank engine and the massive Be6/8 Krokodil of the Swiss Federal Railways. Kit No.3 was for the American 'Old-Timer' The General, a veteran 4-4-0 which did sterling service during the Civil War. Unfortunately, Kitmaster had not properly researched the export market for these kits. All three, together with the later kits of the SNCF 241P Mountain and the DB Class 23 2-6-2 were all produced to the British scale of 4mm to 1ft. Why this fundamental error was allowed to continue into the second year of production is one of the great mysteries of Rosebud Kitmaster. Even T.Eric Smith cannot now remember why it happened. Suffice to say, these models found only limited acceptance in their intended target markets.

### The Models Reviewed
### Kit No.3 - The General HO Scale
The General was a 4-4-0 wood-burning locomotive made famous during the American Civil War. The locomotive was stolen from Big Shanty in the Confederate-held South in April 1862. After a hair-raising chase towards Chattanooga, with another engine in hot pursuit, the Union spies who had captured The General abandoned it, but only after having cut telegraph wires and burned bridges and structures all along the line. The kit is a delightful model of this famous American 'Old-Timer' and as one of only two kits in HO proved popular in the US market.

### Kit No.8 - The Italian State Railways Class 835 Tank engine OO Scale
This popular class of 0-6-0T shunting locomotive could, at one time, be seen all over the FS system and was popularly known as a 'Caffettiera' tank on account of the unusual arrangement of safety valves and domes, which somewhat resemble an Italian coffee-making machine! This 4mm model was also a popular choice for motorisation because the second of the Arby 'Perfecta' kits was designed specifically for the Italian Tank.

### Kit No.12 - Giant Swiss Crocodile OO Scale
The only electric locomotive to be attempted by Kitmaster, the Swiss Federal Railways Class Be 6/8 'Krokodil' was an quixotic choice. The cam-driven cranks and rigid outside coupling rods make this model at once unusual and impossible to assemble in a free running state! The dummy pantographs, whilst a reasonable representation of the prototype in the lowered position, were not conducive to modelling the locomotive as working. Built from 1927 onwards, originally for use on the 1 in 40 gradients of the Gotthard main line, they were displaced in the early 1960s by newer Ae 6/6 traction units. Similar locomotives can still be seen to this day operating on the Central Section of Indian State Railways, with Bombay V.T. being a favourite haunt.

### Kit No.19 - German Class 23 Locomotive OO Scale
The Baureihe 23 (Literally 'Class 23') 2-6-2 locomotives were a lightweight mixed traffic design for the Deutsche Bundesbahn. The distinctive German smoke deflectors, high running plate and articulated bogie tender made this a very distinctive model. Note that in the Kitmaster drawings the tender is shown as a rigid six-wheel construction. Introduced in 1953 as a replacement for the Prussian State Railways Class P8, these locomotives employed novel all-welded construction to reduce weight and were one of the most successful post-war German designs. Yet another 4mm model, it found little favour in its 'home' market as a consequence. The later addition of ex-Prussian B4yge coaching stock (in 3.5mm scale) did little to boost sales and many were remaindered after the company was sold to Airfix.

### Kit No.23 - SNCF 241P 'Mountain' Locomotive OO Scale
A monster kit of a monster locomotive. A personal favourite of the author, the elegant outlines of the Mountain contrast with its bulk and presence. It could almost be British! The last Kitmaster Continental prototype in the fatal 4mm scale, the Mountain portrayed a popular prototype. The 35 locomotives of this class were ordered from Le Creusot immediately after the Second World War and were delivered to the South Eastern Region of SNCF in 1948-49. They were the most powerful passenger steam locomotives operating in Europe at the time and the last steam engines to be constructed for SNCF before their head-long rush to electrification. Displaced from the crack Paris-Lyon-Nice services by electric traction, they were relegated to the Avignon-Marseille portions of such famous trains as Le Mistral, Le Train Bleu

Italian Class 835 Tank (OO).

*Top.* SNCF A9Myfi coach (HO) and DB B4yge coach (HO)
*Below.* Comparing the 4mm Baureihe 23 with the 3.5mm B4yge coach, the scale/gauge ratio is a problem.

and the Paris-Cote d'Azur. The prototype may be seen at the Cite du Train – the SNCF Museum in Mulhouse.

### Kit No.27 - DB type B4yge Coach HO Scale

The first of the 3.5mm scale models. These coaches were formed by re-using ex-Prussian State Railways underframes. Constructed during 1959-60, some two thousand of the remaining four wheelers were used in this project. The resulting HO scale model has a typically Teutonic rustic appearance. The B4yg coaches were built on undercarriages of Prussian bogie coaches, either retaining their Prussian or US type bogies or receiving Minden-Deutz ones. In all, 1,821 such coaches were built commencing in 1935, most of them in Munich. Among them were some 380 with 1st class compartment on one end, and 319 with a luggage compartment in one half of the coach, The first coaches originally were called BC4yg and were upgraded to AB4yg when 3rd class was abolished in 1956. These bogie coaches were the second rebuilding programme. Before and parallel to it, 6,539 old 6-wheelers of all kinds received a new body using the same elements that were later used for the bogie coaches.

### Kit No.29 - SNCF A9myfi/1958 Coach HO Scale

The latest word in air-conditioned first class luxury travel. Introduced for Paris-Lille and Paris-Lyon services these all-steel coaches, over 82 feet long, boasted full public address systems and even radio-telephones in the vestibules! Now superseded by the superior Rivarossi model, these kits were a mainstay of SNCF modelling for many years. These stainless steel coaches are called Inox after the French expression for stainless – 'inoxidisible'. They were built by the Budd Car Company for the SNCF and delivered in 1952 for use on principal services such as Le Mistral and Le Train Bleu as well as express services from Paris to Lille, in the Nord-pas-de-Calais.

### Kit No.34 - New York Central Class J.3 A 'Hudson' Locomotive HO Scale

The J.3 A 4-6-4 was the culmination of a series of 4-8-4 New York Central railroad designs. Constructed by Alco in 1937-38, these 50 locomotives had improved boilers and steaming arrangements as compared with their earlier J.1 and J.2 counterparts. They are perhaps best known for their work at the head of the '20th Century Limited', between New York and Chicago, a train which proudly boasted a throughout average of 60 mph for the journey. The model is a complex kit, reproducing, as it does, a semi-working form of the intricate Baker valve gear and the intriguing boxpok wheel design so beloved of our own O.V.S.Bulleid. These kits have long provided a source of parts for other American-outline locos and are now rather scarce. The Hudson has been a popular prototype and Kitmaster was not the first British company to contemplate such a model. That honour goes to Graham Farish, whose superb working model, tender-driven through a lay shaft, is now a highly-prized collectable in its own right. An entirely new plastic HO scale model in 'snap together' form was introduced by Monogram of the USA in the mid-1980s, available in NYC or C&O liveries.

*Right and middle.* Detail shot of Marcus Archer's built SNCF 241P Mountain loco.

*Below.* The Mountain artwork – the biggest Kitmaster kit to have been issued at that point

*Above.* The mighty Mountain 241P.
*Middle.* The General by Kitmaster built and painted by Marcus Archer.
*Below.* An interesting plan of the new A9myfi stainless steel (INOXidisible) coaches for the Lille and Lyon routes.

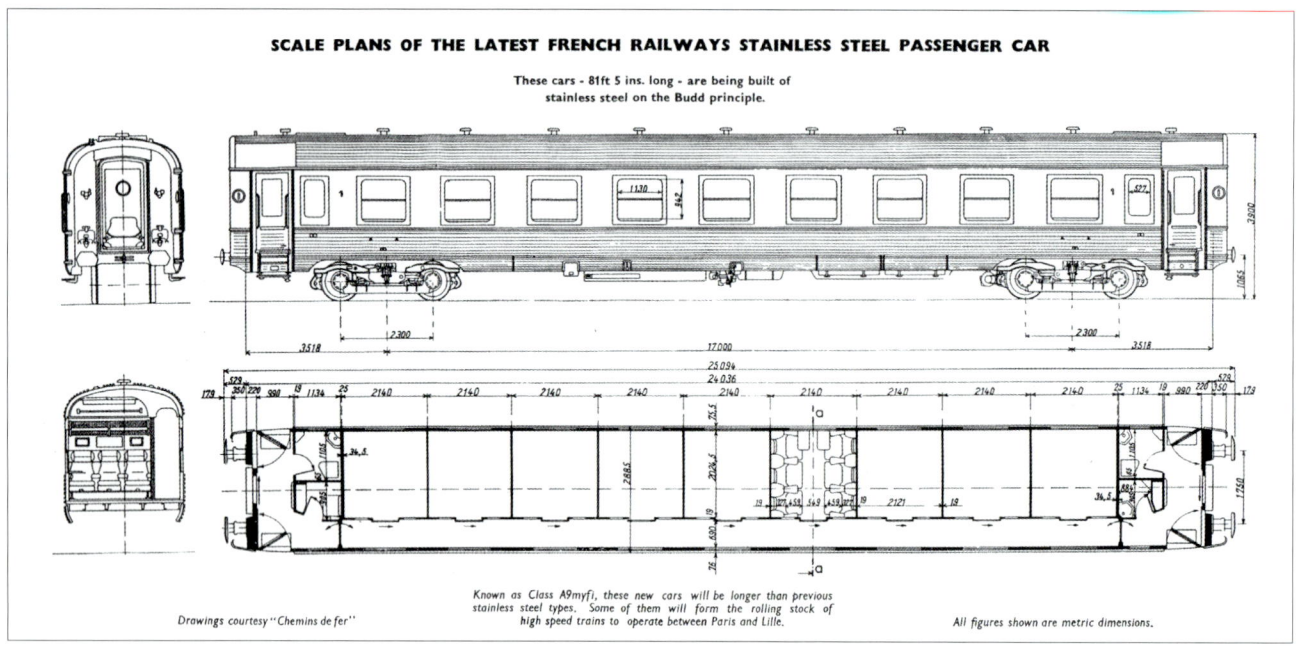

**SCALE PLANS OF THE LATEST FRENCH RAILWAYS STAINLESS STEEL PASSENGER CAR**

These cars - 81ft 5 ins. long - are being built of stainless steel on the Budd principle.

Drawings courtesy "Chemins de fer"

Known as Class A9myfi, these new cars will be longer than previous stainless steel types. Some of them will form the rolling stock of high speed trains to operate between Paris and Lille.

All figures shown are metric dimensions.

*Left.* An 0-10-0T Italian switcher built from two Italian Tank kits.

June, 1960     GAMES & TOYS     51

# KITMASTER REALISM SELLS!

No. 19 Baureihe 23 (00-HO)

**NEW**

**AUTHENTIC MODEL:**

**GERMANY'S**

**"BAUREIHE 23" 10/6d**

**ROSEBUD Kitmaster PLASTIC SCALE MODELS**

Kitmaster models set the highest standards of realism and authenticity. That's why more and more model and railway enthusiasts are collecting them. New models every month bring new customers to your shop... and a profitable increase in turnover. Order "Baureihe 23" now, and check your stocks of models 1 to 18.

ROSEBUD KITMASTER LTD., RAUNDS, NORTHAMPTONSHIRE.    TEL: RAUNDS 444 (10 lines)
KM 16

9F 2-10-0 No.92247 at Banbury shed on 21 August 1965. Photograph Stephen Gradidge.

# The Models In Detail - 12
## No.22 British Railways Standard Class 9F 2-10-0 'Evening Star'

Some fifty years after the nationalisation of British Railways the introduction of standard steam designs to a railway with four hundred and forty-eight disparate steam locomotive classes seems eminently sensible. Under the direction of R.A.Riddles and his team, a series of eleven designs was evolved to cope with the full range of traffic as it was in the post-war period. Many designs 'borrowed' heavily from other successful locomotives in the constituent Big Four companies. For example, the Standard Class 3MT 2-6-2T was a rework of an Ivatt LMS design, but fitted with a standard GWR pattern boiler. A number were entirely LMS designs, only slightly modified. One which was entirely new, although using many standard parts and construction techniques, was the heavy freight 2-10-0 classified as Standard Class 9, with power classification 9F. Riddles and his team excelled themselves to produce a versatile workhorse of an engine that could handle heavy block trains on the Midland and Great Central main lines at reasonable speeds or lift summer Saturday passenger expresses over the gruelling gradients of the Mendip hills with equal ease. The 2-10-0 wheel arrangement was chosen to give maximum route availability by

### Table G - Summary of British model manufacturer's Standard Locomotives in OO/HO

| Class | Wheels | Manufacturer | Status |
|---|---|---|---|
| 2MT | 2-6-0 | Bachmann | Current |
| 3MT | 2-6-2T | Tri-ang | Deleted |
| 3MT | 2-6-2T | Bachmann | Current |
| 4MT | 2-6-4T | HD/Wrenn/Dapol | Deleted |
| 4MT | 2-6-4T | Bachmann | Current |
| 4MT | 2-6-0 | Bachmann | Current |
| 4MT | 2-6-0 | Kitmaster/Afx/Dapol | Current |
| 4MT | 4-6-0 | Palitoy/Bachmann | Deleted |
| 4MT | 4-6-0 | Bachmann | Current |
| 5MT | 4-6-0 | Trix | Deleted |
| 5MT | 4-6-0 | Bachmann | Current |
| 5MT | 4-6-0 | Hornby Hobbies | Current |
| 7P | 4-6-2 | Tri-ang | Deleted |
| 7P | 4-6-2 | Trix | Deleted |
| 7P | 4-6-2 | Hornby Hobbies | Current |
| 9F | 2-10-0 | Hornby Hobbies | Current |
| 9F | 2-10-0 | Bachmann | Current |
| 9F | 2-10-0 | Kitmaster/Afx/Dapol | Current |

Excludes whitemetal or etched kits.

Tom Wright's super-detailed Airfix Class 9F.

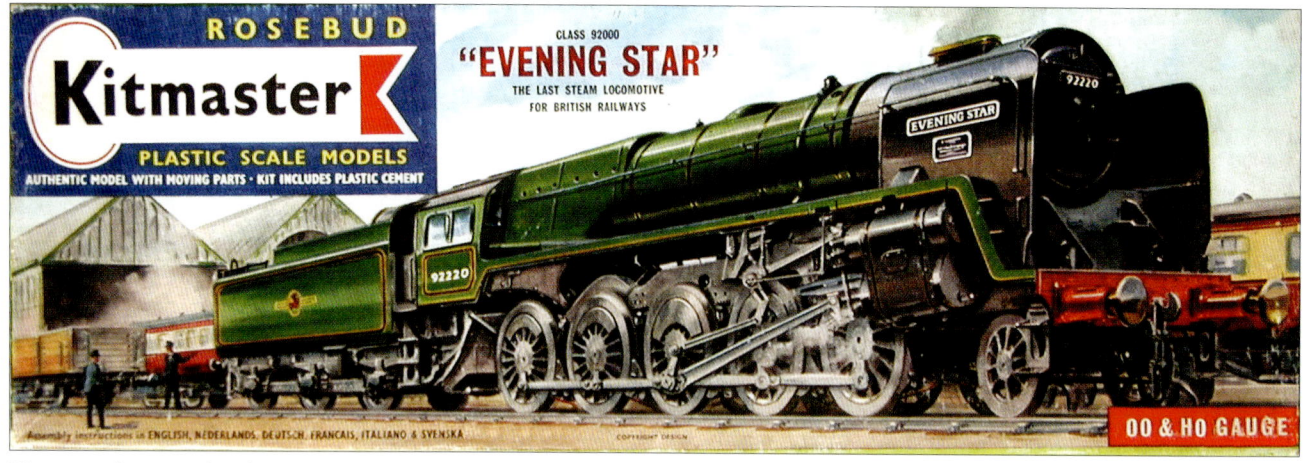

**Kitmaster box top for the 9F.**

minimising the axle loading of these 139 ton behemoths. The smaller wheel diameter also ensured greater torque for handling the heaviest loads. Riddles could not have envisaged, when in January 1951 the first Standard design, Class 7F No. 70000 'Britannia', was rolled out for an admiring press and public, that just nine years later one of his final Standard designs would be the last steam locomotive built in Britain for the nationalised railway. But so it was, when Keith Grand, of the BTC, named Class 9F No.92220 'Evening Star' at Swindon Works on 18th March 1960. No-one, least of all the British Railways Board, was aware that the last steam locomotive to be built would be withdrawn, along with many like her, after shockingly short working lives of just over five years. The Kitmaster instruction sheet carries a quote from Reginald Hanks, Chairman of the Western Region made a the time: 'No other machine somehow is so human and so gentle, yet, when unleashed is capable of such prodigies of strength – nothing quite so graceful in action and nothing quite so romantic. Those of us who have lived in the steam age of railways will carry with us always the most nostalgic memories.'

Altogether, 251 9Fs were built, 178 at Crewe and 73 at Swindon. Although condemned to early extinction, the Standard classes provided ample fodder for the contemporary model manufacturers and continue to be a source of interest today. A short summary of Standard locomotive models follows here.

All of the other designs are available in kit form, as well as conversion kits. With two major sub-classes of Class 9F, these conversion kits have proved to be very useful to modellers. The two variants are the so-called Tyne Dock locomotives, which were dual-braked and fitted with apparatus for operating the iron-ore discharge wagons and, of course the ten locomotives adapted for trials with the Franco-Crosti feedwater pre-heating system. This later modification, along with three other 9Fs fitted with mechanical stokers, proved to be a dismal failure and all were re-converted by 1959.

The Kitmaster model was first shown in the 1960 catalogue. At that time, the locomotive depicted in the catalogue illustration was in conventional unlined BR black, with a single chimney. With 92220 chosen, the 1961 catalogue showed it very differently, named and painted in passenger green. Evening Star, resplendent with Swindon hallmark copper capped double chimney, made a striking model. The Ken Rush portrait on the box lid does the loco no favours, but captures the essential bulk of the prototype. The later Airfix artwork is also unexceptional. Although the loco is the WR allocated Evening Star it is shown hauling stylised Tyne Dock-Consett iron ore discharge hoppers. There are many flaws in the painting which is by Charles Oates. These include a running plate which is not parallel to the cab, the boiler centreline lying over one wheel and numerous other major faults. Still, like the infamous picture of Hardy and Lord Nelson on board HMS Victory, you don't immediately notice how poor the picture is, because the image is certainly very striking and the colouration is vivid.

Evening Star was a natural choice for motorisation projects, being a popular and widely used prototype found on all BR Regions. There was a Wilro chassis for the Airfix version, a Bristol Models chassis for the same and, naturally, a Mike Bryant article on motorising it. Many were done using the K's tender drive unit. In addition there was a very ambitious and interesting article concerning the conversion of an Airfix 9F into the Standard Class 8 Pacific, Duke of Gloucester. Most articles on that subject begin with either the Tri-ang or later Hornby model of the Standard Class 7P Britannia, but the conversion from a 9F is certainly novel.

The Airfix version of the kit was long lived and can be found in several different types of packaging. There is the original Series 4 issue, pattern number R401 of December 1964 in a Type 3 box. With the 1968 re-issue of Biggin Hill in Series 5, the Evening Star kit looked out of place in Series 4 and thus was re-issued in Series 5 with pattern

**Airfix Type 3 Series 4 artwork for Evening Star. It was soon re-issued in the more expensive Series 5 as a "Limited Production" kit; limited only to however many they could sell, it would seem!**

number R502. It then stayed in that Series until its demise in 1978 when, numbered 05652-0, it was issued in a type 7 box. This last issue is rather scarce. The kit has been produced by Dapol in various colours and with three different header styles in the years that they have had the tool. Total production of Evening Star kits now exceeds one hundred thousand, making it one of the truly great kits of all time.

*Above*. Airfix catalogue photograph of their built model from 9th Edition catalogue.

*Below*. Airfix 1976 catalogue artwork by Cliff & Wendy Meadway.

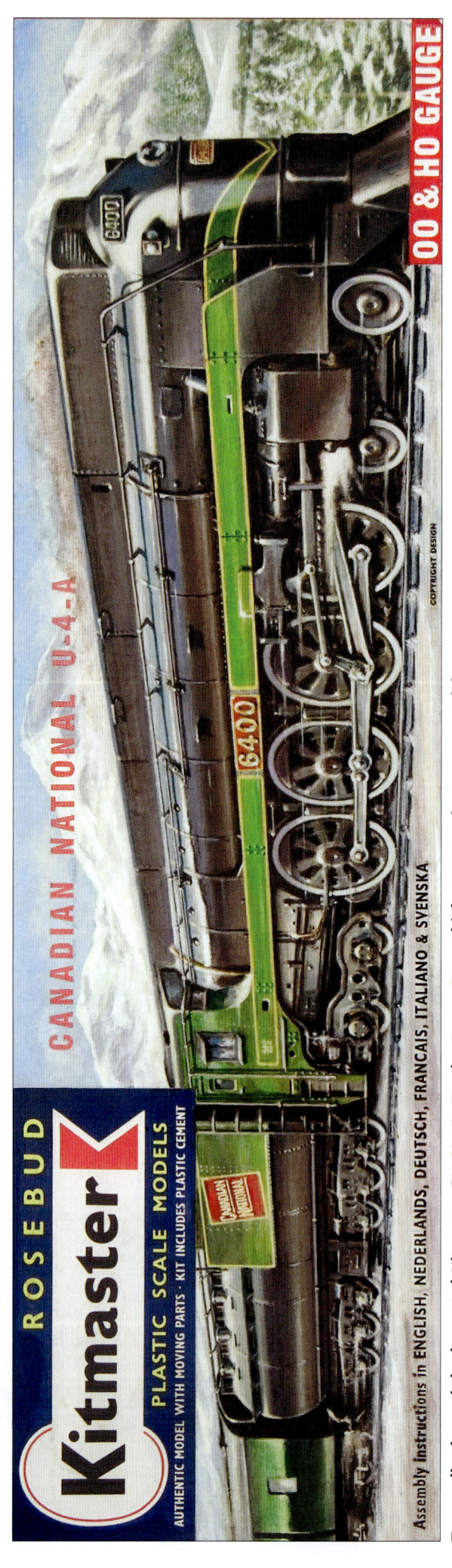

Two realisations of the lamented Kitmaster CN U-4A. Top by Trevor Tremethick, Bottom by Lawrence Blake.

# The Models In Detail - 13

## No.37 Canadian National U4a Class 4-8-4

The Canadian National Railway took delivery of its first 4-8-4 locomotive (road number 6100) in 1927 and used the name 'Confederation' (to celebrate the 60th anniversary of the Canadian Confederation) for this wheel arrangement from the very beginning. In all, forty 'Confederations' were delivered to CNR in 1927, twenty Class U-2-a from the Canadian Locomotive Works and twenty Class U-2-b, from the Montreal Locomotive Works. In 1929, another twenty, Class U-2-c, came from the Montreal Locomotive Works and in 1936 another five, Class U-2-d, also from Montreal were added, making a total of 65. Also in 1936, just five very special streamlined locomotives, the Class U-4-a (road number 6400-6404) were built by the Montreal Locomotive Works. These high speed locomotives had 6ft 5in drivers, 24in x 30in cylinders, 275 psi boiler pressure, a tractive effort of 52,500lb and weighed 155 tons. Between 1940 and 1944 a total of 90 more 4-8-4s, in four batches, were added to the roster giving CNR a total of 160 'Confederations'. There are six survivors; 6153 at the Canadian Railway Museum in Delson, Quebec, 6167 near the CN station in Guelph, Ontario, 6200 and 6400 at the National Museum of Science and Technology in Ottawa, 6213 at the Maritime Museum Exhibition Park in Toronto and 6218 at the Fort Erie Railroad Museum.

With just five units built, it is hard to see why Kitmaster would have chosen this locomotive except for its outstanding streamlined design. The sleek lines are so redolent of 1930s culture, both in North America in the UK, that these are perhaps the epitome of large express locomotive styling. Shown in the catalogue and on all the boxes issued from 1961, the locomotive was much looked-forward to, especially as it would have been in HO scale. Rosebud came late to the conclusion that non-British prototypes should be in 3.5mm rather than 4.0mm, but they did concede this with their final locomotive release – the NYC Hudson.

Their earlier, mistaken, idea had been that 'collectors' would want to build a complete collection of models all to a constant scale of 4mm to the foot. Of course, the 'collectors' were far outnumbered by the modellers who wanted their Continental prototypes modelled in the universally-accepted HO scale. Whilst the first Kitmaster US loco was indeed HO (The General) this was only because Rosebud had shamelessly imitated an existing kit by US-based Advanced Molding Corporation in their 1957 Trailblazers series. After that, they returned to a 'constant scale' of 1/76th. Ironically, it was Airfix Products Ltd who pioneered 'Constant Scale' with their 1/72nd scale aircraft line. In trying to adopt the techniques of their main competitor, Rosebud sowed the seeds of their own destruction – the OO continental kits failed to sell, clogged the warehouse and never recovered their tooling costs, ultimately contributing to the financial meltdown that demanded a sell off to – none other than Messrs. Airfix!

Although this massive locomotive was extensively advertised on Kitmaster boxes and in their catalogues, it did not make it into production. Along with their proposed kits of the Flying Scotsman and the Southern Railway's 'Yankee' tanks (Class USA), it was indefinitely postponed at the Brighton Toy Fair in March 1962. Full artwork had already been prepared. The subsequent sale of the company to Airfix meant that no further development work was undertaken on this project.

*Top.* A super power line up at Montreal shed. *Above.* Canadian O gauge model of the U4a.

*Flying Scotsman* with German deflectors departs Kings Cross.

Smoke drifts through the ironwork as *Flying Scotsman* rushes across the Forth Bridge in this evocative study by Lawrence Blake based on a real Kitmaster monochrome photograph of the proposed box.

# The Models In Detail - 14
## No. 35 LNER Class A3 4-6-2 'Flying Scotsman'

The mythical last three kits that never made in into production have caused more discussion, more argument and more controversy than perhaps any other subject. The artwork reproduced here in colour is that produced from a black and white illustration shown in *Hobbies Annual 1963* and 'colourised' by Lawrence Blake. The Flying Scotsman is caught in amongst the unmistakable ironwork of the famous Forth Bridge in a striking image which is thought to be by noted Kitmaster illustrator Ken Rush.

A lot of the continuing controversy surrounding the kit hinges on unsubstantiated rumours that it was either fully or partly tooled up before Rosebud Dolls decided to dispose of the entire Kitmaster business to Airfix. There are plenty of such rumours and stories, but as yet, very little concrete evidence. What we do know from reliable sources is that both the box art and the decal sheet were completed. Whether Acorn Press was ever called upon to produce the actual box cartons is unknown, but the British Transfer Printing Company of Coventry certainly did print the decal sheets. Remaindered stock was later sold through Graham Shaw's model shop in the town. According to Graham, the sheet included the black and white LNER lining and was considered a useful cheap way to acquire lining by modellers visiting the shop.

Several people have claimed to have either seen or owned a clear test shot of the mould for the A3, but so far, no one has been able to produce a photograph or a real model for inspection, and thus these claims have to be treated with caution. My own belief is that no mould was made. I do think that patterns were completed and the project must have been fairly advanced when Eric Smith took the decision to sell to Airfix. It is important to remember two things here; the Ariel Arrow had just been issued and work was afoot on a Matchless racing machine to accompany it and at this time, Rosebud Dolls was in receievership. The decision of the Receiver would have been needed to invest heavily in more tooling before solving the cash crisis and at least taking some steps to reduce the mountain of unsold stock accumulating at Grove Street and elsewhere.

Going cap-in-hand to the Receiver and asking for another £15,000 (close to £150,000 at today's prices) would have been very difficult when it is estimated that stocks of unsold Kitmaster exceeded one year's sales. For these reasons, one may conclude that the existence of an A3 tool is extremely unlikely. But not impossible, mind!

Turning to the prototype now, one can only be surprised that the Scotsman had not made it into the Kitmaster stable previously. Perhaps this can be explained by the fact that Scotsman, whilst renowned as an ECML performer was not ear-marked for preservation until Alan Pegler stepped in to buy her, thus guaranteeing her legendary status in successive years. We tend to think of it as having always been a famous engine, but in 1960 she was just one of many famed locomotives still operational on Britain's railways. It does seem odd, however, that both the LMS and Southern railways should get their express Pacifics into the first batch of Kitmaster releases whilst the LNER was entirely overlooked.

The original Charles Oakes artwork for the Airfix *City of Truro* issue.

# The Models In Detail - 15

## No.24 GWR City class 4-4-0 'City of Truro'

Reputed to have been the first locomotive to exceed 100 mph in Britain, City of Truro earned herself a place in the Kitmaster line up with distinction. The City class design had already proved itself a formidable performer, with several star turns amongst the ranks. Designed by the celebrated George Jackson Churchward, the City 4-4-0s were the first of his designs to emerge from Swindon works, in 1903. Their free-running characteristics immediately led to a spate of record-breaking runs. The locomotives owed their performance to a number of innovations introduced by Churchward, including double-framing, outside cranks, a large Belpaire firebox and a safety valve column crowning the boiler barrel. But it was the provision of long-travel valves, large exhaust ports and a high working pressure, 225 lb/sq.in., in the novel tapered boiler, which really made the City locomotives stand out. All of these features were new to British locomotive design, so much so that the class was considered to be revolutionary and had a great influence on the many designs of express locomotive to follow.

Although City of Truro is now justly famous, the doyen of the class, 3433 City of Bath, in the year it was outshopped from Swindon, performed remarkably on a Royal Train duty. With the future King George V and Queen Mary safely ensconced with their staff in three suitably appointed coaches, City of Bath was rostered to haul an advance portion of the 10.40 down Penzance express non-stop over the 245 miles from London to Plymouth, via Bristol. The 130 ton train traversed the London-Bristol section in 104 min 42 secs for the 118.4 miles; bettering the timing of the erstwhile Bristolian schedule, which would be introduced in 1935, by half a minute! Topping Whiteball Summit at 50 mph, with Dainton and Rattery at 35 mph, the train arrived in Plymouth some 37 minutes early, much to the pleasure of the Royal Party, who apparently had asked for a 'good run'!

Not content with this performance Churchward determined to improve upon these timings for the commencement of Ocean Mails services between London and Plymouth. On 8 May 1904 City of Truro set out from Plymouth Millbay Docks with a van train comprising 148 tons heading for Bristol. The reckless GWR Driver Clements in charge took the tortuous curves of the South Devon banks at dangerously fast speeds and in so doing set the unbroken record for steam between Plymouth and Exeter, 55min 55sec for the 52-mile sector. More was to come, though, as City of Truro stormed up to Whiteball Tunnel and then, with Charles Rous-Marten esq. recording the timings, descended Wellington Bank at just over 102 mph; the first time in Britain that a train had exceeded 100 mph.

Such was the utility of these powerful 4-4-0 locomotives that the GWR management decided to capitalise on their achievements by introducing a two-hourly schedule from London to Bristol from August 1903. This demanded average speeds of 59 mph throughout; no mean feat in the Edwardian era. Even more demanding, however, was the schedule introduced that summer which became synonymous with the class and later crack express classes of the GWR. This was the longest continuous non-stop run anywhere in the world at that time, 245 miles London-Plymouth in 4 hours 25 mins. The seven clerestory-coach train left Paddington at 10.10 am everyday and was always rostered for a City. With the opening of the Hants & Berks route in 1906, the train was only required to cover 225 miles non-stop and the departure time was accordingly altered to 10.30 am. After a competition was held, the re-timed train was bestowed with its now familiar name – The Cornish Riviera Express.

The Kitmaster model of City of Truro was a mid-range addition and much welcomed by the modelling press and public alike. It was extensively re-tooled by Airfix with the addition of balance weights, brake rigging and numerous other details and survives today in the Dapol range where it is still a popular kit. The Kitmaster artwork is straightforward and not particularly notable, but the Airfix artwork is quite striking. The locomotive is shown, correctly, at Millbay Docks, with a White Star four-funnel liner in the background, hauling suitable Ocean Mails coaching stock. Thought to be by George Oakes, this painting is one of four large canvasses from the Club archives.

*Above.* Original Kitmaster box top. *Top.* A 1960 Kitmaster Trade Display featuring a built *City of Truro* model.

103

## Cadeau
### une magnifique locomotive de collection

**LORD OF THE ISLES**

L'origine de ces machines, prestigieuses pour l'époque, remonte à 1891. Vraisemblablement les plus grandes de ce type, elles furent conçues par William Dean et livrées à la Great Western Railway. Etant donné les différences d'écartement encore présentes à cette époque dans le système des chemins de fer américains (écartement de 7 pieds ou de 4 pieds 8 pouces 1/2) elles pouvaient être adaptées à l'un et l'autre type. Malheureusement la tenue de voie de ces engins était précaire, et l'une d'entre elles, la 3021, dérailla dans le tunnel de Box le 16 septembre 1893.

historique d'après archives Loco-Revue

UNE SOMPTUEUSE COLLECTION DE HUIT MODÈLES

ADLER — 99 — LORD OF THE ISLES — 030.TAO — GENERAL — RENO — 89.DB — J.W. BOWKER

## notre Gadget
### UNE LOCOMOTIVE ANCIENNE DE COLLECTION

**99 "SHIFTING LOCOMOTIVE"**

Cette locomotive de la Pennsylvania R.R. représente un type de machine issu d'études de standardisation faites par la United State Railway Administration et destiné à l'ensemble des compagnies américaines.
Cette standardisation était nécessaire pour faire face à la pénurie de locomotives résultant de la première guerre mondiale.
On trouve encore ce type de locomotive destiné aux services de manœuvres dans la presque totalité des Compagnies de chemins de fer américaines.

historique d'après archives Loco-Revue

dans chaque numéro de télé gadget, une des huit locomotives différentes de votre collection

ADLER — 99 — LORD OF THE ISLES — 030.TAO — GENERAL — RENO — 89.DB — J.W. BOWKER

# The Models In Detail - 16
## The Nescafé/Tele Gadget 4-2-2 'Lord of the Isles' and The General 4-4-0

One of the strangest kit releases of the 1970s must surely be the OO scale (1/76) model of Lord of the Isles by Nestlé France. This remarkable kit was one of a series of eight locomotives which were given away free with the firm's drink brands in France: Nescafé, Nesquick and Ricoré (a chicory based coffee substitute). The models are quite detailed, but amazingly there are no tenders for any of the locomotives that need them. The choice of engines was equally unfathomable. As well as the GWR Dean Single Lord of the Isles, there was Der Adler, The General (again!), the J.W. Bowker and the Reno (these last three all American old-timers) a French steam shunter '030 TAO', a German 0-6-0 '89 DB' and '99', a standard Baldwin 0-6-0 switcher, or shunter.

The locomotives were produced in a variety of brightly coloured plastics; examples of The General 4-4-0 are known in bright yellow and bright blue. Each kit used two different colours so presumably required two separate tools. The original instruction sheets were a multi-coloured affair with all eight locos shown on the front and detailed assembly instructions on the rear. The whole thing was packed in a clear plastic bag and dispatched in a plain carton by post. It is believed that they were issued some time between 1975 and 1978. The kits quickly disappeared from view and nothing more was heard until a French part-works magazine called *Tele Gadget* revived the tools and issued the kits as a free cover mount at some point in the mid-1980s. The instructions were completely redrawn, with the description now showing 'An ancient locomotive to collect' instead of the original 'A magnificent locomotive to collect'. Semantics aside, it was obviously felt that these locomotives were rather old in their appearance. Since all the technical information on the kits is ascribed to the well-respected *Loco Revu* magazine, it seems strange that the selection of locos should be as slanted towards American railroad history as it was.

The model of Lord of the Isles uses rather dull green and black plastics and like all of the locos, has the Nestlé logo on it. In this case it is on the footplate. The *Tele Gadget* locos have this 'plated over' (i.e. polished off the tool). As there is no tender it is straight-forward to match the kit to a Kitmaster City of Truro tender as the basic 3,500 gallon tender of the time will suffice. The French model looks a little too narrow when matched with this tender, but with suitable painting it does look quite respectable. It also makes an interesting comparison with the Tri-ang model. Regarding the USA 4-4-0s, The General is quite a good representation, but all the locos suffer from a lack of fixings on the coupling pins, so that the rods easily fall off. With a bit of work and careful painting, it is possible to produce a decent model of the Dean Single and these kits are today more easily found, thanks to the Internet and Ebay.

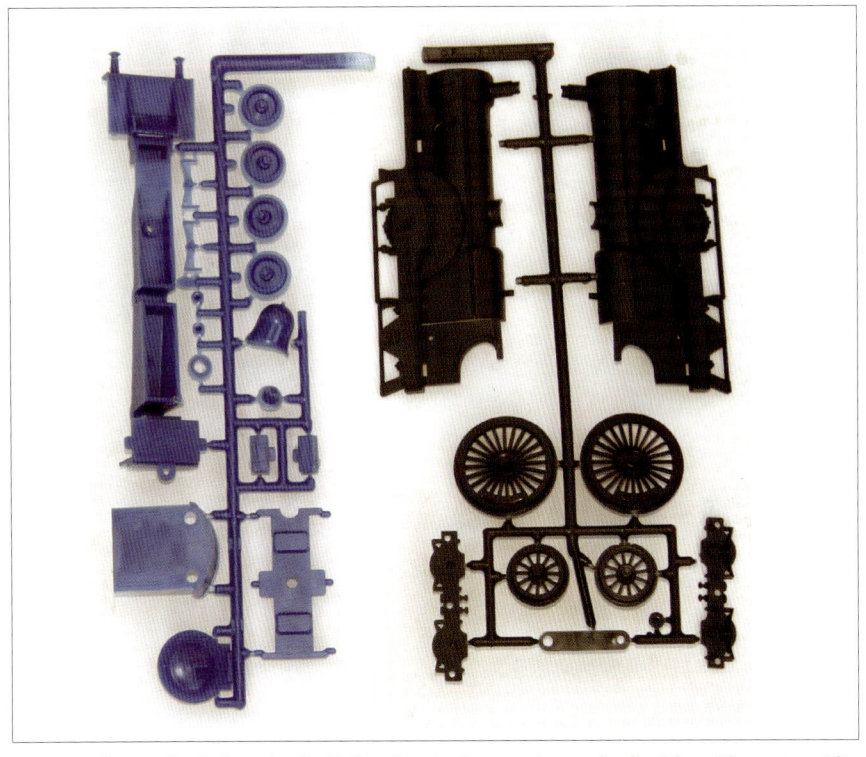

A Nescafé *Lord of the Isles* built by the Author and matched with a Kitmaster *City of Truro* tender. The only other modification needed was the addition of spoke bogie wheels to replace the solid disc French originals seen in the picture of the sprues. These kits were always moulded in two colours – in this case blue and black. Other colours used included green, yellow and red and bore no relation to the authentic livery to be carried.

*Above.* A superbly decorated Stirling Single with lined-out splashers and frames. *Below.* A Stirling Export pack with factory-built model packed in foam and fold-out display stand as supplied to dealers worldwide. *Bottom.* The tasteful Ken Rush artwork for the Stirling Single.

106

# The Models In Detail - 17
## No. 9 – Great Northern '8ft Single' 4-2-2 No.1

The elegant curves, the perfect symmetry of chimney, cylinders and bogie and the pierced paddlebox are all features of this famous design by Patrick Stirling for the Great Northern Railway at Doncaster. The locomotive, with its huge 8 feet 10 inch diameter, single driving wheel was able to achieve very high speeds (albeit with lightly loaded trains) in the 1880s because of the low piston sliding speeds resulting from such a large driving wheel. Stirling Singles raced against the LNWR Jumbos in the famous 'Races to the North' of 1895.

The Stirling has always been a popular kit with modellers. The longevity of the prototype and its celebrated status under the aegis of the LNER and then BR has led many people to attempt a model. The Kitmaster kit, as usual, conveys the basic outline of the locomotive admirably whilst lacking detail in many areas. The moulded lining and handrails would not stand inspection today, but in 1959 were well received. Surprisingly, few detailing kits appear to have been issued, but individual brass fittings for the chimney and dome appeared to be popular. As each of these was split in half on the main body moulding and did not always align correctly, this was a significant improvement.

Power for the Single is invariably from the six-wheel tender. K's were first to promote their excellent tender motor units for this purpose. The firm's 7ft 6in wheelbase unit is a very good fit to the Stirling tender. Comments have been noted from modellers who believe the tender to be too narrow; however, on inspection of the prototype, the Kitmaster models appear to be generally well proportioned. With respect to the size of the tender, the vehicle she was coupled to when first preserved was in such poor condition that when the loco was first run up and down the mileage yard at York in 1938 there were doubts whether this vehicle would stay in one piece. So another GNR tender was quickly found and this is the one she currently has. GNR tenders look very similar, but there are subtle differences. For example, there are three types of large tender, all about 3,500 gallons capacity. Most Singles were fitted with these from the 1890s until withdrawal. Models can therefore be attached to wider higher tenders accordingly.

**Add this new model to your KITMASTER COLLECTION**

Add the world-famous Stirling 8ft. Single to your Kitmaster collection. It was built in 1873 for the Great Northern Railway, had 8ft. diameter driving wheels, and was capable of 80 m.p.h. This authentic model is in all good model and toy shops *now*.

No. 9 Stirling 8ft. Single **7/6**
HAVE YOU MADE THESE EARLIER MODELS?
No. 1. Stephenson's "Rocket" 4/6
No. 2. Diesel-electric shunter 4/6
No. 3. Early American "General" 6/6
No. 5. Schools class "Harrow" 7/6
No. 6. Saddle tank 4/6

**ROSEBUD Kitmaster** PLASTIC SCALE MODELS
Authentic models with moving parts
Can be used on OO and HO gauge tracks
ROSEBUD KITMASTER LIMITED
KINDLY MENTION THE **RAILWAY MODELLER** WHEN WRITING TO ADVERTISERS

**Marcus Archer's built Stirling on Stoke Bank.**

*Above*. Unadorned box top artwork by Roy Cross for The Rocket kit. *Right*. Airfix (top) and Kitmaster (bottom) models compared. *Below*. Airfix Series 2 Type 3 boxed issue. *Bottom*. Original Kitmaster box top.

# The Models In Detail - 18
## No.1 - George Stephenson's 2-2-0 'Rocket'

Still a favourite with many, Rocket has been the subject of several modelling attempts at or near OO scale, but the Kitmaster model remains the granddaddy of them all. When the Liverpool and Manchester Railway was nearing completion, the Directors announced a competition with a prize of £500 for the most efficient railway engine. Tests were held at Rainhill, near Liverpool, and the engines were expected to be able to run at eight to ten miles an hour. There were five different entrants but, in the end, no doubt about the winner. It was 'Rocket,' designed and built in 1829 at the works of Robert Stephenson and Co, Newcastle on Tyne and driven by George Stephenson. This famous engine passed every test in the competition and travelled at the unheard-of speed of twenty-nine miles per hour. Much of the credit for this locomotive must go to George Stephenson himself, but two other people who should be mentioned are George Stephenson's son Robert, who spent a great deal of effort in supervising the construction, and a Mr. H. Booth who suggested that the heat and smoke from the fire should be led through a number of small tubes through the boiler, instead of through one large tube.

As the Kitmaster instructional noted, 'When the Rocket was completed, she was sent by ship from Tyneside to Liverpool and was insured for £500. The boat carrying the engine was so long overdue at Liverpool that she was given up for lost, and the insurance money had actually been paid before she arrived safely.' One of the conditions of the Trials was that each engine, with a load of three times its own weight, was to do ten trips up and down a 1¾ mile level section of line at Rainhill which was the equivalent of a journey from Manchester to Liverpool, and after a pause for refuelling, was to make a further ten trips over the same distance. On 8th October 1829, Rocket carried out the required test and covered the distance at an average speed of 16 miles per hour, which was more than satisfactory, especially as she used only half a ton of coke for the whole 70 miles, and it was for this performance that the £500 prize money was awarded to George Stephenson.

Thus it was that when the line was formally opened in 1830, George Stephenson, who had supervised the construction of the line, drove the first engine. This was 'The Northumbrian,' designed very much like 'Rocket' herself, which hauled the fourth train in a triumphal procession that marked the historic occasion. There was a large crowd, with the Duke of Wellington as the Guest of Honour. The occasion was unfortunately marred by the death of the MP William Huskisson, who failed to get clear of a moving locomotive at the new Liverpool Road station in Manchester. That railway-related fatalities have been with us from the inception of our public railway system is a perhaps a salutary reminder of the forces brought to bear even at low speeds. With the opening of the first passenger railway in the world the Railway Age had dawned.

It is said that the Rocket is the mother of the modern steam locomotive. This is very true if one considers that the idea of allowing the exhaust steam to pass up the chimney and thus produce a strong draught on the fire, and at the same time drawing the hot gasses through a multi tube boiler, was still the basis of most steam locomotive designs even at the genesis of 'modern' era locomotives such as Duke of Gloucester, Riddles' celebrated epitome of good locomotive design.

The Kitmaster Rocket is interesting in several ways. There has been much debate about the actual state and provenance of the locomotive as displayed in the Science Museum. It has been rebuilt, repaired and improved many times in its long life. The engine you see today is not as it first appeared in 1829. The Kitmaster model makes reference to the help of the Science Museum and portrays a typical early configuration. The thick connecting rods are deliberately over scale, to give strength, and were quickly modified by Airfix to a more slender version. However, reference to the painting by Robert Ayton in the 1961 Ladybird Book *The Story of Railways* shows a much thinner connecting rod than even the Airfix model. In addition, ejector piping is evident on both cylinders and the clacks appear to be lower down the boiler. Which is correct is hard to say, but for sure Airfix did make further changes. To simplify manufacturing, the brass chimney stays were replaced by thicker plastic stays integral with the other parts. An extension to the footplate allowed for a Victorian crew to be added. This necessitated a wholesale renumbering of the parts and consequently, a complete revision of the assembly instructions.

In 1963 Tri-ang Railways announced the arrival of a motorised Rocket in their range. The proving model for this used a Kitmaster body on a chassis alleged to have been made by Jack Gain, a freelancer who worked for Rosebud and often motorised the units for his own use. The diminutive locomotive required a new type of motor, the X.500 and together with three matching coaches, Rocket was a big hit. Early locomotives appear to have been popular subjects with model companies as both Academy (Japan) and Arrow Models (USA) produced assembly kits of the Rocket. Academy scaled theirs at 1:50th which is popular in Japan, whilst the Arrow model is in an odd non-metric scale closer to OO scale, possibly American S scale. Both are a testament to the long-lived fame and popularity of this vintage locomotive.

**Wendy Meadway artwork from Airfix 1976 catalogue.**

MODEL RAILWAY NEWS — APRIL, 1959

# AT LAST!

## PLASTIC SCALE MODEL RAILWAY KITS

**Authentic Models with Moving Parts**

**Can be used on OO and HO Gauge Tracks**

Brand-New! Exciting! Just what you've always wanted! Assemble these thrilling new Kitmaster railway kits yourself ... you'll get hours of pleasure and satisfaction. No ordinary models these. They move ... are built to scale ... finely detailed—look just like the real thing. That's why you get that professional finish every time with all Kitmaster models. Start your collection now ... you'll find plenty of thrills and fun with these authentic new Kitmaster plastic scale models.

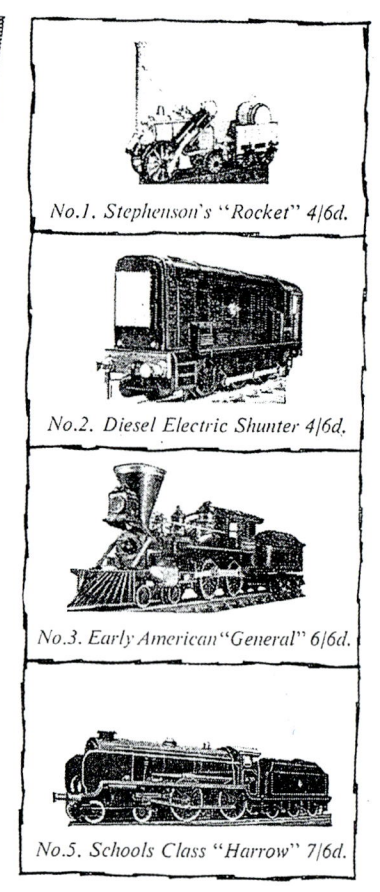

No.1. Stephenson's "Rocket" 4/6d.
No.2. Diesel Electric Shunter 4/6d.
No.3. Early American "General" 6/6d.
No.5. Schools Class "Harrow" 7/6d.

**ROSEBUD Kitmaster PLASTIC SCALE MODELS**

- A fresh, new model is coming out every month
- Step by step instructions, coloured leaflet and transfers included
- Special plastic cement is enclosed for a rigid, lasting fit
- Supplied in all good model shops and toy shops.

ROSEBUD KITMASTER LIMITED
RAUNDS · NORTHAMPTONSHIRE

*Get yours today!*

KMC1

Please mention MODEL RAILWAY NEWS when writing to Advertisers

Kitmaster original issue Schools Class "Harrow", one of the best sellers from the range and still easy to find today.

ROSEBUD Kitmaster PLASTIC SCALE MODELS — "HARROW" SCHOOLS CLASS

AUTHENTIC MODEL WITH MOVING PARTS
CAN BE USED ON OO & HO GAUGE TRACKS
KIT INCLUDES PLASTIC CEMENT

# The Models In Detail - 19
## No.5 - Southern Railway Schools Class 'V' 4-4-0 'Harrow'

The most powerful European 4-4-0 locomotive ever built, the Schools provided power for key semi-fast and express passenger workings in all areas of the former Southern system. Although best remembered for their sterling work on the Kent Coast services from Charing Cross to Dover, Ramsgate and Folkestone, they were also extensively used on the South Western section from Basingstoke and Guildford sheds. Maunsell designed these engines, which were constructed at Eastleigh over 1930-35, to handle mixed traffic services over the entire Southern network. As a result, they were constructed to Restriction 4 loading gauge; the special width restriction used by the Southern for trains working the notoriously narrow Hastings direct route from Tunbridge Wells. Indeed Roy Cross' painting of 'Harrow' on the Airfix box shows the locomotive being 'oiled round' outside a shed said by the artist to be influenced by Tunbridge Wells. This was a favourite haunt for Roy, being just minutes from his home near Groombridge. The width restriction precluded the use of a Belpaire firebox, as used on the earlier Lord Nelson engines, and ensured a sloping tender side and upper cab profile to give maximum clearance through the narrowest tunnels. In addition, Maunsell chose a three cylinder design without large outside cylinders and a four-coupled wheel arrangement to avoid the 'throw-over' of longer six coupled engines on tight curves. The result was a handsome engine which found favour with the public and crews alike.

Named after British public schools, they were officially Class 'V' in the Southern Railway running department. During 1931 all engines then in service were modified as they passed through shops by the addition of smoke deflectors. Downdraught and drifting smoke obscuring the driver's vision was said to be the reason for this change. Engines in the second batch, including Harrow, were fitted with smoke deflectors from new. The Kitmaster model was heralded as a significant gain for Southern modellers. At the time there were few ready-to-run Southern models available, as the 1959 introduction of the 'Schools' predated the Hornby Dublo R1 and the West Country 'Dorchester' and Tri-ang's Battle of Britain and L1. As a consequence, a flurry of motorisation articles appeared, together with a rather good little four-wheel box type chassis from Surrey Model Centre. This item was heavily advertised and probably explains why no Perfecta kit was designed for Harrow. Kitmaster modelled the locomotive in BR black livery with simplified cream lining, but when reintroduced by Airfix, it had a comprehensive transfer sheet covering Southern malachite green livery or BR black. Indeed Airfix units are moulded in green plastic whilst Kitmaster always used black. There are plenty of good colour photographs of these engines in BR lined black, usually flogging up Sole Street bank in Kent with a London-bound boat train, or whistling through Shakespeare Cliff tunnel, with its distinctive neo-gothic portals. Colour photos of these engines in SR green do exist, but none are as good as the Roy Cross painting from a modelling point of view. The painting is shown here without the addition of Airfix branding and box graphics. These engines were again modified by Bulleid, under Southern Railway aegis, when multiple-jet blast pipes were fitted to some of the class. This meant that larger diameter Lemaitre pattern chimneys had to be fitted to the 21 engines so modified from 1939.

A less widespread change was the experimental conversion to oil firing which was tried on 932 Blundell's. The modification involved an extension to the height of the tender and fitting of oil tank filler covers. The experiment was unsuccessful and the engine was re-converted some time later. The Kitmaster instructions omitted oil firing, but did mention the extraordinarily perverse plywood streamlining applied to 938 Sevenoaks for just one month during 1938. Painted as '900 Southern', it was a diabolical mess, but presaged the forthcoming streamlined design for Bulleid's Merchant Navy class, much of which was found wanting as the initial engine, 21 C1 Channel Packet, entered service.

The kit was extensively modified by Airfix before re-issue in May 1968. This was achieved by lengthening a main sprue to encompass extra detail parts. Extra detail included correct shape vacuum pipes, new NMRA buckeye couplers and dummy three-link couplings. In addition, the old Kitmaster style vacuum pipes were shut off at the top of the adjacent sprue. In addition to the Kitmaster/Airfix model, Airfix planned to release a Schools class loco in their Great Model Railways range in 1981. Drawings were prepared and patterns made, but at the Toy Fair that year, Hornby Railways showed their own Schools prototype and as a consequence, cash-strapped Airfix abandoned the project. A rake of Bulleid coaches were to have accompanied this engine and in later Mainline catalogues you can see the ends of the mock-ups in some of the catalogue photographs. They too were aborted when General Mills, owner of Palitoy, cancelled all European product development and effectively withdrew from the UK toy industry during 1982. It was another ten years or more before these coaches finally appeared in the revitalised Bachmann Branchlines range. A new Schools locomotive, in 4mm and to the highest standards, was released by Hornby during 2009.

**Airfix catalogue artwork, 1976, for "Harrow".**

*Left.* Original Roy Cross painting of 30919.
*Bottom.* A fantastically built Kitmaster Schools in the pleasing lined olive green of the Maunsell era.
*Top right.* Airfix Type 7 box artwork for the Schools Class was totally different and used a new air-brushed painting of the locomotive leaving Charing Cross Station. It was the only loco to gain new artwork in this re-issue period.
*Below.* And as it appeared on the Airfix Type 3 box top.

112

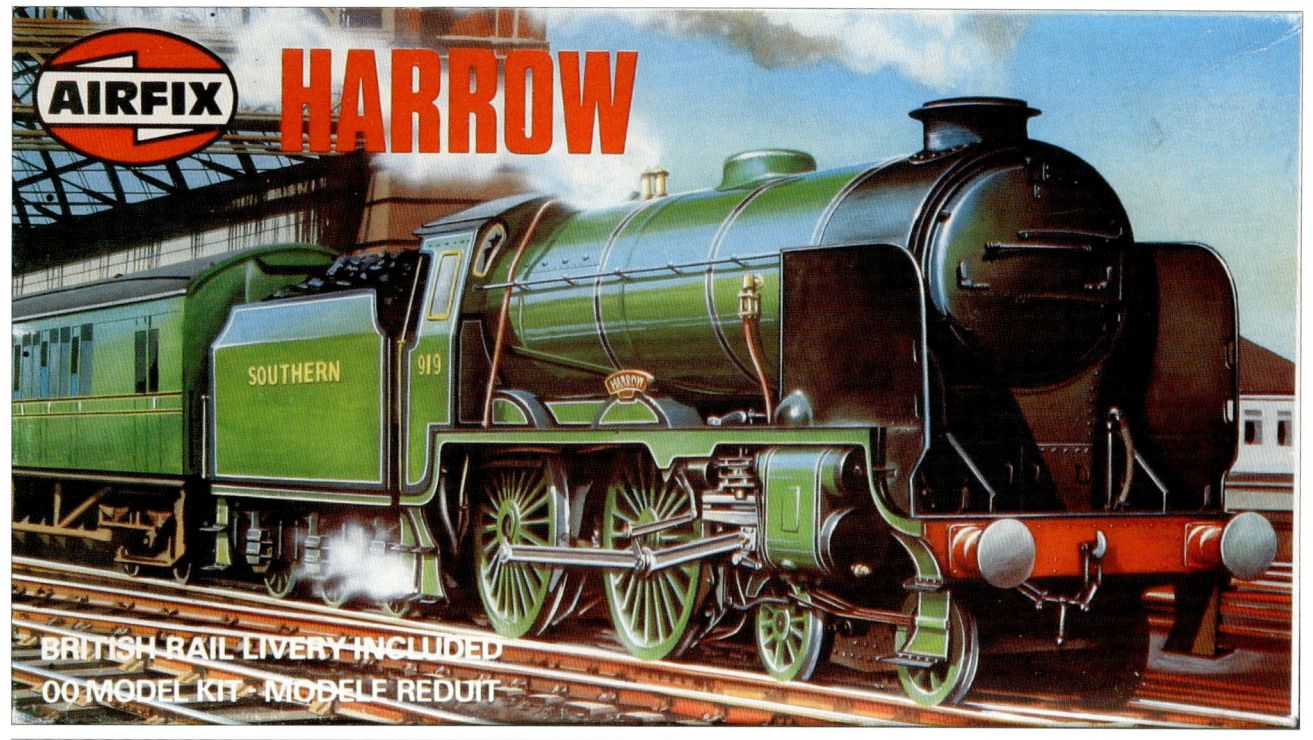

*Left.* And the real thing. "Dulwich" at Weymouth shed in 1961. A.E. West, courtesy Mike King.

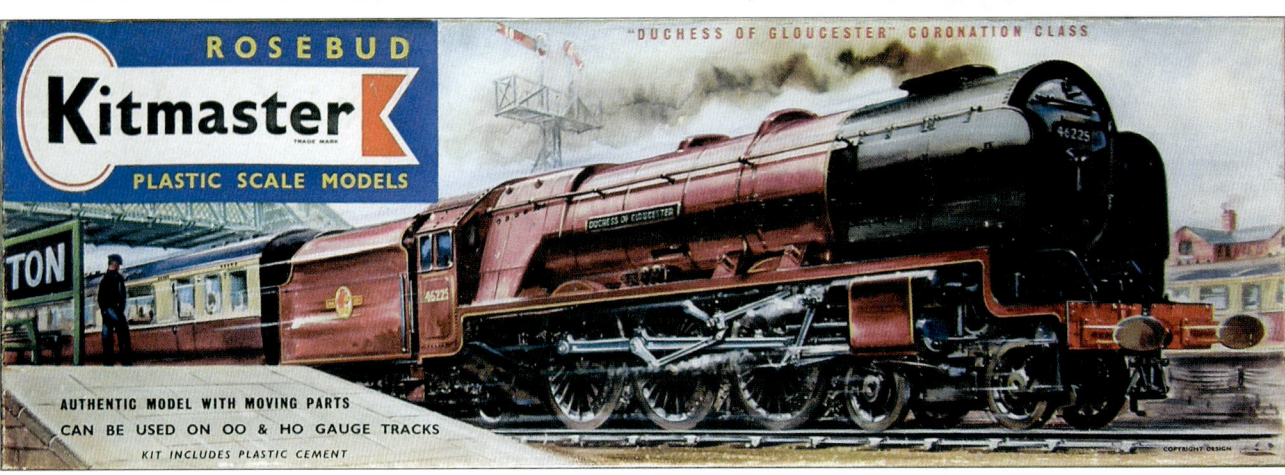

*Top.* Built Kitmaster Duchess in the crimson lake livery with Kitmaster maroon coaches.
*Above.* The striking Kitmaster box top is all exaggerated lines of perspective and speed blur.
*Bottom left and right.* Two more incarnations of the Duchess saw it feature on the P1 Set box top and the 1959 catalogue.

# The Models In Detail - 20
## No.4 LMSR Coronation Class 4-6-2 'Duchess of Gloucester'

One of the most celebrated designs of the 20th century must surely be Sir William Stanier's 'Princess Coronation' Pacific of 1937. Designed for the exacting requirements of the LNWR Anglo-Scottish main line, these engines were the pride of the LMS and later, the LM Region of British Railways. Twenty-four of the thirty-eight built were originally streamlined, the casing later removed to facilitate easier maintenance and to allow certain modifications to the design. Un-air smoothed engines could be seen running with and without smoke deflectors. All of the class were named, some after fine British cities, such as Stoke-on-Trent, Liverpool and Nottingham and some after aristocratic personages of their day. It is this later group which produced the name Duchess of Gloucester, which became synonymous with these locomotives in model form via the Kitmaster model.

The subject of heated debate, this model embodies all of the faults present in the 1948 Roche drawings from which it was prepared, including the wrong tender and the lack of sloping front smoke box which indicated a former streamlined locomotive such as 46225. Frank Roche was a personal friend of both Dennis Franklin, Rosebud's Technical Manager and pattern maker John Marshall. Modellers had the benefit of two other models of these locomotives – the famous Hornby-Dublo version epitomised by Duchess of Atholl/Montrose and City of London/Liverpool, but also the extremely elusive Rowell Duchess, produced in the mid-1950s and also die cast. It is difficult to distinguish from the Dublo version, save for the lack of engraved makers name underneath. Although numbered 4 in the Kitmaster series, the Duchess did not emerge from Grove Street until November 1959, making it the eighth release in the range.

The first locomotives were constructed in 1937 and numbered 6220-4, followed in 1938 by 6225-9. All of these were streamlined as built which meant that the top foremost section of the boiler barrel had to taper down towards the front instead of remaining parallel. In addition all had single chimneys. Later, in 1938, further examples were built without streamlining, numbered 6230-4, also with single chimney. Further streamlined examples were then constructed throughout 1939, 1940 and 1943 numbering a further 13 engines, all built with double chimneys as new. From 1944 to 1948 a further eight engines were built, all un-streamlined and all with double chimneys. During the period from 1946 to 1949 all the former air-smoothed engines were rebuilt without the casing and fitted with double chimneys.

This should be the case for Duchess of Gloucester, but as has been noted, the model portrays a double chimney loco that either never carried air smoothed casing, or had the smokebox rebuilt later. The last of the formerly streamlined Duchesses didn't lose its sloping front until 1960. Duchess of Gloucester's had been replaced several years before the model was issued. so the model is correct for the late 1950s and early 1960s period when it wore the red BR livery. However, only ten engines ever had the continuous footplating that the model bears. Unfortunately, Duchess of Gloucester was not one of them.

When Ian Allan re-issued the Roche drawings as a book in 1968, they made few changes, though one huge error was corrected – a brand new BR-produced drawing of the correct 4000 gallon tender for these classes, replacing the incorrect 5P5F tender previously depicted. The colour of the model is another point of contention. Originally painted in either war-time black or LMS Crimson Lake, these were re-painted by British Railways into several different colours. Express Passenger Blue, Lined Brunswick Green and of course 'Maroon' were all used. However, the Kitmaster instructions talk about 'Red' for the body work. In reality the maroon colour should match the BR coaching stock maroon; lighter colours more akin to crimson or Post Office Red do often occur in model form, but however highly polished and crimson-like the loco may seem in photographs, coach stock maroon is the correct colour. LMS Crimson Lake is also wrong for the BR period and is noticeably too magenta in comparison with maroon.

## Build this scale model

**No. 4 Coronation Class 'DUCHESS OF GLOUCESTER' 10/6**

This famous locomotive, built in 1938, is the eighth to appear in the 'Kitmaster' series of plastic scale model kits of some of the world's most famous engines. How many have *you* collected? All with moving parts, for use on OO and HO gauge tracks.

*Other Kitmaster models*
No. 1 *Stephenson's Rocket* 4/6d
No. 2 *Diesel Electric Shunter* 6/6d
No. 3 *Early American 'General'* 6/6d
No. 5 *Schools Class 'Harrow'* 7/6d
No. 6 *Saddle Tank* 4/6d
No. 7 *Prairie Tank* 6/6d
No. 9 *Stirling 8' Single* 7/6

**Kitmaster** ROSEBUD PLASTIC SCALE MODELS
at all good model and toy shops

ROSEBUD KITMASTER LIMITED

KMC5

961/2/571/225/1159  Published by Ian Allan Ltd., Hampton Court, Surrey, and printed in the United Kingdom by McCorquodale, London, S.E.

*Top.* The grandeur of the mighty Beyer Garratt box art.

*Above.* The built Kitmaster model is from the Author's collection and was one of the first models he acquired – forever stoking his admiration for the Kitmaster range.

*Left.* 4970 with rotating bunker, in 1934 at Cricklewood. It's interesting to see one stabled on a curve for once.

*Below.* 7983 newly shopped makes a magnificent black, brooding beast outside Crewe's Ten Shop, presumably at the end of 1938. Photograph James Stevenson, courtesy Hamish Stevenson.

# The Models In Detail - 21
## No.25 - The Ex-LM.S. Beyer-Garratt 2-6-0 + 0-6-2

Long-term favourite for the most sought-after Kitmaster model, the gargantuan Beyer-Garratt locomotive of the LMSR is certainly impressive. At just over 87ft 10in long, these monster articulated locomotives were the main power for long coal trains from the East Midland coalfields to London and Birmingham for some 30 years. Constructed in two batches, under the direction of Sir Henry Fowler, by Beyer, Peacock & Co Ltd at Gorton Works in Manchester, these machines featured several novel patented devices. Most notable, of course, is the articulated Garratt design whereby two similar 2-6-0 engines are harnessed to one large boiler and bunker. The resulting locomotive had a tractive effort of around 40,250lb as compared to the 46,800lb generated by a pair of LMSR Moguls of the 1933 batch with which the Beyer-Garratt locomotives share many common parts. The other remarkable design feature in these engines was the patent Beyer, Peacock self-trimming rotating coal bunker. Described as being of 'conic frustrum' shape, the bunker was itself driven by a two-cylinder steam engine.

The first three Garratts were built in 1927 and were not originally fitted with rotating bunkers. A second batch of thirty locomotives with minor improvements and modifications was constructed in 1930. Changes introduced included a shorter chimney and dome together with a smaller water tank, reduced from 4,700 gallons to 4,500 gallons. Since the locomotives had bi-directional water scoop apparatus fitted to the leading engine and tank this did not cause problems in service. At the same time, coal capacity was increased from 7 tons to 9 tons, thereby increasing the duty cycle for the class and permitting return workings on the 126 mile Toton-Brent coal run. The Kitmaster instructions are erroneous in regard to water capacity, stating that the later engines have more than the earlier three.

Eventually, all 33 locomotives received the conical bunker, although the first three and some of the 1930 batch were originally constructed with conventional straight-sided bunkers. In order to prevent delays to passenger services on the thirty miles of double track between Kettering and Leicester, fully loaded coal trains needed to maintain a steady 21 mph average on this section. The 5ft 3in driving wheels and four 18½ x 26 inch cylinders of the Beyer-Garratt gave these engines a good turn of speed in addition to plenty of power, enabling them to handle the 1,450 ton coal trains with ease.

Only three locomotives, 4997-9, were fitted with vacuum brake equipment which would have enabled passenger train working. No heating was provided for coaching stock and the design was always only intended as a heavy freight locomotive, although they were expected to maintain 50 mph average speeds over the steeply graded Midland main line with return empties. Whilst these engines were essentially a pair of LMS 8ft 0in x 8ft 6in Mogul chassis running back-to-back, the company did contemplate perpetuating the Garratt design for a larger passenger locomotive of the 4-6-0 + 0-6-4 arrangement similar to those constructed for African railways, but this was not pursued. The Gresley designed LNER 2-8-0 + 0-8-2 Garratt of Class U1 which was introduced in 1926 was destined to remain a solitary locomotive.

Originally allocated LMS numbers 4967-4999, the entire class was renumbered in 1938 into the 7967-7999 bloc, thereby allowing their old numbers to be reused on Stanier Black Five locos then under construction. At nationalisation, each number was increased by 40000. Kitmaster provided number decals for the later LMS 79XX series, as befits a rotating-bunker engine, together with 47994 for the BR period.

Withdrawals began in 1955 with the introduction of BR Standard Class 9F locomotives to the Toton-Washwood Heath and Toton-Brent coal trains and by 1958 all thirty-three Garratts had been withdrawn and cut up for scrap. Today, there are once again narrow gauge Garratts operating in this country (on the Welsh Highland Railway) whilst the sole standard gauge machine in preservation, at Bressingham, is of a much smaller industrial type. However, one cannot fail to be impressed by the repatriated North-British-built Garratt from South Africa which resides in Coatbridge. Whilst only 3ft 6ins gauge, this beast goes some way to conveying the might and power of the Beyer-Garratt design.

In model form there is little to choose from. Apart from the Kitmaster model

*MAY 1961*          *Railway Modeller*

## THE BIG AND THE SMALL

THE latest Kitmaster OO releases are the L.M.S. Beyer-Garratt (12/6) and the Hunslet-designed M.O.S. "austerity" 0-6-0 saddle tank (3/6). Both are to 4mm. scale.

The Garratt represents the only British class of main-line articulated steam locomotive and shows one of them in the later guise with rotating coal bunker. These massive machines were designed for use on the heavy coal trains of the Midland main line to London, but are, alas, no more, having been superseded by the B.R. 2-10-0 9Fs.

This is an excellent kit faithfully reproducing the prototype—even the bunker rotates—and is in itself a fascinating collector's piece, a locomotive that would be tedious to model individually. It would create some problems to motorize this kit, and it obviously requires reasonably large-radius curves if the steps are to remain.

MODEL RAILWAY NEWS         MAY, 1961

**Kitmaster**

THE two "OO" gauge models shown above are the latest from Kitmaster and we know many people who have been waiting for the Beyer Garratt in particular.

This 2-6-6-2T, designed by Sir Henry Fowler and Messrs Beyer-Peacock, has rarely been modelled, this is not really surprising since it is not a particularly attractive locomotive to build from scratch and all possible incentive being considerably dampened when faced with four sets of Walschaerts valve gear!

Now the job is done for you, in plastic of course, but, nevertheless, a reminder in 4 mm. scale of these powerful ex-L.M.S. class of locomotives which were finally withdrawn under nationalisation between 1955 and 1958.

with the rotating bunker, the original K's whitemetal kit is still available from Autocom UK Ltd. This depicts the locomotive is as-built condition with straight-sided bunker. Motorisation was originally with K's HP2M motors at each end, but clearance exists for more modern motor/gearbox combinations. Motorising the Kitmaster model was first tackled by the celebrated Mike Bryant in the August 1961 issue of *Model Railway Constructor*. Mike reported some considerable difficulty in using ready-to-run chassis for this job and in the end resorted to using a scratch-built brass framed chassis. He did comment on the Tri-ang 2-6-2T chassis and the Hornby-Dublo R1 0-6-0T, finding the former easier and cheaper to use for the conversion in this case.

The Kitmaster model is generally a good representation of the prototype and was well received by the press when finally released in March 1961; it had been promised for November 1960. Demand for these kits is as high today as ever it was. With the Autocom model retailing at more than £100 (without wheels etc.) and with a constant stream of modellers wishing to build a motorised Garratt, prices for the original Kitmaster model are likely to stay high for the foreseeable future. As we went to press it was announced that Danish manufacturer Helijan would be producing a ready-to-run Garratt in OO during 2012/13, thereby filling this much-requested gap in the model steam roster.

*Right*. 47969 crosses the Nene at Wellingborough, near the end of a climb with the 'Cargo Fleet' train for the North East, 26 June 1957. Photograph K.C.H. Fairey.

*Below*. The author's Beyer Garratt acquired for the princely sum of £2 from a local swap meet.

*Bottom*. 4999 at Toton on 16 June 1928; Mr Casserley was so impressed he took a few steps back to photograph the thing in all its inordinate length! Early LMS panel. Photographs H.C. Casserley, courtesy R.M. Casserley.

119

*Top.* The Dapol issue of the J94 was very short lived and consequently, is sought-after today. It was produced in two distinct runs, with no makers name and later, engraved with Dapol name. The tool was destroyed in the fire at Dapol's Winsford premises when a large girder fell on it.

*Bottom right.* Marked with their Mainline catalogue number – 937470 "Shunting Loco" are six test shots of the J94 made in Trun by Palitoy. It was never actually incorporated into the range.

*Below.* The Class J94 0-6-0ST was a war time Austerity design that proved to be incredibly versatile. Hundreds were built for war service and many more found their way into industrial and colliery use. Variants were plentiful, including an oil-fired version.

*Bottom.* Outside cylinders from a "Pug" make a pleasing addition to a shortened LNER J94.

# The Models In Detail - 22
## LNER Class J94 Saddle Tank

The "austerity" design of the ex-LNER Class J94 saddle tank is today perhaps one of the most ubiquitous of the 0-6-0 shunters in steam preservation. This is due in part to the huge numbers of locomotives built, by various builders, for industrial use. These include Bagnall, Hunslet, RSH and Vulcan Foundry. Indeed many of today's J94s carry fictitious BR running numbers having never seen front line service with either the LNER or British Railways. Only two of the surviving locos were included in the initial purchase block of 75 purchased by the LNER from the War Department in 1946. Production of the Austerity design finished in 1964, by which time 485 had been constructed.

The Kitmaster model, number 26 in the series, broke ground in several areas. It is one of only two Kitmaster models of steam locomotives that were still in production at the time of issue; the other being the "Evening Star" Class 9F. It was the first to get a Format III instruction sheet in black and red with multiple exploded diagrams. This made assembly so much easier and was then widely adopted by other manufacturers. It was also one of the few kits to have added detail inside the cab, in this case the reverser lever. And it was the first of the smaller locomotives to appear in a directly printed box of the more "floppy" type.

But this charming kit has many more interesting claims to fame. It was only issued by Airfix once, in a Type 3 box with Charles Oakes artwork and it quickly disappeared from Airfix catalogues of the 1970s. It was chosen by Palitoy to be one of the ex-Airfix kits to be introduced into the mainline Railways range and in this guise, the mould was sent to Calais for some test shots to be prepared. These six shots in cream plastic appear elsewhere in this book and they are the only fruits of that particular project, abandoned when Palitoy withdrew from European toy manufacture.

But the stocky little J94 carried on, this time in the portfolio of Dapol Model Railways. "Dapol" was a diminutive of "Dave and Polly", being the names of the company founding Directors, David and Pauline Boyle. When they acquired the J94 tooling, the first thing that happened was grinding off the Airfix logo from the underside. This was a requirement of their sale by Palitoy. However, the tools were not immediately re-engraved with the Dapol logo. So a run of 2000 J94 kits in black and packed in Dapol header bags was produced with no logo on the underside. For the second run, the tool was newly engraved with a Dapol logo in place of the Airfix version and a further 2000 units were produced in a smart new yellow and brown header style.

At this point Dapol Ltd was based in a converted mill in the Cheshire town of Winsford. Unfortunately, when those premises were destroyed by fire one night, a large roof girder fell onto the J94 tooling which was in the factory below and caused irreparable damage. The tool was subsequently scrapped and the two Dapol-produced runs of the J94 instantly became highly-sought after "rare" kits. But that was not the end of the story. David Boyle had chosen this useful maid-of-all-work as the subject for the first fully ready-to-run design produced entirely by Dapol. This proved to be a good, reliable and detailed model which found a further lease of life after Dapol when the tools were acquired and re-used by Hornby Hobbies. This model, which is still in the Hornby catalogue in 2012 can therefore trace it's roots right back to the original Kitmaster issue of 1961.

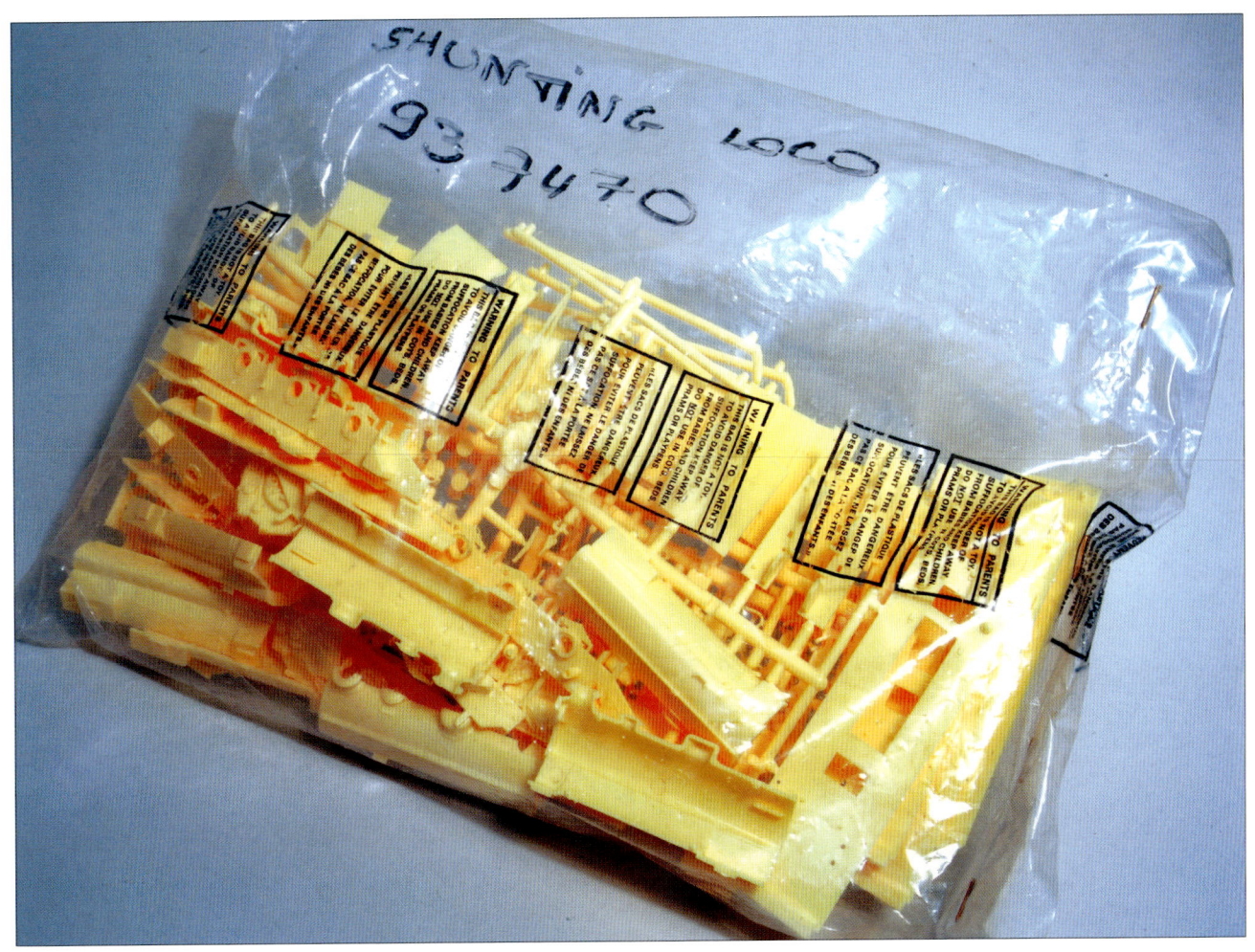

6128 in black livery at Bourne End, en route for High Wycombe, in July 1961. J P Mullett, Colourrail.co.uk

6128 at Southall shed in October 1959. L W Rowe, Colourrail.co.uk

# The Models In Detail - 23
## The GWR Class 61XX Prairie Tank

Of all the classes of Great Western tank locomotives, the large Prairies were certainly the most elegant. Designed in 1931 for rapid acceleration on short- to medium-haul routes on the GW network, the locomotives were frequently required to stop and restart trains on busy main lines with tight headways. The large cylinders and 5ft 8 ins driving wheels gave them a good top speed. Designed by C.B.Collett for and deployed to the London area, th class of 70 locomotives soon became the mainstay of suburban services on the GW mainline and the GW/GC Joint lines. They lasted until 1965 when the Western Region eliminated standard gauge steam completely, only one engine, 6106, was preserved.

The Rosebud Kitmaster model was an early entry into the programme, arriving in October 1959 to near-rapturous criticism. The overall body shape was good and many fixtures and fittings were either moulded on or could be applied separately. Motorisation was relatively simple using the widely available Tri-ang 0-6-0 chassis or sometimes the larger 2-6-2T chassis suitably cut down. Mike Bryant was, as usual, first into print with a "How To" article.

As there were obvious closely-related GWR types that could be converted from the 61XX, more articles soon appeared. However with the advent of the City of Truro 4-4-0 kit more adventurous kit-bashing could be undertaken and it was not long before some wag produced both a Bulldog and an Aberdare from bits of Prairie and Truro. Many more were to follow, making use of Swindon's systemised design philosophy that used standard, interchangeable parts. Motorisation was also helped by the release of Arby Perfecta Kit number 3. This was a popular motorisation pack designed especially for the Kitmaster model and using a Tri-ang XT.60 or X.04 motor.

The Prairie has the special distinction of being the first Kitmaster locomotive kit to be re-issued by Airfix, in October 1963. Only the couplings had been changed, from Kitmaster style to NMRA buckeyes. Later re-issues would sport added detail, but the Prairie was not to benefit from such luxury. It was also the very first Airfix kit of any subject to appear in the smart new "red flash" Type 3 packaging. The painting, which is now in the Kitmaster club archive, is oil on canvas and measures 3 feet by 2ft 6ins, unsigned, it is believed to be by Charles Oakes. The kit was later issued in a modified Type 3 box with the "Limited Production" branding and round Type 4 logos on the end panels. In 1967, Wilro Models introduced a "Simplas" chassis to aid motorisation, the previous Arby kit having been discontinued by then.

When Airfix decided to introduce a ready-to-run system in 1976, the GWR Large Prairie was their choice of steam locomotive with which to launch the range. It was a good and well-detailed model, save for the solid driving wheels, a retrograde step from the earlier kit which always had spoked wheels. Once again, the R-T-R model proved popular and eventually passed to Dapol Model Railways before finding it's way to Hornby Hobbies were it enjoyed a well-earned life extension upgrade that saw it acquire a completely new chassis.

Meanwhile the original kit tool is still in production with Dapol and now offers a choice of running numbers for the first time.

**The Kitmaster Prairie captures the prototype very well and was a popular choice for motorisation.**

What would Kitmaster have produced next if they had not gone into receivership? Lawrence Blake shares some ideas with us… A 1962 letter promised *something of interest to Great Western fans*; with Farish having issued a King, Tri-ang a Hall and Dublo a Castle, could Kitmaster have covered the County Class 4-6-0s? The Airfix issue of the Q1 looks smart – but it was not until 2006 that Hornby finally issued a ready-to-run model.

124

# Chapter 4: Rumours and Postulations

The ever-present theme in the Kitmaster collecting world is the continuous stream of rumours and speculation surrounding the company. Whilst 90% of this is apocryphal, there is a certain element of truth in some of the rumours. Also included here are some of the better substantiated theories about what would have happened next. Rumours can be summarised as:
1. The A3 was produced.
2. The USA Tank was produced.
3. The TT motor bogie was produced.
4. The Motor Bogies were made by Tri-ang Railways.
5. The Coach kit tooling was lost at sea.
6. The CN U-4-a 4-8-4 was produced.

And postulations as:
1 The next design would be a WD 2-8-0.
2 The next boxed set would be the Midland Pullman.

## Rumours

### 1. The A3 was produced
This is the most common rumour and contains some elements of truth. Firstly, let's set the record straight. Full box artwork was produced for the packaging and distributed to the press, although the kit was never on retail sale to the public. However, three different sources claim to have seen a clear plastic 'test-firing' of the mould for the A3. They claim that it was in a clear plastic bag with no markings, decals or instructions. Just as you might expect for a factory test run. Nick Gilman says that the proprietor of a Bedford model shop had one around 1974. These kits, if they exist, would be limited to perhaps half a dozen at most. There is a very strong possibility that they are incomplete. Since more than one tool was required for some kits, Kitmaster may have been in the middle of tooling up when the sale was agreed. This attractive little hypothesis accounts for the existence of one or more (incomplete) test shots and it also explains why this brand new model was never put into production by Airfix. As yet, nobody has been able to show me one first hand, but if they really do exist in some form they would be highly prized collectors items. British Transfer Printing Co Ltd did print the transfers and it is possible that boxes were also completed. The transfer sheet was definitely for Flying Scotsman in LNER livery, including the black and white lining and the number 4472. The LNER insignia were printed inside the tender lining in a similar manner to that for the Class 9F decal sheet. Nameplates were NOT included; presumably, the plates would have been in raised letters as they were on earlier kits, a retrograde step in comparison to the Evening Star and City of Truro neatly reproduced name plates

### 2. The USA Tank was produced
This theory has the same currency as the first, except that nobody is claiming to have seen a test firing. Instead, a source supposed to have worked at Raunds told *Kitmaster Newsletter* that 'six units were made (up) and given to the sales force to show to distributors'. Other sources have been told of nine or twelve kits. This does not, of course, mean that it was tooled up. It just means that several models were mocked up from the pattern or drawings; a normal part of the model makers procedure in any case. Mock-ups should exist for all of the kits, although nobody is looking for them very seriously apart from the USA tank. In any case, if you switch on an injection moulding machine you don't just make a dozen kits; you can't turn it off that quickly!

**Later instruction sheets had a "mini-catalogue" appended at the beginning; here is slightly "expanded" version courtesy of Lawrence!**

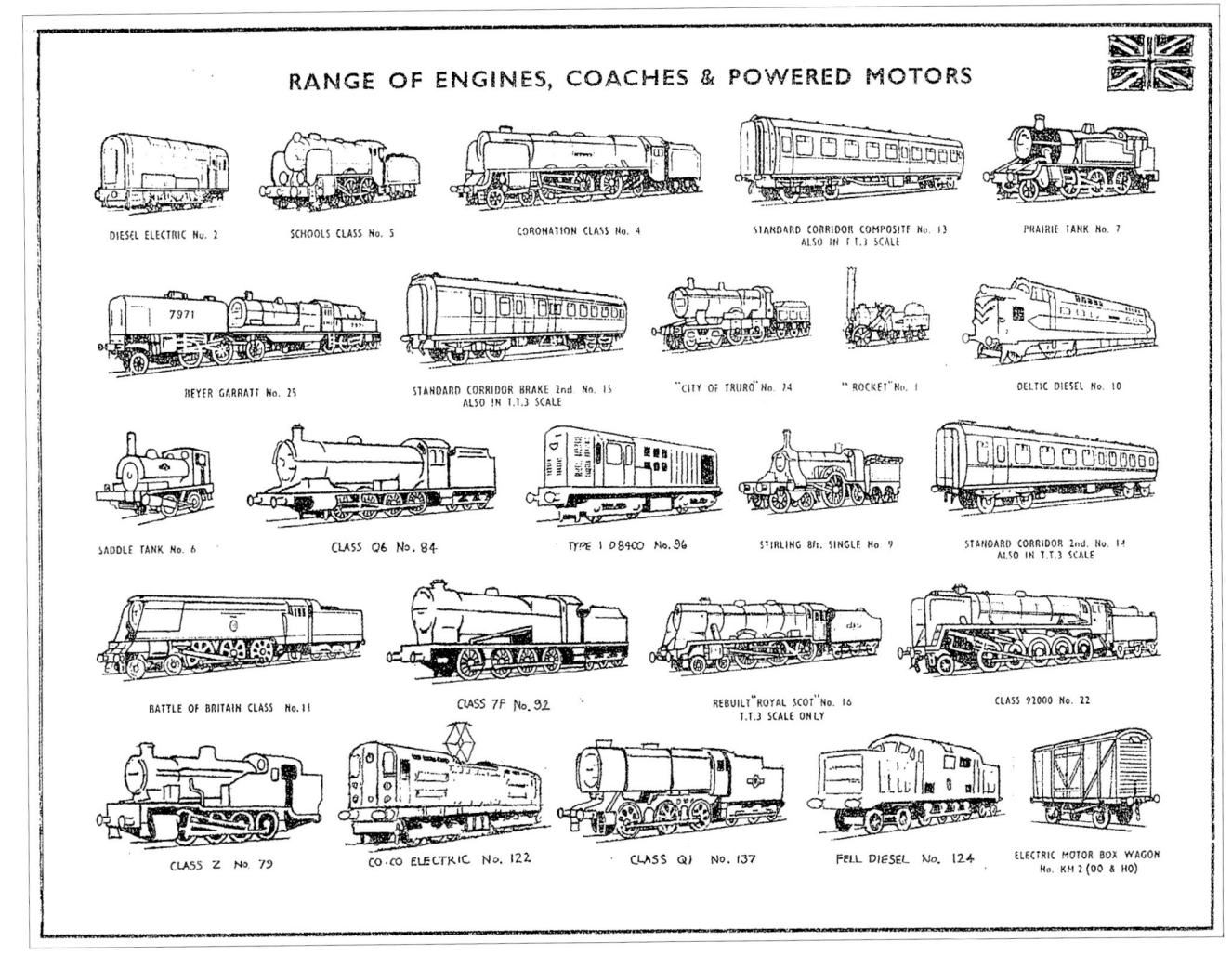

### RANGE OF ENGINES, COACHES & POWERED MOTORS

- DIESEL ELECTRIC No. 2
- SCHOOLS CLASS No. 5
- CORONATION CLASS No. 4
- STANDARD CORRIDOR COMPOSITE No. 13 ALSO IN T.T.3 SCALE
- PRAIRIE TANK No. 7
- BEYER GARRATT No. 25
- STANDARD CORRIDOR BRAKE 2nd. No. 15 ALSO IN T.T.3 SCALE
- "CITY OF TRURO" No. 74
- "ROCKET" No. 1
- DELTIC DIESEL No. 10
- SADDLE TANK No. 6
- CLASS Q6 No. 84
- TYPE 1 D8400 No. 96
- STIRLING 8ft. SINGLE No. 9
- STANDARD CORRIDOR 2nd. No. 14 ALSO IN T.T.3 SCALE
- BATTLE OF BRITAIN CLASS No. 11
- CLASS 7F No. 92
- REBUILT "ROYAL SCOT" No. 16 T.T.3 SCALE ONLY
- CLASS 92000 No. 22
- CLASS Z No. 79
- CO-CO ELECTRIC No. 122
- CLASS Q1 No. 137
- FELL DIESEL No. 124
- ELECTRIC MOTOR BOX WAGON No. KM 2 (OO & HO)

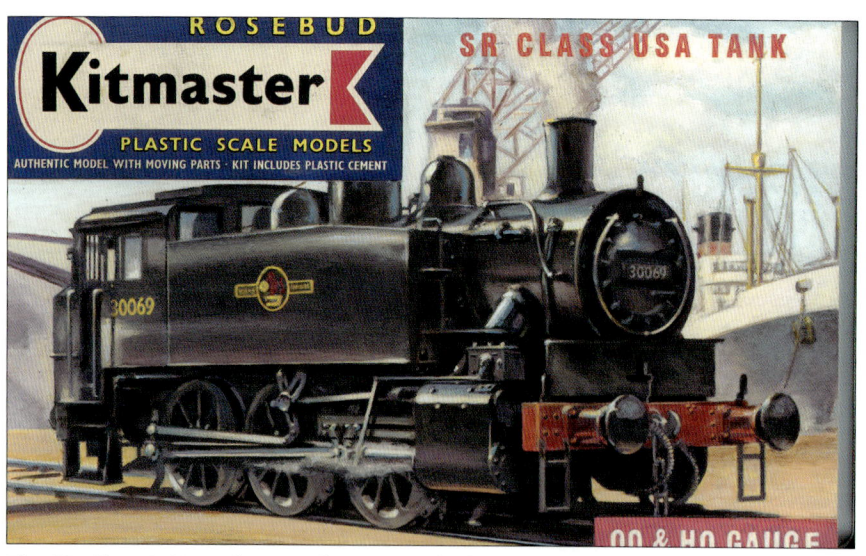

*The SR Class USA tank artwork was supplied to Hobbies magazine for their 1962 Annual, although the kit was cancelled in early Spring 1963.*

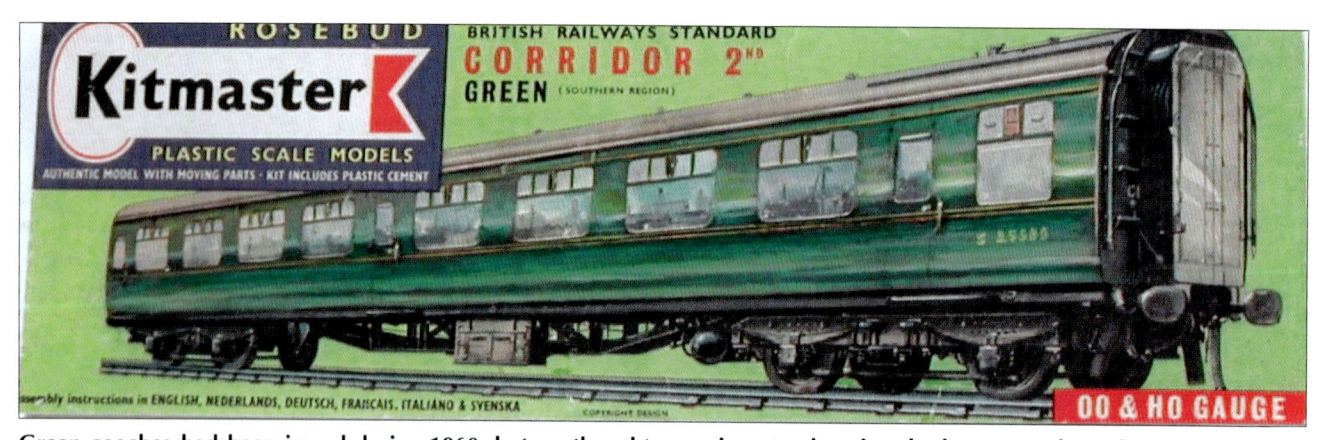

*Green coaches had been issued during 1960, but no thought was given to changing the box artwork – what a shame!*

**5. The tooling for the coaches was lost at sea**

This is an easy one to deal with since it is attributable directly to a true story. The Kitmaster tooling was never sent anywhere by ship until Dapol got hold of it and sent it to Hong Kong. However, Frog did send a batch of tools out to Tri-ang New Zealand on a ship which sank in a tropical storm. The (now somewhat rusty) steel tools continue to lie in 300ft of water on the floor of the Pacific, should you be thinking of a rescue bid...

**6. The CN U-4-a 4-8-4 was produced**

At a Colchester MRC Exhibition, an exhibitor claimed, vociferously, that he had seen a complete box for the CN U4a in a shop called Angels in the Mile End Road in London during 1962. The box was in the window with a label saying 'Coming Soon'. He was quite specific about the artwork, claiming that it was a night scene with the loco travelling right-to-left instead of the Rosebud standard left-to-right. It has not been possible to confirm this story, neither did he see the contents of the box. However, the emergence of the original artwork for the CN U-3-A shows the loco travelling left-to-right, thus discounting this report.

**3. The TT motor bogie was produced**

This is 99% untrue... Kitmaster certainly produced a couple of prototypes for promotion and press reviews, but they abandoned production of the bogie in July 1961 and even issued a press release to this effect, repeated in the *Railway Modeller* of that month.

**4. The Motor Bogies were made by Tri-ang Railways**

This one is easy to lay to rest. I have written confirmation from Richard Lines, proprietor of Tri-ang Railways at the time, who says that at no time did they ever supply parts or bogies to Kitmaster. Indeed, he says that they were not best pleased by the striking similarity of the Kitmaster bogie to their own successful design for the SR EMU and Blue Pullman sets. The design was shamelessly copied by Rosebud and all of the bogies were assembled 'in-house' from parts bought in around the country. Armatures were wound on site at Raunds and carbon brushes were also assembled by the doll workers! It is just possible, however, that Norman Dyson, designer of Tri-ang's motors, also worked on the Rosebud design, since he knew the pattern-maker Jack Gain.

**Postulations**

1 The next design would be a WD 2-8-0
This interesting theory was postulated by Mr Greg Davies of Brighton in a

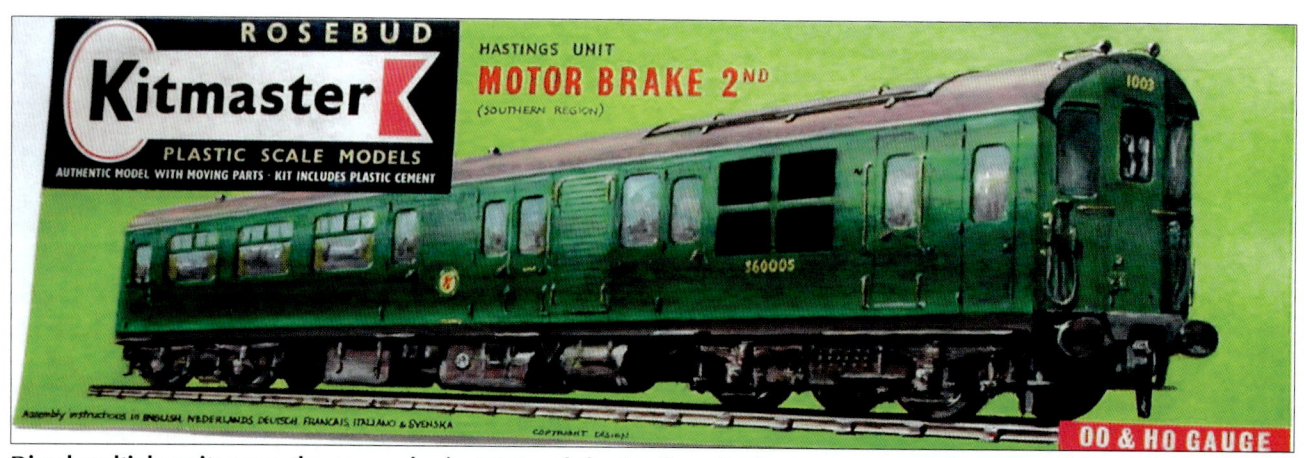

*Diesel multiple units were the new order in 1963 and the Southern Region was no exception. The height of modernity was this fleet of six car express sets for the Hastings route.*

letter to the Club. He says that this was a frequent topic of discussion after the 1962 range had been announced. Certainly, the type would have been a popular choice. Large numbers of these engines were still in service at the time, both at home and, perhaps more importantly for Kitmaster, overseas. The type had not been covered at all by the British manufacturers of ready-to-run equipment and a suitable chassis for motorisation, the Hornby-Dublo Stanier 8F, was freely available from Meccano. Perhaps it was the similar duties and geographical distribution of the self-same 'Eight Freights' which precluded the early choice of an Austerity 2-8-0 for inclusion in the range? We shall never know of course, but a good model of the type would certainly not have gone amiss with the British outline modelling fraternity. However, another correspondent in Wiltshire wrote to Rosebud in 1962 and was told that 'next year's range will include something of interest to GWR modellers'. What this means is of course unclear; it could be another GWR locomotive such as a pannier tank, Manor or Grange to follow the huge success of Truro and the Prairie, or it could have heralded a series of pre-nationalisation coaches. Dennis Franklin, who left Rosebud in 1960, would have liked a King in the range, but it is not known if the idea was ever pursued.

**2 The next boxed set would be the Midland Pullman**
This theory is certainly logical. Bringing

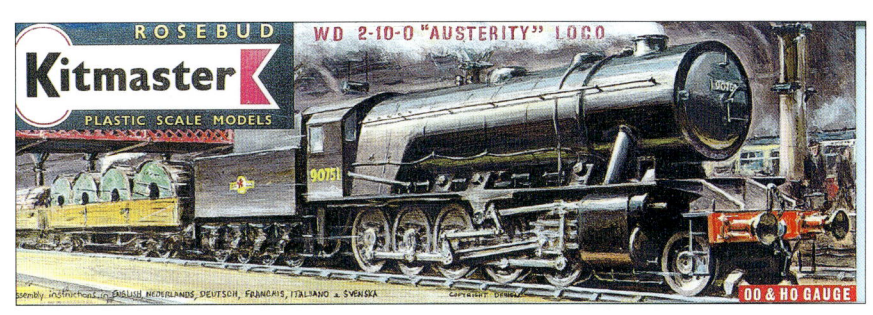

*Top.* The powerful, if somewhat functional, WD Austerity class. The kit proposed was of course for the WD 2-8-0 but the artwork prepared, as can be seen, was for a 2-10-0! *Middle.* Another larger diesel, such as this A1A-A1A Warship would have been popular. *Above.* A Great central 'Director' 4-4-0 had already been earmarked for the National Collection by 1963, in the event it was to be *"Butler Henderson"* rather than *"Luckie Mucklebackit"* that escaped the cutter's torch.

together a 'Complete Train' kit of the six Midland Pullman cars would have been impressive if nothing else. One can speculate as to whether a KM1 (or two) would have been included. This would have taken the approximate cost up to 72 shillings; nearly double the cost of the previous P2 and P3 sets. Even without a power bogie it would come in at around 62 shillings, but what a sight it would have made! Compare this with the rather poor Tri-ang Train Set of the Blue Pullman with just three cars in it and you begin to appreciate what could have been.

**New Artwork**
Not content with these postulations, Kitmaster Club member Lawrence Blake, who is a trained illustrator, produced some splendid 'might have been' illustrations for use in the Kitmaster Club newsletter, *Signal*. When Lawrence sent this superb illustration for a proposed Kitmaster Class Q1, it coincided with the issue of the brand new Hornby model. Lawrence says he deliberately accentuated the perspective and threw in a couple of customary flaws in order to emulate a typical Kitmaster box illustration of the period. Apparently, it's the extraordinary highlights that distinguish early Ken Rush work from later Roy Cross-style boxes. Not content with one Q1, Lawrence then went on to sketch out what Airfix might have made of it had they inherited such a mystical tool. The mouth watering prospect of a retooled Airfix Q1 with Roy Cross artwork had my heart racing for a few seconds before I came back to Earth with a bump…. Gaze and dream on, people….

127

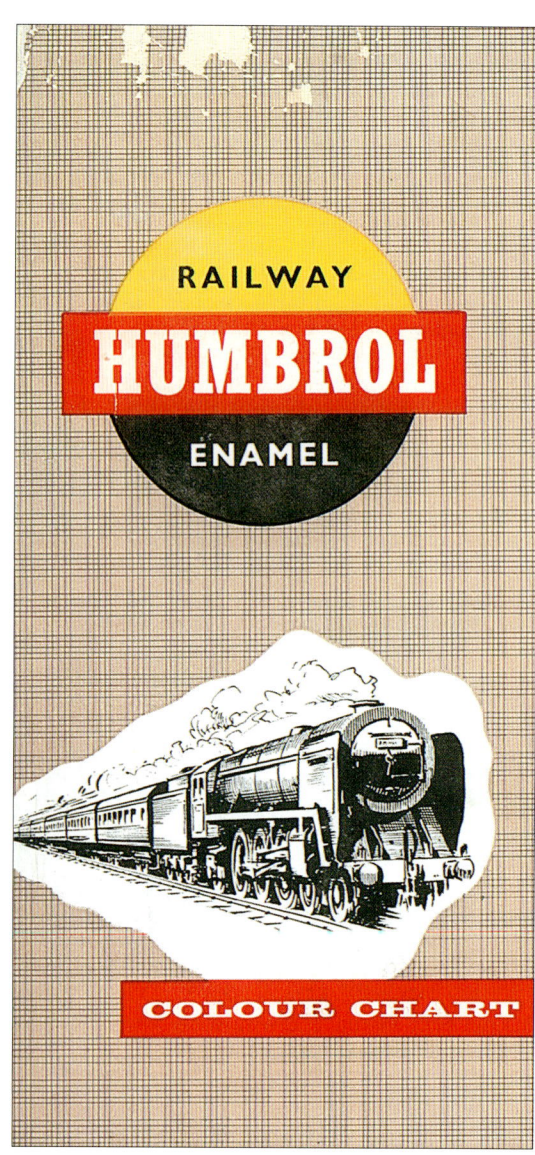

*Top right.* Humbrol Authentic Colours chart featuring a Britannia Pacific drawn by A.N.Wolstenholme, doyen of the Ian Allen ABC Series. *Top left.* A full page colour advert for Fireball XL5 from the back cover of Mecanno Magazine. *Below.* This flyer was packed with the kits as issued and was circulated to suitable confectioners shops.

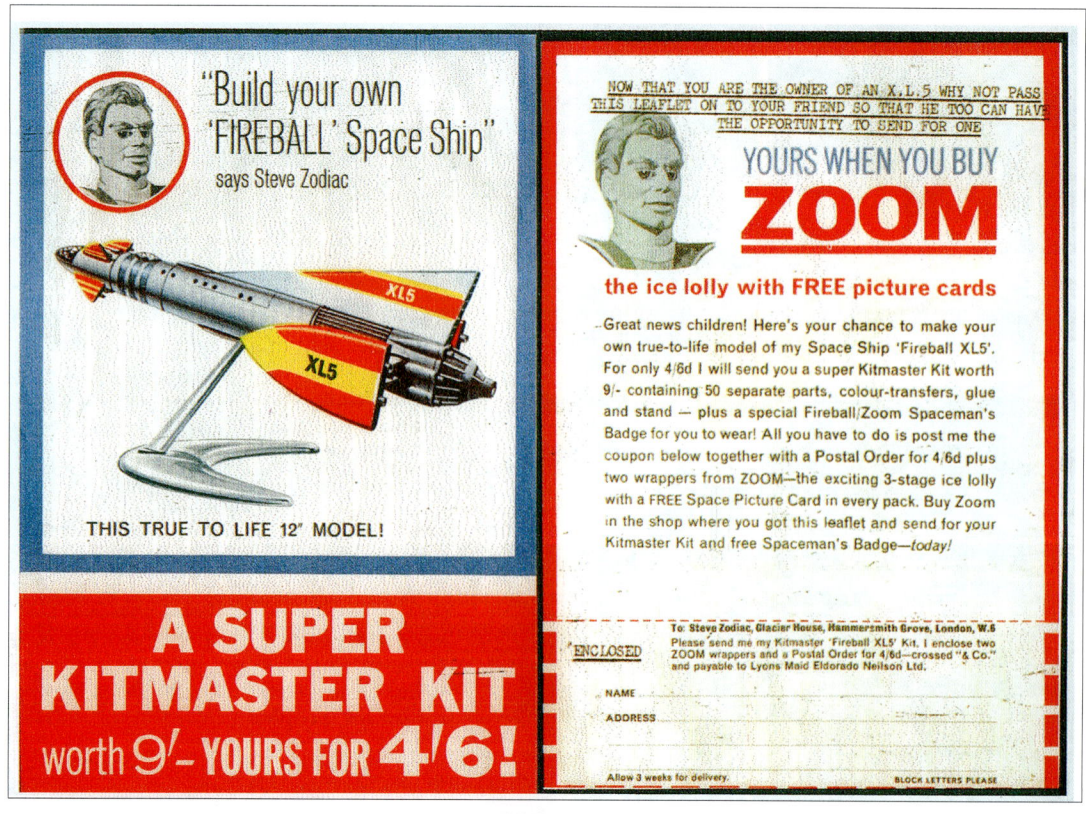

# Chapter 5: Collaborations

### 1. Nabisco and the Hermes Supply Company

The Hermes Supply Company first appears in the Kitmaster story when it used some of the surplus stock from Airfix to fulfil a supply contract with Nabisco Foods. It would appear that HSC was a fully owned subsidiary of the Airfix Holdings Group and is listed as such in the 1973 Airfix Report & Accounts. All the Nabisco kits were actually despatched by Airfix and the two companies both had postal addresses in the same area of south-west London. The mailing boxes carry Airfix postal franking machine labels.

The Nabisco kits were obtained by collecting tokens from packets of *Shredded Wheat* which, together with a postal order, could be redeemed for a 'Train Kit' from a fairly limited selection. There were two types of token on each box. Blue 'X' tokens could be exchanged for an entirely free 'Shunting Locomotive' - actually Kit No.2, the 350HP Diesel Shunter. For the larger kits, yellow 'Z' tokens had to be redeemed with a part-payment of the cost of the loco. The details are shown in the table below.

As can be readily seen from the table, the so-called free shunter actually cost 4d and the others were roughly half-price when the postage is taken into account. Supply of these kits to customers began in January 1963. The Nabisco promotional kits were limited to what was in stock in large enough quantities to fulfil the expected orders from the happy *Shredded Wheat*-eating modellers of the day! Consequently, although you could select the RFO and BSK coaches, you had no choice about the colour. Invariably, it seems, all RFOs were red and all BSKs were green, both in the same box!

Hermes issued their own instruction sheets, based on the latest revisions of

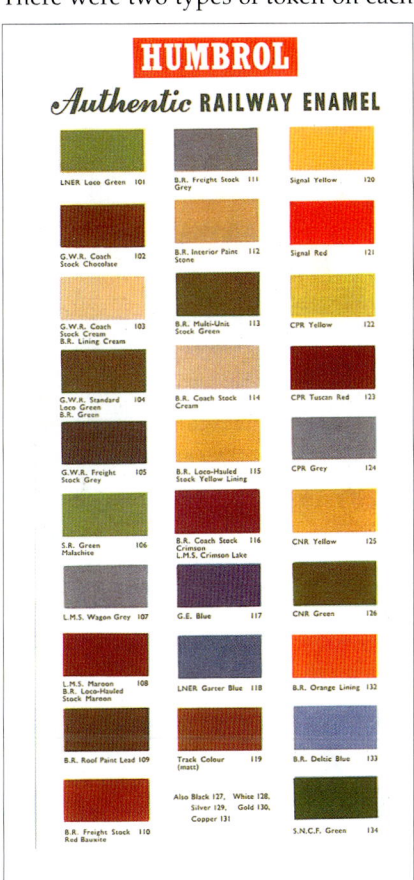

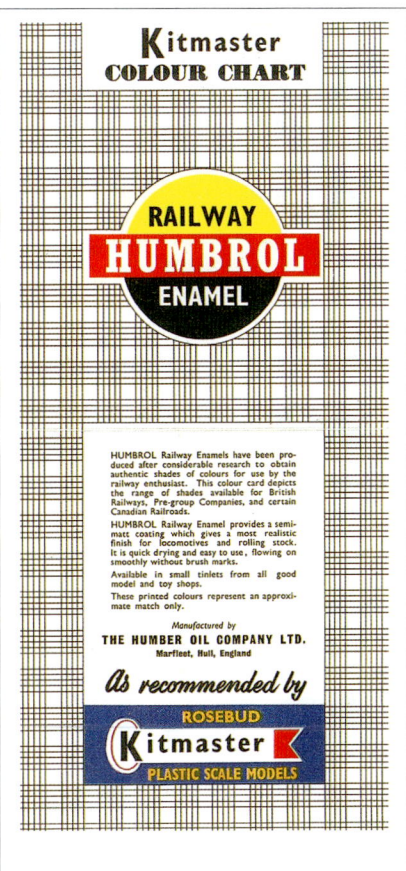

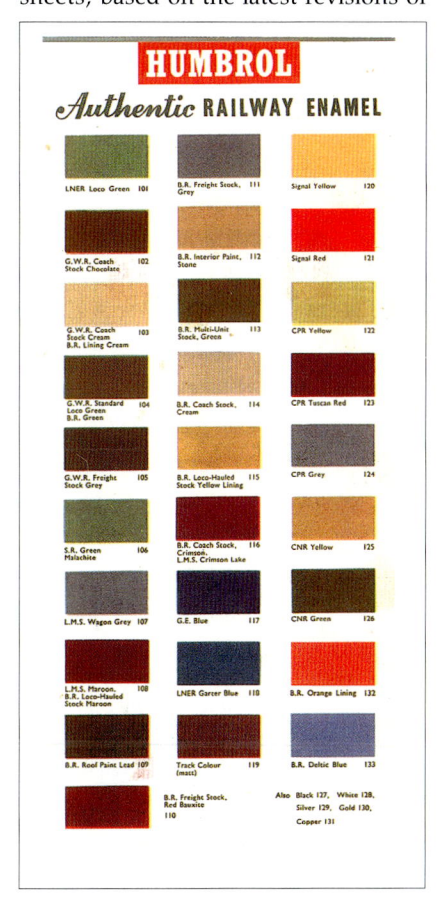

| Kit Number | Kit Colour | Nabisco Description | Token Colour | Number Required | Normal Price | Offer Price | Postage Charge | Postage Cost |
|---|---|---|---|---|---|---|---|---|
| 2 | Black | Free Shunting Engine | Blue | 4 | 4s 6d | Free | 10d | 6d |
| 10 | Blue | Deltic Diesel | Yellow | 2 | 10s 6d | 5s 11d | Free | 10 1/2d |
| 22 | Black | Evening Star | Yellow | 2 | 10s 6d | 5s 11d | Free | 10 1/2d |
| 28 & 15 | Maroon & Green | Dining Car and Corridor Brake coach | Yellow | 2 | 16s 6d | 8s 9d | Free | 1s 4 1/2d |

*Left and right above.* Early Kitmaster/Humbrol colour charts.
*Below left and right.* Part of the Shredded Wheat packaging that enabled free Kitmaster models to be obtained in exchange for tokens.

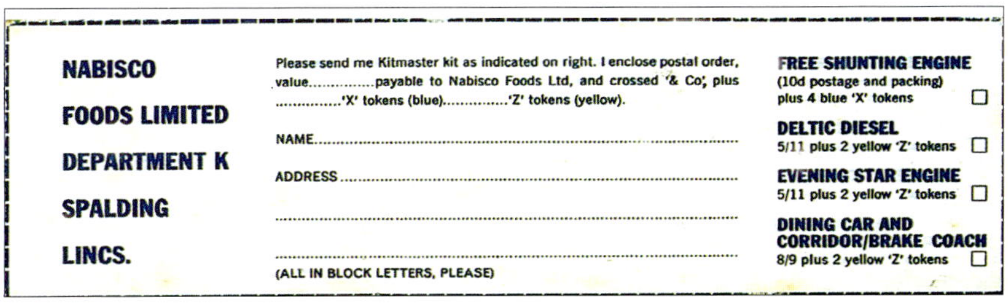

129

*Left.* A very rare Humbrol Authentic Scenic colours gift set, before the switch was made to the familiar "tinlets".

*Middle.* Lawrence Blake takes on Fireball XL5. The publicity for the Lyons Maid issue talks of "nine shillings retail value", but there is no evidence that the kit was ever available to buy elsewhere.

*Bottom.* An unassembled Kitmaster Fireball XL5 kit with decals, instructions and shipping carton.

**Left.** A joint Kitmaster/Humbrol advert featuring the Beyer-Garratt, as the advertising budget dried up, these co-promotions were the only retail adverts to appear. Rosebud did keep on advertising new models in the trade press however. Right up to the Ariel Arrow, adverts were appearing in "Games & Toys" the trade magazine.

the Kitmaster instructionals, for these kits. These were almost certainly drawn by the Airfix drawing office, being stylistically identical to contemporary Airfix Series 4 Type 2 kits. An example of a blue Rosebud Format 1 instruction sheet overprinted with the legend 'With the Compliments of Nabisco Foods' is known to exist for the Deltic kit. They also produced their own complaint slip, which bore a striking resemblance to the Airfix complaint slip. The word 'Rosebud' was carefully removed from the logo on both items. The kits were actually despatched by Airfix, strong evidence of the link between the two companies. The stock was finally exhausted in January 1964, almost two years after the sale of Rosebud Kitmaster Ltd.

Hermes subsequently moved to Sunbury on Thames and, in June 1963, issued the unique Fireball XL5 rocket kit. The 1:100th model of the spaceship was a promotion carried by Lyons Maid on 'Zoom' ice lolly products which resulted in a plastic kit of Steve Zodiac's Fireball XL5 being sent in exchange for tokens. The kit was packed in a clear plastic bag inside a plain Hermes/Nabisco type box only, and does not carry any reference to Kitmaster. However, the advertisements, in *Airfix Magazine* and *Boys Own Paper* all refer to it in the small print of the coupon as '...your Kitmaster Fireball model...'. It was issued in June 1963 by the Hermes Supply Co and is, strictly speaking, not a Kitmaster product. There is a complaint slip from the Hermes Supply Co as per Nabisco kits. Although the tool is no longer known, the kit made a recent reappearance as a resin model with whitemetal fittings thanks to Tony James at Comet Miniatures. They even got Gerry Anderson to help improve some design flaws in the original model! *Collectors Gazette* covered this model in the letters column in 1991 - see bibliography.

So successful was the XL5 promotional kit, that in 1964 they got a contract to produce a similar model of Stingray. Neither of these kits are true Kitmaster models, although the XL5 is often cited as such. In a July 1963 advert in *The Victor* comic, the Lyons Maid XL5 is described (in the small print) as Kitmaster, but the kit carries no indication of this. Interestingly, it also indicates that whilst Lyons Maid customers can obtain the kit for 4s 6d, the 'normal' price is 9s. Add to this correspondence in *Collectors Gazette* from someone who was asked by a dealer 'Is

**Dave Haymen built this Kitmaster Fireball XL5 in the 1960s and still has it to this day.**

131

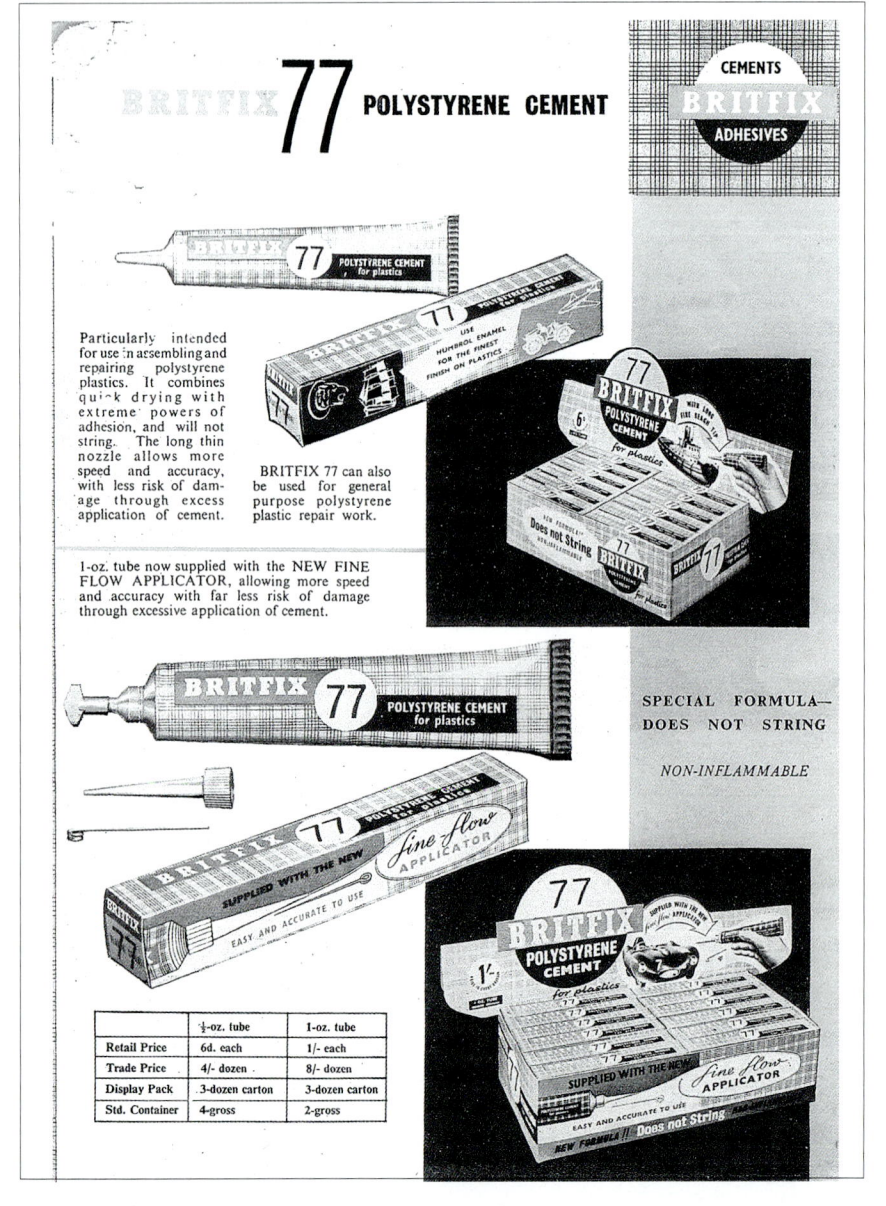

*Above.* The four issued Peco Interior kits. They finished off your Mark 1 coaches to a very high standard, were colourful, versatile and easy to build.

*Left.* A page from the 1960 Humbrol Trade catalogue extols the virtues of Britfix 77 – still the best polystyrene cement money can buy in your author's opinion.

your XL5 in the original box?' and we have strong grounds for suspecting that this kit may also have been supplied direct to the retail trade by Hermes or Airfix. However, all the known XL5 owners contacted by the Club had received the kit in a plain brown mailing box... 'Curiouser and curiouser' as Alice said. Both Stingray and XL5 are extremely rare items now, often commanding in excess of £500 when sold. Now that *is* curious!

132

*Left.* The colourful Humbrol Railway Lining Colours Card provided nine intermixable paints, a plastic palette and a paint brush with detailed mixing instructions for each colour required.

**Collaborations 2 The Humber Oil Company Ltd 'Humbrol'** Kitmaster always recommended Humbrol Railway Colours for completing the models to best effect. Humbrol colours were becoming well established in the late 1950s and early 1960s, and this relationship blossomed. As early as 1960 Humbrol advertisements carried the wording 'Ideal for Kitmaster locomotives'. The joint marketing programme started mid-way through 1960. Firstly, a special chart showing the available colours was produced with both the Rosebud Kitmaster and Humbrol logos and one was packed with every kit from mid-1960 onwards. Secondly, Humbrol produced a convenient card pack which contained eight capsules of enamel paints for lining and finishing the locomotives together with a brush. The reverse side of the card showed nine of the current Kitmaster kits. Both company logos are shown in full colour and the locomotives are reproduced from the original 1959 catalogue artwork. The gelatine capsules contained only basic colours, whilst the details printed inside the sealed card explained how to mix them and the best techniques for applying them. These cards are extremely scarce today.

Finally, joint advertising campaigns promoting Humbrol colours for Kitmaster kits started with a non-specific advertisement in the April 1961 edition of *Railway Modeller*. This was followed by a series of 'specific' advertisements which featured a photograph of a recent Kitmaster release, a stylised Kitmaster logo and text about the suitability of Humbrol paint. These are important because they were the only published advertisements for the J94 saddle tank and the BR Mogul, coming at a time when cash flow was becoming difficult at Rosebud and the advertising budget had been slashed. They are also important because they were the only advertisements for a Kitmaster product ever to appear in *Boys Own Paper*. The complete joint campaign is shown in Table H left.

The Colour Charts were published by Humbrol and included in the kits from 1960 onwards. They show the full range of colours available for railway modellers including some Canadian liveries. Each colour is numbered and Kitmaster refer to these numbers in their later instruction sheets. There were two editions of this 'Kitmaster Colour Chart'. The advent of the French Mountain locomotive eventually led to Humbrol producing SNCF Loco Green to enable this interesting model to be correctly

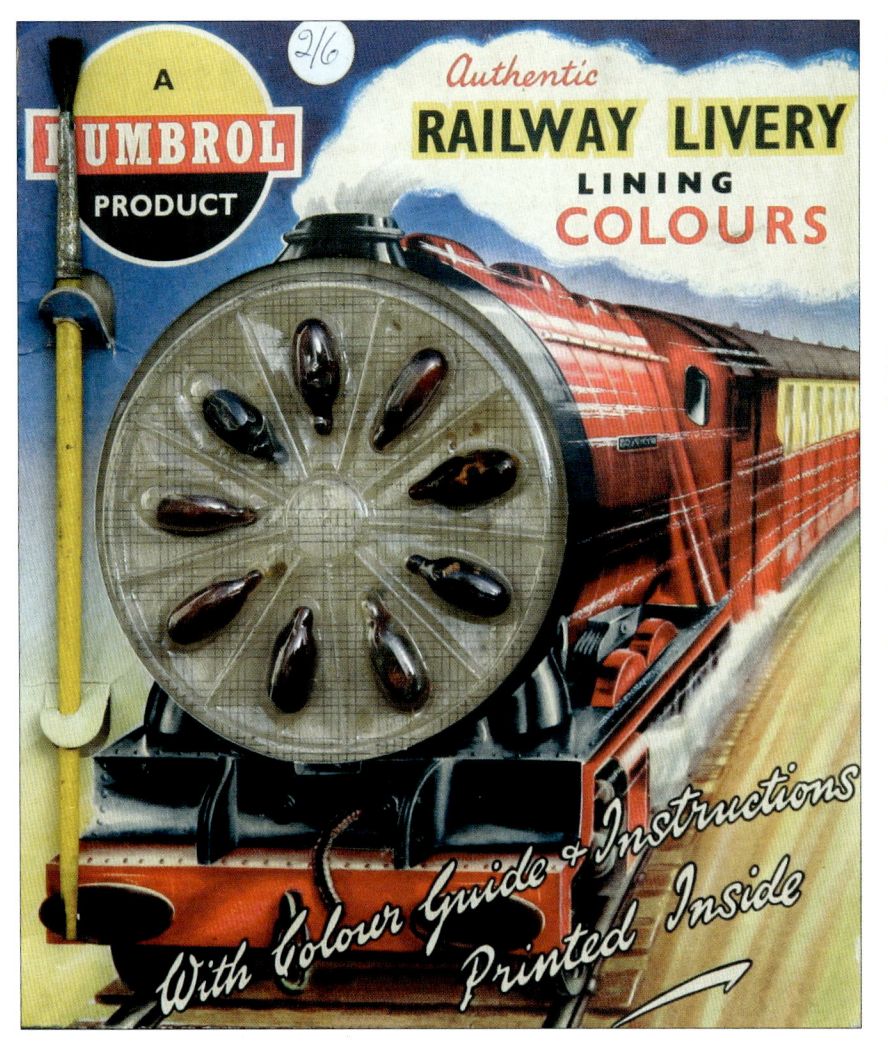

| Table H: Kitmaster/Humbrol Joint Promotional Campaign | | |
|---|---|---|
| Humbrol/Kitmaster Colour Chart | Type A | 1959 -1960 |
| Humbrol/Kitmaster Colour Chart | Type B | 1960-1962 |
| Humbrol Railway Colours Card | | 1960-63 |
| Humbrol / Kitmaster general ad | RM | 4.61 |
| Half page J94 / Humbrol ad | McM | 5.61 |
| Half page J94 / Humbrol ad | BOP | 5.61 |
| Full page J94 / Humbrol ad | BOP | 8.61 |
| Half page J94 / Humbrol ad | MRN | 9.61 |
| Half page 4MT / Humbrol ad | MoM | 9.61 |
| Half page 4MT / Humbrol ad | RM | 10.61 |
| Half page 4MT / Humbrol ad | MRC | 11.61 |
| Half page 4MT / Humbrol ad | RM | 11.61 |
| Half page Pullman/Humbrol ad | MRC | 12.61 |
| Quarter page Pullman/Humbrol ad | MRC | 1.62 |
| Quarter page Pullman/Humbrol ad | AM | 1.62 |
| Full page Pullman/HMS York ad | AM | 2.62 |

*Key to publications:*
AM=Airfix Magazine
RM=Railway Modeller
MRC=Model Railways Constructor
MRN=Model Railway News
BOP=Boys Own Paper
MoM=Model Maker
McM=Meccano Magazine

**FOR AUTHENTIC RAILWAY MODELS—**

*Use A Humbrol Railway Livery Kit*

The Humbrol Railway Livery Kit is made for the authentic lining and decoration of model railway locomotives and rolling stock. And it's particularly suitable for the Kitmaster range of models. In addition to a brush, palette and colour blending chart, the kit includes eight full gloss colours and flatting agent—so any finish from gloss to complete matt is obtainable. Colours are intermixable and the convenient size of the capsules prevents waste so you need never buy more than you require.

*The whole kit costs only 2/6.*

*For Overall Accuracy—Humbrol Railway Enamels*

For overall decoration of railway models always use Humbrol Railway Enamels. Like all Humbrol enamels they dry quickly, without brush marks and last for years. In a range of semi-matt authentic railway colours, they're specially produced to give a more realistic finish to model railways than high gloss paints.

*Price 1/- per jar.*

**HUMBROL** THE ART ENAMEL THAT TURNS MODELS INTO MASTERPIECES

The Humber Oil Company Ltd., Paints Division, Marfleet, Hull

---

painted. This in itself necessitated a reprint of the colour chart to include the new colour, number 134 in the series. This reprint can be dated to July or August 1961 using contemporary advertisements. The two advertisements for the J94 which appear in *Boys Own Paper* (May and August 1961) mark the period during which SNCF Green was introduced. The first advertisement states that there are 33 colours in the range, whilst three months later this had risen to 34 colours.

Surprisingly, the paint in the presentation sets is not branded Humbrol, although that in the P2 set resembles the capsules on the Railway Colours card and the glue in the P2 and P3 sets is Humbrol Britfix 77 packed in specially branded 'Kitmaster' half ounce tubes. These lead tubes are printed in full colour on one side with the Kitmaster logo and on the other side with the Humbrol logo. The Humbrol/Kitmaster relationship appears to have outlasted the Rosebud company by some years. A copy of *Model Railway News* from June 1972 clearly shows a Kitmaster produced 9F, complete with hook and eye coupling, in an advert for Railway Colours! Unfortunately, Humbrol themselves have no record of

134

*Top.* Peco advertised their Interior kits extensively. *Above.* These built Kitmaster Southern Region coaches are set off by the very visible interior kits within. *Below.* The ingenious design included passengers luggage and newspapers!

any of this, as their entire archive was destroyed by a catastrophic fire in 1988.

### Collaborations 3
**The Pritchard Patent Product Co Ltd 'PECO'** The involvement of PECO in the Kitmaster story is twofold; firstly they were the sole agents for the range of Arby Perfecta Kits introduced from 1960 onwards and secondly, they introduced their own interior kits for the Kitmaster Coaches. The Arby 'Perfecta' motorising kits are dealt with in the section covering all chassis and motorisation kits.

**Peco Coach Interiors** The successful introduction of scale-length Mk1 BR coaches in the 1960 Kitmaster range was a great step forward. Enthusiasts everywhere could at last build proper scale models of the modern rolling stock being introduced at that time. However, the kits, whilst offering many innovative features, lacked any sort of interior detail. This led PECO to develop a range of interior kits for the three Kitmaster 'OO' scale coaches. These card kits came as flat packs wrapped in acetate film. Each kit builds one complete interior for either a BSK, SK, SO or CK coach. Both the SK and SO interiors were fitted to the same Kitmaster coach shell, No.14, the Corridor Second. The kits, despite their simple material, were exceptionally well designed and proved very popular. In addition to the major

**More pages from the 1960 Trade Catalogue showing the Railway Lining Colours.**

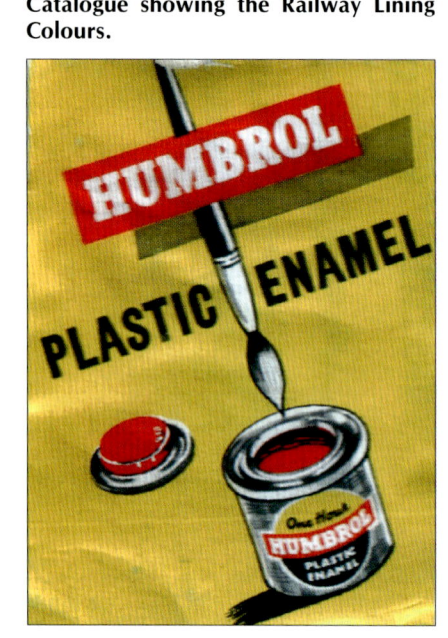

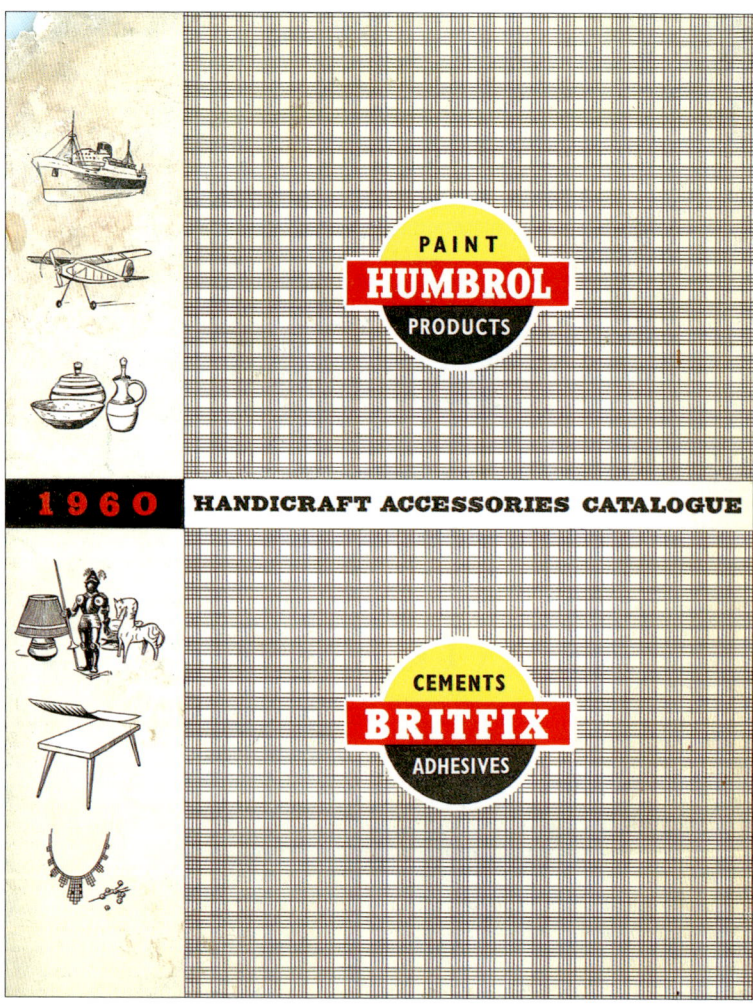

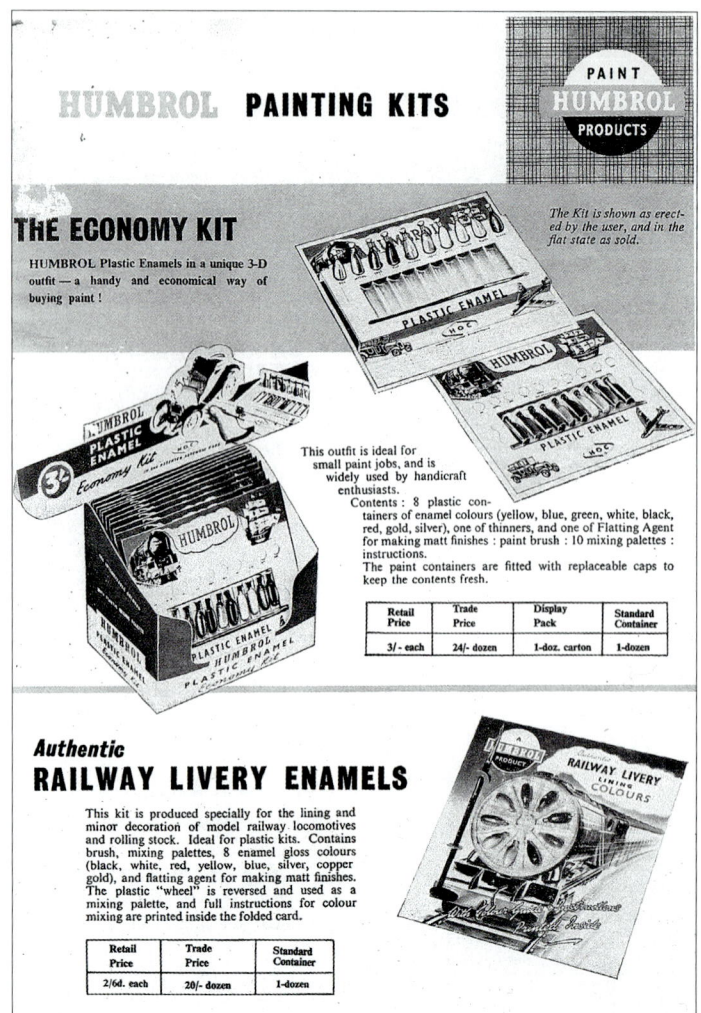

structural components of the coach, the kit provides interior fittings such as toilets, hand basins, periscopes and mirrors. Also included were people and baggage, all folded up from card! When carefully constructed, these full colour interiors look far better than the plain plastic moulding of the Tri-ang coaches.

They lent themselves to other adaptations as well. The CK kit can easily be made to fit the Tri-ang Railways Thompson LNER CK, which never had an interior. They can also be used for a range of other conversions. So successful were they, that they are still in print, in limited numbers, today. PECO extensively advertised them at the time and many different PECO ads exist which refer to the coach kits, often in connection with the aforementioned 'Perfecta' kits. Kitmaster themselves recognised the importance of interiors and with the later introduction of the Mk1 Restaurant First Open coach (No.28) in late 1961 they began to provide interior fittings. Even so, only the Pullman cars were treated in this way; the two HO coaches (No.27 and 29) never had interiors supplied.

PECO also had a marketing alliance with Kitmaster. Many of the early kits included a small black and blue leaflet produced by PECO which promotes the *Railway Magazine* and shows pictures from an article on motorising the Pug. Similar, but longer and printed in black and red, leaflets were also produced by PECO and included in certain Tri-ang Railways TT Train Sets. The text makes it clear that now you have purchased a Kitmaster model, you need to read *Railway Modeller* in order to make it go! In exchange, PECO took the 1960 Kitmaster catalogue as a loose insert in the July issue of that year.

Now rare, Humbrol point-of-sale displays were always very colourful and illustrated many of the hobby areas for which the paint and glue were suitable. At one point in the 1960s a range of moped touch up paint was launched alongside Railway & Military Authentic colours!

137

The four issued Perfecta kits with a motorised Pug.

Eames of Reading motorisation kits for the Airfix Railbus (left) and Drewry shunter (right).

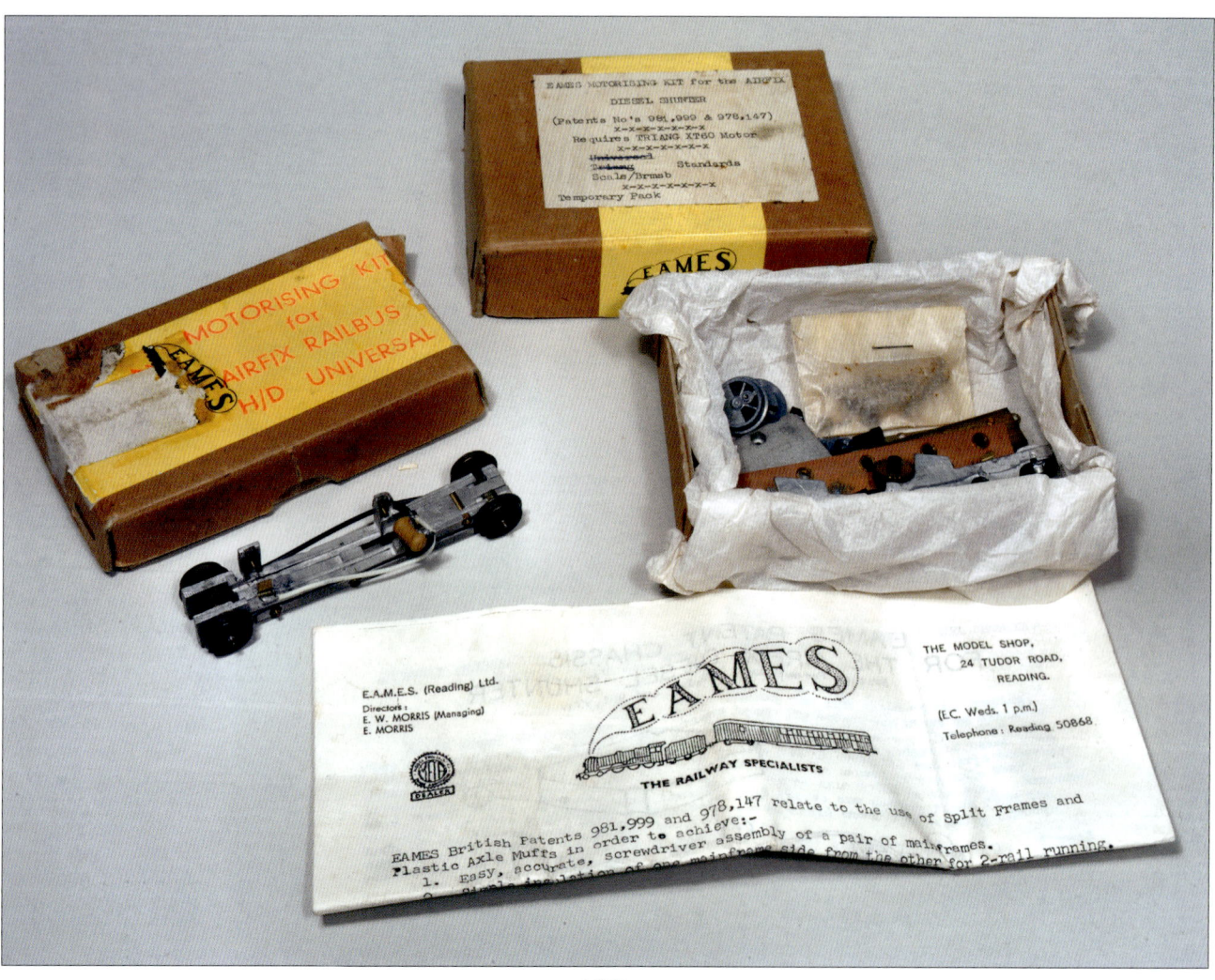

138

# Chapter 6

## Chassis and Motorisation Kits

The advent of a range of inexpensive static locomotive construction kits inevitably led to the introduction of many different products to enable them to run under their own power. We have already considered the Kitmaster solution to the problem – the motor bogie and the motorised box van. Now we shall consider some of the numerous products which emerged throughout the 1960s to enable Kitmaster locos to be motorised. This section is divided into two parts; those kits which provided only a chassis and those which attempted to provide all the necessary parts.

Perhaps the most famous, and sought-after, of all are the original Arby 'Perfecta' kits. Professionally designed and packaged, each Perfecta contained enough parts to modify a Kitmaster locomotive for 12 volt operation. All that was needed in addition was a motor. The sole concessionaires for Perfecta were PECO Products. The Perfecta kits, of which five were produced, but six advertised, came in professionally produced packs featuring a two-colour header card, either red, blue or green on black, with full instructions and diagrams as well as templates for those parts which needed cutting. The kits contain sleeves for axles, metal tyres for the wheels, pick up assemblies, phosphor bronze strip pickups, a cog and worm and even replacement plastic mouldings for certain body parts. These last parts are contained on a single injection moulded sprue in black polystyrene. Although the first kit to be launched was designed for the 'Pug', it was later redesigned for use with the Airfix Railbus. The Railbus was issued in 1961 and the necessary changes to Perfecta kit No.1 were put in place rather rapidly. The re-design resulted in a switch to the Tri-ang XT.60 motor, used in the other four Perfecta kits. The original kit No.1 had used a Romford 'Terrier' motor.

Table I: Arby Perfecta Kits

| Perfecta kit for Kitmaster [Kit No.] | Issued | Priced | Motor |
|---|---|---|---|
| No 1    L & Y Pug [6]       | Oct-59 | 8s 9d  | Terrier |
| No 1a   Pug & Railbus       | Mar-61 | 8s 9d  | XT60 |
| No 2    Italian Tank [8]    | Apr-60 | 8s 9d  | XT60 |
| No 3    Prairie Tank [7]    | May-60 | 11s 8d | XT60 |
| No 4    BoB Pacific [11]    | Jun-60 | 11s 8d | XT60 or X04 |
| (No 5)  Duchess [4]         | Jul-60 | 11s 8d | (X04) |
| No 5    City of Truro [24]  | Mar-61 | 11s 8d | X04 |

There is some uncertainty as to whether Perfecta Kit No.5 for the Duchess Pacific was actually issued. It was never advertised by PECO after the initial introductory range advertisement. Anyone who has one of these kits is asked to contact the Collectors Club. Certainly the fifth kit to be released was for the City of Truro and this has been confirmed by the Club. Although K's never actually produced a 'motorising kit' as such, they did produce a range of motor bogies for Kitmaster locos. These were as follows:

1. General long wheel-base power bogie for large steam locomotive tenders, for example Evening Star and Duchess of Gloucester, introduced in July 1960. 2. Medium wheel-base bogie for the prototype Deltic plus special cast sideframes, introduced in May 1962, priced £2.3.6d + 3s 6d for the sideframes. 3. Short wheel-base bogie for the driving motor brake first of the Midland Pullman plus special sideframes, introduced in February 1962. Price £2.2.9d + 1s 6d for the sideframes. Of these, the tender units are most common today, the Collectors Club has recently handled both a 9F and a Stirling 8ft Single locomotive motorised in this way. The others are extremely elusive. The favourite Deltic motorisation method seems to have been a Tri-ang Class 31

**Wilro Models "Simplas" chassis for the Airfix re-issues, including (centre) the J94 tank.**

139

or 37 chassis or, occasionally, a Hornby-Dublo Deltic chassis. Most Midland Pullmans were done with either the KM1 Kitmaster motor bogie or the Tri-ang DMU motor bogie from which the former was shamelessly copied!

Surrey Model Centre (SMRS) was actually the first into this market with its motorisation pack for the Schools. A straightforward 0-4-0 brass chassis was provided, largely replacing the existing plastic one and having an X.04 motor mount (but no motor). Current collection and transmission of power is all housed in the brass chassis unit, making this an easy conversion. The existing front bogie and valve gear were retained, but a metal coupling rod was provided. Correct scale metal wheels were also included. A quick and neat conversion, but few survive today.

**Chassis Kits**
Many different chassis kits were produced, in whitemetal, brass and, more recently, in etched nickel silver. The best of these are undoubtedly the superb second edition Kemilway chassis for the Mogul and the Bulleid Pacific. Unfortunately, neither of these is currently in production. However, Comet and Crownline do make excellent chassis for the Battle of Britain, whilst Branchlines of Exeter make excellent chassis kits for the Mogul, Class 08, Class 04 and Railbus.

---

*A complete "motorised"*
## TENDER CHASSIS

**ready to run—only 42/- —including P.T.**

Ideal for motorising your KITMASTER tender locos 7 ft. 6 in. x 7 ft. 6 in. for L.M.S. City; 6 ft. 6 in. x 6 ft. 6 in. for Stirling, M. Navy & Schools.

Now that we have redesigned all the loco kits to include full length brass chassis, we are able to offer the chassis as a separate unit. Set includes:
Brass frames, frame spacers, coupling rods (correctly shaped), cast keeper plate, seating block for K's motor, and all screws and washers.

**Price only 10/6 including P.T.**

### Do you know? Humbrol now produce
### 31 different colours for model railways

| | | | | | | | |
|---|---|---|---|---|---|---|---|
| LNER Loco, Green | 101 | LMS Maroon. | | BR Loco-Hauled Stock, Lining | 115 | CPR Tuscan Red | 123 |
| GWR Coach Stock, Chocolate | 102 | BR Loco-Hauled Stock, Maroon | 108 | BR Coach Stock, Crimson. | | CPR Grey | 124 |
| GWR Coach Stock, Cream | 103 | BR Roof Paint, Lead | 109 | LMS Crimson Lake | 116 | CNR Yellow | 125 |
| GWR Standard Loco, Green | 104 | BR Freight Stock, Red Bauxite | 110 | GE Blue | 117 | CNR Green | 126 |
| GWR Freight Stock, Grey | 105 | BR Freight Stock, Grey | 111 | LNER Garter Blue | 118 | Also available:— | |
| SR Green, Malachite | 106 | BR Interior Paint, Stone | 112 | Track Colour (Matt) | 119 | Black | 127 |
| LMS Wagon, Grey | 107 | BR Multi-Unit Stock, Green | 113 | Signal Yellow | 120 | White | 128 |
| | | BR Coach Stock, Cream | 114 | Signal Red | 121 | Silver | 129 |
| | | | | CPR Yellow | 122 | Gold | 130 |
| | | | | | | Copper | 131 |

**All 1/- per tin** Full range always in stock together with K's special track colour at 1/9 per tin.

**K's** PRECISION MODEL ENGINEERS
Hanover Court · 197 Uxbridge Road · Shepherds Bush W.12
Proprietors: N. & K. C. Keyser    Telephone: SHEpherds Bush 5254

★ K's = GOOD VALUE · FINE QUALITY AND DETAILS SECOND-TO-NONE

---

K's motor bogies for (left) the Deltic and (right) the Pullman power cars.

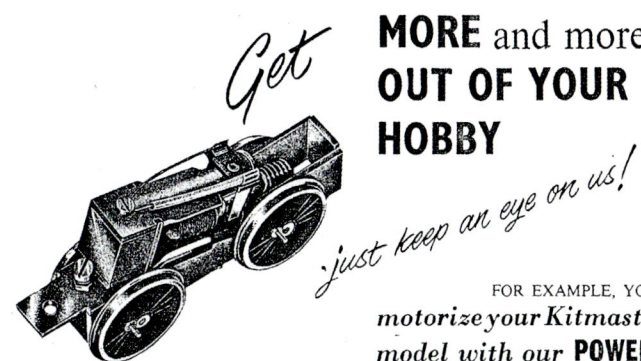

## Get MORE and more pleasure OUT OF YOUR HOBBY

*...just keep an eye on us!*

FOR EXAMPLE, YOU CAN *motorize your Kitmaster "Schools" model with our* **POWER UNIT**

TRI-ANG motor with full scale wheels, complete with full instructions for fitting ... £2/12/6

ALSO AVAILABLE FOR TRI-ANG TRACK ... £2/8/-

### BASEBOARDS

2in. × 1in. machined framing faced with ½in. Sundela semi-hardboard.

| SIZE | PLAIN | MATT GREEN PAINTED |
|---|---|---|
| 6ft. × 4ft. | £3/0/0 | £3/10/0 |
| 5ft. × 3ft. | £2/10/0 | £3/0/0 |

Carriage 7/6 in England.

4 legs 2in. × 2in. with fixing bolts : 15/-

### SETS FOR CHRISTMAS

We can supply sets in Tri-ang or Trix complete with mains transformer unit and either 6ft. × 4ft. or 5ft. × 3ft. baseboard.

Prices from £7 or from 20/- deposit and 8 monthly payments of 16/6.

### REMEMBER

We supply all model railway goods on

**10 WEEKS' or 9 MONTHS' CREDIT**

*Send for* **DETAILED LISTS**

**ALL MODEL RAILWAY EQUIPMENT STOCKED**

TRI-ANG, TRIX, WRENN, MASTERMODELS, FALLER, HORNBY-DUBLO, VOLLMER, MODELCRAFT, AIRFIX, PECO, H & M CONTROLLERS, LILIPUT. Mail orders welcomed. POST FREE

## Surrey Model Railway Supermarket  S. FRENCH & SONS LTD.

Dept. RMT, 450 EWELL ROAD, TOLWORTH, SURREY  Telephone ELMbridge 1325

PLEASE TELL YOUR FRIENDS ABOUT THE RAILWAY MODELLER

---

Others in this field included the 'Simplas' chassis range produced in 1967 by Wilro Models Ltd. of 20 Clarence Road, Clapton, London E5. Messrs Williams and Roland (hence Wil-Ro) designed, manufactured and marketed these Simplas chassis kits from their model shop. The centricast machine was in the back of the shop and these two affable gentlemen persuaded local model builders to donate any unwanted whitemetal scrap parts to their melting pot! They produced at least seven chassis, for the Pug, Evening Star, City of Truro, Biggin Hill, J94, Prairie Tank and Schools, each using the appropriate Romford wheel pack. They were attempting a kit for the Railbus when they split up their partnership and closed the business, so it is therefore unlikely that this kit was marketed. Eames of Reading already had a Railbus chassis kit on the market, so one wonders why they bothered in the first place. Also worth noting is the current production 'Simple Chassis' for City of Truro and Biggin Hill by West Coast Kit Centre. Both Romford and Westward produced packs of wheels and bearings for the Class 9F, although no separate chassis existed. G & G Scale Models produced a chassis pack, which included a turned brass chimney and dome, in etched brass for the Stirling Single, whilst H & N produced a rudimentary kit for the Pug. Current production is limited to the West Coast Kit Centre's 'Simple Chassis' range which includes the BR Mogul, Pug, City of Truro and Battle of Britain.

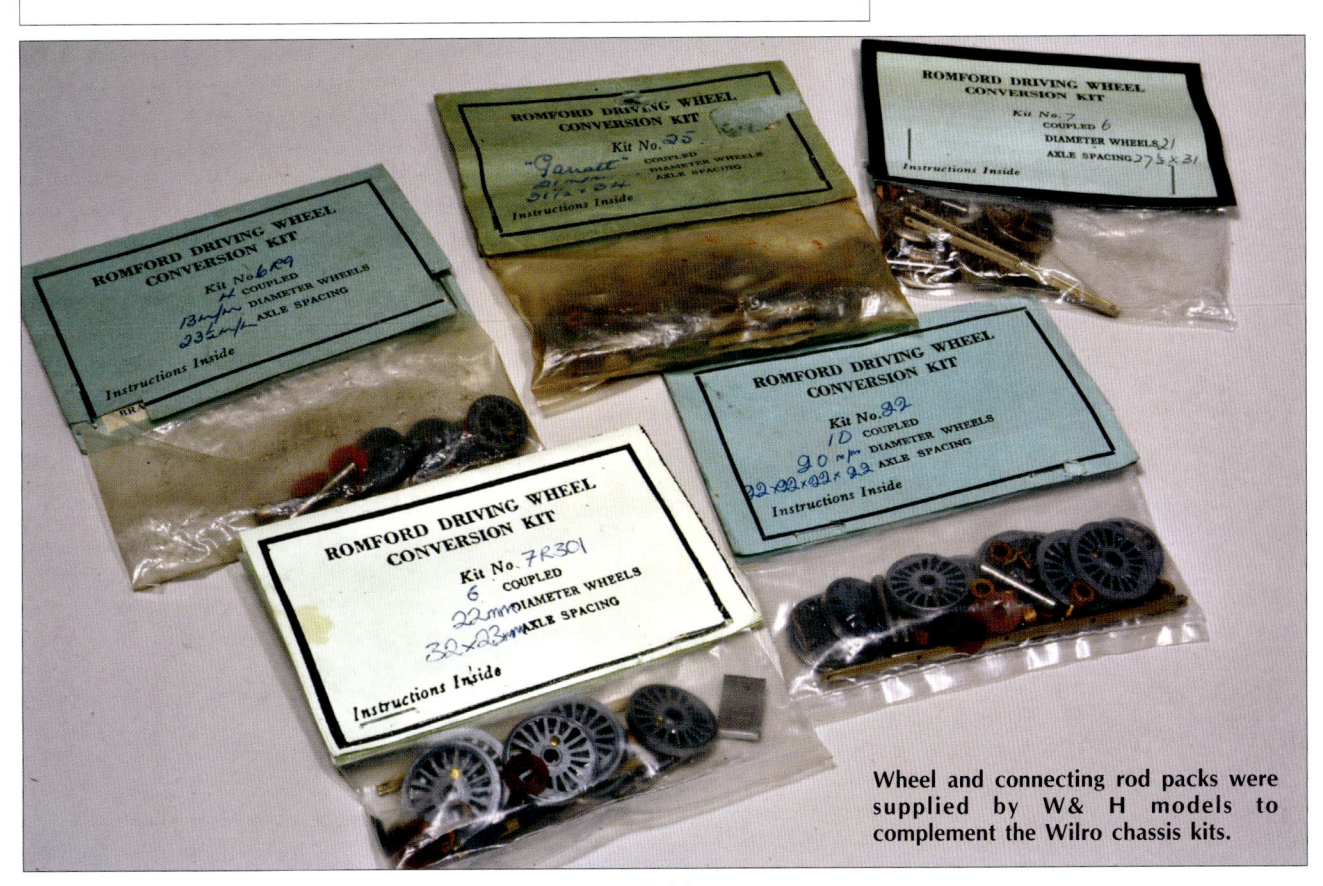

**Wheel and connecting rod packs were supplied by W & H models to complement the Wilro chassis kits.**

141

A fully fitted out Perfecta kit No.4 for the Battle of Britain – their most ambitious design yet.

Brass chassis frames were the highlight of Bristol Models motorising kits; not for the inexperienced modeller.

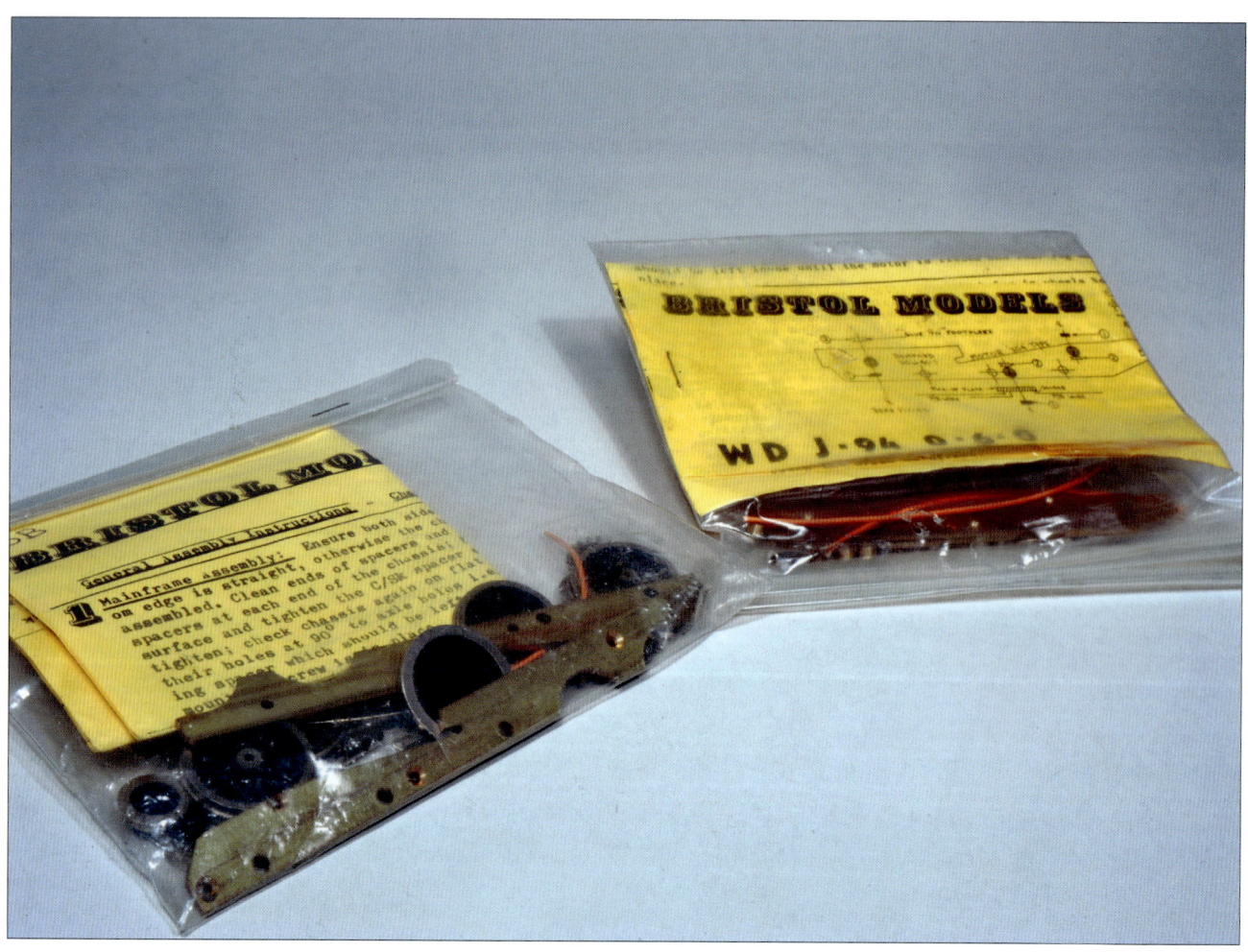

142

# NOW...

*A cut-away model showing the motor installed.*

## 'BATTLE of BRITAIN'

Now you can have the popular Battle of Britain Pacific Locomotive to add to your stud of power-driven Kitmaster models. All the parts you need. Nickel-silver tyres, current collectors, gears, axle sleeves, bearings, wires and weights, plastic parts, etc., conveniently packaged together. Complete with well-detailed, illustrated Instructional. Price only **11/8**, including Purchase Tax.

Apart from the Battle of Britain, there are three other Perfecta Kits to power-drive Kitmaster locomotives. No. 1 for the 0-4-0 Saddle Tank, price **8/9**, No. 2 for the 0-6-0 Italian Tank, price **8/9**, and No. 3 for the ever-popular 2-6-2 Great Western Prairie Tank, price **11/8**. Motors extra. If you have not already obtained these do so without delay as supplies are now limited.

For Kitmaster Coaches—Peco Interiors add the final touch of realism. Four types now available—Nos. 13, 14K, 14SO, 15. All at one price, **2/9** each.

| COMPLETE COST ! | | |
|---|---:|---:|
| KITMASTER LOCOMOTIVE KIT | 10 | 6 |
| PERFECTA KIT ... | 11 | 8 |
| XT60 MOTOR ... ... | 12 | 10 |
| PECO COUPLING HOOKS | 1 | 6 |
| | 36 | 6 |

# PERFECTA KIT ④

COMPLETE REVISED PECO CATALOGUE 1/6, by post 2/-

SOLE SALES CONCESSIONAIRES :—

**TRADE ENQUIRIES TO THE MANUF.**
**THE PRITCHARD PATENT PRODUCT Co Ltd**
**PECOWAY—STATION ROAD—SEATON—DEVON**
TEL. & GRAMS—SEATON 542

PLEASE TELL YOUR FRIENDS ABOUT THE **RAILWAY MODELLER**

The Pressflow cement van artwork, thought to be Charles Oakes, from a transparency retrieved from the skip outside the Coalville factory.

The 10 ton Meat Van artwork exactly matched the official BR photograph supplied byt the Press Office.

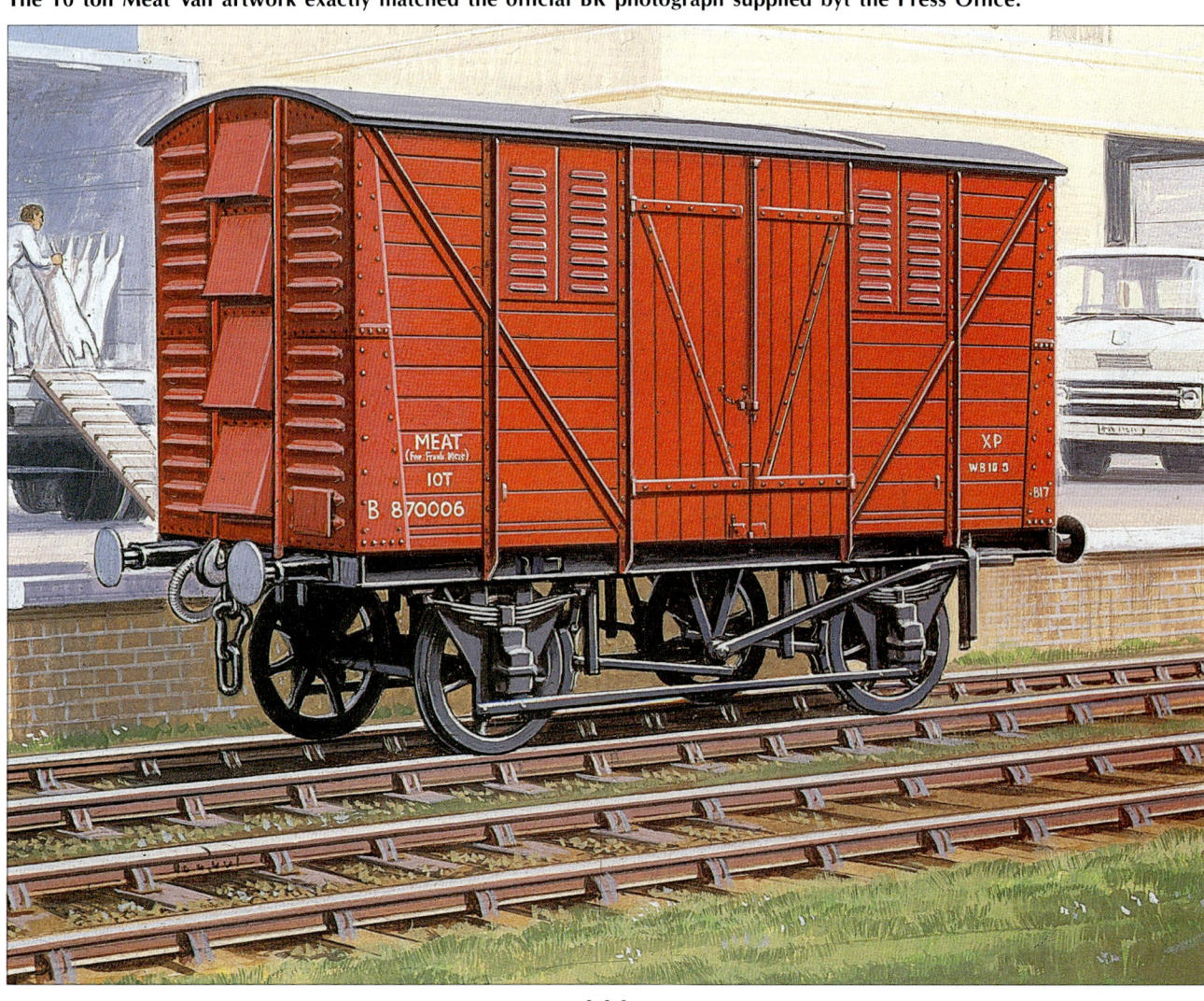

# Chapter 7 - Rise and Fall - The Airfix Reintroductions

**An Introduction to the complex history of Airfix**

It is hard to make money from running a plastic kit business it would seem. Since the very first injection moulded kits were introduced into the UK in 1936, many companies have come and gone. On paper the business model does not look attractive. Invest heavily in expensive steel tools, heavy marketing and promotion to sell a low-cost product with unattractive margins to a public that at best is nit-picking and can even be downright hostile. If you can sell 8-10000 of each model you will recoup your tooling costs.....

Airfix, Kitmaster, Revell GB, Merit, Kleeware, Comet, Lindbergh, Faller, Lincoln, Aurora, KielKraft, Gowland, and FROG have all come and, in most cases, gone again over the past fifty years. Some have changed ownership, some have merged with competitors whilst others have simply disappeared; all of them tried to develop their own range of injection-moulded plastic kits.

So it seems slightly ironic that Hornby Hobbies, one-time owner of Tri-ang Model Land and FROG kits should now be the proprietor of perhaps the most famous kit line of all – Airfix Products. Both companies had dabbled in each other's markets with Airfix introducing model racing cars as early as 1961 and ready-to-run model railways in 1977. These competed directly with Hornby Hobbies' mighty Scalextric and Hornby Railways brands, whilst Airfix kits took on Hornby's FROG construction kits up to 1976.

The history of the two organizations is inextricably interwoven as tools are bartered, sold, swapped, exchanged and even lost between the two protagonists. To try to unravel the story, let's go once more back the early 1950s....

Airfix Products was founded by Hungarian refugee Nicolas Kove to make inflatable toys and later, cheap plastic combs by the revolutionary new method of plastic injection moulding. He chose the name "Airfix" as he believed successful companies should have names that put them at the beginning of trade directories. By 1948, Airfix was the country's largest producer of combs and was approached by Harry Fergusson, the tractor manufacturer, to see if Airfix could produce a cheap plastic model of one of his tractors for use by Fergusson salesmen. The limitations of the early low pressure and rather small injection moulding machines, most of which were hand-operated, meant that the Fergusson tractor had to be moulded as a series of smaller parts which were then assembled by a team of skilled workers into finished models. Fergusson pronounced himself very pleased with the model tractors and allowed Airfix to market them as a new toy under their own brand name "Airfix – Products in Plastics".

Soon it became obvious that more tractors could be sold if the price were lower and the best way to achieve this was not to assemble them, but to supply them as a kit of parts with a set of assembly instructions. Samples were made up in presentation boxes and approved by the Airfix board. However, when the boxed samples were shown to buyers at High Street retailer Woolworths, they were thought to be too expensive and a suggestion was made that the kit be supplied in a simple polyethylene bag with a printed paper "Header Card" which would double as an instruction sheet. Thus was born the very first bagged Airfix kit. It was an instant success and Woolworths buyers began to ask for different subjects to be modeled in the same way.

Tooling began for a small sailing ship, the Santa Maria, and a model of the 4.5 Litre Bentley in 1/32$^{nd}$ scale, both would compete with the new Gowland & Gowland kits of similar subjects, but at more competitive prices.. However, before these could be issued, another special commission was received, this time from the Shaw Savill shipping line. To promote their two new luxury cruise ships, the Northern Star and the Southern Cross, they wanted a plastic scale model to be available in the on board shop. Airfix rose to the occasion with a respectable, if somewhat simplistic, 1/600$^{th}$ scale model of the liner *Southern Cross*, issued in 1955.

The range of poly-bagged kits now included eight galleons, four cars and numerous aircraft, the earliest of which was the Spitfire, coded BT-K, an Me109G, Gloster Gladiator and Westland Lysander. In 1956 a rather good model of the Westland S55 in full BEA markings joined the range, the first of many helicopters. That year also saw the introduction of an entirely new series of Trackside Accessories "for use with OO/HO scale model railways", although in fact they were all 4mm/ft scale. The first six kits featured a Detached House, Country Inn, Thatched Cottage, Service Station, Bungalow and a Signal Box.

*Above and below.* **Two more rescued transparencies, for the Airfix Type 2 boxes; they were re-used for Type 4A re-issues. The Brake Van and the Tank wagon were both long-lived in the range.**

Although there was no interior the Signal Box was heralded by the model railway press of the time as a revolution in structure modeling. The Trackside series eventually ran to more than twenty different models and is covered in detail in "The Airfix Models in Detail, Chapter Eight".

Meanwhile, Airfix diversified into more and more subjects. In the late 1950s

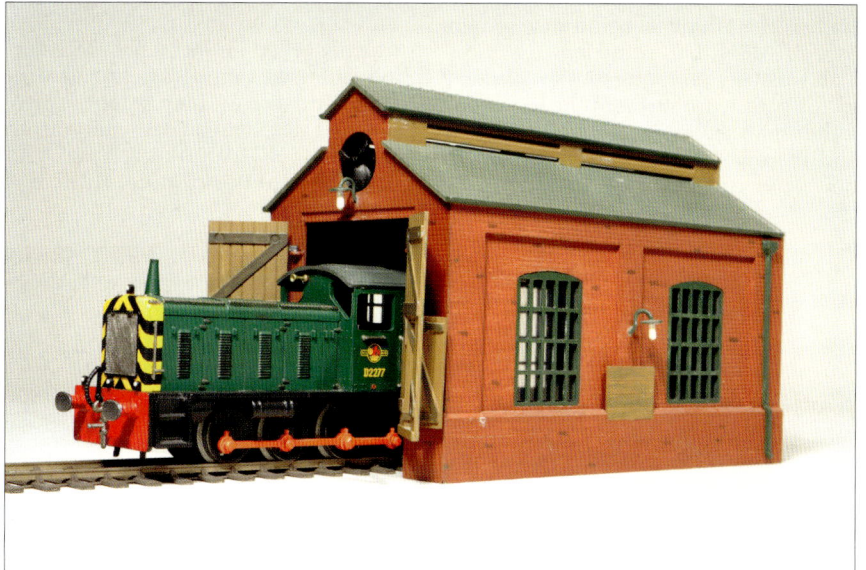

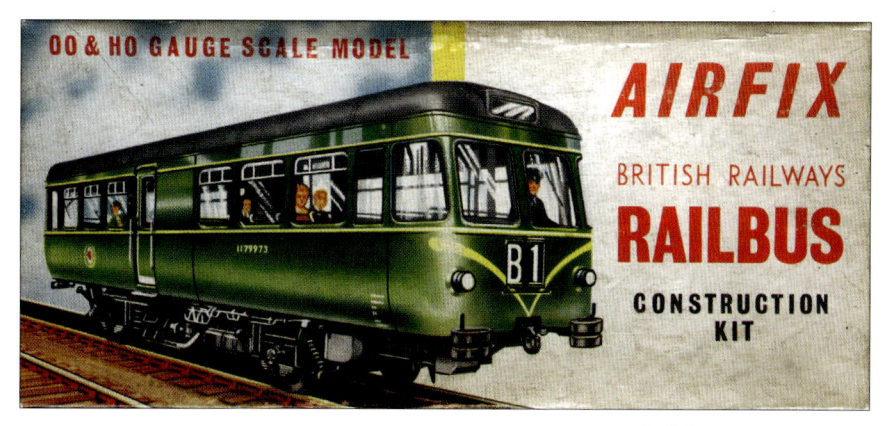

Armoured Fighting Vehicles joined the kit line and polythene ready-made versions of the same joined the Toy Division (always kept separate by Airfix managers). 1960 saw the famous 1/12$^{th}$ scale figures introduced such as Napoleon, Joan of Arc and Henry VIII. Later still came life-size birds, a range of dinosaurs and science fiction subjects. By 1980 there were over 800 tools in the factory although not all of them were in use at once, as subjects came and went from the brightly-illustrated annual catalogues. Indeed some models such as the excellent Scammel Scarab, introduced to the Trackside Series in 1960, exited the catalogue by 1963 never to return, whilst stable mates such as the Mineral Wagon and Brake Van remained in near-continuous production from 1959-1980. In 1963 the ex-Kitmaster tooling gave Airfix their first motorcycle kit, the Ariel Arrow Super Sports in 1/16$^{th}$, forerunner of an entire series in this scale.

Airfix began to produce licensed products in the 1960s. The earliest was the Fireball XL5 model for Lyons Maid in 1963, although this was only a promotion and you could not buy the kit in the shops. It was followed by another Lyons Maid kit for Stingray in 1964. The introduction of the Angel Interceptor, Monkeemobile, James Bond & Odd Job figures and Bond's Aston Martin DB6 showed that Airfix could successfully licence and market film and TV related product.

With interests in plastic shoes, storage containers and children's toys, Airfix was a diverse group. When Mecanno and Dinky Toys were purchased from the Receiver of Dumbee Combex Marx (owner of Tri-ang Hornby Railways) in the early 1970s the group was at its most diverse. It was also financially at its most stretched. The 1977 introduction of the entirely new ready-to-run model train system, Airfix Model Railways (Later "GMR"), was a severe financial burden on the company, with enormous tooling and launch marketing costs. The choice of a Class 31 diesel as the launch locomotive was unfortunate. The model was only slightly better than that already marketed by Hornby and the Mark 2 coaches, whilst well received, were limited in the liveries they could carry. In addition, equal numbers of each type of coach were ordered from the Chinese factory, leading to massive overstocks which persisted long after the demise of Airfix Products Ltd. Indeed, when Palitoy pulled out of the European market in 1982, pallet loads of Mark II brake coaches, which they had inherited as part of the Airfix Railways business, were literally bulldozed into a large pit outside the Coalville factory!

The financial pressure on Airfix led to its first collapse in 1980. A very nice OO scale assembly kit of a London taxi and Leyland Titan bus had been drawn up. (See Chapter 8) They were not to

*Top.* Marcus Archer completed this Railbus to the highest standards. *Above.* A Drewry Shunter is stabled in the charming Airfix Engine Shed, modelled on GWR designs. *Below.* The Airfix Type 2 artwork for the Park Royal Railbus. In later issues, the "M" was retouched out, as all units were by then transferred to Scotland.

**...it even has cab controls!**

*This Airfix OO/HO scale Drewry Shunter is a model of detail that can be motorised. 67-part kit 2/-. It's typical of the realism you get with Airfix models. They're just like the real thing! More than that, though, Airfix give you constant scale, so that the models of every series are proportionately right; and a great ever-increasing range — there are 11 series now, with over 200 kits. At prices from 2/- to 15/-. Airfix are great on value too.*
*For endless modelling fun—make it Airfix.*

**JUST LIKE THE REAL THING!** **AIRFIX** **CONSTANT SCALE CONSTRUCTION KITS**

*From model and hobby shops, toy shops and F. W. Woolworth*

**STOP PRESS!**

**LATEST AIRFIX PRODUCTION — PRAIRIE TANK**
True to the finest detail is this brilliant OO/HO gauge working model of the B.R. 6100 class Prairie tank. Can be motorized. A superb 59-part kit complete with transfers and detailed colour guide. 4/6.
**ALSO NEW:** The U.S. Marines in action! A 46-piece set of OO/HO scale figures. 2/-.

**GET YOUR CATALOGUE** — 32 pages of models, facts and kit details from your dealer - only 9d

PLEASE TELL YOUR FRIENDS ABOUT THE RAILWAY MODELLER

see the light of day, as the assets of Airfix were bought by Palitoy. Kit production was moved to the Heller factory at Trun in France, whilst model trains were consolidated at the Mainline plant in Coalville. Unfortunately, General Mills decided to abandon toy production in Europe in 1984, resulting in Airfix coming back onto the market. Tooling for a ready to run "Schools" class loco and a range of Bulleid coaches was in preparation at Coalville but never issued. This time it was bought by the group which owned Humbrol and Heller, Bordon International. Kit production remained with Heller, but design management moved from Coalville in Leicestershire to Humbrol's HQ at Marfleet, Hull, the trade name Humbrol being an acronym for "HUMBeR OiL company"

It was very tempting for new owners of Airfix to work through the tool store rather than try to develop new models and there was certainly a lack of good new tools until very recently. Only in the last 10 years has Airfix been able to once again develop modern tooling to extend the range. A whole series of superb 1/48th scale models heralded the new era including a Blackburn Buccaneer and a de Haviland Mosquito. These were very well received and the future for Airfix as they passed their 50th Anniversary looked bright. However, Bordon had financially split the group into separate operating companies. Whilst Airfix appeared healthy and was launching fast-selling new products such as the ill-fated, but highly regarded, British Aircraft Coproration TSR-2 in 1/72nd scale, Heller was moribund. As Heller were still producing the mouldings for Airfix, this caused a major headache when in July 2006 Heller suddenly called in the French Receiver. Production was immediately halted in France and try as they might, Airfix could not get hold of kits made from their own tools! Unfortunately, with no end in sight to this dispute, Airfix lost

**The two Airfix original "locomotives" – Railbus and Drewry Shunter make a pleasing pair.**

148

# NEWS from AIRFIX

## The world's greatest value in construction kits

AIRFIX Products Ltd., already Europe's largest manufacturers of scale plastic construction kits, are extending their range to include model railway rolling stock.

The new kits, which will appear from the end of June, conform to OO and HO gauges and, despite their low price of 2s., each possess detail and accuracy hard to find in ready made rolling stock many times the price.

Airfix rolling stock kits may be made up either as Display Models or as fully working units of a scale railway layout, and are fitted with a plastic coupling similar to the N.M.R.A. type. Provision has been made to enable all British Commercial Couplings to be fitted to this chassis.

The first two Airfix Series I OO and HO gauge kits to be introduced are of a British Railways Tank Wagon finished in the colours of Esso and a Presflo Cement Wagon in the livery of the Cement Marketing Company.

### Esso Tank Wagon

Over 800 of this type of wagon were ordered by Esso Petroleum Co. Ltd., from various builders. Two classes were built, Class A for carrying petrol and highly inflammable products and Class B for transporting fuel oils, diesel oils and kerosenes.

The Class B tank barrel is painted black with two white stars to denote acceptance for higher speed working.

In true life it measures 27 ft. 9½ in. long and 12 ft. 6 in. high, and in model form, using Airfix couplings, is 4¾ in. long and 2 in. high.

*The Airfix Esso Tank Wagon*

The kit incorporates 46 parts and uses natural matt black plastic, thus making painting of all but the axle boxes and buffer faces quite unnecessary. An excellent set of correct Esso transfers, wagon numbers and speed stars is also included. The kit comes in a gaily coloured cardboard box which is large enough for storing the completed model when not in use.

### Presflo Cement Wagon

The first of the modern 'Presflo' wagons was designed and built by British Railways at Shildon in 1954 and has since been copied by various well-known rolling stock builders.

During 1955 and 1960 some 60 'Presflos' were built for the Cement Marketing

*The Presflo Cement Wagon*

Company by Butterley Company Ltd., and have several detail improvements over earlier designs to enable speedier and more complete unloading. The cement, incidentally, is loaded by gravity and discharged by air pressure through a flexible pipe either to a storage silo or direct to a road vehicle.

Length over buffers is 19 ft. 11 in. and the height 11 ft. 9 in. The Airfix model measures 4⅝ in. over couplings and 1¾ in. high.

There are 50 parts in the kit, which is produced in canary yellow to eliminate painting of all but the chassis, ladder, catwalk and manhole covers. If the chassis is painted prior to fitting the body a very smart model will result. No fewer than eleven subjects are incorporated on the "Blue Circle" transfer sheet supplied.

## AIRFIX TO PRODUCE ROLLING STOCK SERIES

WHILE samples of all their models were not shown by Messrs. Airfix, we have learnt from them that they are to introduce, apart from their new Lineside items mentioned in January, a series of the most unusual rolling stock. The first of these will be an accurate model of the fifty-seater four-wheeled rail-bus, Park Royal type, fitted with seats and, in fact, all internal detail. Secondly there will be an oil tank wagon, and thirdly a bulk cement wagon. This should make a most attractive model, as it is a hopper-type vehicle having an abundance of angle-iron supporting members and other detail, which will lend itself admirably to plastic production.

In addition there will be other items, but we have been asked particularly to stress that it will be some little time before any of these are released on the market. They will be in their standard self-colour kit form and at their usual very modest prices. Full review will be given as they become available.

---

still very high by later standards, but post-war improvements in production techniques and polymers meant that by 1950 FROG was a leading manufacturer of injection-moulded polystyrene kits.

Throughout the 1950s and 1960s FROG kits sold well, eventually counting some 200 subjects in the catalogue including the R-100 Airship (pictured) airliners such as the Jersey Airlines Dart Herald and Quantas 707, together with the latest military planes such as the V-Bombers, represented here by the Handley Page Victor. The company was fully a part of Rovex Ltd and as such production moved to Margate in 1962. The parent company was Dumbee-Combex-Marx, a wide ranging and poorly managed combine with interests in several sectors of the toy market. When Dumbee Combex Marx was approached by a Russian trade delegation to discuss licensing its old tools, it was FROG kits which made the biggest impression on the men from Moscow. From 1972 until 1976 more and more FROG tools were sent to Russia until eventually there were none left in the UK. The idea was that the Russians would pay for the tools by sending back completed mouldings that could be marketed as cheaper kits in the West. Unfortunately the appalling quality of the polystyrene in use, the over-pressure running of the tools and unfeasibly long delivery times from the inefficient Russian factories all conspired to produce a wholly unsaleable product. Thus ended major kit production at Margate. But not every plastic kit tool had gone to Russia.

Tri-ang Railways had themselves developed a range of plastic assembly kits during 1960 called Real Estate. These were made by IMA at Merton for Tri-ang Railways and depicted a very nice range of buildings for OO and TT model railways (according to the catalogue). As the range grew and more buildings were added, production was transferred to Margate in 1964. This was the height

---

the confidence of their own bankers, who called in their overdraft. This forced the UK company into liquidation as well. Two new moulds, the 1/48th scale Nimrod and a 1/72nd scale Lifeboat were in advanced stages of development, but not actually in the country or under Airfix control.

This was the situation that Hornby Hobbies found towards the close of 2006 and from which they successfully extricated the Humbrol and Airfix businesses. Hornby are well placed to run these as their Chief Executive, Frank Martin, is a former CEO of Humbrol. In addition, Hornby have always had an association with plastic kits ever since 1936. In that year, Lines Brothers, owner of Tri-ang, took an interest in a small company called IMA, International Model Aircraft. Earlier, they had developed a flying scale model aeroplane powered by a patented geared elastic band system with a novel winding handle. The name of this new product

was "Flies Right Off the Ground", or FROG for short.

The idea caught on rapidly in the UK and overseas and every boy wanted a FROG for Christmas. Cheaper versions were produced as well as different models attempting to portray other prototypes. In 1936 FROG decided to introduce smaller, more accurate, but static scale model aircraft. They had been experimenting with a machine for making propellers for the flying models by injection moulding in cellulose acetate. It was suggested that this same, rather primitive, moulding machine could be used to produce the new smaller aircraft models. To distinguish them from the flying models these would be known as FROG Penguins (a non-flying bird). Production was halted by the war, but at that time there were roughly 20 designs in production ranging from a Percival Mew Gull to a large Short Singapore flying boat. Numbers were limited and the cost was

*Left:* The Kitmaster G.W.R. large Prairie has re-appeared as an addition to the Airfix range and is basically the same moulding with only a few detail alterations.

AIRFIX OO
G.W.R. 61XX Class 2-6-2T Kit 4s 6d

Since Airfix took over the Kitmaster stocks and moulds at the end of last year, modellers have waited with interest to see which, if any, of the former Kitmaster models would be reintroduced. The first has now appeared and is the popular 61XX "Prairie" tank. The new kit is basically similar to the original and appears to be produced from the original mouldings. Standard Airfix couplers have been incorporated on the leading and trailing pony trucks and a dummy coupling has also been added. The coupling is, however, of the three link type "instanter" coupling as fitted to certain vacuum brake-fitted wagons to provide loose- or close-coupling, not a screw coupling with which the 61XX locomotives are fitted. We are not pleased to see that the Kitmaster vacuum brake pipe has been retained, for the brake pipe used on some of the Airfix wagons would be almost ideal.

The components are moulded in black plastic and went together without any difficulty and, with a little care in assembling the wheels, the model will run freely when hauled by a powered locomotive. The leading pony did not perform very well on curved track as the axle tended to become jammed and lift one wheel off the track. Motorisation of the kit with a Tri-ang, Hornby or scale chassis is a reasonably easy operation and was described in the October 1959 issue of *Model Railway Constructor*, now out of print. We would not agree with the provision of steps on each side of the bunker. As built, steps were not provided on the bunkers but during the last ten years most of the class have had steps fitted on the fireman's (left-hand) side only. It is a simple matter, of course, to remove the steps on the other side.

The new style instruction sheet, dividing the construction into three stages and incorporating a suggested colour scheme, is provided. A note reminds modellers that the lion of the B.R. totem always faces the front of the locomotive. Although this was the case when the totem was adopted in 1956 it was later discovered to be technically incorrect, as the lion should only face towards the left and from about 1959 totems painted on both sides of a locomotive have the lion facing left. Both transfers supplied with the kit are, in fact, correct! It is pleasing to see that at least two of the former Kitmaster locomotives will be marketed again—these are the J94 0-6-0ST and L. & Y. "Pug" 0-4-0ST which are depicted, Kitmaster fashion, around the attractively designed box, together with the Airfix diesel shunter and mineral wagon.

**THE PROTOTYPE 61XX CLASS**

The 61XX class 2-6-2Ts were a development by Collett of his earlier 5101 class with increased boiler pressure. Seventy were built between 1931-5 for the London suburban services and in addition to A.T.C. apparatus, were fitted with trip apparatus for working over electrified lines. Most have always worked in the London Division, but a few were moved away in early B.R. days. In the mid-fifties some were transferred to other depots including Severn Tunnel Junction, which still has an allocation of three and uses them on the car-carrier services described in the July, 1963 issue of *M.R.C.*, and for assisting freight trains through the Severn Tunnel. In 1932, No. 6116 was experimentally fitted with smaller (5ft 3in) driving wheels, 3ft leading and 3ft 6in trailing pony wheels, instead of 5ft 8in, 3ft 2in and 3ft 8in wheels, respectively. This was to improve the acceleration and formed a basis for the rebuilding of Churchward 2-6-2Ts into the 81XX class.

Unlined green livery was applied to the 61XXs by the G.W.R. and lined black by B.R. until about 1956, when they were repainted lined green. This has remained the livery until recently when, in common with some other ex-G.W.R. types, a reversion to unlined green was made. Although diesel multiple-units have taken over the 61XX's passenger work in the London area, surprisingly few of the class have been withdrawn—18 only in the last five years—and 39 remain in the London Division. All depots in this division have examples on their allocation and use them on freight and general duties.

*Right:* The prototype of the Airfix model is seen here in lined green livery at Paddington. Note the slightly thicker chimney compared to the model and the lack of bunker footsteps on this side of the locomotive.
A. R. Butcher

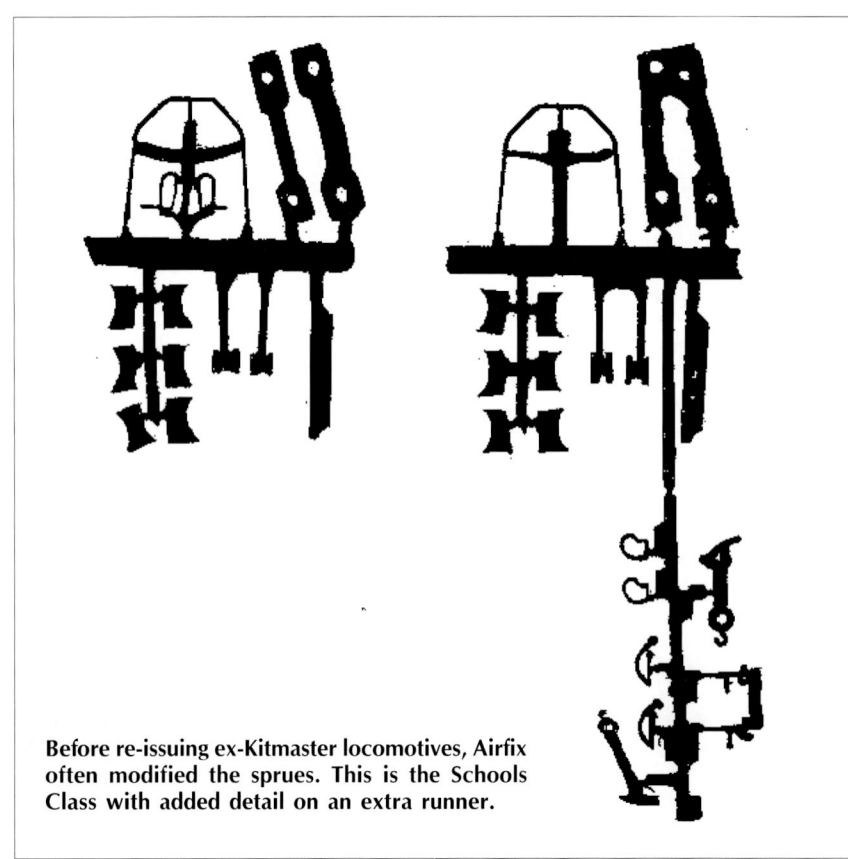

**Before re-issuing ex-Kitmaster locomotives, Airfix often modified the sprues. This is the Schools Class with added detail on an extra runner.**

of the range, which was re-launched as Tri-ang Model Land and now ran to more than twenty different models. The self-coloured plastic kits were easy to assemble and combined traditional dwellings such as thatched cottages and country inns with ultra-modern offices and shops. A church was included in the range and a fine model of an electricity pylon (based on one outside the Margate factory) was introduced. These two kits were to become the last items of Model Land to stay in production, with both marketed by Hornby Hobbies up until the late 1990s.

In 1972 Hornby had licensed a series of trackside structures from German kit company Pola. These included an operating lifting bridge and a coaling stage – both to Continental scale and pattern. Several of the subjects chosen to join the Hornby range had previously been licenced to both Jouef and Playcraft Railways, so had really done the rounds! The rest of the Tri-ang Model Land tools were shipped to Hong Kong at some point in the complicated history of DCM and got separated from the bulk of the Hornby Railways business when it underwent a management buy-out.

The tools eventually returned to the UK only to find their way to Dapol Model Railways in Winsford Cheshire (later at Chirk in Clywd), who had also purchased from Palitoy the Airfix Trackside kits together with Mainline and Airfix GMR trains. Dapol put the former Model Land tools into production as Dapol Land (Imaginative!) although they did re-name some of the kits. When in 1998 Dapol was approached to sell the Airfix GMR and Mainline tools to Hornby, the circle was completed. However, the plastic kit tools remain with Dapol to this day.

So today we have Airfix construction kits being made by Hornby, together with Airfix GMR trains, but not the Airfix trackside kits, which are controlled by Dapol along with the original Tri-ang Model land tools. And what of FROG? Some of their tools were sold off to Revell and Matchbox as the Russians did not want models of "fascist aircraft" whilst others are with Eastern Express and still in production.

After such a long and convoluted history, one wonders what the future holds now for the famous Airfix brand? At least today Hornby Hobbies has sound management and a broad distribution network. Airfix fits well into their portfolio and Hornby has been just the right company to give it the stability it needed to develop and launch the products that are once again making it the most famous kit manufacturer of them all.

***All images right.*** **The bi-lingual Anglo-French issues of Series Two wagons re-used the earlier artwork with a modified Airfix Type 4 logo and layout. The Meat Van was re-introduced, thus gaining the sobriquet "New" when in fact it was 15 years old!**

Almost from their inception, Airfix kits were grouped into 'Series' according to complexity and this was reflected in the price. In Series 1 were the simplest, smallest and cheapest kits, grading up to big expensive complex models in Series 20. The various styles of Airfix packaging are called 'Types' by collectors. Type 2 was in use when Airfix began their rolling stock series, but from 1963 Type 3 boxes began to appear, and lasted ten years or more.

**Airfix Rolling Stock Kits**
The advent of the plastic construction kit after the War has been well documented elsewhere. However, despite their involvement in assembly kits as early as 1949 and the large market for model railways, it was only in 1956 that Airfix Products Ltd began their now-famous association with railway modelling. Even then, the first range to see the light of day was the Trackside Series. A further four years were to elapse before Airfix contemplated a full-blown rolling stock kit. A press release at the March 1960 Toy Fair declared that Airfix would enter the 4 mm rolling stock market with a series of kits. Unusually, it was not a Series One 'pocket money' model, but a larger Series Two kit that was intended to launch the range. This was to be the Park Royal Railbus. However, it was beaten into production by the first of the Series One wagons and was not finally released until November 1960.

The first of the amazing Series One wagons had been given to the press for review in July 1960. Not one, but two models were issued together. These were the Class B Tank Wagon and the Presflo cement hopper. The choice of a tank wagon, whilst on the face of it not very interesting, was an inspired one. All the ready-to-run models lacked detail and did not at that time represent actual prototypes. Consequently, a good and above all accurate model of a modern Class B Tank

151

*Above and opposite.* **When first issued, most Airfix wagons were in Type 2 boxes with a central stripe in a contrasting colour. But by 1980, the squashed oval Airfix logo had appeared on Type 6 packaging. The end of Airfix as an independent company was not long in following. Classic Type 2 boxes shown here include the unique couplings (which was never re-issued) and two Series Two kits: the Booth Rodley Crane and Lowmac with JCB load.**

wagon was an immediate success. These wagons were well distributed around the country and could be seen in the hands of various locomotives. Your author regularly stood in awe on the west end of Basingstoke station watching the impressive Class 33 diesels hauling 30 or more such tankers up from the Exxon refinery at Fawley. I longed to model the whole train but alas, space restricted me to just six or seven tankers! Although Airfix provided markings for three different Esso tankers, they never considered the obvious attraction of issuing the kit in other petro chemical company liveries. That step was left to Dapol, who have recently issued it with BP markings.

The Presflo cement hopper, while similar to a pre-existing Hornby-Dublo model, was a really superb little kit of a distinctive prototype. *The Railway Modeller* looked forward to seeing all that angle iron portrayed in plastic, noting that it was the sort of vehicle exactly suited to injection moulding techniques. The bright yellow plastic and excellent well-reproduced decal sheet made it very easy to depict an example in the Blue Circle cement fleet with minimal effort. However, it was to be the third issue in the series that really caught the imagination of the modelling fraternity. This was the ubiquitous 16 ton steel mineral wagon. Built in their tens of thousands by British Railways and used for carrying all manner of traffic, this kit proved immensely popular. Whole block trains could now be constructed quickly and cheaply, as all these early Series One kits cost just two shillings each. Coming towards the end of 1961, about the time that Kitmaster released their excellent kit for the 9F, this was a modern image modeller's Mecca. All that was needed to complete the train was a standard 20 ton brake van and Airfix duly obliged in late 1961 with a well-received model of the same. Beautifully detailed and moulded in a dark brown plastic ready for painting, this kit set the standard for brake vans that others would have to follow. Not until late 1979, when Mainline introduced their RTR model, was it bettered.

Some of these early kits had extremely long production lives. Indeed, the Tank Wagon appeared in every Airfix catalogue except the final (17th) edition, and has been in production with Dapol for a another ten years since. The Mineral Wagon enjoyed similar favour with Airfix, appearing in 14 of the 17 catalogues. Not so fortunate was the 10 ton Ventilated Meat Van, which had a lamentably short run of just three years in the early 1960s and was then mothballed until the penultimate catalogue in 1979 when it made a welcome return. This model portrayed the louvred ventilators to perfection and even had opening doors. Another popular model was the Cattle Wagon. Though based on an earlier GWR diagram, like all the other kits in this series it was in fact a BR-built vehicle. The traffic in live beasts has long since disappeared from the railways and was steeply declining by the time the model appeared but it was a big seller in the 1960s. Accuracy and attention to detail meant that Airfix designers incorporated a removable partition inside which could be positioned to give a variety of sizes of stall. Naturally, all six doors could be made to open and the chassis had all the correct running gear. Next in line for release was an unusual and now hard-to-find kit. Not so much a kit, in fact, as an accessory pack.

This was R6, '24 Buckeye Couplings'. This pack provided enough extra couplings to convert a dozen wagons to the bizarre Airfix coupling system. According to the 2nd Edition catalogue:

152

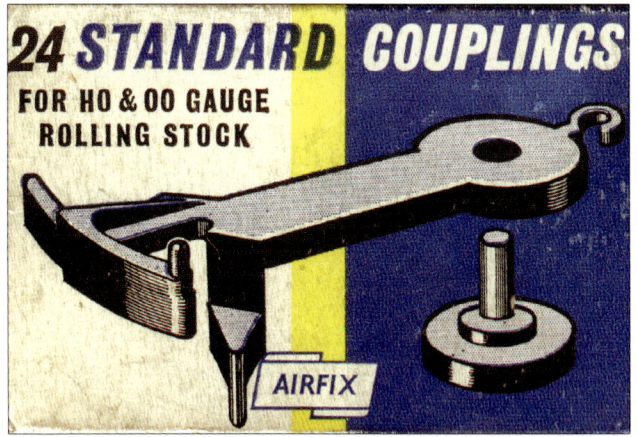

'Airfix have standardised on the NMRA buckeye coupling of type X2F. It allows automatic uncoupling with a simple ramp'. Fine, as long as it works, but as anyone who has tried will know, it doesn't! Understandably deleted after just 18 months in the programme, these couplers must surely rate as one of the most ill-considered ideas of any toy manufacturer. Why NMRA instead of BRMSA or Simplex? Nobody seems to know. like Kitmaster and their hook and eye arrangement, this vitally important part of the model seems to have been left to chance. The only easily fitted satisfactory coupling for these models is the Peco Simplex buckeye. It is close to impossible to fit the Airfix models with the Tri-ang tension lock coupling, which was establishing itself rapidly as the new standard at the time. Today, Dapol supply a useful little adaptor plate that will allow a Dapol or Airfix GMR coupling to be fitted, but frankly it is thirty years too late.

The seventh issue in this series was a milestone in kit history. While the Railbus was technically the first Airfix vehicle to move under its own power, it was not a locomotive as such. That honour fell to the delightful Drewry Shunter, pattern number R7. Classified under the 1970 TOPS system as Class 04, these 204hp diesel-mechanical shunters were a popular and widespread design. An early introduction under the Modernisation Plan and construction in large numbers put them at the head of the queue for a model. However, in reality these shunters were to have relatively short service lives with British Railways, being surpassed by the BR-built Class 03 shunter, with which they share certain similarities. Withdrawals began in the mid-1960s and by 1972 very few survived in capital stock. Many of them did, however, go on to useful lives in industry. Numerous kits were built and motorised, notably with the EAMES of Reading chassis kit and latterly with the Mainline and Bachmann 03 chassis. Now, of course, one can simply buy the excellent Bachmann RTR model off the shelf. The Drewry disappeared from the range after the 5th Edition and only resurfaced under Dapol's aegis. Next in the Series One range was the reissued Kitmaster Pug, No.R9. Priced at just two shillings, this represented great value. Formerly, it had retailed for 4s 6d as a Kitmaster kit.

The final Series One wagon issue was an interesting prototype. The Prestwin Pressure Discharge Silo Wagon is a good model with a wealth of detail. Although Hornby-Dublo had already produced a similar wagon in the Fisons livery, once more the Airfix issue was considerably cheaper and managed to encompass more detail in the walkways and valves on top of the tanks. The late issue date for the Prestwin ensured that it appeared in a rather good Type 3 box. All the previous wagons first appeared in classic Type 2 boxes.

The larger Second Series kits covered some remarkable vehicles. Starting, as noted above, with the Park Royal Railbus, the range served for the introduction of three other very interesting models. The first was the Booth Diesel Locomotive Crane. This unit was a self-propelled diesel-hydraulic crane capable of lifting 15 tons on the jib arm. Unfortunately, no model of the riding truck with the jib runner was forthcoming from Airfix and this remained a 'half-model'. It was rather good in operation, with a winding handle for the winch and a lifting, rotating jib. Mysteriously, this model was listed in the 17th Edition catalogue as a Series 3 kit, but was never issued as such. Next out was the one and only Airfix HO scale model, pattern number R203, the 'Interfrigo' Refrigerator Van. This vehicle, though widely used throughout Europe, had little appeal to the British modeller. A rather insipid pink, white and blue box combined with the chosen HO scaling to make this a distinctly poor seller and it was quickly deleted. Today, it is sought after in certain European circles and etched detailing kits are available from two

**The Presstwin Silo wagon was the only kit to be issued first in a classic Type 3 "red flash" box.**

manufacturers, in Denmark and France, to complete it to modern standards. With the opening of the Channel Tunnel and renewed interest in trans-European freight operations, perhaps the Interfrigo will yet come into its own?

The JCB and Lowmac was last to be introduced and was a truly superb kit. The JCB 3 is an excellent piece of modelling and it set the trend for a long line of outstanding OO scale civilian and military vehicles from Airfix. The Lowmac depicted was of the EU type, which nicely complemented Hornby-Dublo's EB version. Strangely, when Airfix introduced a ready-to-run version in the GMR range, it was of the Lowmac EK, thereby completing the trio. These wagon kits represent a selection of prototypes from the early 1960s. Some were unexciting, everyday types like the mineral wagon or brake van. Others represented the cutting edge of rail transport design. Together, they provide a fascinating snapshot of British Railways freight transport at the height of the modernisation plan.

The acquisition of all Kitmaster moulds and stock was formally announced in the *Railway Modeller* of December 1962, but it was several months before anything happened. Throughout 1963 Airfix continued to sell the stock and to supply orders for the promotional Nabisco models. Postmarks of 21.1.64 and 1.1.64 on Airfix postage labels are known to exist on Nabisco Deltic and 9F kit boxes. After carefully test firing all the tools, Airfix began an evaluation of which kits could be easily reintroduced, which would need some modification and which should be scrapped altogether. The decision was taken to scrap all the TT and Continental prototypes at this point. Due to the unique nature of the Kitmaster hook and eye coupling, and the earlier adoption of the NMRA Buckeye coupling for Airfix trackside rolling stock, there was a considerable delay while the tools were changed to accommodate new couplings. For reasons explained elsewhere, the Rocket kit had all the parts completely renumbered.

Airfix engineers reduced the diameter and shape of the sprue runs and made some additions to the tools, usually by lengthening a main sprue, to encompass more detail in the model. This enabled Airfix to save on the quantity of material used and to run the injectors at much higher pressure. Consequently, the first re-introduction turned out to be none other than the Ariel Arrow motorcycle; ironically, it had been the last kit produced by Kitmaster. Even this early reintroduction did not escape the watchful eye of the Airfix engineers, who introduced solid individual mouldings for the spokes instead of a clear disc of spokes. They also redrew the artwork to show the correct Birmingham registration number, 697 AOH which had always appeared on the decal sheet, even in Kitmaster days – as described earlier. It was advertised in all the railway modelling magazines in July 1963, just six months after the takeover. Initially issued as Series 1 in a bag with an Airfix Type 2 header in blue and yellow, it soon received an excellent Type 3 header with a Roy Cross painting of the bike in a suitably muddy off-road location for a sports bike of this nature. For the Type 4 issue it was boxed and moved up into Series 2, but retained the Cross artwork. It was last produced in 1980.

The first railway kit to reappear was the famous GWR 2-6-2T Large Prairie Tank, re-issued in October 1963. Only one change was apparent on the Prairie, the addition of optional scale three link couplings as well as the NMRA replacement couplers on the pony trucks. This was actually the very first Airfix kit of any subject to appear in the new Type 3 'Ribbon Logo' box style. Conversely, the 'Limited Production' issue was one of the very last reissues in the Type 3 box and actually has Type 4 logos on the end panels, a fate which also befell the City of Truro. These last two kit issues are believed to date from 1972-73. It took several years for the other kits to re-emerge. From then on they were in and out of the Airfix catalogue rather haphazardly, so that in the 16th edition catalogue the reintroduced Pug was described rather mysteriously as 'Ohio Saddle Tank'. One can only assume that they confused 0-4-0 and Ohio phonetically and then failed to spot the mistake. The Airfix decal sheet for the Pug always described it as 'Saddle 1 Tank' for some reason. Alternatively, perhaps the L&Y had shipped 'Pugs' to America without telling anyone! Considering that Airfix had the tools for the entire range, their choice of kits for re-issue was surprisingly limited.

Three of the best locomotives were honoured with Roy Cross paintings - Harrow, the BR Mogul and Biggin Hill. The Cross artwork is dramatically better than that used for the other models, showing far more attention to detail. When compared with Ken Rush's paintings for the original Kitmaster issues, the Cross artwork is in a different league. Indeed, the Cross box paintings show many details which are actually absent on the models, for example cylinder drain cocks on Harrow, various extra fittings on Biggin Hill and much of the ejector piping on the Mogul. Roy's big mistake, as described earlier, was the omission of a coupling rod! These artworks survived the period of Type 4 boxes, but were largely superseded by type 5, 6 and 7 issues. Harrow had a new and very different painting commissioned for the Type 6 issue showing the locomotive leaving Charing Cross Station on a Kent Coast service. Why this was done is a puzzle; the Pug, City of Truro and Evening Star only had modified original artwork in their Type 6 issues.

When Airfix was sold to Palitoy in 1980, all of the surviving moulds were again tested and any that were considered life-expired were earmarked for scrapping. This is the point at which the name of each tool was chalked onto the casing and where the Deltic, which was scheduled for scrapping, was inadvertently marked as the Drewry Shunter. The Beyer-Garratt and Duchess were scrapped at this point.

The main Airfix engineering changes are summarised in Table J. In all cases, new instruction leaflets, retaining the original Kitmaster text, were prepared, new transfers were printed which included the name of the kit and new boxes were designed, primarily for the American market.

During the period of 'limited production' the Prairie and City of Truro were issued as series 4 kits. These later reverted to series 3. Likewise the 9F was issued as series 5 and reverted to Series 4, while the Pug started as Series 1 and went to Series 2. The Rocket was heavily retooled to include plastic stays for the smoke stack and a Victorian crew. Although it was always a Series 1 kit, it appeared firstly in a small box, then in a plastic bag with paper header and finally in a Blister-pack!

### The Airfix Photographic Archive

The secret of good model making, as many people will testify, is having access to good photographs. So it is with good tool and pattern making. One only has to look at the Kitmaster Duchess kit, prepared directly from Frank Roche's drawings, to see what mistakes one can make by relying too heavily on one source. Airfix Products Ltd prided themselves, quite rightly therefore, on having extensive photographic archives from which to develop their models. Indeed, many priceless photographs from the Second World War were included in their collection, including motor-drive sequences of classic sea-borne fighters making carrier landings and take-offs. With newer products such as the 1974 issue of the Morris Marina, access to working drawings, prototypes and photographs was arranged directly with Austin Motors. In a similar fashion, both Airfix and Kitmaster made extensive use of the British Railways Press Office at Euston station for many years. Whilst much of the Airfix photo archive was scandalously destroyed or abandoned by Palitoy when they closed the Coalville factory, Merl Evans was at least able to rescue some of the railway-related material on which he had been working. It is thought that the Museum of Childhood at Bethnal Green has some similar uncatalogued material.

**TABLE J - ENGINEERING TOOL CHANGES**

| No. | Kit | Kitmaster | Airfix |
|-----|-----|-----------|--------|
| 1 | Rocket | Metal stays | 28/29 Plastic stays<br>31/32 crew added |
| 5 | Schools | Moulded name<br>Hook coupler<br>Km steam pipe | 19 Transfer name + nos.<br>33 NMRA Buckeye replaced<br>31 Steam pipes added<br>34 Vac pipes added<br>32 3-Link coupling added<br>33 Injector pipes added<br>22 hole in buffer beam |
| 6 | Pug | Front beam plain<br>Hook coupler | 10A lamp irons added<br>17 NMRA Buckeye replaced<br>17a 3-Link coupling added<br>Whistle added to roof<br>Reversing Rod added<br>Guard irons & Brake gear added |
| 7 | Prairie | Km pony truck | 24/27 NMRA pony truck<br>24a/27a Steam/Vac added |
| 11 | BoB | Hook coupler | 10 NMRA Buckeye replaced<br>27/31 Steam pipes added<br>25 Vacuum pipes added<br>26/32 Scale coupler added<br>27-30 Brake gear added<br>33/34 Front Steps Added |
| 22 | 9F | Front pony Km<br>Rear coupler Km | Front Pony NMRA<br>Rear Coupler NMRA<br>Steam/Vac pipes added |
| 24 | Truro | Hook coupler | NMRA Buckeye replaced<br>Steam/Vac pipes added<br>Brake rods added<br>Wheel Balance weights<br>3-Link coupling added |
| 26 | J94 | Hook coupler | 18 NMRA Buckeye replaced<br>18a 3-Link coupling added |
| 30 | Mogul | Front pony Km<br>Hook coupler<br>KM steam pipe | 38 Front Pony NMRA<br>64 NMRA Buckeye replaced<br>77/81 Steam pipes added<br>78/79 Scale couplings<br>80 Vacuum pipe rear |
| 60 | Arrow | Centre hub clear | Centre hub opaque |

**B.R. (LMR) 10 ton Ventilated Meat Van** This superb 'official' BR photograph of the 10 ton Ventilated Meat Wagon, *(right)* issued by the LMR Mechanical & Electrical Engineers Dept at Derby is undated. The striking resemblance to the final box art is obvious; even the running number is the same as the kit. The model portrays one of the BR-built batch constructed at Wolverton in 1952. The photo is extraordinary in that the white background appears to be physically real; that is, it cuts across the tops of the rails at the right, is partly visible beneath the wagon and rests on the clinker at left. What was it? White painted board perhaps? The high contrast effect that it lends the image is staggering.

Contrast this with the dull, but naturalistic view of a newly completed Lowmac EK machinery *(as above)* wagon taken on a sunny day at Shildon. The low grey hills of Co. Durham form a rather mundane background, whilst the noticeable shadow in the foreground is an oversight that could have been easily avoided. In fact the entire composition is a study in grey tones. The legend on the back of this print shows the origin as the Drawing Office, British Railways, Shildon, although it was once more issued by the BR Press & Publicity department at Euston. It is dated 29 August 1961, although this wagon is one of a batch of fifty-two Lowmacs built during 1952. Whether the vehicle was photographed as it passed through shops at a later date is a matter of conjecture. Interestingly, although the running number is, once again, identical to the kit, the paint scheme is very different. The high visibility white areas were omitted by both Hornby-Dublo and Airfix (both kit & RTR) in their models and it is only now, with the Hornby Hobbies re-issue of the Airfix Lowmac EU that the correct scheme has been applied.

Also derived from an official BR picture is the shot of the Class A Tank Wagon *(Page 157 Bottom Left)*. This particular unit is of the type without internal heating bars and was designed for low-boiling point fuels such as petrol. The Airfix model is of the Class B type for use with heavy fuels such as diesel, fuel oil and kerosene. The internal heating coils were connected to the train steam heat pipes, a fact which prolonged the use of diesel locomotives fitted with either steam-heat or dual-heat apparatus long into the 1980s. This excellent picture is again from official BR sources, this time from Transport Age Vol.1 No.7 of October 1958 published by the British Transport Commission. Large trains of such B Class wagons were a regular feature of Southern Region operations around Fawley Oil Refinery on the Solent. These have now been replaced by standard 100 ton bogie tankers capable of higher speeds, with air-braking. The Airfix archive interestingly also contained the unusual photograph shown on Page 156 *(Middle)*. At first glance, it looks like another oil tanker, but on closer inspection it is revealed as a B Class tanker for transporting Creosote. As such, it is numbered in the Departmental or Internal User number series commencing DB 99XXXX. In all other respects it is identical to the standard Esso Tank wagon finally modelled by Airfix. The builder was Chas Roberts of Wakefield, July 1957. The Prestwin Silo wagon *(above)* was introduced in late 1960 by British Railways to meet the specific requirements of bulk powders that required air discharge, but were not suited to the earlier Presflow design. Prestwin wagons were to remain in service until 1983. The distinctive red oxide finish of these wagons was due to an extra layer of red oxide paint applied on top of the standard wagon grey used elsewhere. The Airfix box artwork follows the official BR colour transparency of the Prestwin, with a mixed industrial background which, once again, appeared in "Transport Age". However, the black and white print found in the archive is different and shows the same wagon (B873001) standing in front of a BR Mark 1 carriage.

Finally we come to two super shots *(right)* from the lens of Pickard of Leeds showing the mighty Booth of Rodley diesel locomotive crane. They appear to have been supplied direct by the company and bear no official BR marks at all. The first thing to notice here is that the underframe is, of course, rigid. This was the pattern adopted for those units supplied by Clyde Crane & Booth Ltd to BR Western Region during 1958-59. The kit, however, portrays a bogied version of the basic design more suited for use in steelworks, yards and sidings where sharper curvature may be encountered. The complete lack of a crane runner in either shot is also interesting. By the late 1950s British Railways had accumulated large numbers of surplus pre-grouping or indeed pre-war coaches. Some of these were stripped to their underframes and rebuilt as bogie crane runners. Maunsell 57ft coach underframes seem to have been popular on the Southern and Western regions, but many others were used. Surprisingly, many of these frames have outlasted the original stock from which they were converted into preservation. It would seem therefore, that when the order for diesel-hydraulic self-propelled cranes was placed, no runners were included, since BR Works would supply them.

### Airfix Catalogue Artwork

During the research for both the first and second editions of this book, it never ceased to amaze me that so much 40-year old material had survived to be rediscovered in the course of my investigations. Four original oil paintings of Airfix artwork were rescued from the closed Coalville factory by Merl Evans *(continued on page 161)*.

157

Illustrated on these pages are some of the wonderful paintings by Cliff & Wendy Meadway for the 1976 and 1980 Airfix catalogues.

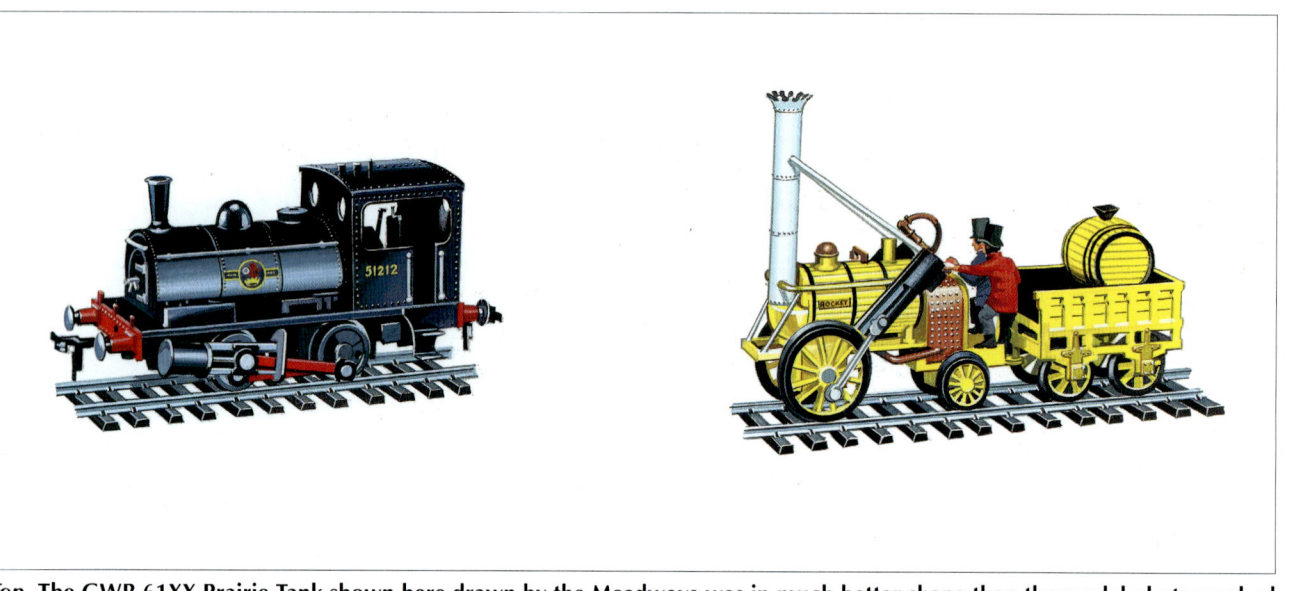

*Top.* The GWR 61XX Prairie Tank shown here drawn by the Meadways was in much better shape than the model photographed by Airfix for the 14th Edition catalogue which had a missing pony truck! *Above.* Two exquisite drawings on one sheet: the L& Y 'Pug' and the re-tooled L&MR "Rocket" with it's Victorian crew. *Below.* This rather wonderful view of the Airfix Trackside range depicting a packed Station with *Evening Star* and a Prairie approaching was used as the back-page illustration in the 1976 catalogue.

*Top.* A group image of the problematic Station Accessories set. Designed for polyethylene moulding and almost impossible to paint!

*Above.* The Airfix Signal Gantry was, rather strangely, designed to cover three tracks.

*Left.* The lovely little GWR Engine Shed could be expanded with extra kits both length- and breadthways. The Telegraph Poles kit remains popular to this day.

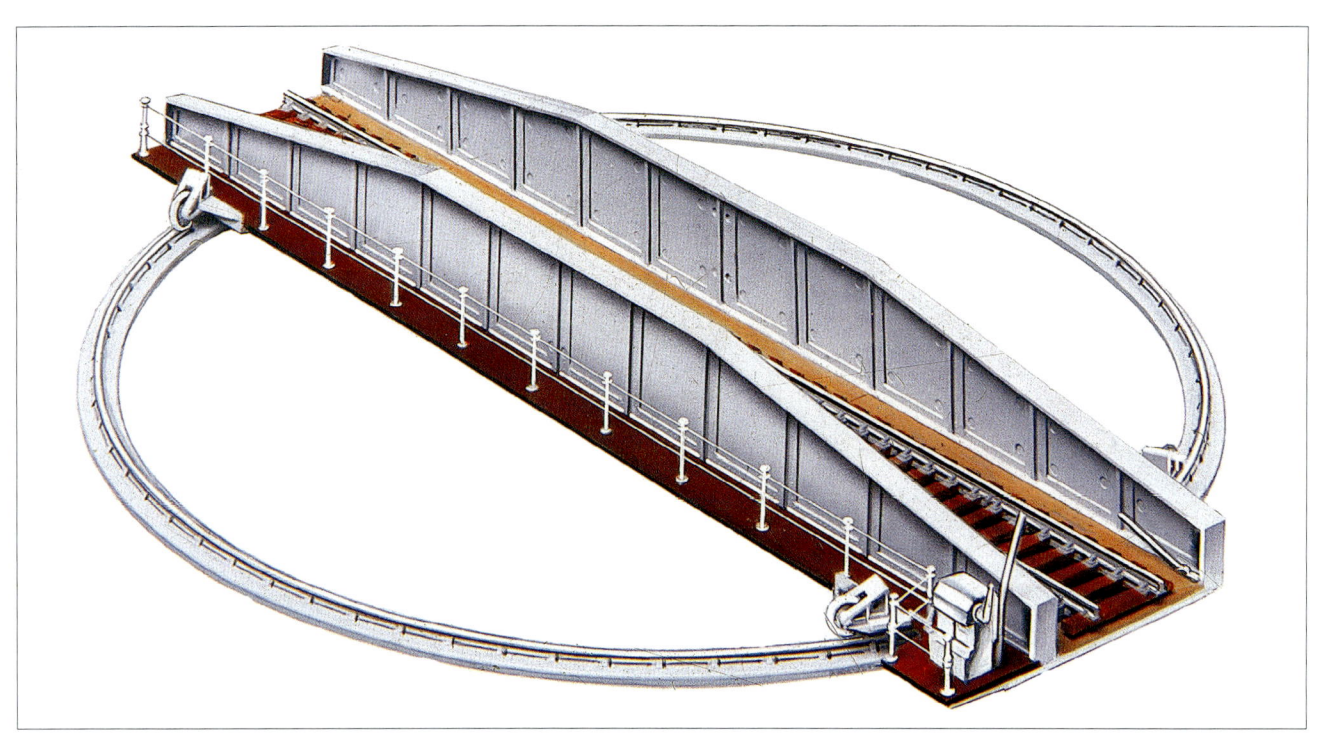

*Above.* The Airfix Turntable has the distinct advantage of being surface-mounted and therefore does not require a hole to be cut in the base-board.

*Left.* The Platform Canopy was illustrated in adverts of the time by the example at Paddock Wood, on the Southern but there were significant differences between the kit and prototype.

*Bottom.* The Dockside Travelling Crane has been a favourite for motorising over the years.

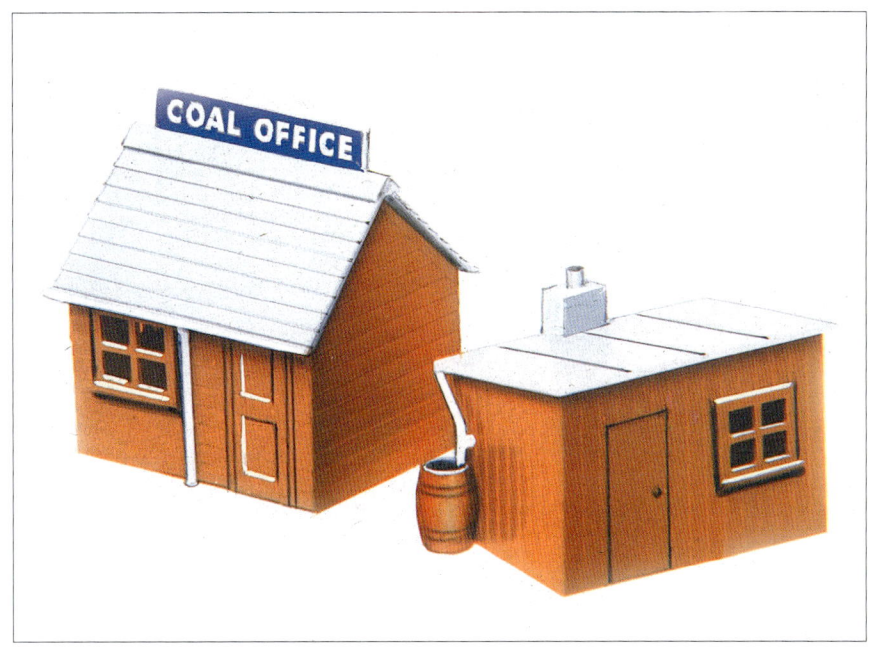

*Left.* The Coal Order Office and Platelayer's Hut adorned many layouts and were partnered with the water crane and loading gauge shown elsewhere.

*Below.* The famous Girder Bridge could also be expanded to make larger bridges. Gerry Anderson frequently used them to make rocket launching towers for his TV 21 productions.

*Bottom.* The Footbridge could also be configured in various ways and was a useful, flexible kit.

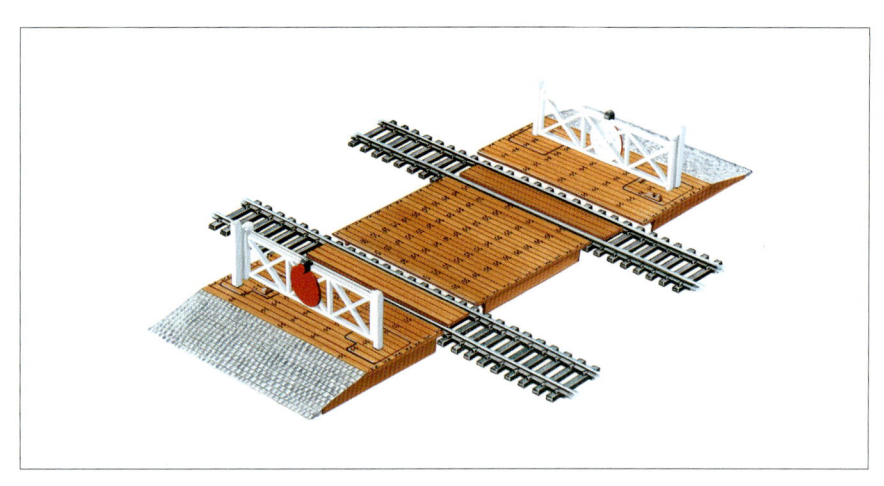

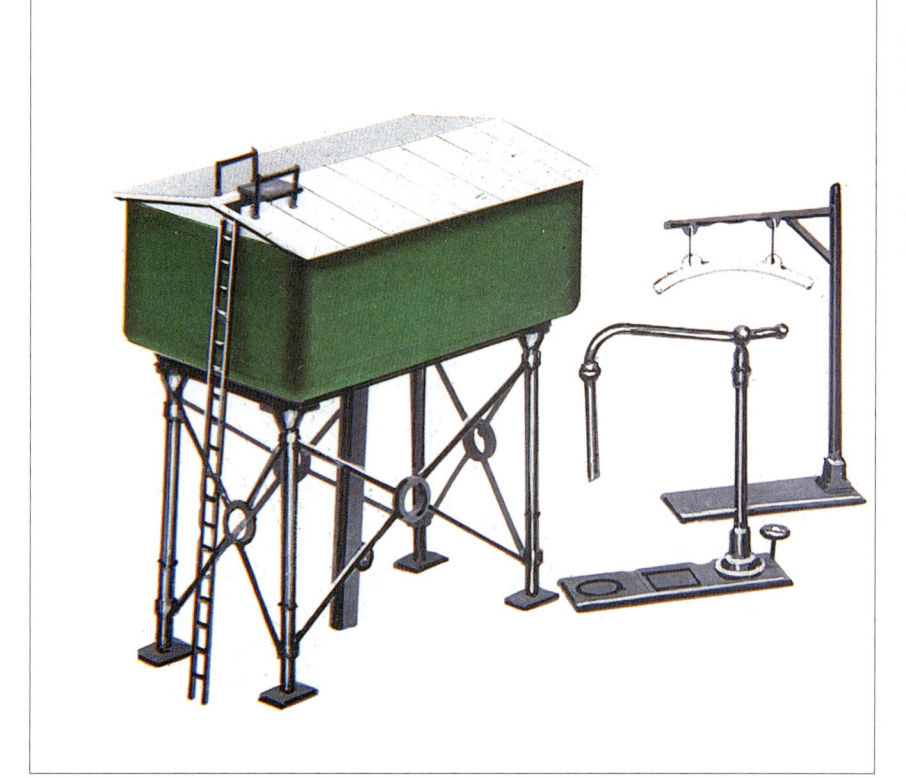

Trackside 'furniture' at pocket money prices were always popular. The Level Crossing could be expanded by adding one more kits to span double tracks. The Station Kiosks were always popular. The Water Tower was impressive in its scale and detail and was a source of many useful spare parts for scratch building. The water crane also came in a separate kit, 'Trackside Accessories'.

The Airfix Service Station was the sixth Trackside kit, dating from 1956.

The Windmill was supposedly based on one on the South Downs.

163

*Above and below*. Platforms and Platform fittings were a valuable addition to any boy's layout and proved an instant hit.

*Bottom*. This famous birds' eye view of the Trackside range first appeared in the Fifth Edition Airfix catalogue and in several more afterwards.

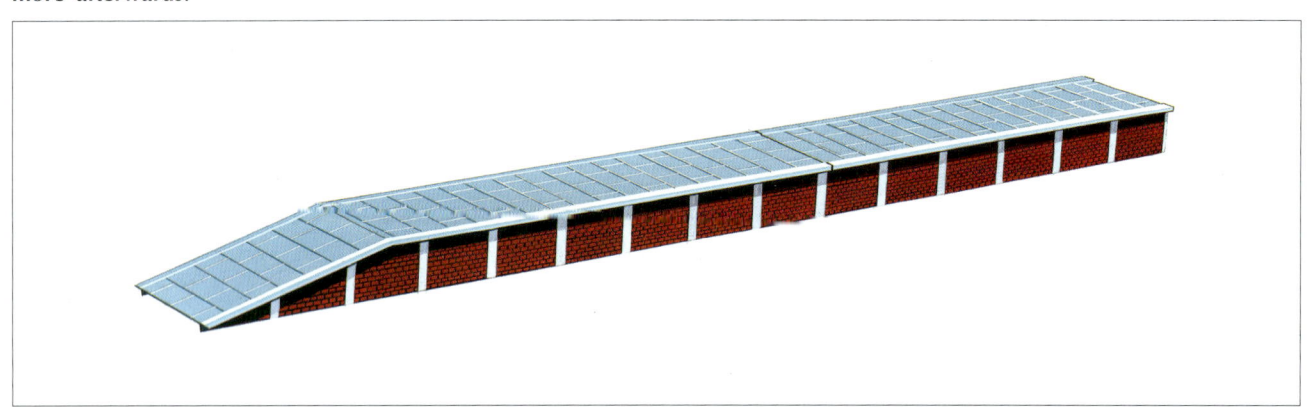

164

**Some classic Airfix Type 2 headers for Trackside kits.**

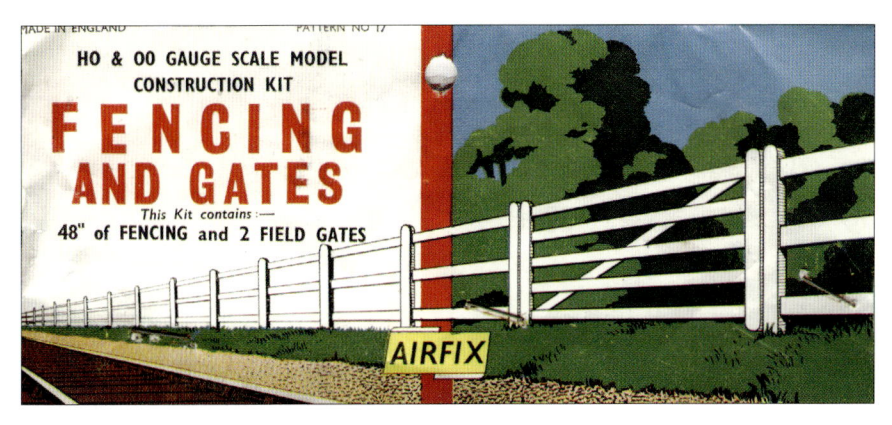

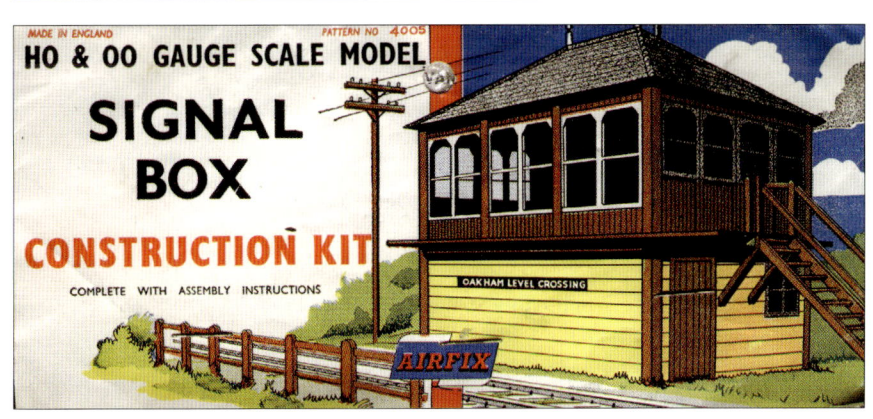

and went on to grace the first edition of *Let's Stick Together*. Just before I set about the re-writing of the second edition, Pat Hammond (he of Tri-ang fame) showed me yet more original Airfix artwork rescued from Coalville. This time, it was the original illustrations for the 1976 Airfix Model Railways catalogue. These were apparently thrown into a skip outside the factory together with a large number of transparencies and even copies of General Arrangement blue prints of British Railways locomotives supplied by the Derby Drawing Office of BR for Airfix use.

Luckily (I've mentioned this famous event elsewhere in the text) the team from Replica Railways were visiting Coalville to collect a consignment of remaindered stock they had bought from Palitoy. According to Godfrey Hayes, the proprietor of Replica Railways at that time, the gate guard informed him that much more material had been deposited in the skip and on pallets just inside the factory and that if he wanted any of it, he was free to take it. Godfrey says he took as many of the G.A. drawings as he could fit into a heavily laden Ford Transit already crammed with surplus Airfix rolling stock. The Airfix transparencies and artwork almost didn't make it; but they finally managed to squeeze in around 30 original board-mounted pieces and a scruffy box of more than 150 transparencies.

Each artwork was prepared on Daler board in watercolours and measures roughly 40cm by 30cm. Some are bigger, some smaller and several boards contain more than one illustration. All of them are by the Portman Artists group of commercial illustrators, mostly done by Wendy and Clifford Meadway, prolific illustrators of childrens books on technical subjects including tractors, aeroplanes and ships. In addition, Clifford was a regular artist contributor to *Look and Learn* magazine.

When well-known railway author O.S. Nock was approached in 1964 by Blandford Press to add a title on British Railway Locomotives their popular Pocket Encyclopaedia series, the prospect of commissioning nearly 200 new paintings of railway locomotives seemed daunting. He wrote in the Preface to that first book in the series: *When the idea of a book illustrating, in full colour, some 200 different locomotives was first put to me I must admit I was incredulous. As the book was intended to cover the entire history of the British steam locomotive, photographs were out of the question. One hundred and ninety-two pictures had got to be painted! It was then that I was introduced to Charles Rickitt and his Portman Artists. Still incredulous I chose*

165

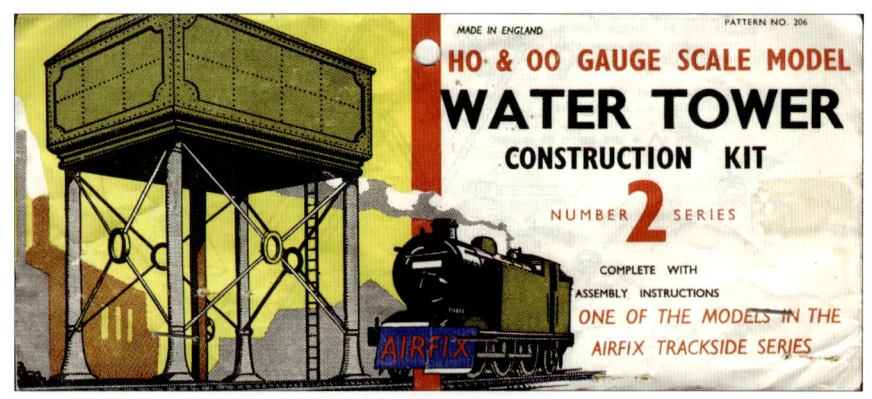

a subject for a trial picture, but when I saw the result my doubts vanished, and the only problem that remained was that of getting the remaining 191 finished in time to meet the production schedule.

But from the very outset I enjoyed the happiest of collaborations with Charles Rickitt, and with his artists Cliff and Wendy Meadway. From the first day, when we picnicked amid photographs, files, reference books and goodness knows what else in my home, locomotives have been painted with a speed and accuracy that could be likened to the production line of a modern factory. What might have been a nerve-racking race against time has been a great pleasure: sending the Meadways subject after subject in rapid succession, and seeing the results so swiftly and beautifully rendered.

It would appear that the Meadways, and Wendy in particular, were very prolific artists and illustrators – they had to be, with 36 subjects needing paintings for the kit section of the 1980 catalogue. Perhaps Airfix were as much impressed by the speed with which these veteran illustrators could turn out superb coloured illustrations rather than any stylistic or artistic considerations? Indeed, so prolific were they, that the Blandford Colour Series eventually ran to twelve volumes covering every aspect of Railways of the World and all illustrated by the Meadways.

Clifford Henry Meadway was born on 6 October 1921 and died in 1999. He had become well known as a painter of railway engines. Titles he illustrated include the Blandford Colour Series books:
British Steam Locomotives in Colour (1964)
Railways of Britain in Colour (1967)
*Railways at the Turn of the Century, 1895-1905* (1969),
*Railways at the Zenith of Steam, 1920-40* (1970),
*Railways in the Years of Pre-eminence, 1905-1919* (1971),
*The Dawn of World Railways, 1800-1850* (1972),
*Railways in the Formative Years, 1851-1895* (1973),
*Railways in the Transition from Steam, 1940-1965* (1974),
*Railways in the Modern Age Since 1963* (1975),
*Great Steam Locomotives of All Time* (1976)
*Great Western in Colour* (1978)
*British Steam Railways and Locomotives* (1983)
all written by O. S. Nock; later titles include
*Guide to Airliners* by Andrew Kershaw (1979),
*Guide to Racing Cars* by Nigel Roebuck (1979),
*Model Railways* by Cyril Freezer (1980),
*Guide to Fighting Ships* by Andrew Kershaw (1980),
*Let's Look at Tractors* by Graham Rickard (1988) and
*Woodland Trees* by Theresa Greenaway (1990).

Wendy Medaway often collaborated on their books but is also a fine nature artist in her own right and illustrated dozens of children's books on animals and other subjects. Steve Holland interviewed Wendy Meadway in 2006 for his excellent book on the history of *Look and Learn* magazine. He kindly gave us permission to reprint his interview with Wendy here.

*My husband, Cliff and I were many years with Look and Learn, nearly always*

**The Girder Bridge (Type 3) and Station Platform (Type 4) both received Roy cross artwork on re-issue.**

166

More Cross artwork – Signal box, telegraph poles and footbridge. The yellow box was a generic design for a general re-issue of the range in Series 3 boxes. Platform Figures was first issued in this box and was the only new issue for 1978 in this range.

167

The Airfix Type 1 "Products in Plastic" headers are popular with collectors for their striking appearance.

illustrating articles that showed how things worked. We covered a great variety of subjects, including the early Walkman, tower cranes, milk parlours, egg grading and packing, loading train containers, testing runways, steam roundabouts in fairgrounds, laying macadam on roadways and many others. This often entailed travelling around in our search for reference for our paintings. I know Cliff went to locomotive depots for the container article and our local farms were helpful for the milk and egg articles. To this day I sometimes see a large piece of machinery and think, "I know how that works!" In my past career I did a five year art course at Harrow Art College, got various diplomas, then went to Portman Artists, a small studio in London, where we did a great variety of things, among them working for the War Office, diagrams for technical books and many, many birthday and Christmas cards. This is where I met Cliff, who had spent 15 years in the R.A.F. as an engineer, so he was always given all the complicated mechanical jobs to do. He had never been to Art School so, did I waste five years training? I don't think so!

**More Type 1 headers including the larger Series 2 issue for the Village Church, modelled on Bonchurch IoW.**

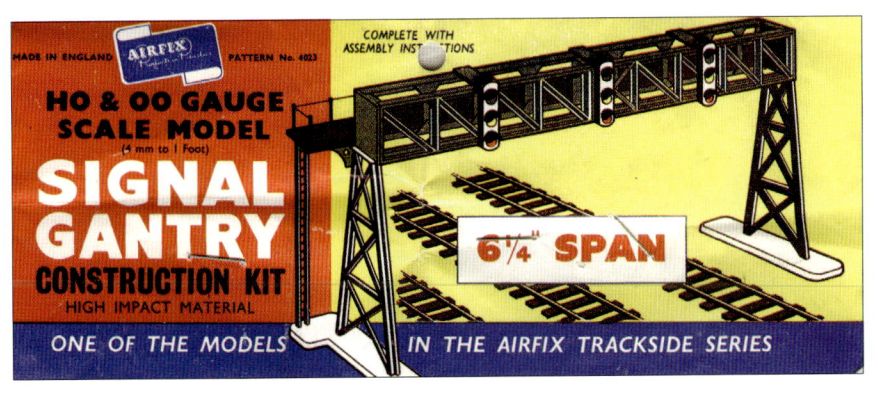

*It was whilst in the studio that we were introduced to Blandford Press and Ossie Nock and the railway books took off, something like twelve all told. Eventually the Studio folded and Cliff & I went freelance. Because deadlines were so tight, Cliff and I often 'shared' a job. This was particularly so with the Blandford books. I did some of the paintings and Cliff did some, and even we couldn't tell them apart. We worked in colour and black and white—when you are freelance you never say you can't do something. In between books we did the usual thing of trudging round publishers with our folio. We never had an agent. I guess my happiest time was painting for the natural history books, as wildlife has always been my great passion, but I also love steam locomotives, so much enjoyed the railway books. When we were 'between jobs' Cliff and I would do paintings for local galleries. Cliff was a very fine landscape artist and had some success with selling his paintings, usually local scenes, in watercolour. I would do animal and flower studies, also watercolour, which is the medium that we always used. In later years, photographs were used more and more in flower, mammal and bird*

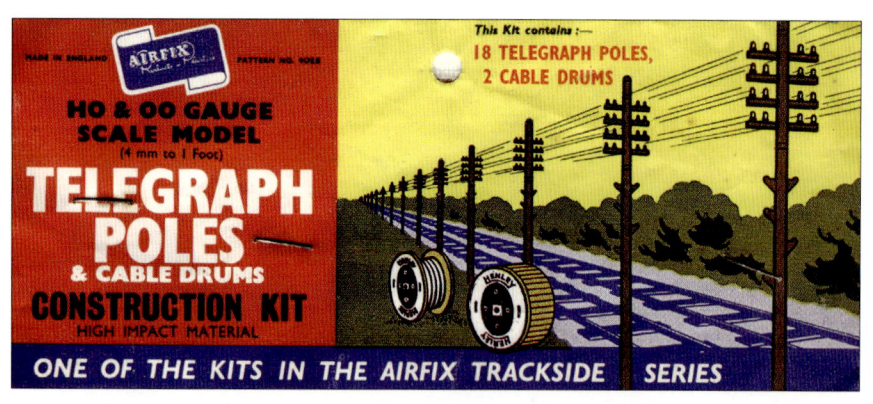

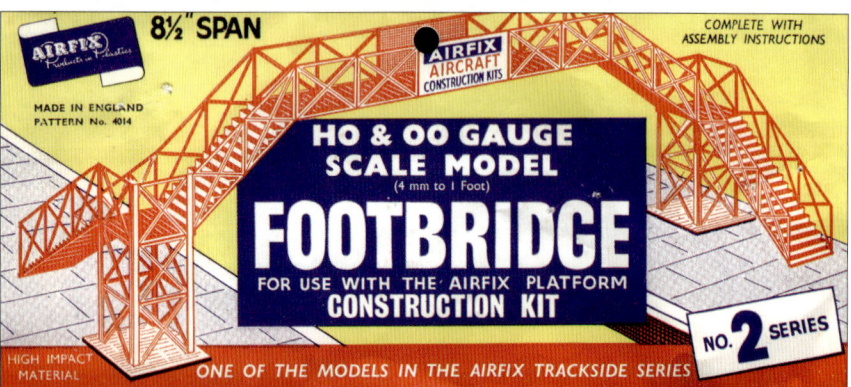

*Left.* Rare German issues of the Trackside Range can occasionally be found. Time to get your tongue around *"Bahnenlagen Zubhorteile"*!

170

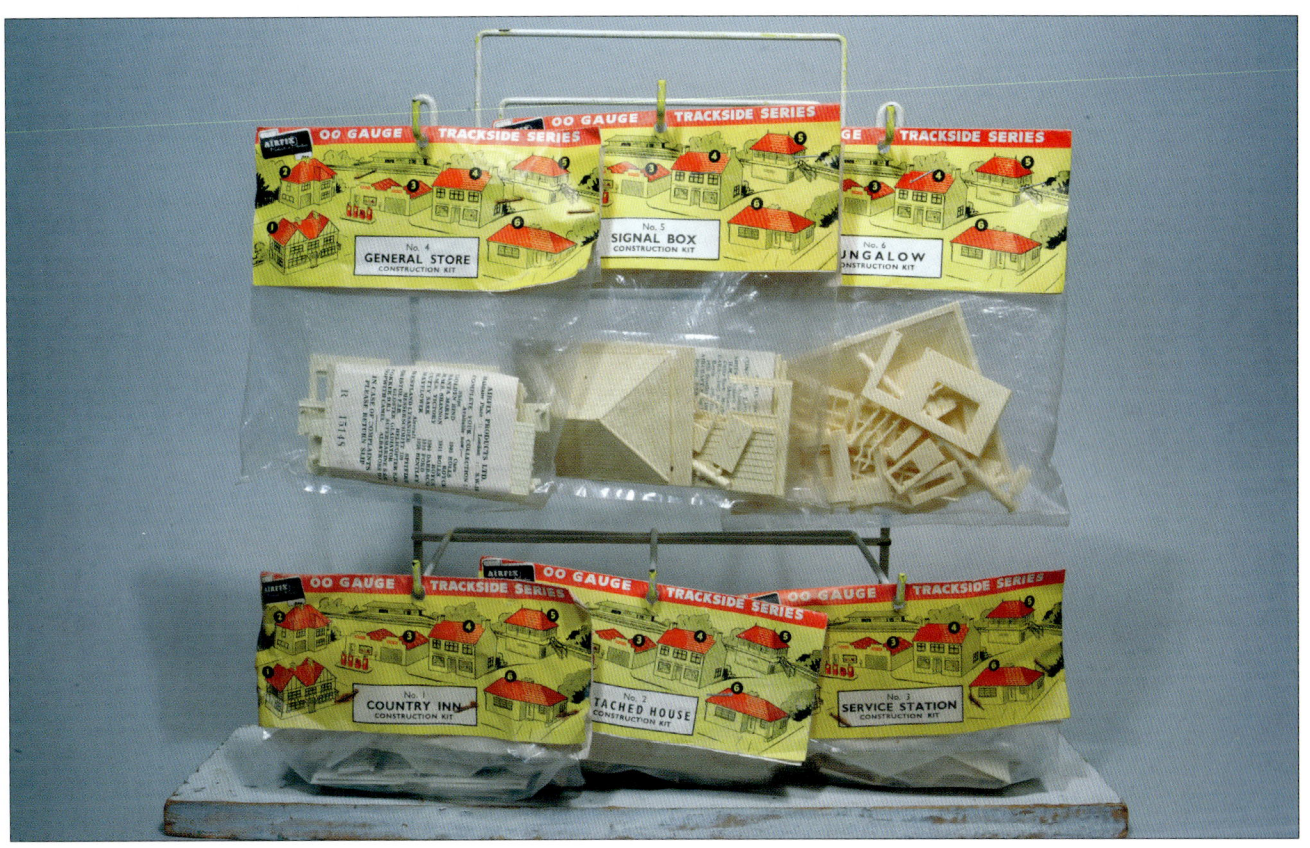

*Top.* The six earliest kits shared a basic header design and date from late 1956.

*Middle.* Take me to the *"Beschrankter Bahnubergang"*!

*Left.* Airfix Plasty, initially a Distributor, eventually became a fully owned subsidiary of Airfix. They frequently repacked British kits by Airfix and Frog in their own outer boxes which have a charm all of their own.

171

*Top.* Scammel Vehicles of Watford found a niche in the 1930s with their successful "Mechanical Horse" designs of three wheel tractor and trailer combinations. The classic 1950s Scammel 1½ ton unit formed the basis of this exquisite kit in the Trackside Range. It provided two different semi-trailers, one flat and one dedicated to Watneys beer.

*Above.* The Airfix Turntable kit has proved very popular since it was launched in the 1960s because it mounts flat the surface of a layout – no well needs to be cut; very useful for model railways mounted on the dining table! Here an Airfix *"Evening Star"* is turned.

*identification books and I lost much work, so turned my hand to commissioned animal portraits instead.*

*They say that artists never retire but, during 2005, I decided to call a halt to my artwork. Cliff died just on 7 years ago, and over the last three years certain things have happened which have made me feel that I must get as much enjoyment out of life as I can, so that's what I am doing—going out a lot and really enjoying myself!*

The completed Airfix watercolours were then photographed on to 35mm transparencies in most cases. Some of the larger drawings, such as the locomotives and the image showing the whole range together, were also photographed on to medium-format stock. We have tried to reproduce as many of these from direct digital scans as we can.

In amongst the transparencies were older Airfix kit artworks including the superb Roy Cross painting of the BR Class 4 Mogul and earlier illustrations of the Presflo Bulk Cement Wagon and Esso Tank Wagon showing signs of the original Type 2 packaging style. Without the added title panels and Airfix logo, far more of the picture can be seen and appreciated. On the Mogul painting, the full turntable with lead-in and lead-out tracks can now be seen, together with Roy's signature in the bottom right-hand corner.

Most of these illustrations eventually found their way into the Airfix GMR catalogues, where they were shown as an adjunct to the fledgling ready-to-run system. Starting with the first edition in 1976, about half of the illustrations were used. By the second edition, most of the kit range was shown, with buildings such as the General Store and the Church now added. The page layouts reached a peak with the third edition of the GMR catalogue where all of these illustrations, together with some of the older rolling stock artwork and a couple of even earlier transparencies (including the broken Prairie tank) all appeared over four pages. By contrast, the final 1980 catalogue pays only passing regard to these kits. In addition, the Turntable and Platform Canopy were also used in the 16th edition kit catalogue and the Turntable on its own in the 17th edition, as the kits came and went from the Airfix range.

It is interesting to see that the built model of the Prairie tank is looking a bit battle-scarred. It has only one operational pony truck; the other is lacking an entire axle! Buffers are missing and the whole is most unsatisfactory as a representation of what could be achieved from the Airfix kit. Nevertheless, it persisted throughout all three catalogues.

We are extremely grateful to Pat Hammond for loaning us this superb artwork for reproduction here, the first time that these drawings have been seen

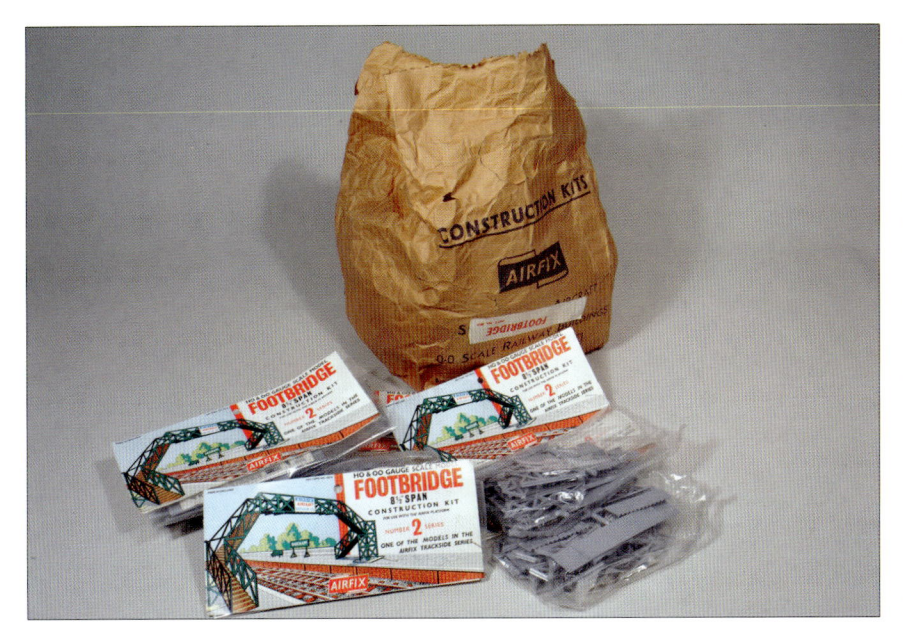

*Top.* Airfix Trackside kits and indeed all their Series One and Series Two bagged kits came in trade packs of 12 kits. These were simply placed in a paper bag with a pasted on label to distinguish the contents.

*Middle and above.* The Airfix OO/HO scale figures range began in 1957/8 with the Guards Colour Party and Guards Band. It was not until much later that they got around to issuing Civilian figures. It was a huge success and went through four different pack styles, two in Type 2 (lower picture), one Type 3 and one Type 4 (Upper picture). Unfortunately, the tool was lost after the Palitoy take-over and has never been found, although a 2009 Hornby Railways catalogue did list Civilians along with Farm and Zoo stock in the Skaledale section. They were never re-issued.

173

in their original form with the benefit of digital enhancement and modern colour reproduction. For completeness, we have also included a scan of the original Schools Class Harrow artwork, also by Roy Cross. This is now in private hands in the West Country.

**Airfix Trackside Range**
Airfix first launched their enormously popular Trackside range in 1956. It eventually comprised thirty-two different models, including two road vehicles (a Scammell Scarab and a motor-scooter), three sets of figures and several 'Manyways' extendable kits which could be combined, such as the Girder Bridge, Footbridge, Engine Shed and Level Crossing. Forty years later they are nearly all still in production with Dapol, a tribute to the original toolmakers. These kits enabled modellers to construct entire towns and villages at modest cost, rapidly and with minimum skill. Indeed, your author well remembers constructing the Booking Hall in an afternoon and being well pleased with the results at the tender age of seven! It is precisely that aspect of the design, the ease of assembly and clear instructions, which has made these kits so endearing over the years. Add to that the unquestionable utility of the various extendable/adaptable kits and you can begin to see why they were so popular. Many famous layouts, from Charford to Acton Mainline, are to be seen sporting suitably cut-up and adapted bits of Signal Gantry and Girder Bridge and one may while away a happy hour at most Exhibitions playing 'Spot the Airfix Kits' with the 4mm scale layouts!

The series began with an initial selection of six buildings, commencing with the Country Inn, and retailing at a modest 1s 9d (7½p). By 1958, a second series of larger kits had been introduced starting with a very useful Footbridge, retailing at 3s (15p). These were all initially in bags, but later Series 2 kits were issued in boxes. Whilst some models, such as the Scammell Scarab 'Mechanical Horse' had regrettably short lives of under three years, several models were in virtually continuous production from 1956 to the present day. These include the Level Crossing and the famous Signal Box, modelled on the Midland Railway prototype at Oakham Level Crossing. Due to the

*Top.* Farm Stock brought together a good selection of farmyard animals and fowl in an attractive Type 2 box.

*Middle.* Brian Knight painted the Farm Animals Type 3 box art with its charming pastoral scene.

*Right.* Type 3 Civilians has the quintessentially English smiling Policeman in a sixties street scene by Brian Knight.

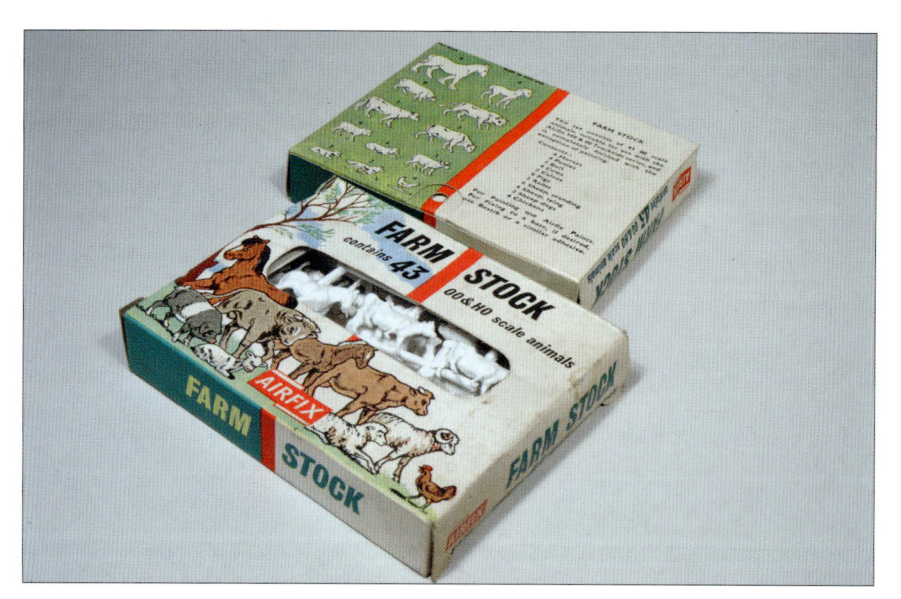

celebrity status of the kit, English Heritage saw fit to grant the box Grade 1 Listed Building status. In fact, the Village Church is also based on a Grade 2 listed building, in this case the beautiful Norman church in the village of Bonchurch, Isle of Wight.

Apart from these two kits, no other specific buildings have been identified. There seems to be no direct link between the 'White Horse' or 'The Chequers' Country Inns and any real life pubs, although a number of the kits represent typical structures of their time, some of which have gone on to listed status in the natural course of events. For example, the classic oval W.H.Smith bookstall in the Kiosks and Steps kit is representative of the type now in preservation at the North Norfolk Railway, whilst at nearby Parham one can see an excellently preserved Second World War Airfield Control Tower of the type covered by the kit. Sadly, Braintree & Bocking station, whilst still in use, no longer has the type of station name boards featured in the Platform Fittings kit, although plenty of enamel running-in boards of this type are to be seen at preservation centres around the country.

Most of the kits are redolent of the 1950s, especially the so-called 'Modern' buildings such as the Detached House, General Store, Shop and Flat and, of course, the Bungalow, complete with VHF TV aerial on the roof! The wide variety of lineside installations, such as Telegraph Poles, Engine Shed and the contents of Trackside Accessories, have provided endless numbers of parts and additional features to improve the detail of many a layout.

When introduced in 1956, the earliest design of packaging for these kits used a common header design carrying line drawings in black on yellow of the first six kits. These distinguish each kit by a central title panel. They are unofficially referred to as Type 0 headers by Airfix Collectors Club members. As the series began to expand a new design of header was required. The Type 1 header prominently features the 'Products in Plastic' logo on the left hand side and is printed in three bright colours – blue and red on a yellow field. Lettering is usually white reversed out on blue, an exception being the Windmill which is predominantly green and red on white. Type 1 headers were used for Series 1 kits 1-19 and the first four Series 2 kits, 201, 204, 4017 and 4019. The latter two are believed to have been allocated Pattern Numbers 202 and 203, but were not taken up.

The first Series 1 in a classic Type 2 header was the Scammell Scarab transporter, No.20. Type 2 is a full colour drawing on a white ground with coloured lettering and a distinctive vertical stripe down the middle of the illustration in a contrasting colour. The Type 2 Girder Bridge kit features a really rather good representation of a green

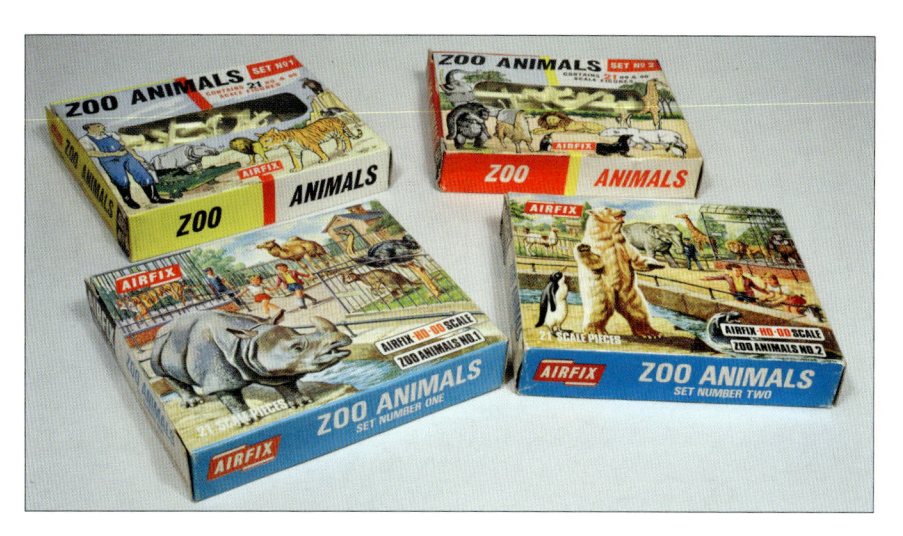

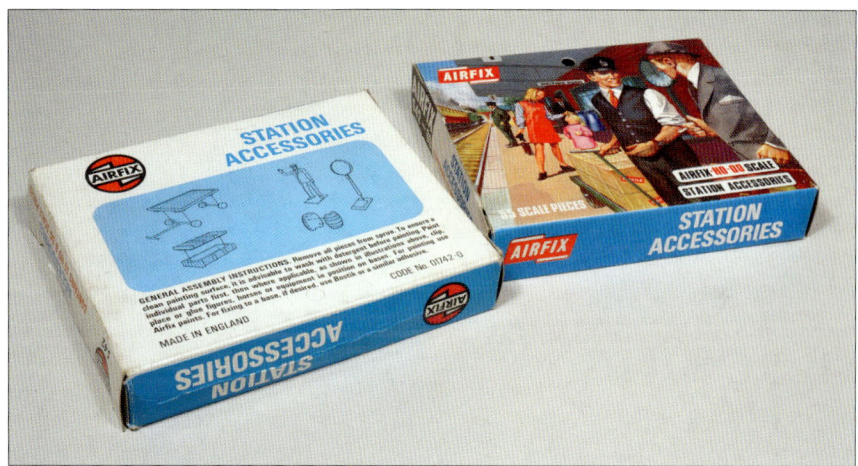

*Top.* There were so many Zoo Animals that they had to be split into two sets. You got a mix of very big (Elephant) and very small (Penguins) in each set. They are much sought-after today. The Type 3 box art is again by Brian Knight.

*Middle.* S46 was a re-issue in the OO/HO Figures range of a set previously sold as a bagged Series One kit: Station Accessories. It had always been moulded in polyethylene, like the figures. It is still in production, in polystyrene, with Dapol.

*Below.* The last civilian figures issue made by Airfix was Railway Workmen in 1980, but in 1978 they tooled a superb set of Platform Figures in polystyrene – much easier to paint and much more durable than polyethylene. This is a catalogue shot of factory-finished figures from that time.

175

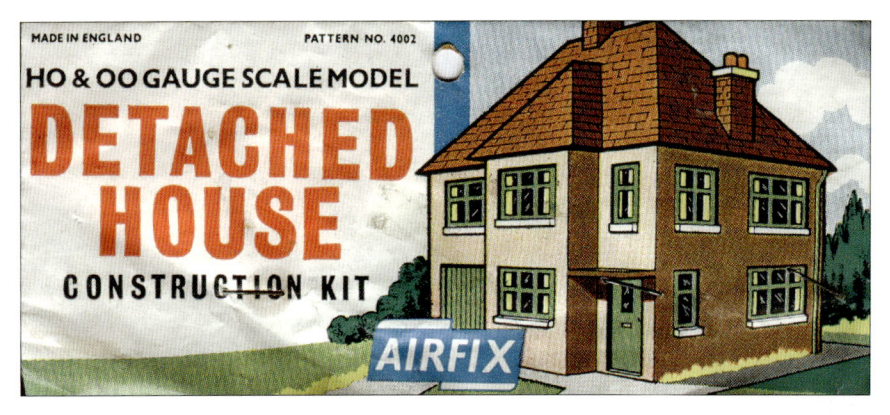

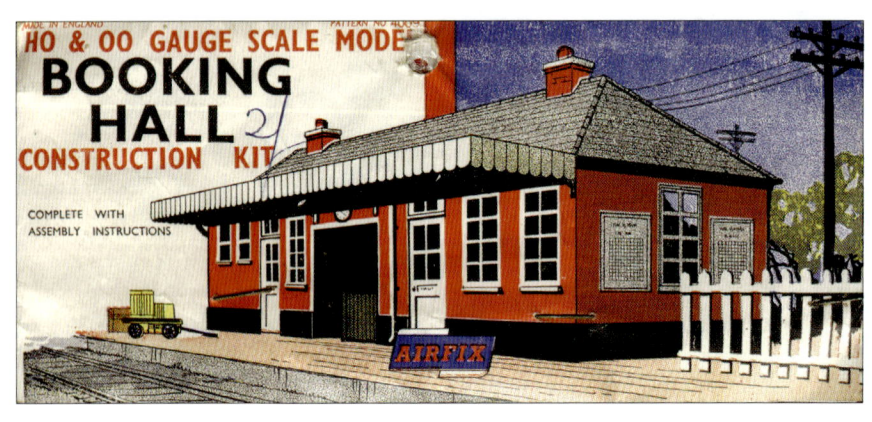

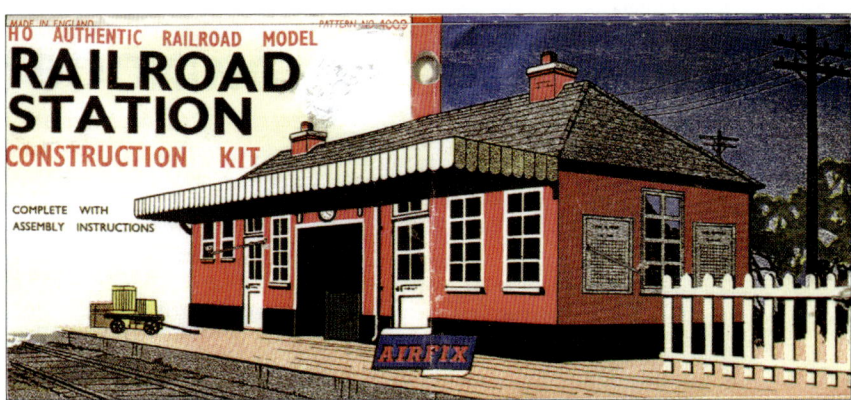

liveried EE Type 4 diesel, by an unknown artist, possibly Charles Oakes. Type 2 was used for all the trackside kits as they were re-issued and all the rolling stock kits as they were introduced until the Prestwin Silo wagon of 1963. The Prestwin is the only one of the original Series 1 wagons in a Type 3 box.

All the re-issued Kitmaster locos appeared in Type 3 boxes at first. Type 3 is the classic 1963-73 design with the so-called 'ribbon' logo for Airfix or 'Red Flash' logo. The original Roy Cross paintings were commissioned by Airfix for Type 3 boxes. Although Roy painted three of the re-issued Kitmaster locomotives, he did not do the rest, that artist was Charles Oakes. Roy was also commissioned for some re-issued Trackside Series 1 kits with Type 3 or 4 header cards. These were the Signal Box, Platform Section, Level Crossing, Telegraph Poles, Fencing and Gates and are all now rather scarce. He also completed artwork for certain Series 2 kits in boxes: the Girder Bridge (Roy's favourite, featuring a blue Brush Class 47), Travelling Crane, Footbridge and Engine Shed. The latter carries a very decent representation of a BR(W) 57XX pannier tank and is one of the best subjects in this series.

Trackside kits were produced in their vintage 1960 Type 2 headers well into the 1970s. After a period of withdrawal from the catalogues, they were reissued en masse in Series 3 during 1978. The Type 6 box is a standard design for all kits and is, frankly, hideous. Bright yellow with a blue 'scene' featuring all the kits, it does little to justify the exorbitant list price of a Series 3 kit, some with as few as 16 parts! Only one new kit was added to the range in this style box, Platform Figures, an excellent moulding of people in various poses, luggage trolleys and station staff, in polystyrene.

The final trackside issue is also rather scarce and is a Type 7 oval logo box showing a Midland Railway Compound locomotive at what might be Bromsgrove, in a blue/black halftone. A picture of the completed kit is superimposed on top. Again this was a new model and once more it was another excellent set of figures, this time Railway Workmen. As with Platform Figures, it was moulded in polystyrene and there were three identical sprues of figures in each kit. It was never catalogued, for Airfix Ltd was sold before this could happen. Both tools are with Dapol.

**Airfix Type 2 Series One headers were always very colourful and carefully drawn to portray more or less exactly what you got in the kit. The Railroad Station ("HO authentic railroad model") is one of four kits re-drawn for the US market, the others being Signal Box (Signal Tower), Telegraph Poles (Telephone Poles), and Shop and Flat (Store & Apartment).**

These last two were very late additions to the range, Platform Figures being introduced in 1978 in a Type 6 box and the un-catalogued Railway Workmen appearing in a Type 6A box in 1979. Both are extremely scarce in original Airfix packaging, but were re-issued by Dapol. They differ from the two sets of figures in the OO/HO figures series in being real polystyrene mouldings, not polyethylene as normally used for figures. The first of that series was the sought-after Civilians set. This featured an excellent Vespa motor scooter and lots of useful people including public service figures such as policemen and a nurse. The second kit is Platform Accessories, which started life as a Trackside kit, but by 1968 had moved into the OO/HO Figures series in a proper blue Type 3 figures box. This later kit is now available from Dapol moulded in polystyrene. In addition, Airfix also produced a very nice set of Farm Stock in the same range. Now with Hornby Hobbies, all three sets were shown in the 2008 Hornby Catalogue for 'Release Quarter 4'; but at the time of writing nothing more has been seen of them and the 2009 catalogue makes no mention of them.

The Airfield Control Tower kit has been the subject of some controversy over the years, as elaborated earlier. Palitoy maintained that it was not a 'trackside' kit, although the 1962 advertisements and the Airfix complaint slip clearly show it in the 'Trackside' range! When released in 1959 Pattern No.4017, it was clearly a trackside kit, but upon reintroduction in the 12th Airfix catalogue it had become 03305-1 numbered in the AFV/Diorama range. Subsequently it became 03380-2 in the 13th Catalogue, but was listed with Series 3 Aircraft Kits! It was reissued again by Airfix in 1991 in the Airfield series. It is the only Trackside tool not owned by Dapol.

**The Un-released Trackside Kit**
According to ex-Palitoy employee, Merl Evans, Airfix had completed a set of drawings for a 'compendium kit', similar to the RAF Emergency, Re-fuelling and Recovery Sets, which was to have been added to the range of Trackside OO/HO scale models. The kit would have had two 4mm scale civilian vehicles; a London Transport bus plus an FX3 or FX4 London Taxi cab. As far as is known, no artwork was prepared and no tooling

**Number 2 Series was introduced for the larger model aircraft, but also encompassed some of the Trackside kits, notably from 1958 the Airfield Control Tower, Water Tower, Windmill, Village Church and the four that would eventually gain boxes – Engine Shed, Girder Bridge, Travelling Crane and Footbridge.**

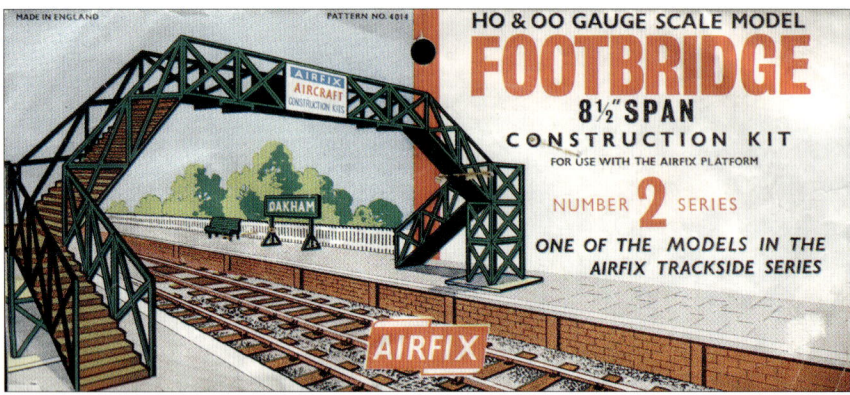

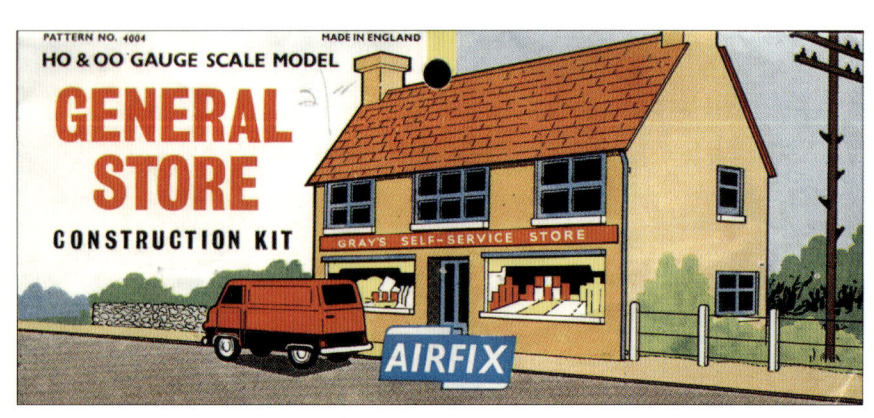

made. Patterns may exist, however. This kit would probably have been a Series 3 issue along with the RAF Recovery Set.

Some interesting minor variations exist amongst the earlier kits, for example Airfix Type 1 Trackside Kits - Station Platform. The earlier Type 1 header carries only simple assembly instructions on the inside beneath the header. The revised version shows several plans of typical platform layouts that can accommodate the new Airfix Booking Hall in addition to the assembly drawings. A quick lift of the right hand flap of the header will either reveal the layout plan (or not) without removing the staples.

**Trackside Fencing and Gates**
With Trackside Fencing & Gates in the Type 1 header, the difference was not so obvious. If you look carefully at the first issue, beneath the words Construction Kit are the words 'High Impact Material'. This is Airfix-speak for Polystyrene. However, the kit contains a red printed note which states: *To improve this item these Fences are now produced in a flexible Polyethylene Compound material, and not in High Impact Polystyrene as originally planned and stated on the cover, should you require to make a permanent fixture to your layout base, Evo Stik Impact Adhesive should be used.* Both kits actually contain polyethylene mouldings and there is no evidence that the kit appeared in polystyrene under the Airfix brand..

**Overseas Issues**
A large number of Airfix Type 1 kits were made available through Airfix-Plasty, the German distributor, either as British kits in German outer boxes or with full German headers. The Trackside range was no exception and the full list of kits with German issues is as follows:

For the USA and Canadian markets, Airfix re-designed their Type 2 Trackside headers to produce four more interesting versions:

| Shop & Flat | - Store & Apartment |
| Booking Hall | - Railroad Station |
| Signal Box | - Signal Tower |
| Telegraph Poles | - Telephone Poles |

All of these are shown in the 1963 AHM catalogue; American Hobby Manufacturing was the local agent before the establishment of US Airfix in 1964. The following Table K (see page 180) summarises the range.

**The Bungalow charmingly sports a VHF TV aerial, whilst the Girder Bridge and Footbridge (along with Level Crossing, Platform, and Engine Shed) were all designed to be extendable through the addition of extra kits. The Service Station came with separate petrol pumps and the General Store had printed interiors for the shop window.**

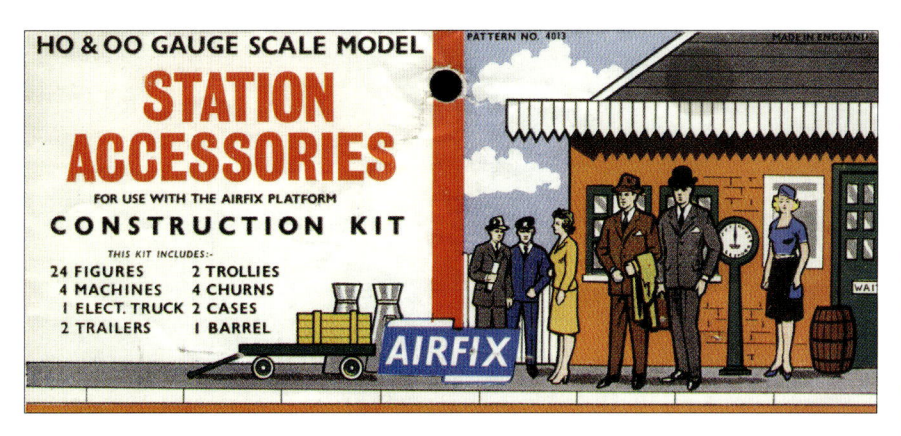

*Left*. Station Accessories, a long-serving figures set, in the original poly-bag.

*Middle*. Another useful set was Trackside Accessories which brought together a water column, loading gauge, coal office and platelayers hut.

*Below*. Bonchurch on the Isle of Wight was the inspiration for the Airfix Village Church. It is small, which made it ideal as a kit subject.

*Bottom*. 1978 saw the Type 6 box reissues which brought *Evening Star* back into the range and allowed *Harrow* a brand new box painting, featuring Charing Cross station.

| German Airfix Trackside kits | |
|---|---|
| Platform Fittings | Bahnsteig Zusatstelle |
| Station Platform | Bahnsteig. |
| Country Inn | Gasthaus |
| Bungalow | Wochenendhaus |
| Trackside Accessories | Bahnanlagen Zubehorteile |
| Service Station | Tankstelle |
| Signal Box | Stellwerk |
| Level Crossing | Beschrankter Bahnubergang |
| Shop & Flat | Geschaftshaus |
| Signal Gantry | Signalbrucke |
| In special "Airfix Plasty" boxes were: | |
| Travelling Crane | Ladekran |
| Girder bridge | Tragerbrucke |
| Engine Shed | Lokschuppen |
| Footbridge | Fussbrucke |

## Table K - The Airfix Trackside Range

| First No. | Later No. | Description of Kit | Original Mould Cost | Date Mould acquired | Box or Bag Type 0 | 1 | 2 | 3 | 4 | 6 | 7 |
|---|---|---|---|---|---|---|---|---|---|---|---|
| **Series 1** | | | | | | | | | | | |
| 4001 | 1 | Country Inn | £1,490.00 | 10.57 | x | x | x | | | x | |
| 4002 | 2 | Detached House | £1,415.00 | 06.57 | x | x | x | | | x | |
| 4003 | 3 | Service Station | | | x | x | x | | | x | |
| 4004 | 4 | General Store | £1,268.00 | 06.57 | x | x | x | | | x | |
| 4005 | 5 | Signal Box | £1,379.00 | 10.57 | x | x | x | x | x | x | x |
| 4006 | 6 | Bungalow | £1,175.00 | 10.57 | x | x | x | | | x | |
| 4007 | 7 | Station Platform | £1,727.00 | 12.58 | | x | x | x | x | x | x |
| 4008 | 8 | Shop & flat | £1,796.00 | 06.58 | | x | x | | | x | |
| 4009 | 9 | Booking Hall | £1,516.00 | 09.58 | | x | x | | | x | x |
| 4010 | 10 | Thatched Cottage | £1,325.00 | 09.58 | | x | x | | | x | |
| 4018 | 11 | Kiosks & steps | £1,223.00 | 05.58 | | x | x | | | x | x |
| 4012 | 12 | Platform Fittings | £878.00 | 09.58 | | x | x | | | x | x |
| 4013 | 13 | Station Accessories | £1,306.00 | 12.58 | | x | x | x (as S46) | x (as S46) | x | x |
| 4021 | 14 | Trackside Accessories | £1,121.00 | 12.59 | | x | x | | | x | x |
| 4022 | 15 | Level Crossing | £1,229.00 | 03.59 | | x | x | | x | x | x |
| 4023 | 16 | Signal Gantry | £1,420.00 | 03.59 | | x | x | | | x | x |
| | 17 | Fencing and Gates | £861.00 | 06.59 | | x | x | | x | | |
| | 18 | Telegraph Poles | £890.00 | 06.59 | | x | x | | x | x | |
| | 19 | Platform Canopy | £1,251.00 | 06.59 | | x | x | | | x | |
| | 20 | Scammell Scarab | £3,036.00 | 03.63 | | | x | | | | |

Note: Numbers 17,19 4017 & 4019 were all current in the same (2nd Edition) catalogue.
Kit 4013 Later issued as S46 in OO/HO Figures range.

| First No. | Later No. | Description of Kit | Original Mould Cost | Date Mould acquired | 0 | 1 | 2 | 3 | 4 | 6 | 7 |
|---|---|---|---|---|---|---|---|---|---|---|---|
| **Series 2** | | | | | | | | | | | |
| 4017 | *202?* | Control Tower | £3,426.00 | | | x | x | | x | | |
| 4019 | *203?* | Windmill | £1,430.00 | 12.58 | | x | x | | | x | |
| 4014 | 201 | Footbridge | £1,829.00 | 09.58 | | x | x | x | x | x | |
| 4015 | 204 | Village Church | £1,568.00 | 09.58 | | x | x | | | x | |
| | 205 | Travelling Crane | £2,076.00 | 12.59 | | | x | x | | x | |
| | 206 | Water Tower | £1,448.00 | 03.60 | | | x | | | x | |
| | 207 | Girder Bridge | £1,792.00 | 03.59 | | | x | x | x | x | |
| | 208 | Engine Shed | £2,246.00 | 09.60 | | | x | x | x | x | |
| **Series 3** | | | | | | | | | | | |
| | 302 | Turntable | £2,694.00 | 12.61 | | | x | | | x | |
| | 03625-2 | Platform Figures | £7,380.00 | 02.79 | | | | | | x | |
| | 03628-1 | Railway Workmen | £13,173.00 | 05.80 | | | | | | | x |
| | n/a | London Bus and Taxi | Not Released | | | | | | | | |
| **Series 1 OO/HO Scale Figures Series** | | | | | | | | | | | |
| | S9 | Farm Stock | | | | | x | x | | | |
| | S17 | Civilians | | | | | x | x | x | | |
| | S24 | Zoo Set 1 | | | | | x | x | | | |
| | S25 | Zoo Set 2 | | | | | x | x | | | |
| | S46 | Station Accessories (Re-issue of 4013) | | | | | | x | x | | |

Still the favourite box art for many collectors: Roy Cross studies for the Class 4MT and SR Schools, both here signed by the artist.

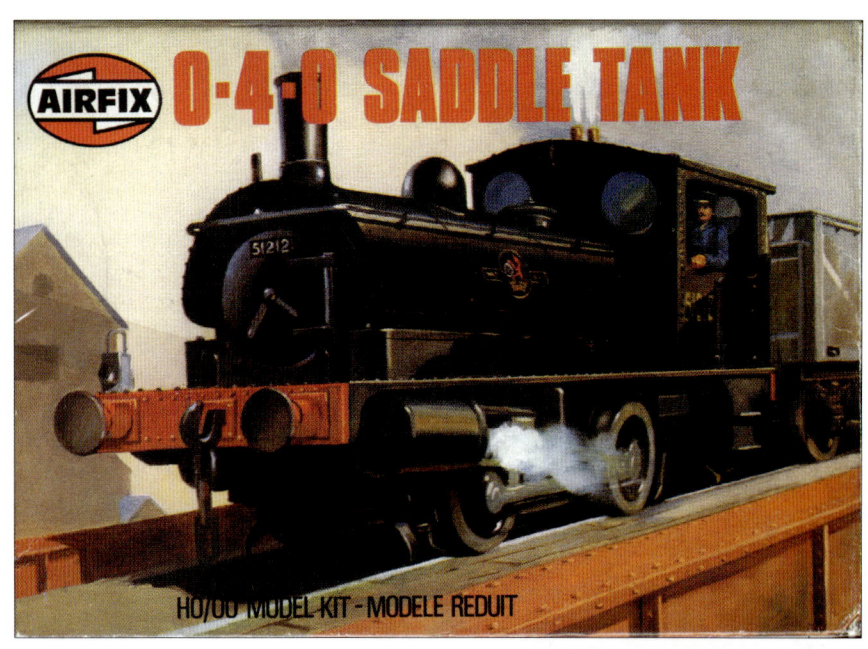

*Top two*. Type 6 boxes for the Pug and Prairie signalled the last high point in the range of locos under Airfix, from here, it was downhill all the way.

*Middle*. Incredibly, nobody at Haldane Place appears to have realised that their "factory built" Prairie model was missing the rear pony truck wheels! It made numerous catalogue appearances in this condition.

*Bottom*. The Airfix Evening Star factory model was, at least, complete, if somewhat garish.

The L&Y Pug was a diminutive loco which was consequently difficult to motorise. Artwork was provided by Charles Oakes and is unfinished in the corners of the canvass – perhaps due to a looming deadline? There were two issues in Type 3 boxes; the upper one here is the original, smaller box. Below it is the so-called "Limited Production" box which was uniform with the larger Series Two wagon issues.

*Below*. The full Pug artwork appears unfinished at lower left.

## SEE THIS AIRFIX HALF PAGE DAILY EXPRESS DECEMBER 3RD & 12TH

*Make it a model Christmas—give AIRFIX*

13,000,000 readers will see this advertisement in the Daily Express *twice* during December as part of the Airfix giant pre-Christmas campaign.

**AIRFIX PRODUCTS LTD · HALDANE PLACE · GARRATT LANE · SW18**

---

## MOTORIZING PLASTIC LOCO KITS

by H. F. Lane

RAILWAY MODELLER 'SHOWS YOU HOW' BOOKLET

**No. 15**

*For the Average Enthusiast*

The plastic loco kit is basically a static model, but inevitably one's thoughts turn towards the idea of motorization. This booklet shows you how to set about the job.

**9d**

---

## AIRFIX — SEE US AT

**BRIGHTON JAN 29 – FEB 2**
GRAND HOTEL BALLROOM STANDS G11–G15

**NUREMBURG FEB 12–17**
2ND FLOOR EUROPA-HAUS STAND 3221

*There's always something new from AIRFIX*

Variety! Non-stop additions to the famous Airfix range of profit makers. See what Airfix has in store for 1967. Motor Racing Sets, Construction Kits, Betta Bilda, New Artist and Dolls. Speciality toys for all ages.

**AIRFIX PRODUCTS LIMITED, HALDANE PLACE, GARRATT LANE, LONDON SW18**

---

## AIRFIX SMASH HITS for 1959!

See them at BRIGHTON—Metropole Hotel, Clarence Vestibule

**AIRFIX BEACH LINES**
BUCKETS · SAND MOULDS · PLAY SETS

★ "COMPLETE ANGLER" FISHING OUTFIT
★ "JUNIOR DRIVER" MOTORING OUTFIT
★ "INVITATION" TEA SET

*AIRFIX TOYS ARE PRESENTED IN COLOURFUL, EYE-CATCHING PACKS!*

**AIRFIX BUILDING SETS**
ATTRACTIVE NEW PACKS
NEW! A GARAGE CONVERSION SET

★ PARKING METER MONEY BOX
★ FLYING TARGET SET
★ "ROUND THE CLOCK" GOLF GAME

*AIRFIX MAKE BRITAIN'S LARGEST RANGE OF CONSTRUCTION KITS!*

**AIRFIX CONSTRUCTION KITS**
'OO' SCALE TRACKSIDE SERIES
Also SHIPS, CARS & 1/72nd Scale AIRCRAFT

Ask to see the complete range

**AIRFIX PRODUCTS LTD**
Haldane Place · Garratt Lane · London, S.W.18
Telephone: VANdyke 7575
Telegrams: Airfixco, Put, London

The full canvas of Charles Oakes Prairie artwork.

*All left hand page. Top left.* Anyone got last Decembers Daily Express? It might have an Airfix ad in it!

*Top right.* Ripe for motorisation, Kitmaster & Airfix kits generated many articles in the modelling press, eventually leading to this little pamphlet from Peco sporting both "*Evening Star*" and "*City of Truro*" on the cover.

*Bottom left.* Watch out! It's "Chippy" the "perky little fellow"! Never seen him? Look in your Fifth Edition Airfix catalogue! A 1968 Toy Fair ad from "Toys and Games".

*Bottom right.* Airfix rarely advertised in colour, but this is a rear cover from "Toys and Games" depicting the Trackside Accessories kit.

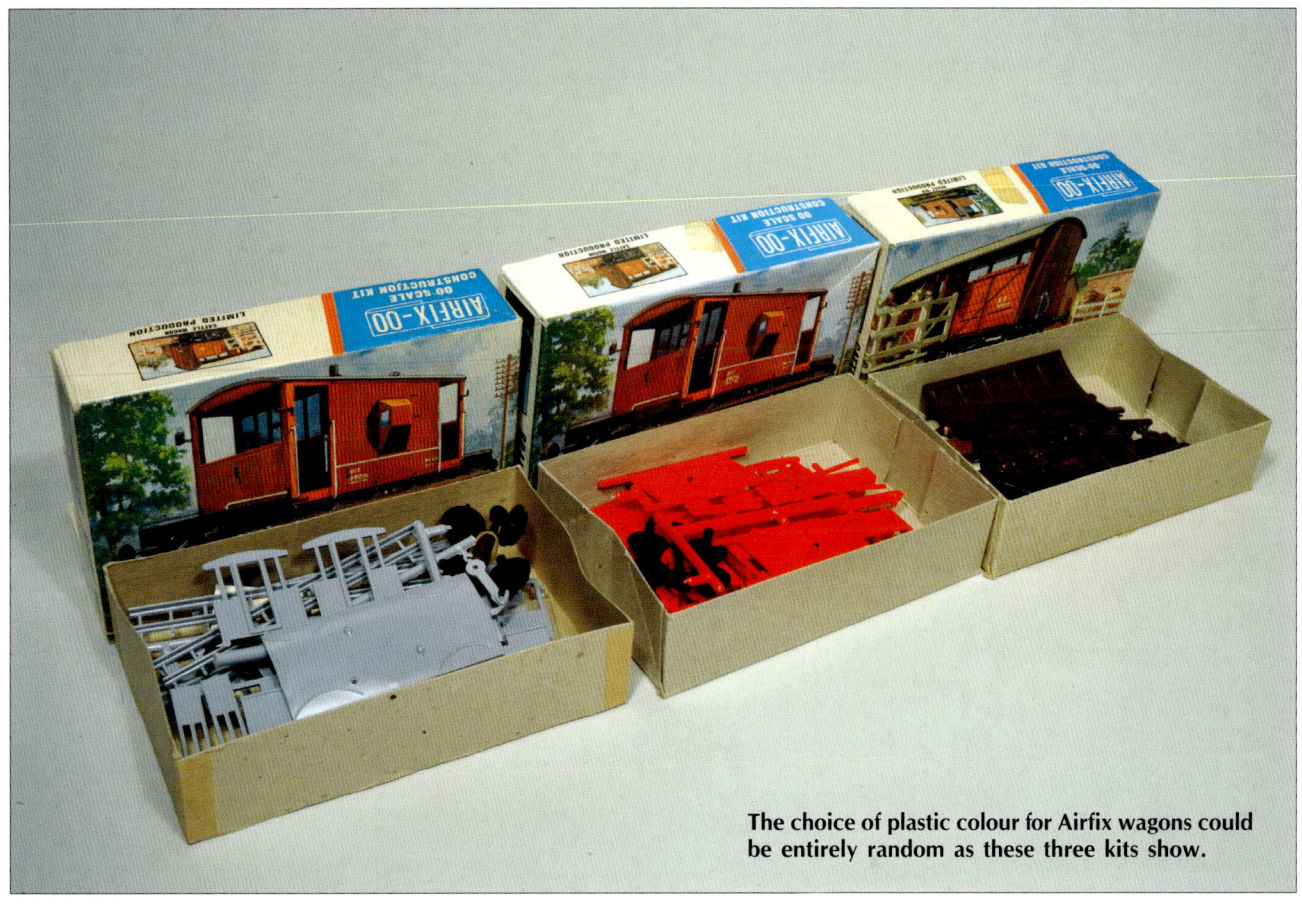

The choice of plastic colour for Airfix wagons could be entirely random as these three kits show.

185

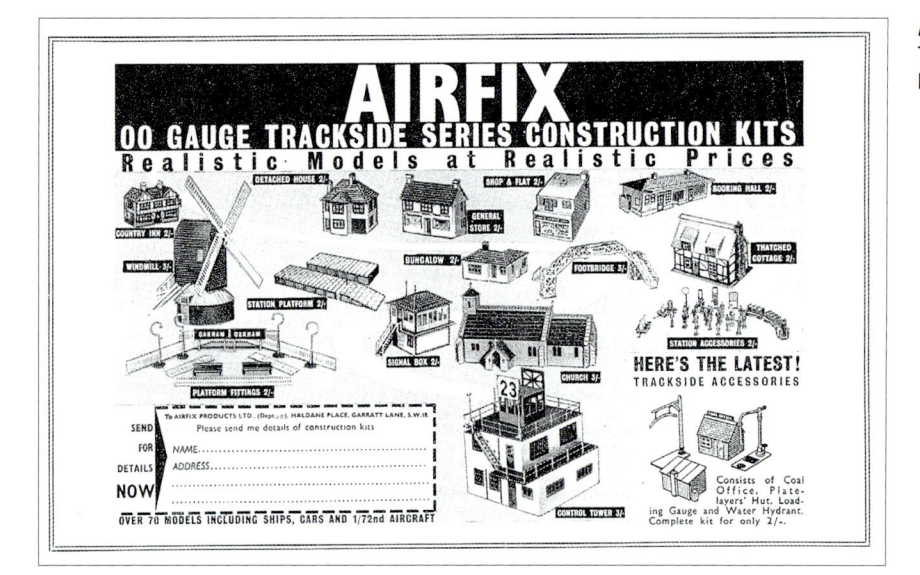

*Left.* A March 1959 half page ad for the Trackside range and a review of Platform Fittings.

## AIRFIX PLATFORM ACCESSORY KITS

WE illustrate below the latest additions to the popular Airfix range of lineside accessories for OO gauge. Two kits are involved, but as they are complementary they should be considered together. For four, six or eight shillings, according to the size of the station, you can fully people and finish the platforms.

The 2/- platform fittings kit comprises 24in. of fencing, two 3in. ramp fences, two nameboards, two platform seats and four lamps. The fence and lamps are provided with bases if the whole affair is to be used with a proprietary train set; scale modellers will, however, discard these and cement the fittings into holes in the platform. Two alternative names are provided, both finished in Eastern Region blue and taken from that region—a small point, but indicative of the designer's care.

The station accessories kit is also wonderful value. For your 2/- you first of all get no less than twenty-four unpainted figures, which in itself is good value—1d. each—even if you don't have a use for the rest! This is, however, most unlikely, for it includes two weighing machines, one for the passengers' luggage, the other a coin-operated personal scale; a chocolate machine of the latest design; and one other slot machine of an indefinite design which could be adapted to most purposes. Then there are an electric trolley and two trailers, two hand trolleys and a small selection of baggage, one barrel, two packing cases and four churns.

We have no hesitation in thoroughly recommending these kits, for they are in our experience unsurpassed in value. There is no reason whatever for bare platforms on 4mm. scale railways!

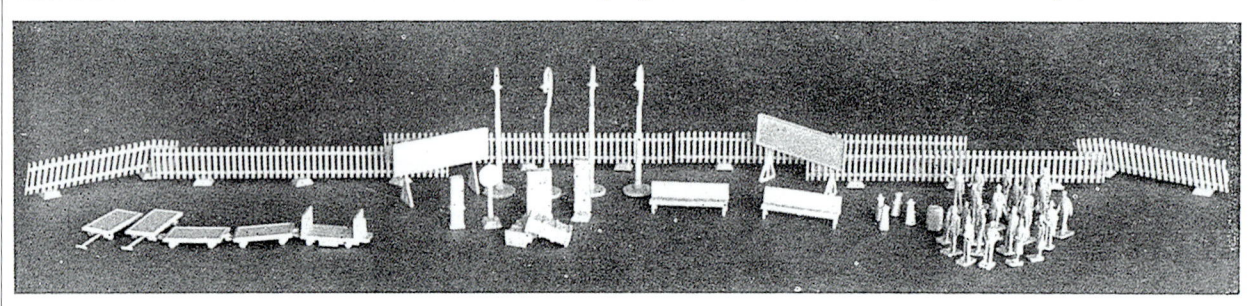

*Above and left.* Although Airfix kits were always described as being for OO and HO gauge, only the Interfrigo was actually modelled in HO scale. It was not successful and quickly disappeared.

186

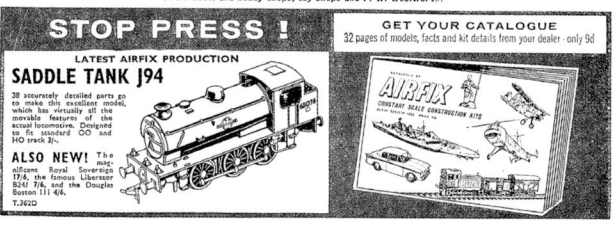

*Above.* Airfix "STOP PRESS!" adverts were used to announce new products. The line drawings were made by hand from bleached-out monochrome photographs of completed models. Later a fully-worked up picture would appear in the "JUST LIKE THE REAL THING" area above as these well-illustrated examples from 1964 show.

*Left.* Almost the end: Mr Farnell was very lucky to receive his *"City of Truro"* kit at this late stage; Airfix were about to enter receivership.

# AIRFIX PRODUCTS LTD
### Manufacturers of Plastic Construction Kits and Toys

HALDANE PLACE  ·  GARRATT LANE  ·  LONDON - S. W. 18.

Telephone VANdyke 7575/6/9
Telegrams: AIRFIXCO,PUT, LONDON.
Code: A.B.C. 7TH EDITION.

YOUR REF:
OUR REF: EHS/MH/HOME                DATE 14th July, 1965.

Mr. R.K. Bickers,
6, Downes Court,
Winchmore Hill,
London, N.21.

Dear Sir,

In reply to your letter of the 4th July, we note that when attending at the Interplas Exhibition recently you were advised of our proposed intention to re-introduce the former Kitmaster models.

As you will be aware from the enclosed Catalogue of our range of construction kits, we have in the last year to eighteen months re-introduced several of the items which were formerly marketed by Kitmaster and whilst we cannot give you any advance information, would advise you that where these items are likely to blend suitably with our own range of rolling stock, etc., future re-introductions may be made. At the moment, however, we cannot give you any firm indication of any future models which are likely to be re-introduced.

Yours faithfully,
AIRFIX PRODUCTS LIMITED

E.H. SPALL
Sales Office Manager

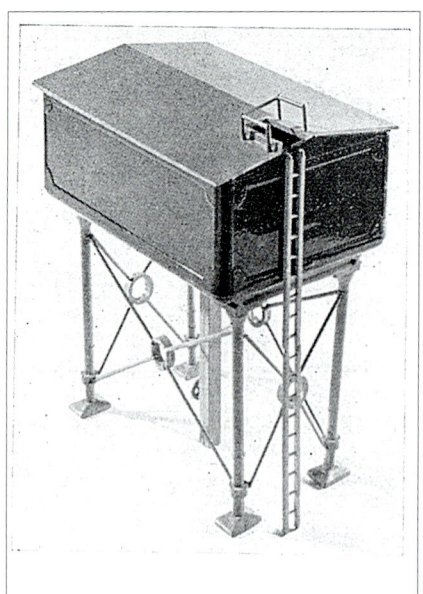

## AIRFIX WATER CRANE

THE latest Airfix lineside accessory is the water tank, which is a No. 2 series model and retails at 3/-. As can be seen from the illustration, it is the conventional design of a rectangular tank supported on cast-iron columns. It is, of course, a very important accessory, and a must wherever water cranes are included in the model. It is also of considerable value for industrial models, while even if one does not need the column the detailed tank can be employed on a home-constructed "brick" foundation.

---

**The era of "Limited Production" kits in Type 3 boxes produced vast quantities of stock which lasted throughout the Seventies. The only limit seems to be how many they thought the Dealers would take.**

J & L Randall of Potters Bar made a super range of OO scale figures and animals, ideal for loading your Airfix wagons, but you do need to butcher the pigs first!

# Realistic Models at Realistic Prices!

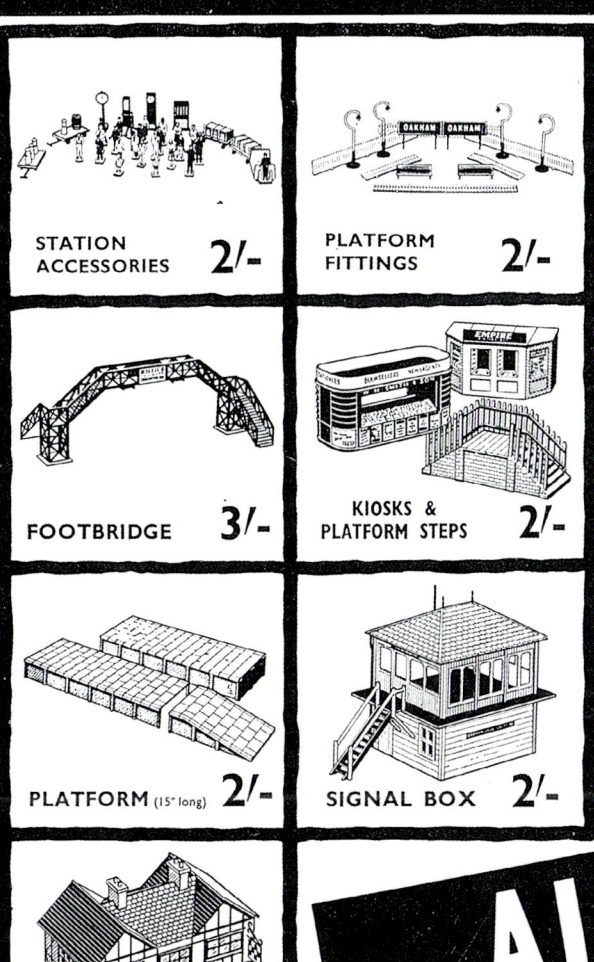

**STATION ACCESSORIES** 2/-

**PLATFORM FITTINGS** 2/-

**FOOTBRIDGE** 3/-

**KIOSKS & PLATFORM STEPS** 2/-

**PLATFORM** (15" long) 2/-

**SIGNAL BOX** 2/-

**COUNTRY INN** 2/-

THERE ARE ALREADY OVER 60 AIRFIX KITS
—and new models are introduced every month!

## OO GAUGE TRACKSIDE SERIES

A really low-priced series of attractive models that will add realism and authenticity to any scenic layout. Moulded in high-impact plastic, in kit form and complete with easy-to-assemble instructions. Terrific value!

*Now available:*

COUNTRY INN
SERVICE STATION
SIGNAL BOX
BOOKING HALL
SHOP AND FLAT
DETACHED HOUSE
GENERAL STORE
BUNGALOW

PLATFORM
THATCHED COTTAGE
KIOSKS AND PLATFORM STEPS
FOOTBRIDGE (No. 2 series)
PLATFORM FITTINGS
STATION ACCESSORIES

## SHIPS, CARS and 1/72nd AIRCRAFT

A finely detailed series of scale models in kit form, moulded in high-impact plastic. Aircraft kits have authentic marking transfers and display stands included. Ships are complete with flags and display stands, and the range of vintage cars are complete in detail down to the number plates. Undoubtedly the finest value in kits today!

★

# AIRFIX CONSTRUCTION KITS
## LEAD IN QUALITY & PRICE

*Ask your dealer for the latest AIRFIX list*

AIRFIX KITS ARE AVAILABLE FROM
**ALL GOOD MODEL SHOPS, STORES and TOY SHOPS**

KINDLY MENTION THE **RAILWAY MODELLER** WHEN WRITING TO ADVERTISERS

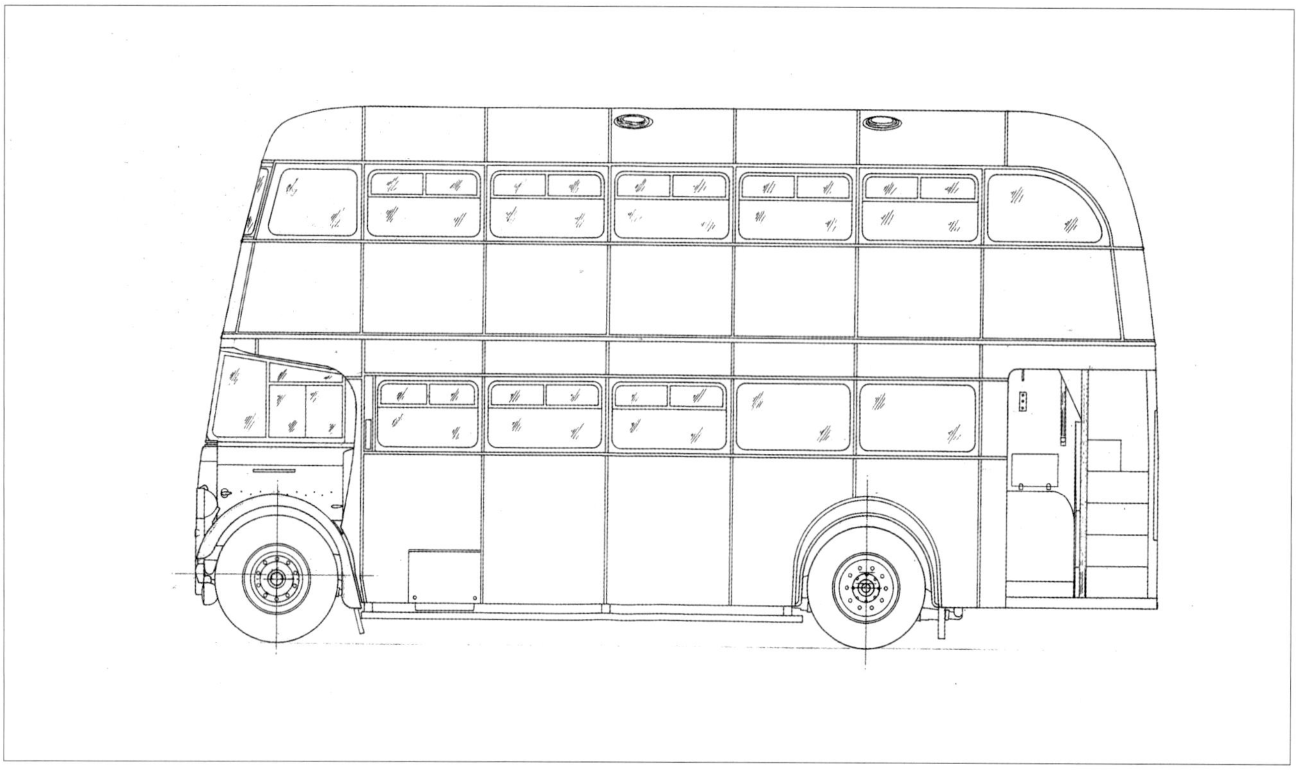

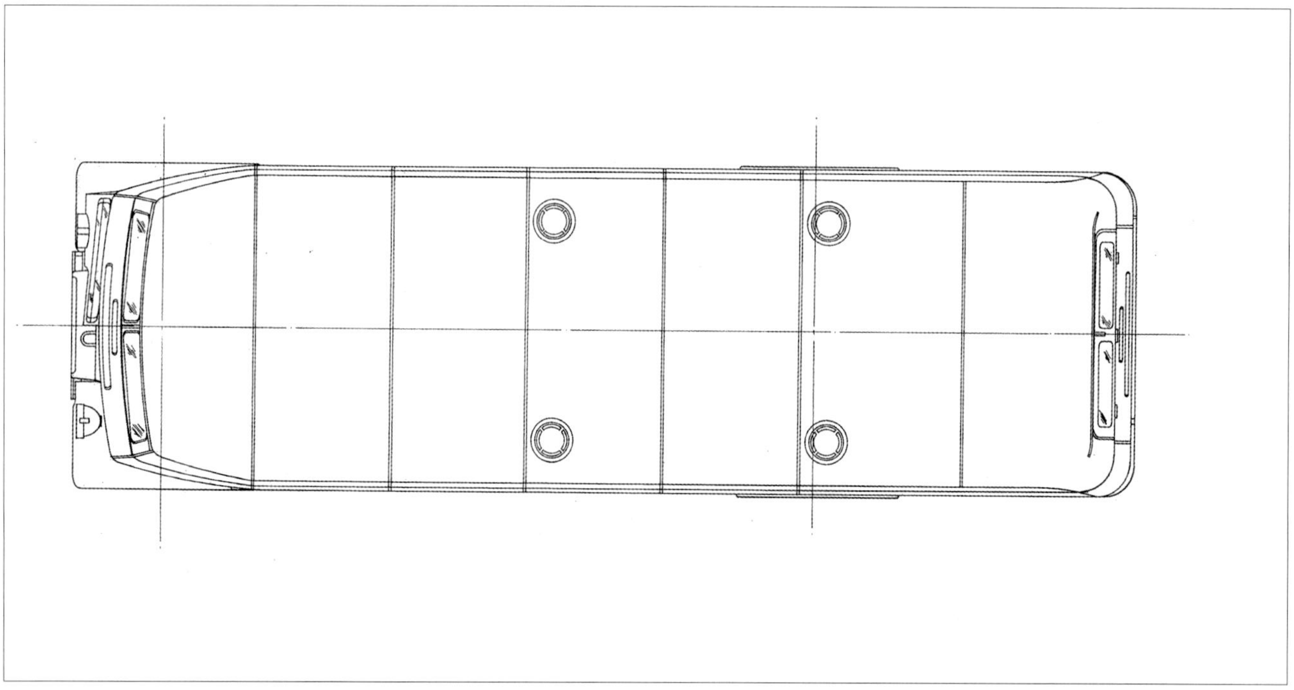

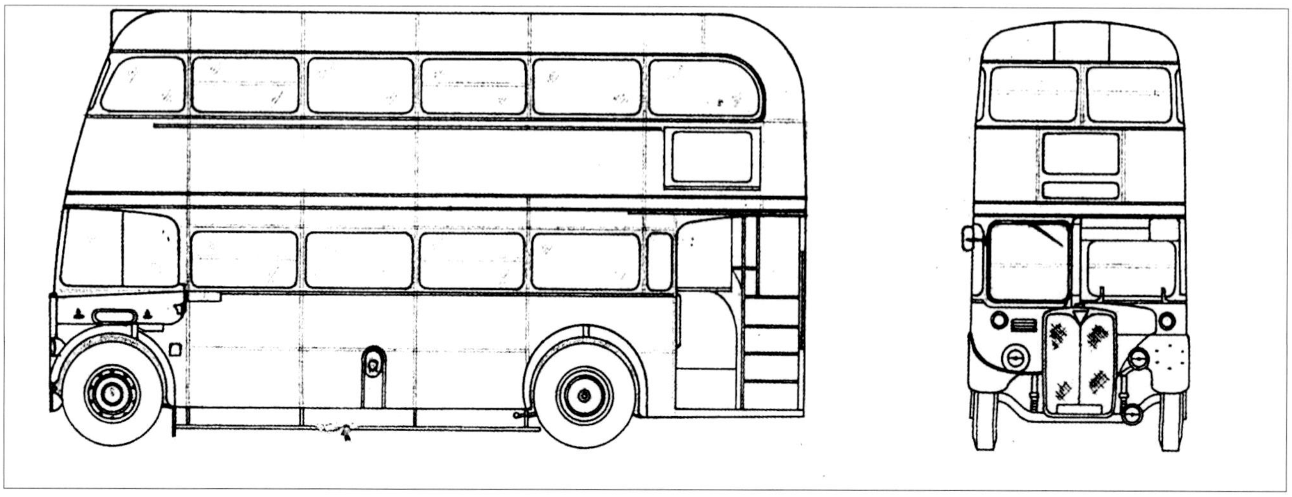

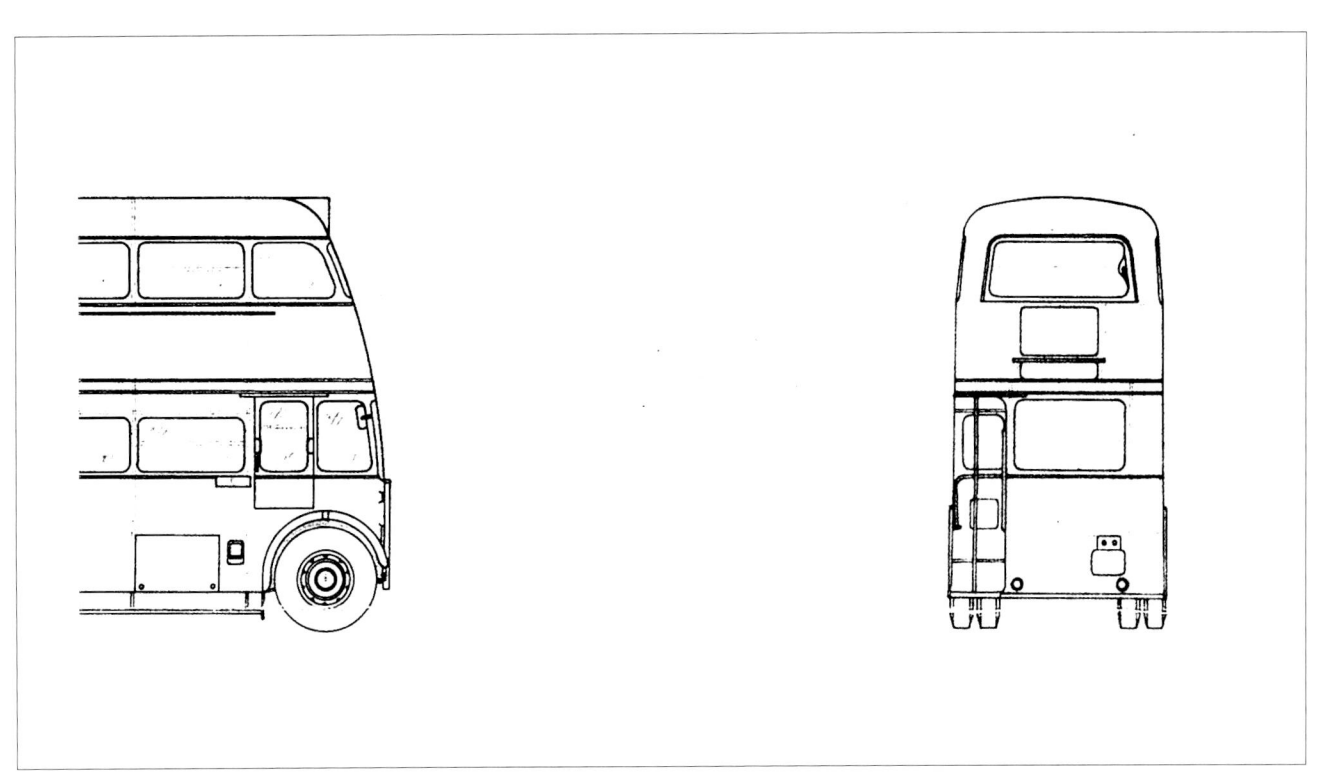

The ill fated Series Three combination kit for an FX3 London Taxi and a Leyland PD2 bus only got as far as this set of remarkable GA drawings, made in late 1980. It would have been particularly popular as it pre-dated widely available OO scale buses by at least 10 years.

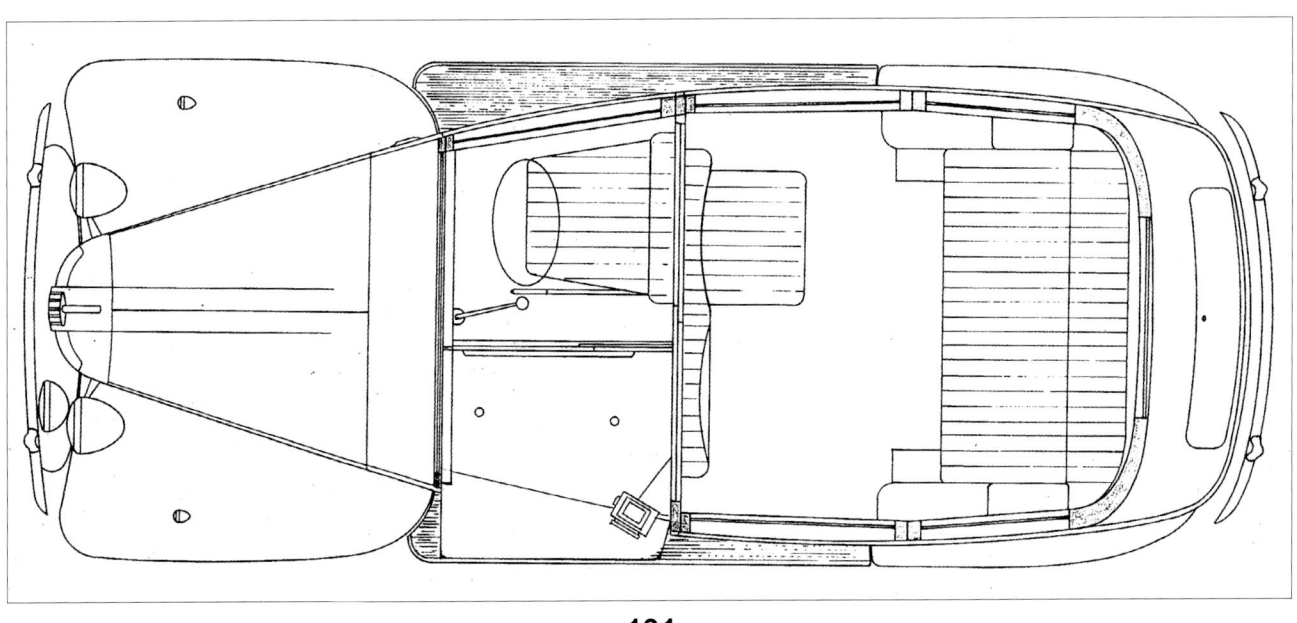

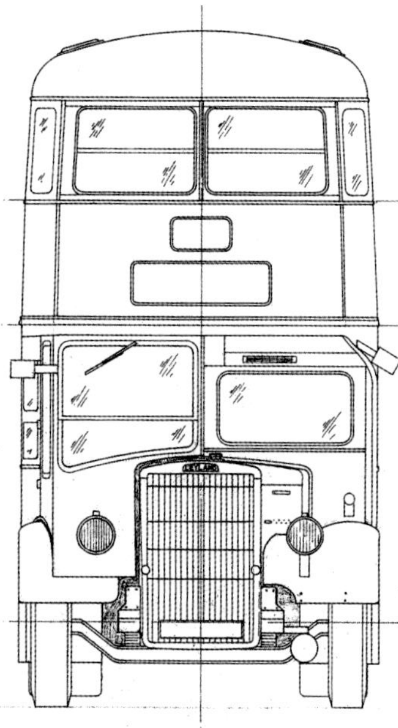

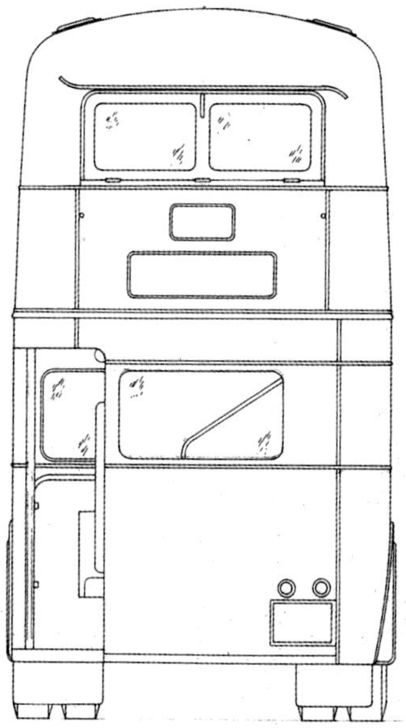

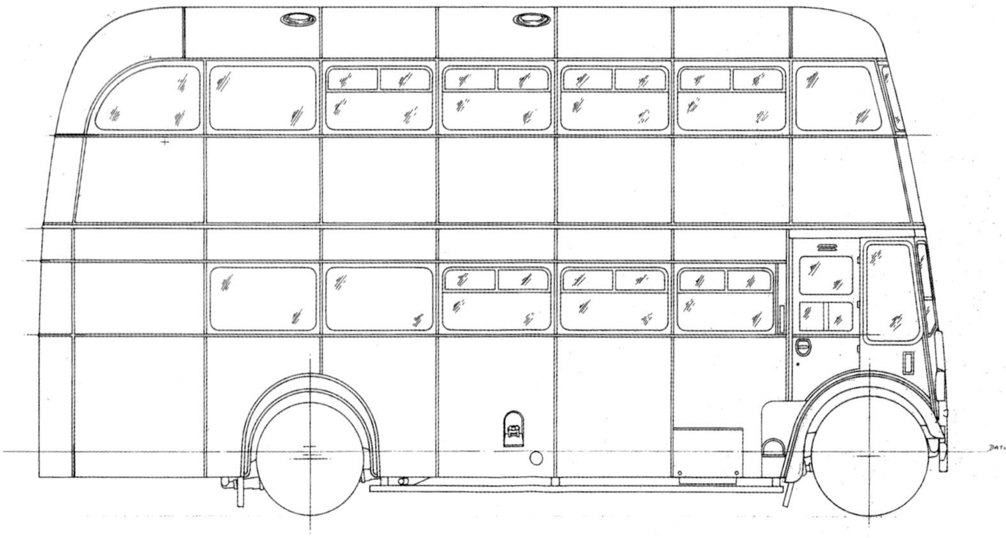

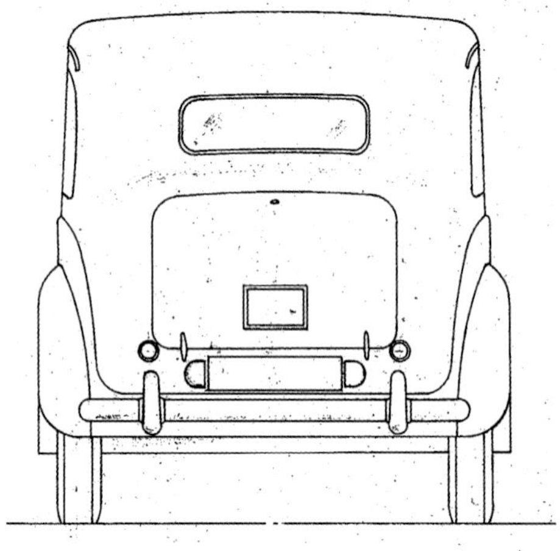

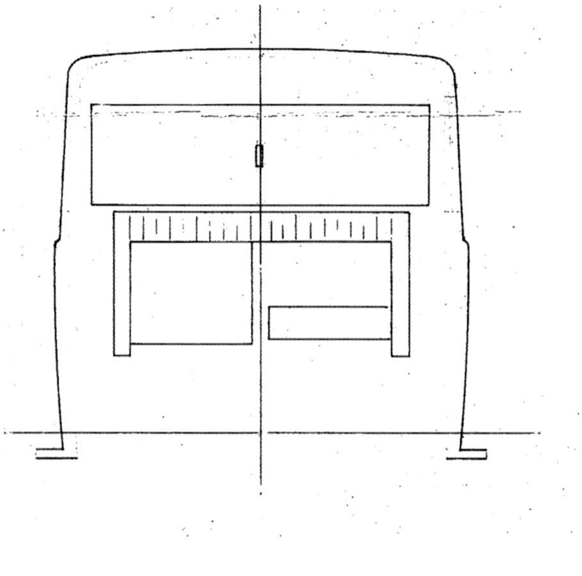

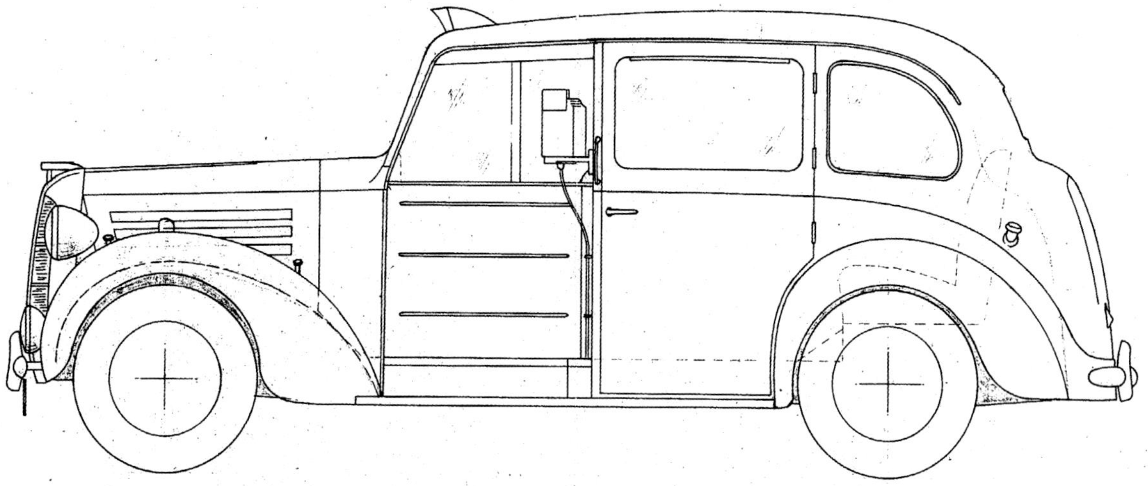

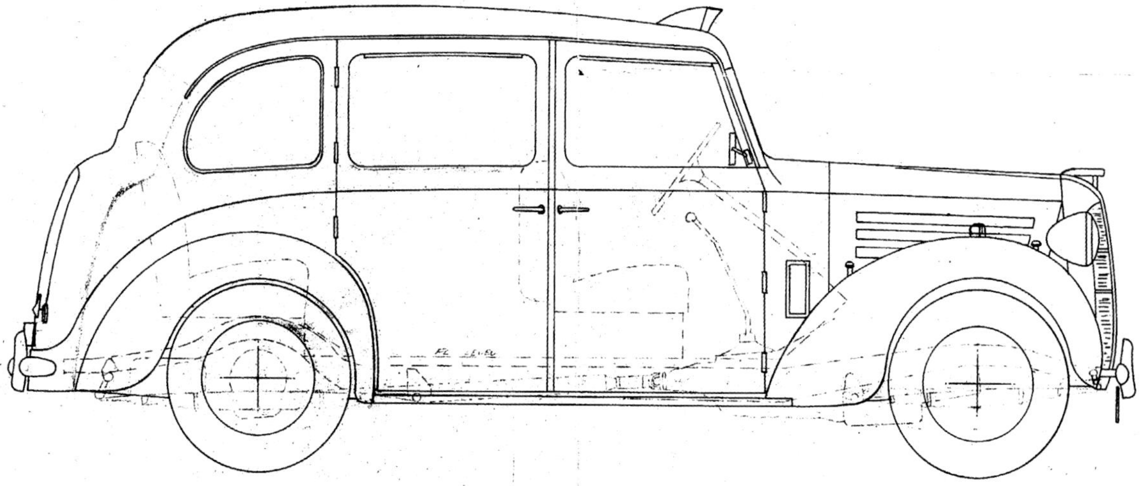

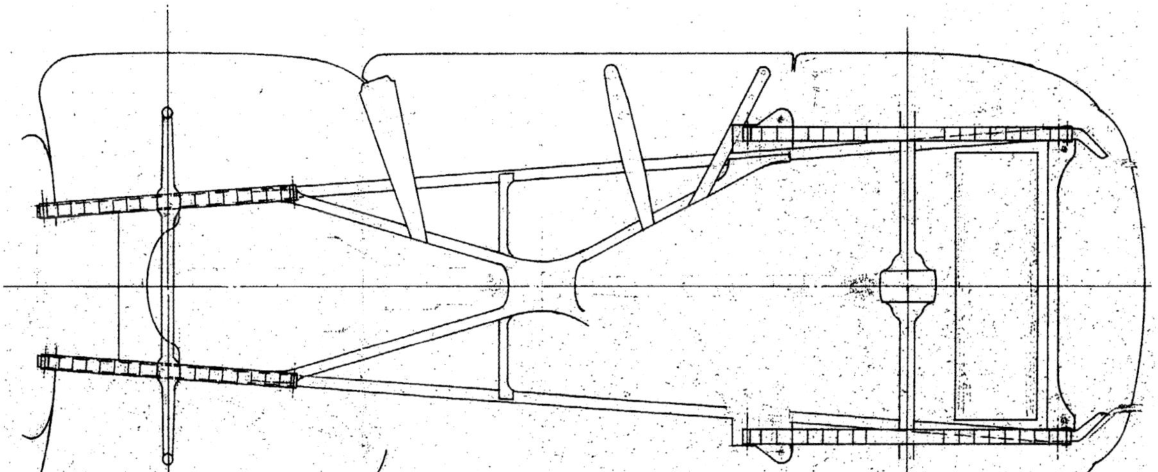

*Above.* Marcus Archer built this Railbus and scratchbuilt an interior. The figures are from Airfix and Merit. A real Railbus, at this time allocated to Bletchley for working Banbury-Buckingham and Bedford-Hitchin services, appears in the Just Like the Real Thing advert. When these lines closed, the Park Royal railbuses were trundled North to see out their days in Scotland.

# Chapter 8: The Airfix Models In Detail
## The Models In Detail - 24
### R201 - The Park Royal Railbus
*A Guest Article by John Wells*

Hailed as the future of rural rail transport, the various rigid four-wheel railbuses introduced by British Railways proved to be great disappointments. This did not prevent Airfix from modelling a version of the railbus built by Park Royal, but it did lead to the early deletion of the model from their catalogue.

In November 1960 the Stop Press column of the then popular, 'Believe it or not' series of Airfix advertisements carried details of the latest Airfix production, which was heralded as: 'A superbly detailed OO/HO scale model of the BR 50-seat Railbus. 7 inches long, it has sliding doors, free-running wheels and can be motorised easily. This 67-piece kit plus nine marking transfers costs 3 shillings.' The kit was enthusiastically reviewed by the railway modelling press of the day and as British Railways were in the midst of their modernisation programme, which would lead, ultimately, to the demise of the steam locomotive in regular daily use, the Railbus fitted in very well with anyone who was trying to portray the railways at that period in time.

The prototype for the Airfix model was the 50 seat Park Royal Vehicles Ltd Railbus, stock number M79971 which was introduced into service in 1958, on the Bedford-Hitchin branch of the London Midland Region. A total of five vehicles was delivered to this design. Four other manufacturers supplied BR with similar vehicles. These were, for the record: A.C. Cars of Thames Ditton, D.Wickham & Co. of Ware, Waggon und Maschinenbau, GmbH. of Donauwõrth, Germany and finally, Bristol Commercial Vehicles, Bristol. The Park Royal cars were powered by an underfloor 150 b.h.p. diesel engine, manufactured by British United Traction (B.U.T.), which was the trading name given to the joint company formed by Leyland Vehicles and A.E.C Ltd. Arguably the Park Royal design was the most handsome and the Bristol, the ugliest.

The main reason that these vehicles were built was to cut operating costs on remote branch lines. The idea of lightweight railcars was not a new one, for they were quite common in some European countries. Unfortunately in the UK they were a commercial disaster, coming too late to save many unprofitable lines. All were withdrawn from service by 1968.

As far as can be established, the Airfix Railbus only ever appeared in a Series 2 box of the second Airfix design (Type 2) carrying pattern number R201. True to form for contemporary Airfix kits, there are two minor box-art variants:

1. Light Malachite green Railbus carrying the -coach number 1179973. (the 11 should of course, be the letter 'M' to signify allocation to the London Midland Region of BR).2. Dark Multiple unit green version with the coach number almost obliterated.

The only indications that Type 3 artwork may have been completed are the small illustrations on the side panels of the Airfix J94 Saddle Tank kit, early issues of the L&Y Pug (small box) and the Series 4 Evening Star kit. The kit comprised 47 parts moulded in green plastic, of which a number of shades exist; the remaining 20 were in clear plastic for the glazing. The darker green mouldings tend to appear, somewhat ironically, within the boxes with the lighter malachite green artwork. A nine subject transfer sheet was provided,

**Guest Author John Wells (left) admires a Bristol Beaufort painting by Airfix artist Roy Cross (right).**

which included coach numbers (M79971), coach crests, frontal 'Speed Whiskers' (the forerunner of the yellow warning panels introduced in the mid-1960s) and technical data markings. The two-character headcode (B1) was not supplied as a transfer, but was instead printed on the instruction sheet, which was presented in the usual Type 2 format. The style and feel of the kit is very similar to that of the superb Rosebud 'Kitmaster' range of BR Mk1 coaches.

R201 appeared in the first (1962), second, third and fourth edition Airfix catalogues and the seasonal leaflets which preceded them. The advent of the fifth edition (3/67) brought with it a general tidying up of pattern numbers, eliminating for the most part the remaining early four digit pattern numbers and introducing fully computerised stock numbers. The other more drastic change was the deletion of the complete range of Series 2 railway rolling stock kits, some of which were destined never again to see the light of day under the Airfix umbrella. Kit number 201 was now the Footbridge, in the trackside series.

That was, therefore, the end of the only model of passenger carrying rolling stock made by Airfix, perhaps echoing the failure of the prototypes, having in the main, one suspects, a rather limited appeal. This, of course, did not prevent several well known names producing motorising kits. Three that we know of are:a) Arby Perfecta - better known for their motorising packs for Kitmaster locomotives.b) The Southgate Hobbyshop, known later as Beatties.c) Eames of Reading.

The Southgate Hobbyshop and Eames conversions both had replacement metal chassis and the Perfecta kit (No.1a) was a modification to the one designed for the Kitmaster 'Pug' loco. All three based their designs around the slightly better Tri-ang XT60 12v DC motor.

The Dapol kits come in a poly-bag complete with header card (similar to the early Airfix series 2 kits) and are mainly moulded in a medium shade of grey complete with the bonus of ready-to-run wheelsets with pin point metal axles. The transfers are exactly the same as the original Airfix sheet. Artwork for the 1st Dapol header card was taken directly from the Airfix launch advert printed in maroon, as most Dapol instructions and headers were, making the pre-printed 2 character headcode appear rather inauthentic when used on the model. As with the original kit, motorising conversions have been manufactured for the Dapol model, by Branchlines of Exeter, who also produce an interior detailing kit.

An interesting twist in the tale concerns the doyen of the class, M79971, which ended its revenue earning days operating on obscure lines in Scotland. After withdrawal from service in 1968 it did not follow the fate of its stablemates by being reduced to scrap metal, but instead the body was separated from the chassis, grounded and used as a messroom in Millerhill marshalling yard until 1981. Because of the levels of asbestos present in the body, it could not be broken up in the normal manner, so it was taken to Pattersons Tip at Bishopbriggs, in Glasgow, where it was unceremoniously buried in the ground.

**AIRFIX**
# DREWRY 204 H.P. DIESEL SHUNTER
## CONSTRUCTION KIT

**HO & OO GAUGE SCALE MODEL**

As Airfix lauded the Drewry Shunter, the re-issue Kitmaster Prairie was making its debut in the "Stop Press!" box.

### ...it even has cab controls!

*This Airfix OO/HO scale Drewry Shunter is a model of detail that can be motorised. 67-part kit 2/-.* It's typical of the realism you get with Airfix models. They're just like the real thing! More than that, though, Airfix give you constant scale, so that the models of every series are proportionately right; and a great ever-increasing range — there are 11 series now, with over 200 kits. At prices from 2/- to 15/- Airfix are great on value too.

For endless modelling fun — make it Airfix.

**JUST LIKE THE REAL THING!**   **AIRFIX**   **CONSTANT SCALE CONSTRUCTION KITS**

*From model and hobby shops, toy shops and F. W. Woolworth.*

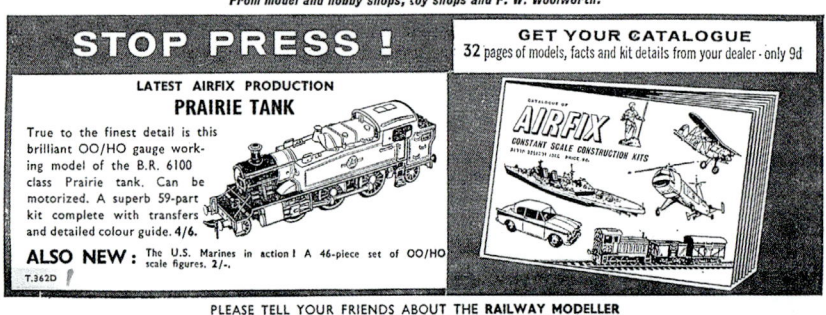

**STOP PRESS !**

**LATEST AIRFIX PRODUCTION — PRAIRIE TANK**
True to the finest detail is this brilliant OO/HO gauge working model of the B.R. 6100 class Prairie tank. Can be motorized. A superb 59-part kit complete with transfers and detailed colour guide. 4/6.

**ALSO NEW:** The U.S. Marines in action! A 46-piece set of OO/HO scale figures. 2/-.

T.362D

**GET YOUR CATALOGUE**
32 pages of models, facts and kit details from your dealer - only 9d

PLEASE TELL YOUR FRIENDS ABOUT **THE RAILWAY MODELLER**

# The Models In Detail - 25
## Airfix R7 Drewry 204 HP 0-6-0 Diesel Shunter

Airfix released their first 'real' locomotive kit to rapturous applause in October of 1961. Contemporary reviewers heralded the wealth of detail in a kit that could be used on just about any layout and at a remarkable price – just two shillings would buy you this brand new Series 1 kit. The Drewry kit arrived in a striking Type 2 box, which was the same size as the popular series of railway wagons that preceded it. Unlike the wagons, however, the Drewry shunter had a lamentably short catalogue life with Airfix and as a consequence, it never appeared in any other packaging style. Just imagine what a fine sight a Ken Rush or Roy Cross Type 3 Drewry would make!

The Drewry Car Co first built a prototype of their hugely successful 0-6-0 diesel mechanical design as long ago as 1947. The locomotive was extensively trialled on the LNER and later Eastern Region of BR before being returned to the manufacturer. This first unit differs from the later production Class 04 and the kit in having square windows. Original units had only one cab side window whilst later units had improved visibility cabs with two side windows and tapered lower front cab windows. CME of British Railways, R.A.Riddles envisaged a fleet of small and versatile locomotives of this type to replace large numbers of steam shunting engines on duties in restricted places such as docks, steelworks, depots and on general shunter duties. The Class 04, as it became known under the 1967 TOPS numbering, was ideally suited to the job, having a short wheelbase of just nine feet and a powerful Gardiner diesel engine centrally mounted and driving through a jackshaft.

The design proved so popular when bulk deliveries commenced in 1952 that British Railways perpetuated their own version of the basic locomotive, as Class 03. All in all, 142 04s were built up to 1961, of which many have survived in preservation and in industrial revenue-earning service. There are many detail differences between individual locomotives, including progressively larger wheels throughout the period of construction. The first three locomotives, then numbered 11100-11103, were delivered to BR Eastern Region to replace ancient GE steam 'tram' locomotives on the Wisbech & Upwell Tramway and at Ipswich Docks. Hence these engines were fitted with 'tram' skirts covering the motion.

The kit represents a later locomotive after the 1960 revision to the numbering system, when all diesel and electric locomotives gained either a D or E prefix to distinguish them from steam classes. In addition the 'stove' pipe chimney is prominent on this locomotive whereas in reality many different variations existed for the smoke cowl. In 1999, Bachmann Industries Europe Ltd produced a super ready to run version of the locomotive, re-using the chassis from their existing Class 03 shunter. Prior to release, catalogue shots showed professionally built Airfix kits finished in appropriate liveries.

**Airfix Drewry shunter leading a short freight on Tony Wright's Little Bytham layout.**

*Left.* An early BRCW diesel hauls the first two prototype Roadrailer units finished with blue name boards.

*Below.* Three different brandings were used on the Roadrailer fleet as seen here. Although the kit comes with AEC Mandator prime mover, the Bristol FCG6 unit was much more prevalent in service. A Bedford S type tractor was also used.

*Bottom.* The crew manhandle the portable air compressor in to position to activate road/rail wheel changeover.

198

# Chapter 9: Middlesex Toy Industries - Scalecraft

Another manufacturer of plastic assembly kits using injection moulded polystyrene, Middlesex Toy Industries introduced the Scalecraft name with a range of 1/48th scale snap-together racing cars. These included a Mini Cooper and a Lotus Formula 1 racing car. Packaged in red and black boxes about 5in by 4in, they proved popular. Each kit included a motor and gears whilst the one piece body moulding included clips for AA batteries. These appear to date from 1960-63.

David Jane worked for Middlesex Toy Industries, starting work there in October 1964 as a model maker at Twickenham. The Middlesex Toy Industries factory was under the railway arches in Twickenham and had been a higgledy-piggledy collection of workshops in a previous life. The frugal attitude of MTI and the boss, Derek Baldwin, made model making an interesting task. David's job was to re-use as many standard components as possible in any new model. He was the junior of three model makers there, and had to think up ideas for new models in the Scalecraft range, make working prototypes and try to sell the ideas to the MD of Seddon Bros. David says it was a fascinating job, sometimes a frustrating job when the idea he had been working on was turned down and then consigned to the back of the cupboard.

'We spent a lot of time sorting out problems experienced by purchasers of the kits who couldn't get them to work properly. I remember that the Centurion Tank was the worst. The gearbox was difficult to complete with all the gears in the right order, although when it worked it was a very impressive model. The Traction Engine was another dodgy one, I recall, but most of the others were quite simple and didn't cause problems.' The tools were all produced in-house at first, but by the time David joined them they were already being sent out to Hong Kong, following the course taken by so many British toy companies at that time. In late 1961, Middlesex Toy Industries introduced a further range of Scalecraft products, this time in 1/76th (OO) scale. These were exclusively licensed for distribution by The Pritchard Patent Product Co 'PECO'. The series consists of three kits on the subject of the new Road-Railer train. The Road-Railer was developed by the Pressed Steel Company and undertook trials extensively on the Eastern Region during 1961-62, before the advent of the now ubiquitous Freightliner. A special station yard test site was constructed at Takely, on the Bishops Stortford to Braintree branch (closed 1967) where the experimental units could transfer from road to rail and vice-versa. The other end of the line was Canning Town in London. where a similar Road to Rail transfer siding was built. This operation involved using a portable air-compressor unit to provide the pneumatic force for the exchanging of road and rail wheels. The Scalecraft RoadRailer series was advertised extensively by PECO from mid 1961 until the early 1970s and came in three distinctly packaged kits:
Kit No.1 RoadRailer - Complete Kit introduced Dec 1961

**These photographs feature three semitrailers and the Adaptor Bogie built from Scalecraft Kits by Marcus Archer and photographed by Tony Wright.**

199

Contents: AEC Mandator Prime Mover, Rail Bogie, Box Van trailer, 7s 6d
Kit No.2 Accessory Kit - Box Van introduced Dec 1961Contents: Box Van trailer, 3s 0d
Kit No.3 Accessory Kit - Prime Mover introduced April 1962Contents: AEC Mandator Prime Mover, Rail Bogie, 4s 6d
Kit No.4 Accessory Kit - Compressors - Not Released. Introduction autumn 1962Contents: 3 x trackside air compressor, 2s 0d
Kit No.5 Accessory Kit - Platform Wagon - Not Released. Introduction laterContents: Flat Bed trailer with Packing case, 3s 0d
Kit No.6 Accessory Kit - Tanker - Not Released. Introduction LaterContents: Tanker Trailer, 3s 0d

Rapid containerisation of rail freight led to an abrupt curtailment of the RoadRailer project, but the three kits proved extremely popular. In fact, the RoadRailer project gripped the imagination of the rail-minded public to such an extent that there was even a ready-to-run version in the Tri-ang Minic range (now much sought after by collectors) which allowed automatic docking and would run on Minic Motorway or Tri-ang Railways tracks! The Scalecraft model is the only proprietary model kit of the AEC Mandator vehicle ever produced. It is of the original deep window cab, there being a later Mandator cab with more normal windscreens. Mandators also saw use as Blue Streak missile transporters, but apart from their use in this and the RoadRailer project, they appear to have had only a short working lifetime.

It seems that the Bristol HG6L tractor unit of the FCG/1 Longwell Green type constructed in 1957 was a much more normal pairing with the RoadRailer trailers than the AEC Mandator included in the Scalecraft kit. A BR publicity photograph, apparently taken at the experimental Canning Town RoadRailer hub, depicts unit XYY 137 (Fleet number 1A 114) which was part of a fleet of 60 such units allocated to the BRS depot at Kentish Town. These tractors were intensively used on Anglo-Scottish freight using the newly opened M1 motorway. Units from London worked as far as Coventry or Stonebridge (near the NEC) where a Birmingham-based unit took over. The RoadRailer trials used one of these tractors each day and apparently put considerable strain on the fleet by removing a spare tractor from available service and tying it up each day.

Scalecraft RoadRailer Kit No.1 came in a similar type of box to their racing cars, whilst the two accessory kits were bagged with card headers rather like a Perfecta kit. The boxed kit instructions feature an unusual design on the cover and drawings of DB diesel locomotives inside and are copied exactly from the original Pressed Steel Co. sales brochure for the RoadRailer.

At the 1962 Toy Fair in Brighton, the Peco stand was exhibiting an electric road/rail axle changeover system to fit in the box van. It appeared to be operated via a switch from the Minic roadway track supply. At the same show, Peco were forecasting a new kit containing three of the trackside compressor units and then in the future a 'Platform Lorry' and a Tanker. These two kits were said to be in preparation by Scalecraft, awaiting the finalisation of the real design by Pressed Steel. In the event, this never saw the light of day and the project was cancelled along with the real thing. The withdrawn trailers were kept in a shed at Stratford Depot for several years before being cut up quietly. Some of them ended their days at a factory adjacent to the Lea Valley line, north of Temple Mills yard, where they were used as storage units. At least one body survived on a Northamptonshire farm until 2002! The fate of Middlesex Toy Industries and Scalecraft was to be absorbed into the Airfix group of companies in the mid-1970s.

****

The RoadRailer liveries are very well covered by Cambridge Custom Transfers which are highly recommended: **Cambridge Custom Transfers, 206 Nuns Way, North Arbury, Cambridge CB4 2NS** (Sheet BL20). Both the 1960 prototypes and the 1962 production vehicles are included, as are all known liveries. Even the unique and little-known low-sided RoadRailer is there. The sheet provides enough lettering for up to fifteen RoadRailers and pairs of numbers for all sixty RoadRailers and converter wagons are included. In addition CCT also produce alternative number and logo sets for the Airfix Esso Class B Tank Wagon (Bitumen, Oil A and B plus Regent Oil B) as well as the Presflos and Prestwins.

**A selection of bagged and boxed Scalecraft Roadrailer kits**

The complete train is hauled by a Kitmaster Class 08 shunter.

Left is the Scalecraft unit and it compares very well with (right) the Minic Motorways unit by Tri-ang. The Minic adaptor bogie made use of a standard BR Mk1 coach bogie to save costs.

201

# MOTORISED BOGIE AND BOX WAGON
RUN YOUR KITMASTER MODELS ON ANY 2 RAIL TRACK 12-15v. DC

Now every Kitmaster collector can cheaply and easily motorise his models to run on 00/H0 or T.T. Tracks, thanks to the new electric Motor Bogies and motorised Box Wagon.

The Motorised Bogies are ready to run and are complete with detailed instructions for assembly into the Corridor Brake 2nd. Kit No. 15. 00/H0 or Kit No. 17 T.T.

The motorised Box Wagon comes to you ready to run, complete with snap fit buffers, vacuum pipes and hand brakes.

**K.M.1.   00/H0   32/6**
ELECTRIC MOTOR BOGIE
To be used with Kit No. 15 Corridor Brake 2nd

MOTORISED BOGIE FITTED TO COACH No. 15

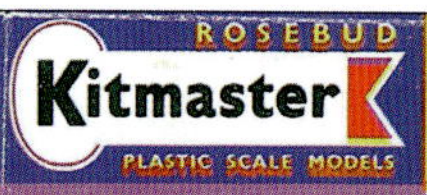

**K.M.2.   00/H0   39/6**
ELECTRIC MOTORISED BOX WAGON
To be used with Kitmaster Freight Engines

## Kitmaster — PLASTIC SCALE MODELS
### THE RIGHT APPROACH TO MODELLING

* AUTHENTIC DETAIL
* MOVING PARTS
* BRITISH & FOREIGN LOCOS & COACHES
* POWER BOGIES
* EASY-TO-ASSEMBLE NUMBERED PARTS

Whether for the beginner, assembling his first kit, or for the enthusiast building for his O.O. or T.T. layout, Kitmaster provides the perfect medium for railway modelling.
Each kit will build a true-scale, fully detailed loco or coach—each component is numbered and the instructions are clear and easy to follow.
The finished models will run on any make of track of the appropriate gauge and power units are available to operate them.
Now!—twelve new models at the same standard—but more exciting than ever!

**only KITMASTER can give you all this . . .**

---

## TT3
### FIVE KITS FOR THE TT GAUGE ENTHUSIAST

Each one a masterpiece of scale engineering, see the fine detail of the rebuilt 'Royal Scot' plus a power bogie for Motorising to run on all makes of track
Packed in attractive full colour boxes to meet the growing demand for TT.
If you are thinking of trying a change to TT, here is the ideal pilot set complete in every detail.

**16 REBUILT "ROYAL SCOT"   6/11**
The famous locomotive is a rebuilt version of the 1927 "Royal Scot". Now transferred to the Midland Region of British Railways.

**17 CORRIDOR BRAKE SECOND COACH   5/11**
With four compartments to seat 24 passengers, plus guard and luggage compartments.

**18 CORRIDOR COMPOSITE COACH   5/11**
With seven compartments — three 2nd class and four 1st class.

**20 CORRIDOR SECOND COACH   5/11**
With eight compartments, each seating six passengers.

**21 RESTAURANT FIRST COACH   6/6**
Able to seat 42 first class passengers. An important item in any train or layout.

### T.T.3. MOTORISED BOGIE

**K.M.3.   T.T.   32/6**
ELECTRIC MOTOR BOGIE
To be used with Kit No. 17 Corridor Brake 2nd

### PRESENTATION SETS

**P1** 100 YEARS OF BRITISH STEAM.
This interesting set contains the Rocket of 1829, the Stirling 8 ft. Single Wheeler of 1870, the 1937 Coronation Class "Duchess of Gloucester" and a booklet "The Steam Locomotive", specially written for this set.   **27/6** (00/H0 Gauge).

**P2** "Battle of Britain" Class Loco. and Three Coaches; Corridor Composite, Corridor 2nd., Corridor Brake 2nd. in the Southern Region Livery.   **37/6** (00/H0 Gauge).

**P3** A T.T. Gauge Set to construct models of the Rebuilt Royal Scot and Four Coaches; Corridor Composite, Corridor 2nd., Corridor Brake 2nd. and Restaurant 1st.   **37/6** (T.T. Gauge).

All these exciting sets are complete with detailed assembly instructions, with a history of each vehicle; cement, paints, brush, tweezers and file. Packed in Presentation Boxes.

---

**ROSEBUD KITMASTER LTD**
GROVE STREET · RAUNDS · NORTHAMPTONSHIRE · ENGLAND

## ROSEBUD Kitmaster
PLASTIC SCALE MODELS

### Catalogue 1961
PRINTED IN ENGLAND

---

## MIDLAND PULLMAN
### BRITAIN'S MOST MODERN TRAIN
### HO & OO

These trains are the latest word in luxury, comfort and speed which British Railways now offer. They have been specially designed with the inter-city travel requirements of the modern businessman principally in mind.
The coaches are most distinctive in appearance and the elegant decor of the interiors is restful and relaxing to the traveller. All passenger accommodation is fully air conditioned. There are roomy individual reclining seats, adjustable at the touch of a small lever.
The Kitmaster models capture the exciting beauty of this train in all its colour and detail.

**31 MIDLAND PULLMAN POWER CAR   10/6**
**32 MIDLAND PULLMAN KITCHEN CAR   10/6**
**33 MIDLAND PULLMAN PARLOUR CAR   10/6**

# Chapter 10: The Kitmaster and Airfix Compendium

This part of the book attempts to list all known production kits and planned kits identified in promotional material. A key to the abbreviations used in the text is given here. For an explanation of the symbols in the Notes column, please see 'Notes to Tables' which follows. 'Kit Colour' is the colour of the plastic used to mould the kit; as shown in table [a].

**Table [a]: Colours of plastics used by Kitmaster**

| | |
|---|---|
| A = Apple Green | B = Black |
| Br = Brown | C = Clear Glazing |
| D = Dark Brunswick Green | G = Light Emerald Green |
| I = Pink (Pale Red) | K = Dark Grey |
| L = Light Grey | M = Metal parts |
| N = Nanking Blue | O = Dark Olive Green |
| P = Beige (Pale Yellow) | R = Red |
| S = Silver | U = Ultramarine Blue |
| W = White | Y = Yellow |

### Packaging and Box Type

Box type refers to the dimensions of the boxes. Two materials were used. Earlier models were housed in strong cardboard boxes with the design printed on a paper surface covering the cardboard, but with kit number 26 (J94 Saddle Tank) a change to card boxes (which were generally larger and more floppy) was made. These have the design printed directly on to the surface. A change was also made to the colour specification for the box designs. TT Scale models are printed with yellow logos on a pale blue background, whilst OO Scale models are Royal Blue on pale greenish-yellow backgrounds. From 26 onwards the Kitmaster logo was re-designed to take up slightly less room on a Type 1 box, the new condensed logo was also printed in deep violet blue instead of royal blue and the background colour changed from greenish-yellow to yellowish-green (i.e. more green). The motor bogie and box van always had a smaller condensed logo due to lack of space on the box. These boxes were probably printed by a different firm from the others as the colours are paler and have a dull matt finish.

From 1960 onwards, all the boxes were sealed in an acetate wrapper similar to cellophane. It is still possible to find kits in the original wrapper. Additionally, some kits had the parts enclosed in a plastic bag. This tended to be in the Presentation Sets, where the lack of box lids would otherwise have caused a problem. Examples of kits packed in plastic bags bearing the original Rosebud logo (used for the Dolls range) are known to exist. All Nabisco kits were despatched in plastic bags inside a plain brown box stamped with the name of the kit. Several sizes were used, depending on the number of kits ordered.

### Design Patents

Rosebud always sought to protect their famous box designs from competitors and cheaper imitations. To this end, each instruction sheet carried the legend 'The box illustration on the front of this kit is the subject of a Registered Design Application.' Early kits in the series also had the appropriate Application Number included. Interestingly, The General and the Pug were the first two to be registered, as shown in the table below. The applications were lodged by Rosebud's Patent Agent, Messrs.

**Table [b]: Principle Box Types - Dimensions**

| Type | L W H mm | L W H ins | Used for kits: |
|---|---|---|---|
| 1 | 144 x 93 x 39 | 5.75 x 3.75 x 1.5 | 1/2/6/8/26 |
| 2 | 208 x 93 x 39 | 8.25 x 3.75 x 1.5 | 3/7 |
| 3 | 370 x 126 x 39 | 14.50 x 5.00 x 1.5 | 4/10/11/12/19/22/28/31/32/33 |
| 4 | 297 x 92 x 39 | 11.75 x 3.75 x 1.5 | 5/9/13/14/15/24/30 |
| 5 | 240 x 92 x 39 | 9.50 x 3.75 x 1.5 | 16 |
| 6 | 255 x 80 x 39 | 10.00 x 3.25 x 1.5 | 17/18/20/21/ 27/29 |
| 7 | 420 x 126 x 39 | 16.50 x 5.00 x 1.5 | 23/25 |
| 8 | 424 x 126 x 39 | 16.75 x 5.00 x 1.5 | 34 |
| 9 | 152 x 102 x 36 | 6.00 x 4.00 x 1.0 | 60 |
| 10 | 442 x 216 x 39 | 16.50 x 8.50 x 1.5 | P1 |
| 11 | 660 x 225 x 39 | 25.50 x 8.75 x 1.5 | P2 |
| 12 | 750 x 216 x 39 | 30.00 x 8.50 x 1.5 | P3 |
| 13 | 116 x 93 x 39 | 4.25 x 3.75 x 1.5 | KM1/KM2 |
| N1 | 152 x 102 x 45 | 6.00 x 4.00 x 1.7 | Nabisco 2 |
| N2 | 342 x 137 x 56 | 13.50 x 5.33 x 2.3 | Nabisco 22/11 |
| N3 | 275 x 140 x 88 | 11.00 x 5.50 x 3.5 | Nabisco 28/15 |

**Table [c]: Printing Colours of Kitmaster Boxes**

| Scale | Kit Numbers | Logo Colour | Background Colour |
|---|---|---|---|
| OO | 1-15,19,22-25,P1 | Royal-Blue | Greenish-Yellow |
| TT | 16-18,20-21, P3 | Deep Yellow | Pale Duck Egg Blue |
| OO | 26,28,30-33, P2 | Violet-Blue | Yellowish-Green |
| HO | 27,29,34 | Violet Blue | Yellowish Green |
| OO | KM1 & KM2 | Matt Royal Blue | Pale Greenish-Yellow |

**Table [d]: Registered Design Applications**

| Kit No. | Application No. | Date of Application | Date Registered | Certificate Issued |
|---|---|---|---|---|
| 1 | 891075 | 13 Nov 1958 | 13 Nov 1958 | 27 April 1959 |
| 2 | 891076 | 13 Nov 1958 | 13 Nov 1958 | 27 April 1959 |
| 3 | 891073 | 13 Nov 1958 | 13 Nov 1958 | 27 April 1959 |
| 4 | 891077 | 13 Nov 1958 | 13 Nov 1958 | 27 April 1959 |
| 5 | 891078 | 13 Nov 1958 | 13 Nov 1958 | 27 April 1959 |
| 6 | 891074 | 13 Nov 1958 | 13 Nov 1958 | 27 April 1959 |

'Article in respect of which design is registered: A box primarily for a toy construction kit.'

Haseltine, Lake & Co. of 28 Southampton Buildings, Chancery Lane, London, W.C.2.

Unfortunately, the 'Statements of Novelty' relating to these designs have now been destroyed and are no longer in the Designs Registry. After this point there were no Application Numbers shown, even on the later redrawn sheets for the Battle of Britain and Deltic. According to the Patent Office there are no more applications in the name of Rosebud Kitmaster Ltd.

### Instruction Format

Several different instruction formats were used for Kitmaster kits. The first twelve had Format 1 sheets. These are an early version of the instruction sheet with a large Kitmaster logo in the top left corner, surmounting a black and white half-tone of the finished locomotive. Step-by-step instructions in English are given, together with a brief description of the class. The reverse side has an exploded assembly diagram; exceptions are some examples of the Italian tank which were erroneously packed with single sided sheets. These Format 1 sheets were used for the first twelve models throughout 1959 and 1960 but, commencing in December 1960, certain popular kits, including the Schools and Battle of Britain, had their sheets reprinted in the multilingual Format 2. The necessity to reprint the Battle of Britain sheet in Format 2 was caused by the issue of the P2 Presentation Set. On the outside of that set the instructions are quoted as being in six languages. Whilst this was not a problem with the coaches, it was for the locomotive, which had first been issued with a Format 1 sheet. The Deltic, Schools, Stirling, Italian Tank, Pug, Duchess and Battle of Britain are all known with Format 1 sheets printed in blue ink. We can deduce, by dating these examples from catalogues and decals, that they were first printed in Format 1 in black, then Format 1 in blue and finally in Format 2.

The second style only has the exploded diagram on the reverse side, but has a 'mini catalogue' of drawings showing other available kits on the front side; normally in the top right corner. These multilingual sheets are very large and have detailed assembly instructions and the class description in English, French, German, Dutch, Swedish and Italian. This type of sheet was used exclusively for kits 13-25, released in 1960, as well as the reprints mentioned above. Starting with the 1961 programme of introductions, new reduced sheets were introduced. The J94 Saddle Tank (26) appeared with one of these later sheets, which were two colour (normally red and black) to indicate glue lines and moved away from the primitive single exploded diagram to a more 'user-friendly' series of assembly diagrams. This is Format 3, but it dispensed with the long multi-lingual instructions and shortened the description, so that the entire sheet would fit on a single side of foolscap paper. Previously the Format 2 instructions covered both sides of an Imperial folio sheet. Quite a drastic revision! The final retail kit to be produced, the Ariel Arrow, has a double sided two colour instruction sheet with multiple diagrams, akin to early Airfix offerings. This is Format 4.

The Nabisco versions of the kits had their own entirely different instruction sheets, designated Format N. These have only a small Kitmaster logo, minus the Rosebud name, positioned centrally. In addition they have the wording 'With Compliments of Nabisco Foods Limited'. They comprise full assembly instructions and an exploded diagram only and are very similar to Airfix Type 2 kit instruction sheets. It is interesting to note that the Nabisco version of the OO gauge Restaurant Car is a single diagram, whereas the actual Kitmaster sheet was a multi-diagram offering. In fact, all of the Nabisco sheets included entirely new drawings, which were often superior to the original sheet. Thus the Deltic kit has an extra diagram showing how to assemble the bogies, something not available in the Format 1 kit instructional. We can postulate that this sheet and that for the Diesel Shunter (2) were actually prepared for the 1961 Format 2 reprints of the Rosebud sheets, but neither of these kits with that reprint is confirmed as yet. Alternatively, they could have been drawn by the Airfix drawing office, as they do bear a strong resemblance to Airfix Type

203

2 kit instructionals. There is also evidence for a blue Format 1 Deltic sheet overprinted in black 'With the compliments of Nabisco Foods Ltd.' in the top right-hand corner.

Unrelated to any of this is the Fireball XL5 sheet. This Format 5 sheet is a crude hand drawn single exploded diagram with no descriptive text, just the bare essentials for assembly. It carries no reference to Kitmaster, and was despatched by the Hermes Supply Co.

Motor Bogie and Motor Box Van instruction sheets fall into two categories. Both products share a common sheet which details care and maintenance of the motor. Glued to the inside of the box lid is a sheet showing how to fit the alternative Peco or Tri-ang couplings. Finally, the Motor Bogie has separate monochrome instructions on how to fit the Bogie to the coach shell.

**Table [e]: Sheet Formats**

| Type | Style |
|---|---|
| 1 | Large picture and one exploded diagram |
| 2 | One exploded diagram and mini-catalogue |
| 3 | Two colour exploded multiple diagrams, single side |
| 4 | Two colour exploded multiple diagrams, double side |
| 5 | Fireball XL5 - Hand drawn single exploded diagram |
| 6 | Motor Bogie fitting sheet |
| 7 | Motor maintenance sheet |
| N | Nabisco instruction sheet |

**Transfer Sheets**

As far as can be ascertained, all the transfer sheets were printed in Coventry by British Transfer Printing Co. Ltd of Harefield Road, now part of the Eyelith group. They also printed decals for the unreleased A3 kit as well. There are several variations to the transfer sheets (decals) included with some kits. The first production of British locomotives in British Railways livery contained the 1957 'totem' emblem of the Lion on Wheel heraldic device facing both left and right. However, the College of Arms had only granted to the British Transport Commission the left-facing emblem as a corporate mark, so from 1960 onwards, all locomotives had the right-facing emblem replaced by a second left-facing one. Kitmaster also reprinted the transfer sheets for kits 2, 4, 5, 6, 7, 11 and 16 accordingly. There is no indication on the sheet that the decals have been reprinted and the kits were otherwise identical. Later kits such as 22, 25, 26 and 30 were only produced with left-facing lions.

Type LR = left and right facing emblems, used up until mid-1960

Type LL = both left facing emblems used after this time.

## Notes to Tables in the Compendium

**Tables One and Two**

Afx indicates that this kit was released by Airfix.
Dap indicates that this kit was released by Dapol.
Nab indicates a confirmed issue of a Nabisco branded kit by Hermes Supply Co.
Com indicates that a resin model made from the original Hermes model has been issued by Comet miniatures.
6 The Stirling Single was moulded in two different colours of green, which are quite distinct. The early models were in Apple Green, but this was changed to Light Emerald Green around 1960, it is thought. There are no other detail differences. Both colours were used for kits in the P1 Box Set. During 1962, G & G Scale Products produced an etched brass chassis kit for the Stirling at a price of 25s which included a brass boiler dome and safety valve unit.
7 Although Airfix had the Deltic mould, it was never put into production. See also The Models in Detail - 4.
9 Pullman Cars: See The Models in Detail - 2. These kits had three alternative colours for the seat mouldings, pink, white and beige.
10 Power bogies - see The Models in Detail - The KM1 & KM2 Motor Bogies.
13 See also The Models in Detail - 7 - The Ariel Arrow Motorcycle
15 See also The Models in Detail - 9 - British Railways 350HP Shunters

**Table Two Only**

1 Peco introduced two interior kits for the Corridor 2nd. The first was introduced in March 1960, for the SK interior, priced at 2s 9d. This was followed in October 1960 by the SO interior, also at a price of 2s 9d.

**Table Three**

2 Simplas Chassis were produced and marketed by Wilro Models Ltd. 20 Clarence Road, London E5
3 Humbrol advertised the J94 with a picture to promote Humbrol Railway Colours in MRN 9/61
4 Humbrol advertised the Mogul with a picture to promote Humbrol Railway Colours in RM 10/61 and 11/61
5 Referred to in an article in RM 10.62 page 242 as the introduction date.
8 Humbrol advertised the Pullman Power Car with a picture to promote Humbrol Railway Colours in Airfix Magazine 2/62

**Table Four and One**

14 See also The Models in Detail - 1 - BR Mk1 Coaches. Other numbers for vehicles with this body shell (First Class Open) with Mk1 BR1 bogies would be: 1953- build year: M3000/1/2. All regional prefixes were carried by these vehicles. Note: Build year 1953, FO's 3003-3007 were outshopped with a centre door added. This was the only change to the vehicle as supplied in the kit. All FO/RFO outshopped after this differ considerably in ventilator positions and internal arrangement. RFO kit No 28 was produced with both white and pale pink interiors and, in several cases, Deltic's ultramarine blue plastic interior!

**Table Five: Airfix Re-Releases**

Table Five gives information about the Airfix production of Kitmaster locomotives as well as their own tooled-up kits for the Drewry Shunter, Railbus and wagons of varied descriptions. Airfix originally catalogued all of their kits by 'Pattern Number' which was engraved on the tool. However, as office automation began to have an impact on Haldane Place during the early 1970s, the Type 4 boxes started to show the Pattern number together with a computerised number. This eventually became the standard number for cataloguing the kits. Since the first digit after the leading zero is the Series number, if a kit changed Series, it was given a new number. This was also true of the old Pattern Number system as applied to the larger kits. Hence Pattern No.R401 is a Railway Series 4 kit, whilst R502 is the same kit, but in a Series 5 box. Airfix periodically withdrew their rolling stock kits only to reintroduce them again later, and many box variations exist. Some of the earlier reintroductions are marked 'Limited Production' on the box cover, although all subsequently went into mass production. Limited Production kits are not as rare as those without this marking!

Airfix Box types -
1958-1962 Type 2 Has yellow/blue stripe down the middle.
1962-1973 Type 3 Has a red flashed rectangular Airfix logo
1967-1973 Type 3LP Has Limited Production wording next to logo.
1973-1977 Type 4 Has a circular Airfix logo, the colour of the box art
1977-1978 Type 5 Red/white/black logo English/French wording White border to box
1979-1982 Type 6 Has red/white/black oval logo on full colour box. with no border

It should be noted that the Ariel Arrow kit and Evening Star, together with all the Series 1 wagons and some of the others, changed series during their lifetime. When first re-introduced, the Arrow was packed as a Series 1 kit in a clear plastic bag with a paper header/instructions. When last produced, in 1981, it was packaged as a Series 2 kit in a conventional box with a separate instruction sheet. Many Airfix Series 1 kits reverted to Series 2 during their production life-spans. The Evening Star kit was designated a Series 5 model with Pattern No.R502 for the limited production run, having moved up from a short spell in Series 4, upon which it was allocated Pattern No.R401; both are tabulated above. In 1979 it was issued in a Type 6 box in Series 5; this is a scarce kit. Only the Rocket ever appeared in a Series 1 'Blister-Pack' The Lowmac & JCB was issued with two different instruction sheets due to a numbering error on diagram 2 of the sheet, which resulted in all numbers being increased by 1. This was quickly reprinted with the correct numbering.

*The Diesel Crane in a Series 3 box was clearly shown in the first few Airfix GMR ready-to-run catalogues, in the kit section. It even appeared in the text of the Railways section of later Kit catalogues, but is thought not to have been issued. None of the Series 2 Airfix rolling stock ever appeared in the Roy Cross style Type 3 packaging, although the Railbus was certainly redrawn for a Type 3 issue – it can be seen as such on the side panels of the larger locomotive kits. Consequently these Type 2 Series 2 boxes remained in production for much of the 1960s, long after all the other kits had progressed to Type 3 artwork. Interestingly, the Prairie Tank locomotive was the first Airfix kit to appear in Type 3 boxes. It was also one of the last; when re-issued as Limited Production, the end panels were already drawn as Type 4 (with a circular Airfix logo) but the front panel remained Type 3, one of the very last to do so.

## TABLE ONE: Kitmaster Production details

| No. | Scale | Livery | 1959*/1960 Catalogue Description | Notes | Kit Colours | Box Type | Inst. Format | Nabisco | Airfix | Dapol | Comet |
|---|---|---|---|---|---|---|---|---|---|---|---|
| 1 * | OO | | "Rocket" | | YM | 1 | 1 | | x | x | |
| 2 * | OO | | Diesel Electric - 2-lights | 15 | B | 1 | 1 | | | | |
| 2 * | OO | | Diesel Electric - 4 lights | 15 | B | 1 | 1 | | x | | |
| 3 * | OO | | Early American General | | BM | 2 | 1 | | | | |
| 4 * | OO | | Coronation Class | | B | 3 | 1 | | | | |
| 5 * | OO | | Schools Class | | B | 4 | 1 or 2 | | x | x | |
| 6 * | OO | | Saddle Tank | | B | 1 | 1 | | x | x | |
| 7 * | OO | | Prairie Tank | | B | 2 | 1 | | x | x | |
| 8 * | OO | | Italian Tank | | B | 1 | 1 | | | | |
| 9 * | OO | | Stirling 8ft Single | 6 | A/G | 4 | 1 | | | | |
| 10* | OO | | Deltic Diesel | 7 | CU/L | 3 | 1 | x | x | x | |
| 11* | OO | | Battle of Britain Class | | B | 3 | 1 or 2 | | x | x | |
| 12* | OO | | Swiss Crocodile | | CB | 3 | 1 | | | | |
| 13 | OO | Maroon | Standard Corridor Composite | | BCRK | 4 | 2 | | | | |
| 13 | OO | Green | Standard Corridor Composite | | BCDK | 4 | 2 | | | | |
| 14 | OO | Maroon | Standard Corridor 2nd | | BCRK | 4 | 2 | | | | |
| 14 | OO | Green | Standard Corridor 2nd | | BCDK | 4 | 2 | | | | |
| 15 | OO | Maroon | Standard Corridor Brake 2nd | | BCRK | 4 | 2 | | | | |
| 15 | OO | Green | Standard Corridor Brake 2nd | | BCDK | 4 | 2 | x | | | |
| 16 | TT | | Rebuilt "Royal Scot" | | M B | 5 | 2 | | | | |
| 17 | TT | Maroon | Standard Corridor Brake 2nd | | BCRK | 6 | 2 | | | | |
| 17 | TT | Green | Standard Corridor Brake 2nd | | BCDK | 6 | 2 | | | | |
| 18 | TT | Maroon | Standard Corridor Composite | | BCRK | 6 | 2 | | | | |
| 18 | TT | Green | Standard Corridor Composite | | BCDK | 6 | 2 | | | | |
| 19 | OO | | Baureihe 23 (German) | | B | 3 | 2 | | | | |
| 20 | TT | Maroon | Standard Corridor 2nd | | BCRK | 6 | 2 | | | | |
| 20 | TT | Green | Standard Corridor 2nd | | BCDK | 6 | 2 | | | | |
| 21 | TT | Maroon | Standard Restaurant 1st | | WBCRK | 6 | 2 | | | | |
| 21 | TT | Green | Standard Restaurant 1st | | WBCRK | 6 | 2 | | | | |
| 22 | OO | | Class 92000 | | B | 3 | 2 | x | x | x | |
| 23 | OO | | 241P Mountain (French) | | B | 7 | 2 | | | | |
| 24 | OO | | "City of Truro" | | B | 4 | 2 | | x | x | |
| 25 | OO | | Beyer-Garratt | | B | 7 | 2 | | | | |
| 26 | OO | | J94 0-6-0ST | | B | 1 | 3 | | x | x | |
| 27 | HO | | DB B4yge Coach | | CBO | 6 | 3 | | | | |
| 28 | OO | Maroon | Standard Restaurant 1st | 14 | IWBCRKU | 3 | 3 | x | | | |
| 28 | OO | Green | Standard Restaurant 1st | 14 | IWBCDKU | 3 | 3 | | | | |
| 29 | HO | | SNCF A9 myfi Coach | | CS | 6 | 3 | | | | |
| 30 | OO | | BR 4MT Mogul Class 76000 | | B | 4 | 3 | | x | x | |
| 31 | OO | | Midland Pullman Power | 9 | IWPCBKN | 3 | 3 | | | | |
| 32 | OO | | Midland Pullman Kitchen | 9 | IWPCBKN | 3 | 3 | | | | |
| 33 | OO | | Midland Pullman Parlour | 9 | IWPCBKN | 3 | 3 | | | | |
| 34 | HO | | New York Central Hudson | | B | 8 | 3 | | | | |
| 35 | OO | | SR Class USA Tank | 11 | Not Released | | | | | | |
| 36 | OO | | A3 Flying Scotsman | | Not Released | | | | | | |
| 37 | HO | | CN U-4-A | | Not Released | | | | | | |
| 60 | 1:16 | | Ariel Arrow Motorcycle | 13 | PC | 9 | 4 | | x | | |
| -- | 1:100 | | Fireball XL5 | 12 | SC | N3 | 5 | | | | x |

### Presentation Sets including Set No & Contents

| P1 | 1/4/9 | | 100 Years of British Steam | | MYGB | 10 | 1 | | | | |
| P2 | 11/13/14/15 | | Battle of Britain Set | | KCBD | 11 | 1 or 2 | | | | |
| P3 | 16/17/18/20/21 | | TT3 Royal Scot Set | | MKIWCBR | 12 | 2 | | | | |

### Ready-to-Run Motor Bogie "Kits"

| KM1 | OO | | Motor Bogie | 10 | - | 13 | 6 | | | | |
| KM2 | OO | | Motor Box Van | 10 | Br | 13 | 7 | | | | |
| KM3 | TT | | Motor Bogie | 10 | Not Released | | | | | | |

## TABLE TWO: Release Dates and Prices

| No | 1961 Catalogue Description | Release Dates In Cat. | Actual | Original Price | 1961 Price | 1960 Trade | Peco Kit |
|---|---|---|---|---|---|---|---|
| 1 | Rocket | 2.59 | 4.59 | 4s 6d | 3s 6d | 2s 7d | |
| 2 | Diesel Electric Shunter | 1.59 | 4.59 | 4s 6d | 3s 6d | 2s 7d | |
| 3 | Early American "General" | 1.59 | 4.59 | 6s 6d | 5s 0d | 1s 11d | |
| 4 | Coronation Class | 8.59 | 11.59 | 10s 6d | 10s 6d | 5s | 11s 8d |
| 5 | Schools Class Harrow | 3.59 | 4.59 | 7s 6d | 10s 6d | 4s 3d | |
| 6 | Saddle Tank | 5.59 | 5.59 | 4s 6d | 3s 6d | 2s 7d | 8s 9d |
| 7 | Prairie Tank | 7.59 | 10.59 | 6s 6d | 5s 0d | 1s 11 | 11s 8d |
| 8 | Italian Tank | 9.59 | 12.59 | 4s 6d | 3s 6d | 2s 7d | 8s 9d |
| 9 | Stirling | 6.59 | 9.59 | 7s 6d | | 4s 4d | |
| 10 | Deltic Diesel | 10.59 | 1.6 | 10s 6d | | 5s | |
| 11 | Battle of Britain Class | 11.59 | 2.6 | 10s 6d | | 5s | 11s 8d |
| 12 | Giant Swiss Crocodile | 12.59 | 3.6 | 10s 6d | | 5s | |
| 13 | BR Standard Corridor Composite | 2.6 | 4.6 | 6s 6d | | 2s | |
| 14 | BR Standard Corridor Second | 2.6 | 4.6 | 6s 6d | | 2s | 2s 9d 1 |
| 15 | BR Standard Corridor Brake 2nd | 2.6 | 4.6 | 6s 6d | | 2s | 2s 9d |
| 16 | Rebuilt Royal Scot | 4.6 | 5.6 | 6s 11d | | 4s | |
| 17 | BR Standard Corridor Brake 2nd | 5.6 | 6.6 | 5s 11d | | 1s 5d | |
| 18 | BR Standard Corridor Composite | 5.6 | 6.6 | 5s 11d | | 1s 5d | |
| 19 | German Baureihe 23 | 6.6 | 7.6 | 10s 6d | | 5s | |
| 20 | BR Standard Corridor Second | 7.6 | 8.6 | 5s 11d | | 1s 5d | |
| 21 | BR Standard Restaurant 1st | 7.6 | 8.6 | 6s 6d | | 2s | |
| 22 | BR Class 92000 | 8.6 | 9.6 | 10s 6d | | 5s | |
| 23 | French 241P Mountain | 9.6 | 10.6 | 12s 6d | | 7s 2d | |
| 24 | City of Truro | 10.6 | 11.6 | 7s 6d | | 4s 4d | |
| 25 | Beyer-Garratt | 11.60/Sp 61 | | 12s 6d | | 7s 2d | |
| 26 | ER Saddle Tank Class J94 | Sp 61 | | 3s 6d | | | |
| 27 | German Coach Type B4yge | Sp 61 | | 7s 6d | | | |
| 28 | BR Standard Restaurant 1st | Sp 61 | | 9s 6d | | | |
| 29 | French Coach Type A9 myfi/1958 | Sum 61 | | 8s 6d | | | |
| 30 | BR Mogul Class 76000 | Sum 61 | | 7s 6d | | | |
| 31 | Midland Pullman Power Car | Sum 61 | | 10s 6d | | | |
| 32 | Midland Pullman Kitchen Car | Sum 61 | | 10s 6d | | | |
| 33 | Midland Pullman Parlour Car | Sum 61 | | 10s 6d | | | |
| 34 | New York Central Hudson Type J3a | Win 61 | | 3s 6d | | | |
| 35 | SR Tank Class USA | Win 61 | No kit | 13s 6d | | | |
| 36 | ER Gresley A.3. "Flying Scotsman" | Win 61 | No kit | 10s 6d | | | |
| 37 | Canadian National Railways Type U-4A | Win 61 | No kit | 13s 6d | | | |
| 60 | Ariel Arrow Super Sports Model | N/A | March 62 | 5s 11d | | See Note 13 | |
| -- | Steve Zodiac's Fireball XL5 | N/A | July 62 | 4s 6d | | See Note 12 | |

### Presentation Sets

| | | | | | | | |
|---|---|---|---|---|---|---|---|
| P1 | 100 Years of British Steam | 10.59 | 11.59 | 27s 6d | | 15s 9d | |
| P2 | Battle of Britain Set | 4.60 | 10.60 | 37s 6d | | 21s 5d | |
| P3 | TT3 Royal Scot Set | 8.60 | 12.60 | 37s 6d | | 21s 5d | |

### Ready-to-Run Motor Bogie Kits

| | | | Actual | Advance | | |
|---|---|---|---|---|---|---|
| KM1 OO Motor Bogie | 7.60 | | 32s 6d | 27s 6d | 15s 9d | |
| KM2 OO Motor Box Van | 7.60 | | 39s 6d | 35s 0d | 20s | |
| KM3 TT Motor Bogie See Note 10 | 7.60 | | (32s 6d) | 27s 6d | 15s 9d | |

Note that the "Actual" price shown for the Motor Bogies is the price given in the Retail catalogue for 1960/61, whereas the "Advance" prices are those shown as being the suggested retail prices for 1960 in the 1960 Trade Price List. This reflects the increased supply costs of the motorised items to Rosebud.

| TABLE THREE: Press Coverage | | | | | | | |
|---|---|---|---|---|---|---|---|
| No. | Short Description | First Advert | Reviews RM | MRN | MRC | Interior or Perfecta | Simplas Chassis | Airfix Re-intro |
| 1 | Rocket | 4.59 | 4.59 | | 4.59 | | | 10.64 |
| 2 | 08 Shunter | 4.59 | | | 3.59 | | | |
| 3 | General | 4.59 | 4.59 | | 4.59 | | | |
| 4 | Coronation | 11.59 | 12.59 | 11.59 | 11.59 | 7.60 | | |
| 5 | Schools | 4.59 | | 7.59 | 6.59 | | ?1968 | 5.68 |
| 6 | L & Y Pug | 5.59 | 5.59 | 7.59 | 12.59 | 9.59 | 3.67 | 3.64 |
| 7 | Prairie Tank | 10.59 | 10.59 | 10.59 | 10.59 | 5.60 | 10.67 | 10.63 |
| 8 | Italian Tank | 12.59 | 12.59 | | | 4.60 | | |
| 9 | Stirling | 9.59 | 10.59 | 10.59 | 8.59 | | | |
| 10 | Deltic | 01.60 | 03.60 | 03.60 | | | | |
| 11 | B o B | 02.60 | 02.60 | 02.60 | 02.60 | 06.60 | ?1968/9 | 4.68 |
| 12 | Crocodile | 03.60 | 04.60 | | | | | |
| 13 | Mk1 CK | 04.60 | 03.60 | | | | | |
| 14 | Mk1 SK | 04.60 | 03.60 | | | 03.60 | | |
| 14 | Mk1 SO | 04.60 | 03.60 | | | 10.60 | | |
| 15 | Mk1 BSK | 04.60 | 05.60 | | | 07.60 | | |
| 16 | Royal Scot | 05.60 | 07.60 | 08.60 | 08.60 | | | |
| 17 | Mk1 BSK | 06.60 | 08.60 | 08.60 | 08.60 | | | |
| 18 | Mk1 CK | 06.60 | 07.60 | | | | | |
| 19 | Baureihe | 07.60 | 09.60 | | 10.6 | | | |
| 20 | Mk1 SK | 08.60 | 08.60 | | | | | |
| 21 | Mk1 RFO | 08.60 | 07.60 | | | | | |
| 22 | 9F 2-10-0 | 09.60 | 1.61 | 1.61 | 1.61 | | 10.67 | 12.64 |
| 23 | Mountain | 10.60 | 2.61 | 4.61 | 4.61 | | | |
| 24 | City of Truro | 11.6 | 3.61 | 4.61 | 3.61 | 4.67 | | 4.65 |
| 25 | Beyer-Garratt | 5.61 | 5.61 | 5.61 | 6.61 | | | |
| 26 | J94 0-6-0ST | 5.61 | 5.61 | 5.61 | 5.61 | 10.67 | | 1.64 |
| 27 | DB Coach | 7.61 | 7.61 | 7.61 | 7.61 | | | |
| 28 | Mk1 RFO | | 7.61 | 7.61 | | | | |
| 29 | A9 myfi | | 8.61 | 8.61 | | | | |
| 30 | BR Mogul | 10.61 | 10.61 | 11.61 | 10.61 | | | 7.71 |
| 31 | Power Car | 2.62 | 12.61 | 12.61 | 12.61 | | | |
| 32 | Kitchen | | 12.61 | 12.61 | 12.61 | | | |
| 33 | Parlour | | 12.61 | 1.62 | 12.61 | | | |
| 34 | Hudson | | 2.62 | | 3.62 | | | |
| KM1 | Motor Bogie | 7.61 | 7.61 | 12.61 | | | | |
| 60 | Ariel Arrow | 7.63 | | | | | | 7.63 |
| P2 | Battle of Britain | 1.62 | | | | | | |
| | | | | | | | | |
| RM | | Railway Modeller | | | | | | |
| MRN | | Model Railway News | | | | | | |
| MRC | | Model Railway Constructor | | | | | | |

| No | Instruction sheet name: | Notes | | Alternative Names & Numbers |
|---|---|---|---|---|
| | TABLE FOUR : Names and Numbers | | | |
| 1 | George Stephenson's Locomotive "Rocket" | | Rocket | Rocket |
| 2 | BR Standard 350HP Diesel Electric Shunting Locomotive | | D3421 | D3421 |
| 3 | The Early American "General" Locomotive | | No 3 | No 3 The General |
| 4 | British Railways (London Midland Region) 4-6-2, "Coronation" Class Locomotives | | 46225 | 46225 Duchess of Gloucester |
| 5 | "Schools" Class Locomotives | | 30919 | 30919 Harrow |
| 6 | 0-4-0 Saddle Tank | | 51212 | 51212 |
| 7 | British Railways (Western Region) 6100 Class Prairie Tank Locomotive | | 6167 | 6167 |
| 8 | Italian State Railways Class 835 Tank Locomotive | | -- | 835 162 |
| 9 | Stirling 8ft "Single" Locomotive | | No 1 | GNR No 1 |
| 10 | English Electric 3,300HP Deltic Locomotive | | Deltic | Deltic |
| 11 | British Railways (Southern Region) "Battle of Britain" Class Locomotives | | 34057 | 34057 Biggin Hill |
| 12 | Swiss Federal Railways "Crocodile" Series Be6/8 | | 13305 | 13305 |
| 13 | BR Standard Corridor Composite | | M16001 | M15627/019/243 W15111/598/430, E15307/144/16017 |
| 13 | SR Green version only | | M16001 | S15042/573/888/903/580/873 |
| 14 | BR Standard Corridor Second | | M25589 | M24133/405/861 W24165/341/719, E24222/531/25027 |
| 14 | SR Green version only | | M25589 | S24320/305/169/326/318/311 |
| 15 | BR Standard Corridor Brake 2nd | | M35114 | M34090/105/671 W34152/297/763, E34422/590/35157 |
| 15 | SR Green version only | | M35114 | S34256/621/158/945/279/35020 |
| 16 | Rebuilt Royal Scot Locomotive (ex LMSR) | | 46100 | 46100 Royal Scot |
| | | | | 46110 Grenadier Guardsman |
| | | | | 46169 The Boy Scout |
| 17 | BR Standard Corridor Brake 2nd | | M35114 | M34090/105/671 W34152/297/763, E34422/590/35157 |
| 17 | SR Green version only | | M35114 | S34256/621/158/945/279/35020 |
| 18 | BR Standard Corridor Composite | | M16001 | M15627/019/243 W15111/598/430, E15307/144/16017 |
| 18 | SR Green version only | | M16001 | S15042/573/888/903/580/873 |
| 19 | German Federal Railways Class 23 Locomotives | | 23014 | 23001 23008 23014 |
| 20 | BR Standard Corridor Second | | M25589 | M24133/405/861 W24165/341/719, E24222/531/25027 |
| 20 | SR Green version only | | M25589 | S24320/305/169/326/318/311 |
| 21 | BR Standard Restaurant 1st | 14 | M5 | M4/5/6/S9/W7/8/E1/2/3/10/11 |
| 21 | SR Green version | 14 | M5 | M4/5/6/S9/W7/8/E1/2/3/10/11 |
| 22 | BR Standard Class 92000 Locomotive | | 92220 | Star |
| 23 | French 241P Mountain | | - | 241P.026 241P.027 241P.029 |
| 24 | GWR "City" Class Locomotives | | 3440 | 3440 City of Truro |
| 25 | Beyer-Garratt 2-6-6-2 Freight Locomotive (Ex-L.M.S.) | | 7971 | 7971, 7987, 47994 |
| 26 | ER Saddle Tank Class J94 | | 68022 | 68022 68028 68051 68076 |
| 27 | German Coach Type B4yge | | - | - |
| 28 | BR Standard Restaurant 1st | 14 | M5 | M4/5/6/S9/W7/8/E1/2/3/10/11 |
| 28 | SR Green version | 14 | M5 | M4/5/6/S9/W7/8/E1/2/3/10/11 |
| 29 | French Coach Type A9 myfi/1958 | | - | - |
| 30 | BR Mogul Class 76000 | | 76000 | 76000, 76093, 76114 |
| 31 | Midland Pullman Power Car Type 1 First Class | | M60090 | - A F |
| 32 | Midland Pullman Kitchen Car Type 4 First Class | | | - B E |
| 33 | Midland Pullman Parlour Car Type 6 First Class | | | - C D |
| 34 | New York Central Hudson J3a Locomotive (4-6-4) | | 5405 | 5405 |
| 60 | Ariel Arrow Super Sports Model | | ONV 989 | 697 AOH |

## TABLE FIVE: Airfix Re-Releases. Reissued Kitmaster Rolling Stock:

| Km No | Airfix No | Dapol No | Airfix Description | Series | Type | Colour | Reissue |
|---|---|---|---|---|---|---|---|
| 1 | R11 | C46 | Stephenson`s Rocket | 1 | 3 Box | Y | 12.64 |
| 1 | R11 | C46 | Stephenson`s Rocket | 1 | 3 Bag | Y | 1966 |
| 1 | 016612 | C46 | Stephenson`s Rocket | 1 | 4 Blister | Y | 1973 |
| 5 | R402 | C35 | Schools Class Harrow | 4 | 3 | D | 05.68 |
| 5 | 046527 | C35 | Schools Class Harrow | 4 | 4 | D | 1970 |
| 5 | 046527 | C35 | Schools Class Harrow | 4 | 6 | D | 1978 |
| 6 | R9 | C26 | Saddle Tank Pug | 1 | 3 | B | 03.64 |
| 6 | R9 | C26 | Saddle Tank Pug | 1 | 3LP | B | 1965 |
| 6 | 026602 | C26 | Saddle Tank Pug | 2 | 5 | B | 1980 |
| 6 | 026602 | C26 | Saddle Tank Pug | 2 | 6 | B | 1982 |
| 7 | R301 | C62 | Prairie Tank | 3 | 3 | D | 10.63 |
| 7 | 036561 | C62 | Prairie Tank | 3 | 3LP | D | 1965 |
| 7 | 046556 | C62 | Prairie Tank | 4 | 4 | D | 1972 |
| 11 | R501 | C48 | Battle of Britain Class | 5 | 3 | D | 04.68 |
| 11 | 056517 | C48 | Battle of Britain Class | 5 | 4 | D | 1970 |
| 22 | R401 | C49 | Evening Star | 4 | 3 | B | 1966 |
| 22 | R502 | C49 | Evening Star | 5 | 3 | B | 12.64 |
| 22 | 056520 | C49 | Evening Star | 5 | 4 | B | 1970 |
| 24 | R302 | C61 | City of Truro | 3 | 3 | B | 04.65 |
| 24 | 036524 | C61 | City of Truro | 4 | 3LP | B | 1972 |
| 24 | 046543 | C61 | City of Truro | 4 | 6 | B | 1978 |
| 26 | R205 | C34 | Class J94 Saddle Tank | 2 | 3 | B | 01.64 |
| 30 | R403 | C59 | BR Mogul | 4 | 3 | B | 07.71 |
| 30 | 046530 | C59 | BR Mogul | 4 | 4 | B | 1973 |
| 60 | 1635 --- |  | Ariel Arrow Motorcycle | 1 | 2 | P | 07.63 |
| 60 | 014805 |  | Ariel Arrow Motorcycle | 1 | 3 | P | 1968 |
| 60 | 024811 |  | Ariel Arrow Motorcycle | 2 | 4 | P | 1978 |

### Original Airfix production rolling stock:

| Airfix No | Dapol No | Airfix Description | Series | Type | Colour | Issue | Mould Cost | Date Aquired |
|---|---|---|---|---|---|---|---|---|
| R1 | C36 | 12t Oil Tank Wagon | 1 | 2 | B | 07.60 | £2,073.00 | 07.60 |
| 02656-3 | C36 | 12t Oil Tank Wagon | 2 | 3 | B | 1978 |  |  |
| R2 | C40 | "Presflow" Cement Wagon | 1 | 2 | Y | 07.60 | £2,057.00 | 06.61 |
| 02662-8 | C40 | "Presflow" Cement Wagon | 2 | 3 | Y | 1978 |  |  |
| R3 | C37 | 10t Mineral Wagon | 1 | 2 | L | 03.61 | £1,515.00 | 03.61 |
| 02657-6 | C37 | 10t Mineral Wagon | 2 | 3 | L | 1978 |  |  |
| R4 | C38 | Brake Van | 1 | 2 | Br | 05.61 | £1,615.00 | 06.61 |
| 02658-9 | C38 | Brake Van | 2 | 3 | Br | 1978 |  |  |
| R5 | C39 | Cattle Wagon | 1 | 2 | Br | 05.61 | £1,656.00 | 06.61 |
| 02659-2 | C39 | Cattle Wagon | 2 | 3 | Br | 1978 |  |  |
| R6 |  | 24 Buckeye couplings | 1 | 2 | B | 01.64 | £1,445.00 | 03.61 |
| R7 | C60 | Drewry Shunter Class 04 | 1 | 2 | B | 10.61 |  |  |
| R8 | C41 | 10t Meat Van | 1 | 2 | R | 08.62 | £1,802.00 | 12.62 |
| 02661-5 | C41 | 10t Meat Van | 2 | 3 | R | 1978 |  |  |
| R10 | C43 | "Prestwin" silo wagon | 1 | 3 | Br | 04.64 | £4,963.00 | 03.64 |
| R201 | C47 | Park Royal Railbus | 2 | 2 | D | 12.60 | £3,261.00 | 12.60 |
| R202 | C28 | 15 ton Diesel Loco. Crane | 2 | 2 | R | 03.61 | £4,098.00 | 03.62 |
| 03622-3 | C28 | 15 ton Diesel Loco. Crane | 3 | 6 | R | 1980* |  |  |
| R203 | C42 | "Interfrigo" Refrigerator | 2 | 2 | W | 07.62 | £2,479.00 | 12.62 |
| R204 | C45 | 14t Lowmac with JCB Load | 2 | 2 | Br/Y | 07.63 | £6,655.00 | 09.63 |

| Date of Issue | Railway Modeller | Model Railway News | Model Railway Constructor | Model Aircraft | Meccano Magazine | Model Maker | Ian Allan Publications | Trains Illustrated | Express Weekly | Issue Date | Hobbies Weekly | Issue Date | The Eagle | Aero Modeller |
|---|---|---|---|---|---|---|---|---|---|---|---|---|---|---|
| 04/59 | KMC1 | KMC1 | - | | | | Range Ad | KMC1 | | 8.4.59 | KMC1 | 4.4.59 | KMC1 | |
| 05/59 | KMC2 | KCM2 | | | | | ABC Directories | KMC2 | | 6.5.59 | KCM2 | 2.5.59 | KMC2 | |
| 06/59 | KMC2 | KM2 | - | KCM2 | | - | ~ | KMC2 | | 10.6.59 | KCM2? | 6.6.59 | KMC2 | |
| 07/59 | ~ | - | - | | - | | ~ | | | | ~ | Printing | - | |
| 08/59 | - | - | | | ~ | - | | | ~ | | ~ | Strike | | |
| 09/59 | KMC3 | KMC3 | KMC3 | | KMC3 | - | ~ | KMC3 | | 9.9.59 | (KMC3) | 5.9.59 | KMC3 | |
| 10/59 | KMC4 " | KMC4 | - | | KMC4 | ~ | ~ | KMC4 | | 7.10.59 | KMC4 | 3.10.59 | KMC4 | |
| 11/59 | KMC5 | KMC5 | - | KMC5 | KMC5 | - | KMC5 | KMC5 | | 11.11.59 | KMC5 | 7.11.59 | KMC5 | |
| 12/59 | KMC6 | KMC6 | | KMC6 | KMC6 | - | ABC Directories | KMC6 | | 9.12.59 | KMC6 | 12.12.59 | KMC6 | |
| 01/60 | KC10 | KC10 | KC10 | | KC10 | KC10 | - | | | | | | | |
| 02/60 | KC11 | KC11 | KC11 | | KC11 | KC11 | ~ | | | | | | | |
| 03/60 | KC12 | KC12 | KC12 | | KC12 | KC12 | ~ | | | | | | | |
| 04/60 | KC13 | KC13 | KC13 | | KC13 | KC13 | - | | | | | | | |
| 05/60 | KC14 | KC14 | KC14 | | KC14 | KC14 | ~ | | | | | | | |
| 06/60 | KC15 | KC15 | KC15 | | KC15 | KC1S | ~ | | | | | | | |
| 07/60 | KC16 | KC16 | KC16 | | KC16 | - | - | | | | | | | |
| 08/60 | KC15 | KC15 | KC15 | | KC15 | KC17 | ~ | | | | | | | |
| 09/60 | KC17 | KL17 | KC17 | | KC17 | - | ~ | | | | | | | KC15 |
| 10/60 | KC18 | KC18 | KC18 | | KC18 | - | ~ | | | | | | | |
| 11/60 | KC19 | KC19 | | | KC19 | - | Range Ad | | | | | | | |
| 12/60 | KC20 | KC20 | K20 | | KC18 | | Book of Model Railways | | | | | | | |

After this point, there were no more advertisements placed by Rosebud Kitmaster themselves, except in Toys and Games

**TABLE SIX - Media Campaign for the Kitmaster Launch.** This table summarises the advertisements appearing in support of the Kitmaster launch during 1959/60

Rosebud Kitmaster launched their famous range of kits with a spectacular, not to say expensive, advertising campaign. During the spring and summer of 1959, it was impossible to miss this barrage of advertising. Each month a different and highly original advert would appear in the major magazines of the period. In the second year of production, the campaign continued, but in a different selection of titles. Out went *Model Aircraft* magazine and in came *Model Maker*. This impressive launch campaign, covering as it did twelve separate publications, ensured that Kitmaster was the name on everyone's lips by the end of 1960. At that point, all paid-for advertising ceased and Kitmaster relied heavily on editorials and reviews. There was no shortage of these either, as the kits afforded plenty of opportunities for conversions and motorisation. After the initial wave of motorisations, a second series of articles appeared from 1967 onwards as Airfix progressively re-introduced their range of modified kits. The last advertising to be done by Rosebud was a joint campaign with Humbrol which ran throughout 1961 and into early 1962. The table summarises the majority of the initial Kitmaster launch campaign. Each advertisement carried a code letter and number combination, usually in the bottom left-hand corner. These are shown in the table and are decoded below. KMC 5 was used for two entirely different ads for the Duchess. One is a full page portrait format and used exclusively for Ian Allan ABC spotters guides, the other is landscape format and was in wider use. We are lacking any information on the issues left blank. The symbol ~ indicates that nothing appeared in that issue, as verified by the Club. Persons with information on the vacant cells in the table are asked to contact the Secretary at the usual address. An updated table will be published when we have checked all the issues concerned. Due to a nationwide printing strike, no journals appeared in July 1959, save for 'Emergency Issues' of some Ian Allan titles.

## Catalogues

Rosebud produced three catalogues, one for each year of their existence. All of them were printed on a single sheet of paper, double sided in 4 colour photolithography.

### Catalogue 1 1959-1960

This familiar little catalogue was included with most of the early kits. There are at least ten known versions, including four UK reprints, plus two Irish, two US export, several French and Italian versions and even an Austrian version! The reprints were necessitated by poor reproduction and the need to add the Raunds address block to the rear panel. Different typefaces were used for the second and third reprints.
Dimensions: 125 x 90 mm closed 250 x 90 mm opened flat
Type A Early 1959. Address block missing. Kit number 2 is spaced with 2 dots only.
Type B Mid 1959. Address block added, upper and lower case letters. Kit number 2 is spaced with 3 dots.
Type C Late 1959. Address block is 4 lines all capital letters. Kit number 2 is spaced with 3 dots.
Type D Early 1960. Full address block, plus the name of the printer added to it. All in caps.
Type E USA 1 1959. Text includes OO scale, US address added, prices in US $
Type F USA 2 1960. Text reset to exclude OO scale, US address added, prices in US $
Type G Eire 1. Type A, but carries bold type inside 'Prices only valid in Eire' with higher £ prices shown. Kit 10 spaced with two dots, Regd. TM is above Made in England.
Type H Eire 2. As above, except kit 10 has no dots, Made in England is above Regd. TM This was included with some P1 sets.
Type AI1 Italian. As type A above, but text in Italian; Lire price of Prairie is LT575
Type AI2 Italian. As type AI1, but price of Prairie corrected to read LT825
Type AI2b Italian. As type AI2, but text now printed in blue ink throughout.
Type AU Universal. As type A above, but no prices. English text. Used in Canada.
Type AUb Universal. As type A above, but prices blocked out in black overprint.
Type AS Swedish. As type A above, but text in Swedish Confirmed.
Type AD German. As type A above, but text in German.
Type AA Austria. As type A above, but text in German, prices in Schillings, confirmed.
Type AF French. As type A above, but text in French Confirmed.
Type AN Dutch. As type A above, but text in Dutch Confirmed.

### Catalogue 2 1960-1961

This is the more elusive 1960 catalogue. It was packed with the P2 and P3 Presentation Sets and was also distributed free with the July 1960 *Railway Modeller*. It does not seem to have been included with any other kits. It is slightly larger than the 1959 catalogue and opens out to twice the size. It has all the TT kits and the power bogies included and goes up to kit number 25, the Beyer Garratt. Note that, at this stage, the BR 9F is shown in BR black livery and is not Evening Star, that the OO coaches are shown as available in green and maroon, whilst the TT coaches are shown only in maroon. The bogies are wrongly described as being for 12.15 Volt operation instead of 12-15 Volt use!. It was also produced in all the major languages; the Archive contains Dutch and Italian copies.
Dimensions: 145 x 75 mm closed 285 x 145 mm opened flat.

### Catalogue 3 1961-1962

The most impressive yet. Full colour illustration of Evening Star on the front cover, opens in a peculiar manner to a full A3 sheet. Shows all railway kits including 35, 36 and 37 not produced, but not the motorcycle. Was printed in all the languages used by Kitmaster, Confirmed printings

included German, French, Italian and Swedish in KMCC archives, also an interesting South African version with prices in Sterling and in Rand.
Dimensions: 140 x 190 mm closed 280 x 380 mm opened flat

### Dealer Catalogues
These are certainly known to exist for 1959 and 1960, and were also presumably available for 1961. The 1959 catalogue is like a large version of the 1959 retail leaflet, with the same artwork of Pug and Duchess, but bigger, measuring 194 x 244 mm in the closed position. It is printed in full colour and is in the form of a simple four page folder. The first twelve kits are illustrated. It details the advertising campaign for the initial launch and promotes special shop display units featuring an 0-6-0 diesel emerging from a tunnel mouth on a special plinth, which can also hold a kit box. It is extremely rare, far more so than the 1960 catalogue, but why this should be is not apparent.

The 1960 catalogue is like a large version of the 1960 Retail leaflet, with the same artwork of Pug and Duchess with the date 1960 in the top right corner. However, this 12 page booklet is the same size as the 1959 trade catalogue. It is printed in full colour throughout and describes the range in some detail, including the Presentation Sets, with a mock up of the TT3 Set box. Special displays are promised and much is made of the new introductions planned for 1960. It comes with a separate smaller 4-page Trade Price List, printed in black and red, featuring the Deltic artwork first used for advertisement KMC 12.

### Collecting Kitmaster Models
If you are thinking of beginning a collection, there are some basic rules. Firstly, condition is very important. A good collection would ideally contain 'one of everything' in pristine condition. This may mean wrapped in cellophane or just in very clean boxes without any damage. It is often very satisfying to buy a model which you don't yet have regardless of condition; after all, you can probably improve on it later

You should try to buy models which are as complete as possible. For example, missing parts may be replaced from other examples of the kit or from scrapped models. However, it is very difficult to replace transfer sheets and damaged instruction sheets Likewise, the presentation sets are often lacking in their track, paint and brushes, glue, files and *The Steam Locomotive* booklet.

Think about how you want to display your kits. The colours of the boxes fade quite rapidly with exposure to daylight. Arrangement of the kits is up to you of course, but my favourite is still in numerical order from 1 to 60! Original Kitmaster models are becoming more and more collectable and ever more difficult to come across in mint, boxed condition. Market prices are increasing all the time for unbuilt mint, boxed Kitmasters. Prices will continue upwards as more of the better examples are snapped up, so if you want to collect Kitmaster kits, you had better start soon or you may not be in a position to afford them!

### Valuing your Kitmaster Models
Placing a value on a model is a fine art. One has to consider the condition and nature of the kit, as well as the scarcity. There are often surprising, for example, a good Stirling Single will fetch twice as much as a City of Truro, despite that they both cost the same in 1961.

Mint, boxed kits in the original cellophane are going to command a premium price, whilst a badly-painted assembled kit with no box may seem to be 'going cheap.' As a general rule, the larger and later the kit was issued, the more it is going to fetch. When assessing kits, these are the questions to ask.

1. Is the box in good condition? After 1960 all kits were shrink-wrapped in cellophane, whilst earlier boxes will show signs of sellotape damage.

2. Is the kit still on the sprues? A good clean kit with the majority of parts still on their sprues indicates a kit that has been properly stored. It also makes checking for completeness a lot easier.

3. Is the instruction sheet in good condition? Kitmaster's larger instruction sheets were multi-lingual affairs and are often found with the bottom chopped off. This seriously affects their value, as does over-enthusiastic checking-off of the parts.

4. Are the decals present? A cut or missing decal sheet always detracts from value.

5. Are the metal parts present? Three of the kits, Rocket, The General and the Hudson, were supplied with metal handrail wire and the Scot had metal valve gear.

These notes should help you to determine whether a kit is worth the asking price, but in the end, only you can decide if it is a useful addition to your collection or a filler to be replaced at a later date.

An Important Note: Made-up unboxed examples of kits still in production with Dapol are virtually worthless. These include: Pug, Schools, Prairie, City of Truro, Evening Star, Class 4MT Mogul, J94, Rocket, Drewry shunter, Railbus and all Airfix wagon kits

When valuing your collection, it is important not to overlook the accompanying paperwork. Early paperwork, catalogues, leaflets and flyers are now much in demand. The 1961 Kitmaster catalogue now commands £10 in good condition, whilst the smaller 1960 catalogue routinely fetches £5-£6. The two trade catalogues, 1959 and 1960 are considered to be very scarce.

## For the first time anywhere!

**ROSEBUD Kitmaster PLASTIC SCALE MODELS**

**RAILWAY KITS**

A "Do-It-Yourself" locomotive kit moulded in plastic that's specially designed to appeal to modellers everywhere. Enthusiasts of all ages will obtain hours of pleasure and satisfaction from assembling these engines themselves. Packed in attractive boxes, complete with step by step instructions, these models are precision moulded and authentic in every detail. Kitmaster's special plastic cement is provided with all kits. Order your Rosebud Kitmaster stocks now.

**AUTHENTIC MODELS — WITH MOVING PARTS**

CAN BE USED ON OO AND HO GAUGE TRACKS

## GREAT NATIONAL ADVERTISING CAMPAIGN!

Specially planned to reach millions of boys & model enthusiasts!

**WHOLE PAGE ADVERTISEMENTS every MONTH**

starting April in :

Hobbies Weekly — Railway Modeller
Model Railway News — Trains Illustrated
Aero Modeller — Model Aircraft
Meccano Magazine — ABC British Locomotives

Also large advertisements every month in 'Eagle' and 'Express Weekly'

---

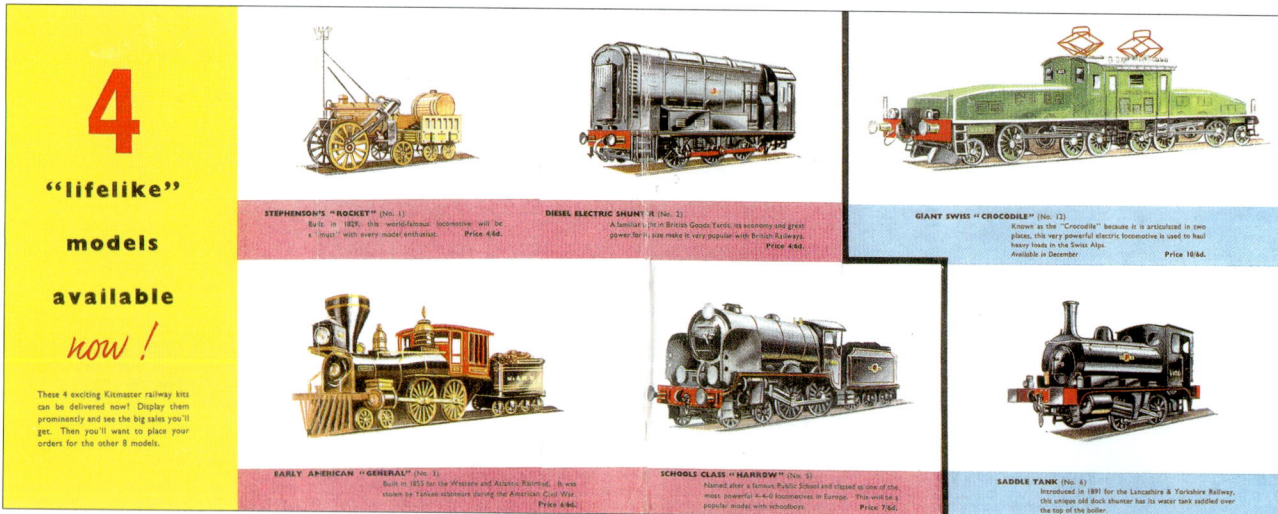

## 4 "lifelike" models available now!

These 4 exciting Kitmaster railway kits can be delivered now! Display them prominently and see the big sales you'll get. Then you'll want to place your orders for the other 8 models.

**STEPHENSON'S "ROCKET"** (No. 1)
Built in 1829, this world-famous locomotive will be a "must" with every model enthusiast. Price 4/6d.

**DIESEL ELECTRIC SHUNTER** (No. 2)
A familiar sight in British Goods Yards, its economy and great power for its size make it very popular with British Railways. Price 4/6d.

**GIANT SWISS "CROCODILE"** (No. 12)
Known as the "Crocodile" because it is articulated in two places, this very powerful electric locomotive is used to haul heavy loads in the Swiss Alps. Available in December. Price 10/6d.

**EARLY AMERICAN "GENERAL"** (No. 3)
Built in 1855 for the Western and Atlantic Railroad, it was stolen by Yankee raiders during the American Civil War. Price 4/6d.

**SCHOOLS CLASS "HARROW"** (No. 5)
Named after a famous Public School and rated as one of the most powerful 4-4-0 locomotives in Europe. This will be a popular model with schoolboys. Price 7/6d.

**SADDLE TANK** (No. 6)
Introduced in 1891 for the Lancashire & Yorkshire Railway, this unique old dock shunter has its water tank saddled over the top of the boiler.

---

## presentation boxes

Here are three handsome Kitmaster Presentation Boxes — containing three, four and five kits each — to please everyone in search of special presents for model makers. They are just the thing to recommend for birthdays and Christmas! The attractive display boxes feature dramatic and original locomotive paintings in full colour that are guaranteed to catch the eye of all your customers. Kitmaster Presentation Boxes deserve their own window and counter displays.

**PRESENTATION BOX No. P.1.** "100 YEARS OF BRITISH STEAM" containing The Rocket, Stirling 8 foot, Single, and Coronation Class.

**PRESENTATION BOX No. P.2.** containing Battle of Britain Class, with Corridor Composite, Corridor Second and Corridor Brake Second Coaches.

**PRESENTATION BOX No. P.3.** containing T.T.3 series models of rebuilt Royal Scot and Corridor Composite, Corridor Second, Corridor Brake Second and Restaurant First Coaches. Available August.

## now Kitmaster introduce motors!

Now every Kitmaster collector can cheaply and easily motorize all his models to run on OO, HO and TT tracks—thanks to the new Coach Electric Motor Bogies. It's another exciting "first" from Kitmaster to create enormous interest among your customers! Sold as complete units with easy-to-follow instructions for fitting, and for use with the Corridor Brake Second Coach.

**OO-HO and TT3 COACH ELECTRIC MOTOR BOGIES**
Kit No. KM1 ... OO-HO unit Available July
Kit No. KM3 ... TT3 unit Available July

★ KITMASTER POWER UNITS ARE FOR TWO RAIL 12-15 VOLTS DC SUPPLY

**KIT NO. KM2 Available July**
**OO-HO ELECTRIC MOTORIZED BOX WAGON**
To be used with Kitmaster Freight Engines. Sold as a complete unit with instructions for use.

---

## ROSEBUD Kitmaster PLASTIC SCALE MODELS

At last! A do-it-yourself train kit moulded in plastic. And these models that Rosebud Kitmaster bring you can actually be used on OO and HO gauges. They will delight both children and model-railway enthusiasts. They are so easy to assemble. You just follow the simple instructions and use the Kitmaster special plastic cement for a perfect model every time. Each model is built to scale, finely detailed with actual moving parts. Paint them, and they look just like the real thing. Choose your model from the range illustrated here.

Recently introduced T.T.3 scale models are illustrated on the opposite page

## ROSEBUD Kitmaster PLASTIC SCALE MODELS

**RE-BUILT "ROYAL SCOT" No. 16** ... $1.50 AVAILABLE APRIL 1960
**STANDARD CORRIDOR BRAKE 2nd No. 17** ... $1.35 AVAILABLE MAY 1960
**STANDARD CORRIDOR COMPOSITE No. 18** ... $1.35 AVAILABLE MAY 1960
**STANDARD CORRIDOR 2nd No. 20** ... $1.35 AVAILABLE JULY 1960
**STANDARD RESTAURANT 1st No. 21** ... $1.50 AVAILABLE JULY 1960

**T.T.3 SCALE**

212

# Appendix One - Index to Railway Journal Entries

## [A] Railway Modeller

| Date | /page | Description |
|---|---|---|
| 3.59 | XV | Review of range and [2] |
|  | VI | H A Blunt Retailers announcement of [1] [2] [3] [5] |
| 4.59 | XIII | KMC1 Full page ad for [1] [2] [3] [5] |
|  | 100 | Review of [1] [3] |
| 5.59 | VII | KMC2 Full page ad for [6] |
|  | 124 | Review of [6] |
| 6.59 | IX | KMC2 Full page ad for [6] |
|  | 148 | Article: Changes in P.T. - Kitmaster not affected |
| 7.59 | 157 | Feature: Motorising the Kitmaster Pug |
| 9.59 | X | KMC3 Half page ad for [9] |
| 10.59 | V | Peco Perfecta (1) for [6] |
|  | VIII | KMC4 Half page ad for [7] |
|  | XI | Ad for Surrey Models motorising kit for [5] |
|  | 224 | Review of Perfecta kit (1) |
|  | 226 | Review of [9]. |
|  | 227 | Review of [7]. |
| 11.59 | XVII | KMC5 Half page ad for [4] |
|  | XII | Ad for Surrey Models motorising kit for [5] |
|  | 251 | Mention of [4] |
| 12.59 | VIII | KMC6 half page ad for [8] |
|  | 276 | Letter suggesting [6] is not a Pug |
|  | 251 | Review of [4] [8] |
| 1.60 | 18 | Article: Notes on Kitmaster Models [4] |
| 2.60 | VI | KC 11 Half page ad for [11] |
|  | 42 | Letters: Answers to Pug letter (qv 12.59) |
|  | 47 | Review of [11] |
| 3.60 | X | KC 12 Half page ad for [12] |
|  | XXV | Gamages ad for [13/14/15] |
|  | 74 | Review of OO & TT Coaches & [10] |
|  | 74 | Peco announce Perfecta kits for : |
|  |  | (2) Italian Tank Available Apr |
|  |  | (3) Prairie May |
|  |  | (4) BoB Pacific Jun |
|  |  | (5) Duchess Jul |
|  | 74 | Photograph of [10] |
|  | 75 | Review of Peco Coach Interiors |
| 4.60 | VII | Peco ad for coach interiors + Perfecta (2) for [8] |
|  | XVI | KC 13 Half page ad [13] [14] [15] |
|  | 98 | Review of [12] |
| 5.60 | VII | Full page ad for Perfecta (2) for [8] |
|  | X | KC 14 Half page ad for [16] |
|  | 121 | Review of Perfecta (2) for [8] |
|  | 121 | Review of [13] [15] |
| 6.60 | II | KC 15 Half page ad for [16] [17] [18] |
| 7.60 | X | KC 16 Half page ad for [19] |
|  | 171 | Review of [16] [18] [21] |
|  | 169 | Review of BSK interior kit & [16] |
| 8.60 | VI | KC15 Half page ad [16] [17] [18] [20] [21] |
|  | 195 | Review of [17] [20] |
| 9.60 | V | Full page ad Peco Perfecta var. & interiors |
|  | 218 | Review of [19] |
|  | XIII | KC17 Half page ad for [22] |
| 10.60 | VIII | Peco ad for SO Interior |
|  | XXXI | KC18 Ad for [23] |
|  | 232/3 | Feature: Motorising Old Timers (The General) |
| 11.60 | VII | Full page ad for Perfecta (4) |
|  | 266 | Article: The Kitmaster Lamp |
|  | 206 | Motorizing the Railbus with a Rivarossi motor |
|  | 271 | Review of (4) for [11] |
|  | XVII | KC19 Half page ad for [24] |
| 12.60 | III | Peco ad for interiors & Perfectas |
|  | XIV | KC20 Half page ad for [22] |
| 1.61 | XXI | H A Blunt composite prices for Km/Perfecta |
|  | 14 | Article : Kitmaster Variations |
|  | 23 | Review of [22] |
| 2.61 | 40/1 | Motorizing the Railbus with Perfecta kit No 1 |
| 3.61 | 78 | Review of [24] [23] |
| 4.61 | X | Kitmaster/Humbrol Ad |
| 5.61 | 112/3 | Feature: Motorising the City of Truro |
|  | 122 | Article: Kitmaster Modifications |
|  | 122 | Article: Replacing Kitmaster Coach Windows |
|  | 129 | Review of [25] [26] |
|  | 129 | Airfix introduce cattle wagon & Brake van |
| 7.61 | V | Retailer Ad for [27] [28] |
|  | 169 | Article: EM-ing the Kitmaster Coaches |
|  | 175 | Review of KM1 & [27] |
|  | ??? | Situations Vacant - Modelmaker required apply Rosebud Kitmaster! |
| 8.61 | V | Full page Peco interiors ad |
|  | 191 | Article: Bringing the Deltic up to date |
|  | 191 | Article: Lining Km Coaches |
|  | 192 | Article: Flexible coach connections |
|  | 193 | Article: Fitting Km coach windows |
| 10.61 | XXVI | Humbrol/Kitmaster ad featuring the Mogul |
|  | 235/6 | Feature: Motorising the Mogul |
|  | 253 | Review of [30] |
| 11.61 | XXVIII | Humbrol/Kitmaster ad featuring the Mogul |
| 12.61 | VI | Ad for Perfecta (1) |
|  | 302 | Review of [31] |
|  | 305 | Southgate chassis for Railbus intro |
| 2.62 | 39 | Kitmaster Prairie to 4-4-2 Atlantic! |
|  | XIX | K's Pullman motor bogies and sideframes |
| 3.62 | FC | 'A Corner Station'- pic shows four Km locos |
|  | 54 | Charford - pic is 'denationalised' 21C157 |
|  | 64 | A Sludge Tender - conversion from Schools |
|  | 64/5 | Corridor connections for Km Coaches |
|  | 65 | Kitmaster Diesel Pullman |
|  | 67 | Motorising the Prairie |
| 4.62 | 91 | Duchess to Jubilee |
|  | 98 | Brass motorising kit for Stirling |
| 5.62 | 115 | 'Painting Simplified' Stirling/9F etc.. |
|  | 117 | Motorising the J94 |
|  | 118 | Transformer wagon with Km parts |
|  | 118 | Airfix couplings on Km coach bogies |
| 7.62 | 170 | W & H announce wheel kits for Km locos |
| 8.62 | 175 | Layout- Belindavon and LLanderek - many Km |
| 10.62 | 240 | A Kitmaster-Fleischmann conversion - Hudson |
| 11.62 | 259 | Various Pug conversions |
|  | 266 | Extra weight for plastic kit locos |
| 12.62 | 297 | Announcement: Airfix purchase moulds and stock |
| 3.63 | 57/58 | Various Km in action |
| 6.63 | 134 | Kitmaster coach windows |
|  | 143 | Tender conversion using [4] parts |
| 7.63 | VII | Ariel Arrow reintroduced by Airfix |
|  |  | Airfix introduce Lowmac & JCB |
| 8.63 | IX | Tri-ang Blue Pullman introduced |
| 9.63 | FC/198 | 'The Long Thin Look' 6-car Pullman set pics |
| 10.63 | VII | Ad for Airfix Prairie Tank |
|  | 232 | 'A 4 Car EMU' Pic of KM1 in use |
|  | 252 | News of the Airfix Prairie [7] reintroduction with new pic |
| 11.63 | XIX | H A Blunt Prairie Pack ad Kit/Romford wheels/Phantom motor |
| 1.64 |  | Airfix reintroduce [26] |
| 3.64 |  | Airfix reintroduce [6] |
| 12.64 |  | Airfix reintroduce [1] |
| 5.65 |  | Airfix reintroduce [24] |
| 12.65 | 317 | Midland Pullman in action |
| 4.68 | ??? | Beatties of London offering KM2 at 25s each. |
| 3.81 | 80/1 | Motorising the City of Truro |
| 12.89 | 544 | Plastic Surgery for Archaeologists - Stirling conversions. |

## [B] Model Railway News

| Date | Page | Description |
|---|---|---|
| 3.59 | xxiii | Gamages ad featuring [2] [3] Press shots |
|  | 69/70 | DEJ3 Intro foretold |
| 4.59 | iii | KMC1 full page ad |
| 5.59 |  | KMC2 full page ad for [6] |
| 6.59 | vii | KM2 full page ad for [6] |
| 7.59 | 166/7 | Review of [5] & [6] |
| 9.59 | xix | KMC3 half page ad for [9] |
| 10.59 | vii | SMRS motor ad for [5] |
|  | ix | Peco announce Perf.(1) for [6] |
|  | 210 | Reviews of [7] [9] |
|  | xxvii | KMC4 for [7] |
| 11.59 | x | SMRS |
|  | 236 | Review of [4] with pic |
|  | 242 | Pug letters |
|  | xxi | KMC? half page ad for [4] |
| 12.59 | xii | Peco ad inc (1) |
|  | xxxiii | KMC6 half page for [8] |
| 1.60 | xvii | KC10 1/2 page ad for [10] |
| 2.60 | xii | KC 11 for [11] |
|  | xiii | SMRS |
|  | 73 | Review of [11] |
|  | 74 | pic of [11] |
| 3.60 | vi | KC12 half page ad for [12] |
|  | 95 | Review of [10] with pic. |
|  | 118 | Gamages ad for [13-16] |
| 4.60 | vii | Peco ad for interiors & (2) |
|  | 130 | Brighton Fair - Kitmaster pavillion reviewed prototype of box van |
|  |  | shown. Pics of 15/13 & interiors. Announce Croc & 1960 Catalogue |
|  | xxiii | KC13 for [13/14/15] |
| 5.60 | XXV | J.N. Maskelyne biog |
|  | X | KC14 half page ad for [16] |
|  | XII | Half page ad for Perfecta (2) for [8] |
|  | XIX | Bradshaws ad inc 1960 KM releases and pic of [14] |
|  | 176 | The Last One by J N Maskelyne |
| 6.60 | iii | Southgate ad for Motorised Utility Van 'Southgate Special' |
|  | xiii | KC15 half page ad for [16][17][18] |
|  | xvi | K's ad for tender drive units |
|  | 225 | Jennings introduce wheels for [2] |
| 7.60 | ix | Airfix intro of Cement/Oil wagons |
|  | xi | KC 16 for [19] |
|  | xiv | K's tender chassis |
| 8.60 | xi | KC 15 for [16-21] |
|  | 278 | J N Maskelyne - An Appreciation |
|  | 300 | pic [16] Reviews [16][17] |
| 9.60 | xiii | Perfecta (2) ad |
|  | xiii | KC 17 for [22] half page |
| 10.60 | xvi | KC18 for [23] half page |

213

| | | |
|---|---|---|
| 11.60 | xiv | KC 19 for 24 |
| | 410 | pic of [19] |
| | xxiii | Peco ad for Perf. (4) for [11] |
| 12.60 | xviii | KC20 for [22] Half page |
| 1.61 | 9 | Review of [22] |
| 4.61 | 15 | Review of [23] [24] |
| 5.61 | 179 | Review of [25] [26] |
| 7.61 | 272 | Review of [27] [28] |
| 8.61 | 301 | Review of [29] |
| 9.61 | XXV | Humbrol ad featuring J.94 |
| 11.61 | 416 | [30] picture only |
| 12.61 | 455 | [31] picture |
| | 458 | [31] [32] reviewed |
| 1.62 | 22 | Pic of [32][33] |
| 5.62 | xiv | K's Deltic chassis/sideframes ad |
| 7.62 | iv | W & H ad for wheel kits [6] [7] [30] |
| 7.62 | 266 | Airfix announce Interfrigo and Meat Van |
| 8.62 | xiii | H A Blunt ad for Romford [7] |
| 9.62 | 361-4 | An Approach to good kit construction -[4] |
| 12.62 | xi | Romford kits for [5] [25] |
| 8.63 | iii | Airfix ad for intro of Lowmac/JCB |
| | | Airfix Re-introduce Ariel Arrow |
| 10.63 | 52 | Airfix preview of Prairie [7] reintro |
| | 56 | Photograph of new Prairie [7] |
| 1.64 | 175 | Painting the Prairie |
| 2.64 | iii | Re-intro of J94 [26] Ad |
| | 242 | Review of J94 [26] |
| 3.64 | iii | Re-intro of Pug [6] Ad |
| | 279/80 | Review of Pug [6] |
| 4.64 | iii | Intro of Prestwin Silo wagon Ad |
| 5.64 | 325 | Airfix at Nuremberg Toy Fair |
| 8.64 | 469 | Airfix at Central Hall |
| 12.64 | iii | Re-intro of Rocket [1] Ad |
| | 622 | Rocket [1] & 9F [22] Reintro noted |
| 10.67 | 475 | New ad for Airfix Prairie |
| 6.72 | ins F/C | Humbrol ad featuring a Kitmaster 9F [22] |
| 8.74 | ins F/C | Humbrol ad featuring an Airfix Schools |

[C] Model Railway Constructor

| Date | Page | Description |
|---|---|---|
| 3.59 | 69 | Review and pic of [2] |
| 4.59 | 76/7 | Mechanising the Rosebud Kitmaster diesel |
| | 90/1 | Review & photos of [1] [2] [3] |
| 3/4.59 | | Review of [2] |
| 6.59 | 132/3 | The General goes to town (with a Terrier motor) |
| | 140/1 | Reviews & photo of [5] [6] |
| 7.59 | 162 | Pugs motorised |
| 8.59 | 174 | Motorising the Schools |
| | 183 | Pic of [9] |
| 9.59 | ix | KMC3 ad for [9] |
| | 194/5 | A Stirling Loco (Motorisation) |
| | 208 | Review of [7] & [9] |
| 10.59 | ix | SMRS |
| | 216/7 | Motorising the Kitmaster Prairie |
| | 228 | Review of Perfecta (1) for [6] |
| 11.59 | | Review of [4] |
| 12.59 | ix | SMRS |
| | 261 | Fairlie Pug! |
| | 271 | Review of [6] with pic |
| 1.60 | viii | KC10 ad for [10] |
| 2.60 | vi | KC11 ad for [11] |
| | 44 | Review of [11] |
| | 45 | Fiddlers end - Pug to NG 0-4-2! |
| 3.60 | VI | KC12 half page ad for [12] |
| | 52-53 | Motorising the Deltic |
| | 69 | Kitmaster 1960 News pic of [12] [15] |
| 4.60 | iv | 1/2 page ad KC13 for coaches |
| | 96 | Review of CK + [12] + pics |
| | 97 | Trade report- Km1 Perfecta & interiors |
| 5.60 | vi | 1/2page ad KC14 for [16] |
| | 122 | [14] noted |
| 6.60 | iv | KC15 1/2 page ad for [16][17][18] |
| | 134 | Photo of [9] |
| | 139 | 'From a Swedish Enthusiast' Comical text accompanies shot of motorised Pug & Shunter! |
| | 146 | Review and phot of [15] |
| 7.60 | IV | KC16 half page ad for [19] |
| | V | Airfix introduce Presflow Cement & Oil Tank |
| | 170 | Peco interior kits review with pic |
| 8.60 | 192 | Review of [16] |
| | 193 | Review of Tank & Presflo |
| | 194 | Review of [17] |
| 9.60 | vi | 1/2page ad KC17 for [22] |
| | 198/9 | Motorising the TT Scot |
| | 215 | Review of Peco BSK interior |
| | 216 | Review of Perfecta (2) for [7] |
| 10.60 | vi | Taylor McKenna ad including P2 Set |
| | vii | KC18 half page ad for [23] |
| | 226 | Motorising the DB 23 |
| | 240 | Review of [19] |
| 11.60 | 251/2 | A4 into Bulleid Light Pacific |
| | 252 | Kitmaster BR Standard Coaches |
| 12.60 | v | Airfix Railbus intro ad |
| | vi | 1/2page ad K20 for [22] |
| | 287/8 | Motorising the Railbus |
| | 293 | Review of Peco SO interior |
| | 295 | Mike Bryant letter on Perfectas |
| 1.61 | 7-9 & FC | 4-CEP unit from Kitmaster coaches I |
| | 20 | Review of [22] |
| 2.61 | 47 | Letters on Bryant motorising article |
| 3.61 | 49 | Photo of 241P |
| | 56 | Motorising the Kitmaster 2-10-0 |
| | 58 | A Full Brake Van Kitmaster Conversion |
| | 65 | Review of City of Truro [24] |
| | 68 | Kitmaster 1961 Trade Fair report - review of range |
| | 69 | Airfix intro Booth Crane & Mineral wagon |
| | 70 | PECO Perfecta changes intro of (5) for [24] and (1a) for Railbus/XT60 |
| 4.61 | vi | Airfix intro ad for Booth crane |
| | 96 | Kitmaster conversion 1 - SO to RMB |
| | 87/8/9 | Kitmaster conversion 2 - GW Mogul from Prairie & Truro |
| | 100 | Review of [23] and Booth |
| 5.61 | v | Airfix intro of Cattle wagon |
| | 129 | Review of Cattle & Brake |
| 6.61 | 143/4 | Kitmaster BCK conversion |
| | 152 | Review of [25] |
| | 156 | Letter on GW Mogul conv. |
| 7.61 | 174 | Finishing touches for Kitmaster Couplings |
| | 180 | Review of [26] with pic |
| | 181 | Review of [28] & [27] with pics |
| 8.61 | 198/9 | Motorising a Kitmaster Beyer-Garratt 2-6-6-2 |
| | 203 | Review of [29] |
| 9.61 | 218/9 | City of Truro pics |
| | 226 | First Open conversions - FO, FK, BFK |
| | 231 | Duchess pic |
| 10.61 | iii | Airfix intro of Drewry |
| | 239/40/1 | Motorising the Kitmaster J94 |
| | 244 | 4-BEP conversion & MLV |
| | 257 | Review of [30] & Airfix 04 with pics |
| 11.61 | ix | Humbrol ad for [30] |
| | 280/1 | Motorising the Kitmaster 4MT Mogul |
| 12.61 | xi | Humbrol ad for [31] |
| | 304 | Motorising the Airfix Drewry Shunter |
| | 311 | Review of [31] [32] [33] [KM1] |
| 1.62 | F/C | [31] in action! |
| 3.62 | | Review of [34] |
| 5.62 | 135 | Letter 'More Market Research'; bigoted reactionary bullshit! |
| 7.62 | iii | Airfix intro of Interfrigo & Meat |
| | vi | Romford kits for [7][26][30] in W&H ad |
| | 165-7 | Kitmaster catering vehicle conversion RB & RF |
| | 182 | Review of Interfrigo & Meat |
| 8.62 | III | Airfix introduce 10t Meat Van |
| | IV | [31] in Alan Brett Canon ad |
| | 197 | A Kitmaster Open Brake Second BSO |
| 10.62 | 249 | A Kitmaster Unclassed Restaurant Car |
| | 256 | Kitmaster coach lighting |
| 11.62 | iii | Airfix intro of Scarab |
| | vii | Romford kits for [5] + [25] in W & H ad |
| | 292 | Review of Scarab |
| | 293 | Review of Airfix Old Bill Bus! |
| 12.62 | | A Kitmaster Kitchen Buffet RKB/KB |
| 6.63 | ? | Conversion of Km coaches & Airfix Railbus to Class 301 Clacton Set |
| 7.63 | ? | Conversion of Km coaches & Airfix Railbus to Class 301 Clacton Set II |
| 2.64 | iii | Airfix J94 reissue ad |
| | 242 | Airfix J94 review |
| 12.64 | iii | Airfix 9F reissue ad |
| | 321 | 'Maurice Onions - Designer' Pug Conversions |
| 4.65 | 106 | Prototype pic of [27] |
| | 108 | Review of Airfix Truro noting tool changes |
| 11.67 | iv | W&H 1/2 page ad for re-imported Km 4/5/8/9/10/11/12/KM1 |

[D] Airfix Magazine

| | | |
|---|---|---|
| 6.60 | 39 | Review 13/14/15 |
| 7.60 | 78 | Pic of Km Deltic |
| | 84 | Airfix intro of Tank/Presflo |
| 8.60 | 127 | Photo of Pug |
| 9.60 | 191 | The Kitmaster Story |
| 11.60 | 258 | TT reviews |
| | 274/5 | Motorising the Railbus |
| | 276 | Railbus review |
| 12.60 | 302 | Review of [22] with pic |
| 3.61 | 466 | Future production |
| | 467 | Review of [23] [24] |
| 4.61 | 504 | Breakdown Crane Conversion |
| 5.61 | 572 | Review of [26] with pic |
| | 576 | Motive Power photo |
| 6.61 | 35 | Reviews of [27] [28] |
| 8.61 | 134 | Review of [29] |
| 10.61 | 232 | Review of [30] |
| 11.61 | 278 | Review of [31] with pic |
| 12.61 | 328 | Review of [32] with pic |
| 1.62 | 373 | Review of [33] with pic. |
| 2.62 | 417 | Full page Humbrol Britfix/[31]/HMS Eagle ad |
| 3.62 | 447 | Review of [60] with pic |

214

|       |      | 448 | Review of [34] with pic |
|-------|------|-----|------------------------|
| 6.62  |      | 10  | Working dockside crane Pt1 |
| 7.62  |      | 42  | Working dockside crane Pt2 |
| 8.62  |      | 88  | Review of Romford motorising kits for [9] [22] [26] |
| 12.62 |      | 206 | Scarab variations |
| 1.63  |      | 236 | Variations on the Drewry Diesel motorisation |
| 7.63  |      | B/C | Full colour ad for XL5 |
| 8.63  |      | 74  | Working Overhead Travelling Cranes Pt1 |
| 9.63  |      | 10  | Working Overhead Travelling Cranes Pt2 |
| 10.63 |      | 40  | Motorising Airfix Railbus |
| 1.64  |      | 152 | Motorising Airfix Prairie Tank |
| 2.64  |      | 188 | Modelling Airfix BR Scarabs |
| 5.64  |      | 290 | Pug narrow gauge conversion |
| 6.64  |      | 308 | Motorising the Pug |
| 9.64  |      | 8   | Motorising the J94 |
| 1.65  |      | 141 | Motorising Evening Star Pt1 |
| 2.65  |      | 168 | Motorising Evening Star Pt2 |
| 7.65  |      | 329 | Motorising City of Truro |
| 9.66  |      | 8   | Making Plastic valve gear run smoothly |
| 11.66 |      | 80  | Motorising Drewry Shunter |
| 2.67  |      | 200 | Detailing City of Truro |
| 5.67  |      | 320 | GW Mogul from Truro + Prairie |
| 6.67  |      | 366 | Motorising 4MT Mogul |
| 8.67  |      | 450 | Variations on the Mogul |
| 9.67  |      | 14  | Truro to Aberdare 2-6-0 |
| 11.67 |      | 98  | Truro to County |
| 12.67 |      | 136 | Truro to Bulldog |
| 2.68  |      | 216 | Truro to Curved-frame Bulldog |
| 3.68  |      | 260 | More Bulldog Bird variants |
| 4.68  |      | 316 | Dukedog from Truro + Prairie |
| 5.68  |      | 342 | Prairie to 2-8-0 42XX |
| 6.68  |      | 384 | Truro to Flowers & Atbaras |
| 9.68  |      | 24  | Prairie + Triang 0-6-0 to 56XX |
| 10.68 |      | 60  | Pug to crane tank |
| 1.69  |      | 212 | Motorising Biggin Hill Pt1 |
| 2.69  |      | 254 | Motorising & Detailing Biggin Hill Pt2 |
| 3.69  |      | 298 | Tender detailing for Biggin Hill |
| 5.69  |      | 410 | Converting Pugs to narrow gauge |
| 7.69  |      | 488 | Fireless locos from Pugs |
| 12.69 |      | 164 | Schools to Thompson B1 |

[E] Model Maker
3.59        Publicity HA Blunt ad for range [1] [2] [3] [5]
4.59        Publicity HA Blunt ad for range [1] [2] [3] [5]
5.59        Publicity HA Blunt ad for range [1] [2] [3] [5]
6.59        Publicity Mail Order Models [1][2][3][5][6]
9.59        Publicity HA Blunt [9[
12.59       Publicity HA Blunt ad for [6][9] and Perfectas for [6]{4]
1.60        Publicity KC 10 1/2 page ad for [10]
2.60        Publicity KC11 1/2 page ad for [11]
3.60        Publicity KC12 1/2 page ad for [12]
4.60        Publicity KC13 1/2 page ad for [13]
5.60        I.F.C KC14 1/2 page ad for [16]
6.60        Publicity KC 15 1/2 page ad for [16][17][18]
8.60        Publicity KC17 1/2 page ad for [22]
12.60       Publicity HA Blunt ad for [22[
8.61        441 Review of [29]
9.61        Publicity 1/2 page Humbrol/Kitmaster ad featuring [30]
1.62        45 Review of [31][32][33]

[F] Meccano Magazine
| 9.59  | iv    | KMC3 1/2 page ad for [9] |
| 10.59 | viii  | KMC4 1/2 page ad for [7] |
| 11.59 | x     | KMC5 1/2 page ad fot [4] |
| 12.59 | xiv   | KMC6 1/2 page ad for [8] |
| 1.60  | xv    | KC 10 full page ad for [10] |
| 2.60  | xi    | KC 11 full page ad for [11] |
| 3.60  | xvii  | KC 12 full page ad for [12] |
| 4.60  | xv    | KC 13 full page ad for [13][14][15] |
| 5.60  | xv    | KC 14 full page ad for [16] |
| 6.60  | xiii  | KC 15 full page ad for [16][17][18] |
| 7.60  | xv    | KC 16 full page ad for [19] |
| 8.60  | ix    | KC 15 full page ad for [16][17][18][20][21] |
| 9.60  | xv    | KC 17 full page ad for [22] |
| 10.60 | xiii  | KC 18 full page ad for [23] |
| 11.60 | xv    | KC 19 full page ad for [24] |
| 12.60 | xxi   | K 18 full page ad for [22] |
| 5.61  | viii  | 1/2 page Humbrol/Kitmaster ad for J94 |
| 9.61  | xvii  | 1/2 page Humbrol/Kitmaster ad for J94 |

[G] Boys Own Paper
| 5.61 | 9   | Humbrol/J.94 Half page ad |
| 8.61 | 59  | Humbrol/J.94 Full page ad |
| 7.63 | B/C | Full page colour ad for XL5 |

[H] The Victor
29.6.63   #123   1/2 page b/w ad for Fireball XL5

[I] European Railways
| No1 1960 | 22 | Reviews of 1960 range |
| No3 1960 | 24 | Reviews of [16] [19] |
| No2 1961 | 24 | Reviews of [24][23] and 1961 range |
| No4 1961 | 23 | Reviews of [25] [27] |

[J] Ian Alan Publications
ABC British Railway Locomotives
Summer 1959 Editions
Parts 1-4 Ins B/C        Range ad featuring [1] full page
Winter 1959/60 Editions
Parts 1-4 B/C            KMC5 full page for [4]
The Ian Allan Book of Model Railways, by Mike Bryant.
1960        43      Full Page Kitmaster ad, no code, 'Improve your layout'.
            45-47   Full description of Kitmasters with many pics inc. motorisation
                    by author.

[K] Montezuma Magazine
November 1962    Reprint of Model Railroader review of [34]

[L] Model Aircraft
| 6.59  | ix  | KCM 2 (sic) for [6] full page |
| 11.59 | xiv | KMC5 for [4] half page |
| 12.59 | xiv | KMC 6 for [8] half page |

[M] Hobbies Weekly
| 8.4.59   | 11  | KMC1 for [1][2][3][5] full page |
| 6.5.59   | BC  | 'KCM2', should be KMC2 for [6] full page |
| 10.6.59  | ?   | KMC2? This should exist, but has not been checked/found yet. |
| 9.9.59   | 301 | Half page ad for [9], no ref, but is KMC3. |
| 7.10.59  | 13  | KMC4 for [7] 1/2 page ad |
| 11.11.59 | 105 | KMC5 for [4] 1/2 page ad |
| 9.12.59  | 184 | KMC6 for [8] 1/2 page ad |

[N] Trains Illustrated
| 04.59 | b/c | KMC1 for [1][2][3][5] full page |
| 05.59 | III | KMC2 for [6] full page |
| 06.59 | b/c | KMC2 for [6] full page |
| 09.59 | ii  | KMC3 for [9] 1/2 page |
| 10.59 | xi  | KMC4 for [7] 1/2 page |
| 11.59 | iv  | KMC5 for [4] 1/2 page |
| 12.59 | x   | KMC6 for [8] 1/2 page |

[O] The Eagle
| 4.4.59   | 14 | KMC (1) Range ad 1/2 page |
| 2.5.9    | 14 | KMC 2 for [6] |
| 6.6.59   | 4  | KMC2 for [6] |
| 5.9.59   | 7  | KMC 3 for [9] 1/2 page |
| 3.10.59  | 4  | KMC 4 for [7] |
| 7.11.59  | 19 | (KMC 5) for [4] |
| 12.12.59 | 16 | (KMC 6) for [8] |

[P] Model Railway Collector
Issue 2      All Stuck Up - Collecting Kitmaster Scale Models
Issue 3      Deltic Doodlings - The Kitmaster Deltic
Issue 5      Pullman Pulling Power - The Kitmaster Pullmans
Issue 6      Getting the Presentation (Sets) Right

[Q] British Railway Modelling
May 1993     Collecting Kitmaster Models
June 1993    Battle of Britain Class in Detail
August 1993  Kitmaster 3mm Models in Detail
Oct 1993     Blue Movers - The Pullman Cars
Nov 1993     Deltic Details - The Prototype Deltic
Jan 1994     Diesel Shunters

[R] Collectors Gazette
12.90    Sean Rothman article on Gerry Anderson - XL5
03.91    Andrew Burford et al. photo of XL5 kit
07.91    Letter about XL5 boxes

[S] Model Railway Enthusiast
| 10.94 | 25-30 | Profile of the L&Y Pug |
| 61    |       | Models that might have been [34] |
| 04.95 | 9-14  | The Story of Kitmaster full colour pics |
| 01.96 |       | Kitmaster Spin-Offs 4 pages with pics |
| 09.96 |       | Kitmaster Continental prototypes 6 pages with colour |

[U] Practical Model Trains
03.87    27-32    A Tale of Three Cities - motorizing the Airfix/Kitmaster City of Truro

[V] Rosebud News
Vol 1
#1    Sept/Oct 1953
#2    Nov/Dec 1953
#3    Jan/Feb 1954
#4    Summer 1954
#5    Winter 1954
#6    Winter 1955

[W] Model & Miniature Railways
Partworks p.425-7 Plastic Kits Part 2: Locomotives & Rolling Stock, by Paul Towers.

[X] Northamptonshire Evening Telegraph
June 16th 1964 Front Page        Receiver Appointed for Rosebud Dolls

# Sweet dreams are made of this!